A PRACTICAL GUIDE TO APPELLATE ADVOCACY

Aspen Coursebook Series

A PRACTICAL GUIDE TO APPELLATE ADVOCACY

Fourth Edition

MARY BETH BEAZLEY
Professor of Law
Moritz College of Law
The Ohio State University

Wolters Kluwer
Law & Business

Printed in the United States of America.

2 3 4 5 6 7 8 9 0

ISBN 978-1-4548-3096-2

Library of Congress Cataloging-in-Publication Data

Beazley, Mary Beth, 1957- author.
  A practical guide to appellate advocacy / Mary Beth Beazley, Associate Professor of Law, Moritz College of Law, The Ohio State University.—Fourth edition.
    pages cm
  Includes bibliographical references and index.
  ISBN 978-1-4548-3096-2 (alk. paper)
  1. Legal briefs--United States. 2. Appellate procedure—United States. I. Title.
  KF251.B42 2014
  347.73'8—dc23

                                        2014017665

About Wolters Kluwer Law & Business

Wolters Kluwer Law & Business is a leading global provider of intelligent information and digital solutions for legal and business professionals in key specialty areas, and respected educational resources for professors and law students. Wolters Kluwer Law & Business connects legal and business professionals as well as those in the education market with timely, specialized authoritative content and information-enabled solutions to support success through productivity, accuracy and mobility.

Serving customers worldwide, Wolters Kluwer Law & Business products include those under the Aspen Publishers, CCH, Kluwer Law International, Loislaw, ftwilliam.com and MediRegs family of products.

CCH products have been a trusted resource since 1913, and are highly regarded resources for legal, securities, antitrust and trade regulation, government contracting, banking, pension, payroll, employment and labor, and healthcare reimbursement and compliance professionals.

Aspen Publishers products provide essential information to attorneys, business professionals and law students. Written by preeminent authorities, the product line offers analytical and practical information in a range of specialty practice areas from securities law and intellectual property to mergers and acquisitions and pension/benefits. Aspen's trusted legal education resources provide professors and students with high-quality, up-to-date and effective resources for successful instruction and study in all areas of the law.

Kluwer Law International products provide the global business community with reliable international legal information in English. Legal practitioners, corporate counsel and business executives around the world rely on Kluwer Law journals, looseleafs, books, and electronic products for comprehensive information in many areas of international legal practice.

Loislaw is a comprehensive online legal research product providing legal content to law firm practitioners of various specializations. Loislaw provides attorneys with the ability to quickly and efficiently find the necessary legal information they need, when and where they need it, by facilitating access to primary law as well as state-specific law, records, forms and treatises.

ftwilliam.com offers employee benefits professionals the highest quality plan documents (retirement, welfare and non-qualified) and government forms (5500/PBGC, 1099 and IRS) software at highly competitive prices.

MediRegs products provide integrated health care compliance content and software solutions for professionals in healthcare, higher education and life sciences, including professionals in accounting, law and consulting.

Wolters Kluwer Law & Business, a division of Wolters Kluwer, is headquartered in New York. Wolters Kluwer is a market-leading global information services company focused on professionals.

To my parents,
who made it possible;

to David,
who made it probable;

and to Betsy and Annie,
who make it all worthwhile

Summary of Contents

Contents

CHAPTER EIGHT

PROFESSIONALISM: FOLLOWING FORMAT RULES   165

Using the Examples in This Book

This book is meant to guide law students and others who are new to writing briefs. It attempts to make the writing process easier by examining the various decisions a brief-writer must make, and by articulating criteria that will help the writer to make those decisions. The book contains numerous excerpts from student-written briefs that illustrate various aspects of brief-writing. Although following examples too closely can be dangerous, I know that many good writers learn through imitation. Therefore, I offer the following caveats:

1
SOME EXAMPLES ARE "BAD" EXAMPLES

Do not presume that the principle illustrated in each example applies to the brief you are currently writing. First, the examples in the book are not meant to represent the current law on any subject. They come from a variety of student briefs written over several years. Some of the cases cited in the examples are fictional. Second, some of the examples are "bad examples," that is, they were adapted to show how *not* to do something. Unfortunately, some students, in a hurry to complete a project, will consult a textbook and imitate its examples slavishly, including "bad examples." To try to avoid this problem, the bad examples are carefully labeled—with the words "bad example" and with a downward arrow—so that you will not mistake a bad example for a good example. Most, if not all, of the bad examples are paired with a good example to show how to address the problem illustrated in the bad example. These are labeled with the words "good example" and an upward arrow.

The examples that are not paired are labeled with the words "example" and an arrow pointing to the example. Virtually all of these examples are good examples, but even these examples must not be followed unquestioningly. Just as the same law applies differently to different fact situations, the guidelines in this book may apply differently to briefs addressing different issues. For that reason, I have used examples from a variety of cases; no one case aptly illustrates every type of brief-writing problem. The majority of the examples in the text come from student briefs written for four Supreme Court cases: *Minnesota v. Carter,* 524 U.S. 975 (1998); *Knowles v. Iowa,* 525 U.S. 113 (1998); *Miller v. Albright,* 523 U.S. 420 (1998); and *Rubin v. Coors Brewing Co.,* 514 U.S. 476 (1995) (argued as *Bentsen v. Adolph Coors Co.*). There are also scattered examples from student briefs written for *Ohio v. Robinette,* 519 U.S. 33 (1996); *City of Chicago v. Morales,* 527 U.S. 41 (1999); *Holloway v. United States,* 526 U.S. 1 (1999); and *City of Indianapolis v. Edmond,* 531 U.S. 32 (2000). Many of the motion brief examples are based on a fictional case, *Garrett v. Kirkby,* in which the issue is whether a supervisor can be held individually liable under Title VII as an "employer" as that term is defined in 42 U.S.C. §2000e(b).

Even the good examples may not be perfect, but they represent good attempts by law students to write effectively. The sample briefs in Appendix C contain marginal notes that point out passages that are particularly effective, as well as passages that might be made even more effective if the writer had made certain decisions differently. Some marginal notes try to explain why certain peculiarities about the case may have led the writer to choose a certain writing or organizational technique. Thus, when you are deciding whether to imitate an example, you should first consider whether the example is effective; second, decide whether your case presents the same types of writing concerns as the case used in the example.

2

NOTE THE TONE AND WRITING STYLE CONVENTIONS IN THE GOOD EXAMPLES

Generally, you should imitate the tone and writing style in the good examples and not in the text itself. Tone and writing style should change to reflect the needs of particular types of documents and of particular audiences, and only the examples are purposely written in the style that is appropriate for brief writing. Your writing teachers may have already told you not to imitate judicial writing styles because the needs of judges and clerks (the audience for a brief) differ from the needs of the readers of judicial decisions. Similarly, you should not model your brief-writing style after the writing style of the *text* in this book. Unlike the good examples in this book, I did not write the *text* material in formal brief style. Although I followed many conventions that also apply to brief writing, I used a tone and writing style that is more like the one that I use when

I write comments on student papers. I use contractions, attempt humor, and include unusual metaphors, many of which could easily hinder the effectiveness of a brief. Thus, you should use a particular writing technique only when that technique is consistent with the rules and conventions of the court to which you are writing.

Bearing these caveats in mind, the examples should provide an opportunity for you to see how various writing decisions play out in the context of real cases and real (student) briefs. I hope that you find them helpful.

Acknowledgments to the First Edition

I would like to recognize and thank the following people who helped me in many different ways as I worked on this book:

Those of us who teach legal writing are blessed by the existence of a strong corps of supportive colleagues. I am grateful to the founders of the Legal Writing Institute, Anne Enquist, Laurel Currie Oates, and Christopher Rideout, of Seattle University. They were instrumental in the profound changes that have occurred in the teaching of legal writing over the past 20 years; without those changes I would not be teaching legal writing or writing about it. I also thank the colleagues whose work first taught me that there is a doctrine of legal writing that can be analyzed and communicated to others: Elizabeth Fajans, Jill Ramsfield, Mary Barnard Ray, Marjorie Rombauer, Helene Shapo, and Marilyn Walter. At Legal Writing Institute Conferences and, later, at conferences of the Association of Legal Writing Directors, I have been able to learn and grow through the exchange of ideas with colleagues who became friends: Coleen Barger, Linda Edwards, Richard Neumann, Terri LeClercq, Grace Tonner, Christy Nisbett, Sue Liemer, JoAnne Durako, Steve Johansen, Terry Seligmann, Jane Kent Gionfriddo, Ellen Mosen James, Anita Schnee, Steve Jamar, and Jan Levine. I am grateful to Judy Stinson and Samantha Moppett, who field-tested the book with their students, to my first colleagues, Julie Jenkins and Mary Kate Kearney, and to my first teachers of legal writing and how to teach it, Nancy Elizabeth Grandine and Teresa Godwin Phelps.

I thank my current and former colleagues at Ohio State who provided support, read drafts of this document, and gave advice early and often: Doug Berman, Debby Merritt, Camille Hébert, Chris Fairman, Nancy Rapoport, Cre Johnson, Terri Enns, Steve Huefner, Kathy Northern, and Ruth Colker. I also thank the three Ohio State deans who have affected my life in significant ways: Frank Beytagh, who hired me; Gregory H. Williams, who appointed me to the tenure track; and our current dean,

Nancy Hardin Rogers, who provided critical support at a crucial time in my career. Liz Cutler Gates, Art Hudson, and Loraine Brannon provided technical support, and Nancy Darling, Shirley Craley, Carol Peirano, and Michelle Whetzel-Newton provided administrative support. Finally, I would like to recognize Kimberly Town Abels, now of the University of North Carolina at Chapel Hill, who suggested that the "macro-micro-final draft" method would be suitable for legal writing, and Jacqueline Jones-Royster, Associate Professor of English and Vice Chair for Rhetoric and Composition at the Ohio State University, who suggested that I develop a self-grading instrument for my students.

I have been teaching legal writing since 1982, and I have learned so much from my students over that time. Students at Ohio State have been field testing versions of this text for the past two years, and versions of the self-graded draft since 1993. I want to thank especially the students at Ohio State who have allowed me to use and adapt their work for the examples in this text: RonNell Jones, Tiffany C. Miller, Peter Nealis, Timothy G. Pepper, Rebecca Woods, Bridget Hayward Kahle, Steven Webb, Michael Duffy, Andrew Kruppa, and Christopher Snyder. I am also grateful to the students whose work gave me insight into appellate advocacy, and who sent me examples of good and bad writing after they entered the practice of law, including Glenda Gelzleichter, John Lowe, Peter Rosato, Kevin Kessinger, Angelique Paul, Kathleen Lyon, Cynthia Roselle, Yvonne Watson, and Sean Harris. I particularly thank Jen Manion, research assistant extraordinaire.

I have learned something from each of the many adjuncts with whom I have worked over the years, but especially from Robert Burpee, Peggy Corn, Cynthia Cummings, Hilary Damaser, Ken Donchatz, Rita Eppler, Sean Heasley, Dan Jones, Randy Knutti, and Stephen Wu.

I thank the people at Aspen who guided and encouraged me along the way, including Lynn Churchill, Betsy Kenny, Carol McGeehan, Jay Boggis, Michael Gregory, Peggy Rehberger, and George Serafin. I am also grateful to the anonymous reviewers who gave helpful advice about the manuscript.

Finally, I thank the people at the home front who helped and supported me, including my parents, Ben and Pat Beazley; Trish and Dick Sanders, Mike and Julie Beazley, Marlene and Rick Fields, Mary Slupe, Laura Sanders, and Laura Williams; and of course, my daughters, Betsy and Annie Pillion; and my dear husband, David Pillion.

Acknowledgments to the Second Edition

I give special thanks to the anonymous reviewers who sent suggestions for the second edition, and to the people who sent comments and suggestions for the book or who inspired changes in other ways, including Steve Abreu, Kristopher Armstrong, Thom Bassett, Susan DeJarnatt, Steve Hardwick, John Paul Jones, Jennifer Lavia, Katy Liu, Pam Lysaght, Joan Mathews, John Mollenkamp, Sara Sampson, Steven Tung, and Chris Wren. I am particularly grateful for the work and generosity of Kate Gills, and for the wise counsel of Ken Chestek, Shawn Judge, Terrill Pollman, and Paul A. Woelfl, S.J. I also thank the people at Aspen for their hard work, including Betsy Kenny, Lisa Wehrle, and Christie Rears.

Acknowledgments to the Third Edition

Once again, I give special thanks to the anonymous reviewers who sent suggestions for the third edition. I also thank the students, teachers, and practitioners who sent comments, notified me of typos, or who inspired changes in other ways. I fear listing some, for fear I will leave out someone important, but they include Mark Armstrong, Theresa Cunniff, Susan DeJarnatt, Terri Enns, Paul Giorgianni, Terry Hagen, Traci Martinez, Sheridan McKinney, Amanda McNeil, Marek Pienkos, Pierce Reed, Sarah Ricks, Carla Scherr, and Beth Uhrich.

My colleague at Ohio State, Monte Smith, provided wise counsel and guidance on occasions too numerous to count. I am also thankful for the help of many at Aspen, and I am particularly grateful for the guidance—and necessary nudging—provided by Dana Wilson.

You will see the name "Kobacker" and "Marvin Kobacker" sprinkled throughout the examples in the text and in Appendix C. The "honor" of being used in these entirely fictional contexts was an auction item at an event benefitting Ohio State's Public Interest Law Foundation and was purchased as a gift by his son, James Kobacker.

Acknowledgments to the Fourth Edition

Once again, I give special thanks to the anonymous reviewers who sent suggestions for the fourth edition. I also thank those who sent comments, reviewed edits, or inspired changes in other ways. I fear listing some, for fear I will leave out someone important, but they include Terry Hagen, Terri Enns, Traci Martinez, Pierce Reed, and Katherine Kelly.

Matt Cooper provided invaluable research assistance, especially with regard to procrastination and digital reading issues. My colleague at Ohio State, Monte Smith, once again provided wise counsel and guidance on occasions too numerous to count. I am also thankful for the help of many at Aspen, and I am particularly grateful for the guidance provided by Dana Wilson.

You will see the name "Restrepo" and "Susan Restrepo" sprinkled throughout the examples in the text. Susan purchased the "honor" of being used in these entirely fictional contexts at Ohio State's Public Interest Law Foundation auction in the spring of 2014.

I dedicate this edition to the memory of my mother, Pat Beazley, who died this past February. She "bloomed where she was planted," and three generations have benefitted from her love and wisdom.

A Practical Guide to Appellate Advocacy

Chapter One

INTRODUCTION

1.1
BEFORE WE BEGIN

Okay, I'm going to start out by violating a principle of legal writing and ask you a question: Why are you reading this book? Let me guess—because you have to. You've been given a reading assignment in a course, or someone told you that you should read it to improve your writing. As much as the fond author might hope that her readers look forward to reading her book with delight, the hard reality for textbook authors—and brief writers—is that people read their writing for a *purpose*, and not for pleasure. So here's the first lesson of this text: People read differently when they read for a purpose, and because they read differently, you have to write differently.

This book is about the practical side of appellate advocacy and brief writing, about recognizing the limits that every legal writer works with: factual limits, legal limits, and time limits. It's also about recognizing and understanding the important decisions that you make every time you write a brief, so that you can do a better job making those decisions.

We all make thousands of decisions every day, both consciously and unconsciously. On some level, you have decided that your eyes are going to move across this page to read these words, and that at the end of each line, you will move your eyes to the left to start reading the next one. Many of your decisions are unconscious, or become unconscious, and they need to—you would go crazy if you had to decide consciously to read every word or to take every step when you walk. Just being reminded of the decisions we make, however, can help make us conscious of those decisions. I'm guessing, for example, that some of you became conscious of your eyeballs moving from left to right as you read this paragraph.

If we want to be better writers, we need to identify the important decisions that must be made, so that we can make them consciously and thus more effectively. Too many of us go into default mode when we write. We don't think about which issue we want to argue first, second, or third. We don't identify what our best points are, and so we don't consciously decide to state them as effectively as we can or to put them in the places in the document where we know that readers will be paying the most attention.

And that's the other thing most of us don't think about, either: the people who read our briefs. We know that we're writing a brief to a court, but too many of us, I fear, have some vague, dreamy notion that our brief is being read by a panel consisting of Oliver Wendell Holmes, Thurgood Marshall, and Sandra Day O'Connor—at the peak of their judicial and intellectual powers and on a free day with nothing to do but wonder at the fascinating complexities of our arguments.

Well, life's not like that. First of all, many of your briefs will be read by law clerks as well as judges, and sometimes by law clerks alone. Your readers will be real people with real lives. People who have phones that ring and beep, computers that bring them e-mail messages, and colleagues who knock on their doors and interrupt their work. Your readers are people with families and deadlines. They're people a lot like you, except they're a little further down the road than you are now, if you're a law student, or they took a different road from yours, if you're a practitioner.

So instead of reveling in the complexities of your argument or throwing a bunch of authorities at a busy law clerk, you have a different job to do. You have to look at those complexities and make them easy. You need to find and explain the rules and policies that govern your argument and show explicitly how they connect or don't connect to your client's case, and do it so clearly that the judges will wonder why they didn't notice before how obvious the answer is. You'll follow the law, of course—it's no good writing clearly about legal rules that don't exist. You'll follow the court's rules, too, so that unprofessional errors won't distract the reader from your tight, clean argument. And you'll use honest persuasive techniques to make sure that your readers get the best opportunity to read and understand your arguments.

You'll remember that the audience for a brief wears two hats. You have to write for both the *reader* and the *user*. Most of us think of law clerks (and judges) as readers, who read the brief sequentially from beginning to end. At some point, however, they act as users: They are hunting for a particular authority or argument, or they want to know immediately what each sentence, paragraph, or section is about, because if it isn't about what they care about, they want to skip it. So when you write and revise, you have to remember both the reader and the user, and write in a way that helps them both.

Furthermore, when considering the differences between readers and users, you need to consider whether they will encounter your text as a paper-and-toner document or in digital form. And of course that digital form may appear on a desktop or laptop computer, on an iPad or similar tablet, or on a smartphone. Modern readers are in a transition stage between paper text and digital text. For this reason, you should write for both paper and digital readers.

You should also be practical about your own behavior as a writer and self-editor. You'll learn how to identify the important decisions that you have to make, and to take steps that will help you to recognize what information you've included and what information you've left out of your argument.

By being practical about both your audience's needs and your needs, you can learn how to use the resources available to create documents that are easy to read and easy to use.

1.2
KNOW YOUR AUDIENCE

At this point in your law school career, you have probably written at least two kinds of documents: an office memo and a case brief. As you know, a typical office memo is a document that an attorney writes to a supervising attorney. The memo analyzes one or more legal issues and predicts how a court would rule on those issues. A case brief, in contrast, is an organized set of notes on a court decision, and the writer essentially has himself or herself as an audience. Now you are being asked to write a brief to a court. Briefs of this kind are written to persuade courts to take certain actions or make certain decisions. Although the formal purposes for appellate briefs and motion briefs are different, they are often similar to each other in use of authority and persuasive techniques, and they are both similar to office memoranda in analytical structure.

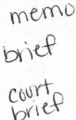

memo
brief
court brief

An *appellate brief* is written to an appellate court. As you know, both state and federal court systems include at least one level of appellate review; most include both an intermediate appellate court and a court of last resort. For example, in the federal system, when a federal district court issues a final order, the losing party may appeal to a United States Court of Appeals in the relevant circuit. When the Court of Appeals issues its decision, the losing party may file a writ of certiorari that asks the United States Supreme Court to review the decision of the Court of Appeals.

The party that brings the appeal may be called the *appellant*, because he or she is *appealing* to the higher court to review the decision. The party opposing the appeal is often called the *appellee*. In some courts, the party bringing the appeal is called the *petitioner*, because he or she is *petitioning* to the higher court to ask it to review. In those courts, the other party is often called the *respondent,* because he or she is *responding* to the petition for review.

The audience for a *motion brief,* in contrast, is usually a trial court. Attorneys write motion briefs to argue that a court should *grant* or *deny* a particular *motion.* A motion is a formal request that the court take an action or make a decision relevant to a case before the court. Whenever a party wants the court to take any action in the case (other than the decision on the merits), it must *move* the court or file *a motion.* The parties may file a motion to ask the court to postpone the trial date, to limit the kinds of evidence that may be heard in a case, or to decide in favor of one party or the other without a formal trial. The more significant the motion, the more likely it is that the parties will support the motion with a *motion brief.*[1]

In a motion brief, the attorneys support their arguments by analyzing how the controlling law applies to certain agreed-upon facts (usually the facts that the plaintiff provided in the complaint; sometimes these facts may be supplemented by affidavits or other documents). The party who filed the motion (often the defendant) is sometimes referred to as the *movant* or the *moving party.* The moving party writes the *Brief in Support of the Motion.* The party who did not file the motion, sometimes referred to as the *opponent* or the *non-moving party,* writes the *Brief in Opposition to the Motion.* The parties are also referred to by their categorizations of *plaintiff* or *defendant,* as appropriate. Although many motions are decided on the basis of the briefs alone, the court may ask counsel to participate in an oral argument to help it decide the issues before it.

Whether you are writing to an appellate court or a trial court, you are writing to a busy reader. The United States Supreme Court, for example, hears approximately 80 cases per term. Consider that each case requires reading several documents. The petitioner submits a brief accompanying the petition for writ of certiorari, and the potential respondent often submits a brief in response. If the Court grants the petition, there will usually be three briefs on the merits: petitioner's brief on the merits, respondent's brief on the merits, and petitioner's reply brief on the merits. Furthermore, various parties may submit amicus briefs, and counsel for the parties will submit documents to support or oppose the various motions that may accompany Supreme Court practice.

Thus, even estimating conservatively that each case generates around seven documents, Supreme Court Justices and their clerks are reading over 500 briefs per year. Of course, this statistic does not take into account the reading required when the Justices review the joint appendix (selected elements of the case record) and the statutes, cases, and other sources cited in the briefs. It also does not take into account the time spent reviewing

---

[1]Note that these documents are sometimes given other labels, including *Trial Briefs* and *Memoranda of Points & Authorities.*

the thousands of certiorari petitions that are ultimately denied or—by the way—the time spent writing opinions.

The numbers are equally impressive in other courts. Judge Boyce F. Martin, Jr., of the United States Court of Appeals for the Sixth Circuit, estimated in 1999 that the average judge on the Sixth Circuit sits on 32 panels and hears 192 cases a year.[2] The Federal Court Management Statistics for the United States Court of Appeals revealed that in 2012, the average circuit judge was responsible for deciding hundreds of cases and writing 59 signed opinions and 75 unsigned opinions.[3] At the state-court level, an intermediate appellate judge may write anywhere from 50 to over 100 opinions each year.[4] Presuming that these judges sit on three-judge panels and that the opinion-writing duties are evenly spread, even judges who write fewer opinions may hear 150 to 300 cases per year.

An associate justice in Maine's highest court noted that during her first six months on the court, she and her colleagues heard 114 oral arguments and conferenced 181 cases on briefs alone, in addition to reviewing 120 petitions for review of workers' compensation matters.[5] A former Wisconsin Court of Appeals judge estimated that he read 24 *sets* of briefs per month, or almost 300 sets per year.[6] Although cases submitted to lower courts may not generate the same number of documents as cases submitted to the United States Supreme Court, the number is still daunting: The average intermediate court judge will read 600 briefs per year, while the average federal circuit judge may read as many as 900 briefs per year.

Writers of motion briefs should not presume that their trial judges have ample time to read, either. One trial judge observed that, while hearing and deciding motions is "but a small part" of the work of a trial judge, it

---

[2] Boyce F. Martin, Jr., *In Defense of Unpublished Opinions,* 60 Ohio St. L.J. 177, 182 (1999).

[3] Federal Court Management Statistics, http://www.uscourts.gov/uscourts/Statistics/Federal CourtManagementStatistics/2013/appeals-fcms-summary-pages-march-2013.pdf. Note that the median number of signed opinions was 42.3, with the median number of unsigned opinions at 82.5. *See also* Honorable Ruggero J. Aldisert, Meehan Rasch & Matthew P. Bartlett, *Opinion Writing and Opinion Readers,* 31 Cardozo L. Rev. 1, 7 (2009) (citing the 2008 report and noting that the average federal circuit judge wrote 152 opinions in 2008).

[4] *See* the 2012 Annual Report of the Indiana Court of Appeals, which indicates that each judge who served for the entire 12 months wrote over 100 majority opinions. http://www.in.gov/ judiciary/appeals/files/annual-report-2012.pdf.pdf. *See also* 2009 Oregon Court of Appeals Annual Report, http://www.publications.ojd.state.or.us/2009CAReport.pdf (last visited Mar. 28, 2010) (noting that in 2009, the ten Oregon Appellate Judges "closed 3,609 cases, issued 2,173 case dispositional decisions, and issued 503 authored opinions"); Honorable Edwin H. Stern, *Frustrations of an Intermediate Appellate Judge (and the Benefits of Being One in New Jersey),* 60 Rutgers L. Rev. 971, 980 (2008) ("Each judge now writes an average of 108 opinions a year, independent of the cases disposed of by motion, sua sponte, or other order"); Daniel J. Foley, *The Tennessee Court of Criminal Appeals: A Statistical Analysis,* 66 Tenn. L. Rev. 427, 442 (1999) (citing National Ctr. for State Cts., Court Statistics Project, State Court Caseload Statistics, 1994, at 133-36 (1996)).

[5] Leigh Ingalls Saufley, *The Judicial Process: Amphibians and Appellate Courts,* 51 Me. L. Rev. 18, 19 (1999).

[6] William Eich, *Writing the Persuasive Brief,* 76 Wis. Law. 20, 22 (Feb. 2003).

has become "overwhelming."[7] A federal district judge noted that "[a]t any given time," on her own docket she carries "approximately 500 civil and another 75 criminal cases."[8] Scholars who analyzed statistics from state and federal courts recently concluded that "[t]rial courts handle approximately 98% of the thirty-five million cases that the federal and state courts resolve each year."[9]

Think about these statistics when you make every decision—from whether to file a motion or an appeal,[10] to the number of issues to argue, to (especially) how to organize and write the brief. Your goal should be to produce a document that can be understood by a busy reader the first time through without reference to outside sources.

1.3
FOLLOW AN EFFECTIVE WRITING PROCESS

Because your reader is so busy, you should keep four policies in mind as you make your brief-writing decisions:

(1) **The *law* upon which you base your argument should be complete and accurate.** No judge wants to waste time considering arguments that must be rejected. Furthermore, if you have failed to identify a significant legal authority or an important legal, ethical, or policy argument, you should presume that no one else will dig it up either.

(2) **Your arguments must be *organized and written* in a way that makes them easy to read and understand.** Write with your audience in mind, and presume that your audience is intelligent but ignorant of the specifics of your case. If your readers can't understand your point without a struggle, they probably won't understand it at all.

(3) **You must avoid *mechanical* problems of all types.** First, as a matter of professionalism, you should follow the local rules of the court about format requirements and other ancillary matters. In some courts, failure to follow the rules will get a case dismissed; in others, it may result in your brief being returned so that you can try again to comply with the rules.

---

[7] Honorable Helen E. Hoens, *Writing Persuasively at the Trial Court Level: Practical Tips on Style and Substance,* 210 N.J. Law. 9 (Aug. 2001).

[8] Honorable Sarah Evans Barker, *Beyond Decisional Templates: The Role of Imaginative Justice in the Trial Court* (Hallows Lecture), 92 Marq. L. Rev. 667, 674 (2009).

[9] Chris Guthrie, Jeffrey J. Rachlinski & Andrew J. Wistrich, *Blinking on the Bench: How Judges Decide Cases*, 93 Cornell L. Rev. 1, 4 (2007) (citations omitted).

[10] This book is meant to advise on methods of brief-writing and oral argument. For advice on preserving issues for appeal and deciding whether to appeal, you should consult a reference geared to the jurisdiction in which you are practicing. *See, e.g.,* Kristen Brown, G. Ronald Darlington, Kevin McKeon & Daniel Schuckers, 20 Pennsylvania Appellate Practice 2012-2013 edition chs. 1-13 (West); Paul G. Ulrich, *Federal Appellate Practice: Ninth Circuit* (2d ed., West 1999) (most recent update 2013).

Even if you escape these sanctions, you hurt your credibility with the court when you make technical mistakes.[11] Second, proofread carefully to avoid typographical errors, citation form errors, and mistakes in citations (e.g., transposed page or paragraph numbers). Although these errors may not seem legally significant, they waste time and hence annoy the reader.

(4) **You should use *persuasive techniques* that make the most of your facts and your arguments but that do not violate ethical rules or otherwise hamper your credibility with the court.** If your persuasive methods go too far, all of the work you have devoted to writing a legally valid, well-organized, and error-free document will be wasted. The court may well discount valid arguments, or even stop reading your brief, if it believes that you cannot be trusted.

Not coincidentally, these four policies represent four different focuses in the writing process. It is impossible to make each of these focuses totally separate. For example, you cannot help but notice your content while you are reviewing your organization. By forcing yourself to pay special attention to each of these areas, however, you make it easier to create an effective brief.

Keeping these concepts in mind may be easier if you connect them to a little bit of writing theory. Although there are many more sophisticated ways of talking about the schools of writing theory, two schools are particularly significant for legal writing. One is the *cognitivist* school, and another is the *social perspective* school.[12]

The cognitivist school teaches that writing is a way to think about things and to learn about them. If you are thinking in cognitivist terms as you write, you are not writing for someone to read your writing; you are merely writing to figure out what you know about something or to generate new knowledge about your topic. Although many people used to think that writing was merely a way for us to record our already completed thoughts,[13] we now realize that writing is more than the hands taking dictation from the brain. When we write, we engage in brainstorming with ourselves. We question and challenge our presumptions, discover new ways of thinking about something, and gain insights that had not occurred to us before we began to write.

The cognitivist theory of writing helps legal writers to understand the benefits of multiple drafts. Writing multiple drafts of the same document allows you to let at least one of the drafts be a "working draft" or a "thinking draft"—that is, a draft you can write without worrying about what the reader thinks or about whether the reader will understand you. In this

---

[11] *See generally* Judith D. Fischer, *Bareheaded and Barefaced Counsel: Courts React to Unprofessionalism in Lawyers' Papers*, 31 Suffolk U. L. Rev. 1, 20-36 (1997).

[12] *See generally* J. Christopher Rideout & Jill J. Ramsfield, *Legal Writing: A Revised View*, 69 Wash. L. Rev. 35 (1994).

[13] Philip C. Kissam, *Thinking (By Writing) About Legal Writing*, 40 Vand. L. Rev. 135, 138 (1987).

way you can use the process of writing to understand your issues better, discover what aspects of your writing need more research and analysis, and clarify your legal thinking.

The second school of writing theory that is particularly relevant to legal writing is the social perspective school. The social perspective school tells us that writers must understand the needs and expectations of their audiences and write in a way that meets those needs and expectations. For example, if you were asked to draft an opinion letter for a client who happens to be a lawyer, you would write it very differently than if you were asked to write a similar letter for a client who is not a lawyer.

The social perspective school of writing theory reminds you to think about "readers" and "users" and about judges' workload and attention span. When legal writers are writing an appellate brief, for example, they may have particular formal requirements that they must meet. They could be required to include a table of contents, a table of authorities, a statement of the case, a statement of the issue, an argument, and a conclusion. Judges and the clerks might be confused, frustrated, or even angry if the brief-writer violated their expectations by not including the required elements.

Writers who keep writing theory in mind will first allow themselves to spend time researching, brainstorming, drafting, and using other techniques to think about the problem in creative ways, so that they fully understand the message that they intend to convey. Only after gaining sufficient understanding of the message will they pay close attention to the reader's needs and requirements. Of course, legal writers should keep the reader's needs in mind from the early stages of the process. Paying attention to many of the reader's needs—for example, the need for clear articulation of the rule, the need for discussion of one issue at a time, the need for an explication of the meaning of the legal rule—will also help the writer in the cognitive stages to gain a fuller understanding of the legal issues that the case presents.

1.4
HOW TO USE THIS BOOK

In this book, you will learn about techniques to help you to advance each of the policies noted previously and thus to write a better brief, whether for an appellate court or a trial court. (To see a sample of both an appellate brief and a motion brief, consult Appendix C.) Although you are writing with the complete end product in mind, your end product will usually be better if you follow a writing process that focuses your attention on only one task at a time.

As you begin your writing process, focus your attention on gaining an understanding of the legal issues that your case presents and of the legal authorities that govern those issues. Get to know the facts of the case, and plan and execute your research. Chapter Three will give you advice on getting to know your record and planning your research.

When your research is fairly complete, focus your attention on how to structure your argument. You might even write a rough draft of your argument as a method of trying to understand how the law and the facts relate. After you have gained an understanding of how the legal issues of your case relate to the legal authorities, use the rewriting stage of the writing process to think about how best to organize the document so that your reader will be able to understand the legal issues as well as you do. You can do this by writing a draft of just the argument section of the document that (1) uses the arguments and authorities that you think are necessary, (2) uses an effective large-scale organization, and (3) includes a full analysis of each legal issue. Because this type of draft is focused on large-scale, or macro, concerns, you may wish to think of it as a *macro draft*. Chapters Four and Five will help you as you rough out your argument and plan its structure.

After you have created a macro draft of some kind, review and revise your written argument a few times, focusing on these two important features of content and organization. Check your authorities, and supplement your research if necessary. Eliminate weak arguments, and devote your attention to the strong ones. Make sure that each section of the argument is focused on just one point. Chapter Six will help you to examine your use of authority, while Chapter Seven will help you to review your argument for focus and completeness.

Next, create a draft of the entire document, including everything from the cover page to the certificate of service. Because this type of draft broadens its focus to include small-scale, or micro, concerns, you may wish to think of it as a *micro draft*. Chapter Eight identifies and describes the elements that courts commonly require in appellate briefs and motion briefs.

After you have created your micro draft, review the way that you have presented your arguments. For example, make sure that you have laid out your arguments clearly and organized them well. Take a look at the signals you are sending to the reader and the user through your headings, roadmaps, and topic sentences, and revise them as needed. Evaluate your statement of the case to verify that it presents the facts in a positive light without stretching the truth. Review each element of the brief in this way to make sure that you are presenting an accurate and effective legal argument. Chapter Ten will help you to make your document more user-friendly, while Chapters Nine and Eleven will help you to use persuasive writing techniques both in the argument and in those special elements such as the question presented, statement of the case, and the summary of the argument.

In the polishing stage of the writing process, pay attention to sentence structure, grammar, citation form, and format details so that you create a final draft that is complete, well structured, and free from distracting technical errors. Chapter Twelve will give you guidance on objective techniques you can use to make your document error-free.

Even before you are finished writing the brief, you should be considering the oral argument. Of course, the brief, in large measure, will dictate the oral argument, but a practice oral argument can also help you to write your brief. You may want to hold a moot court while you are still writing the brief, perhaps even while you are working on the first draft of your argument. Preparing for an oral as opposed to a written presentation will force you to confront your issues and arguments from a different point of view. As you argue, you may realize the strengths of certain arguments and the weaknesses of others. The process can result in significant substantive or structural changes in your written product. Chapter Thirteen gives you advice on preparing an effective oral argument; Chapter Fourteen addresses using oral argument and brief-writing skills in moot court competitions.

As you work on all of these tasks, you might keep in mind one of Aesop's lesser-known fables, about an argument between the sun and the wind:

> The Wind and the Sun were disputing which was the stronger. Suddenly they saw a traveler coming down the road, and the Sun said: "I see a way to decide our dispute. Whichever of us can cause that traveler to take off his cloak shall be regarded as the stronger. You begin." So the Sun retired behind a cloud, and the Wind began to blow as hard as it could upon the traveler. But the harder he blew the more closely did the traveler wrap his cloak round him, till at last the Wind had to give up in despair. Then the Sun came out and shone in all his glory upon the traveler, who, finding it too hot to walk with his cloak on, soon took it off.

The moral of this fable is that "kindness effects more than severity,"[14] or, to put it another way, "you catch more flies with honey than with vinegar." Like the sun and the wind, you are trying to get someone to do something when you act as an advocate. To be most effective as an advocate, however, you must be both the sun *and* the wind. As the wind, you use the law and the facts to show the court that it *must* reach a decision in your client's favor. As the sun, you use persuasive writing techniques to help the court realize that it *wants* to reach that decision.

---

[14] http://aesopfables.com/cgi/aesop1.cgi?srch&fabl/TheWindandtheSun (last visited Oct. 14, 2013).

1.5
SUMMARY

People read and use briefs in a different way than they do books or newspapers, and brief writers should write in a way that takes audience needs into account. No process can guarantee a perfect result, but it is practical to use a process that requires you to focus your attention on certain aspects of the document at the appropriate time. Just as you probably would not paint the trim of a house before deciding what color to paint the walls, you should not fuss with grammar problems and format concerns before you have decided which authorities and arguments will be most effective in your case. By following an effective writing process, you help to ensure that—given the inevitable limitations of the law, the facts, and the deadlines—you will submit the best brief possible.

Chapter Two

APPELLATE JURISDICTION AND STANDARDS OF REVIEW

Understanding some basic principles about the various courts and their powers will help you to make decisions as you prepare your written and oral arguments. Your arguments will be different if you are writing a brief to a trial court as opposed to an appellate court. Even within the appellate system, you may argue differently to an intermediate court of appeals as opposed to a court of last resort. On the one hand, intermediate courts of appeals must hear every appeal (with few exceptions)[1] and must follow the decisions of the courts above them. Courts of last resort, on the other hand, usually have some authority to decide which cases they will hear[2] and the authority to make new law.

[1] *See, e.g.*, Tenn. R. App. P. 3; Fed. R. App. P. 3.
[2] *See, e.g.*, Ohio Sup. Ct. Prac. R. 5.01 (discussing "appeals of right"); 5.02 (discussing "jurisdictional appeals"); 5.03 (discussing "certified conflict cases"); and 5.04 (discussing certified questions of state law from federal courts). *See also* U.S. Sup. Ct. R. 10 (governing certiorari).

This chapter briefly explains principles of appellate jurisdiction before discussing how writers can use the appropriate standards of review in both appellate briefs and motion briefs.

2.1
JURISDICTION IN COURTS OF LAST RESORT

A "court of last resort" is the highest court in a particular legal system. It is the last court to which litigants can resort when seeking resolution of a legal issue. In the federal system, the United States Supreme Court is the court of last resort, and the majority of its cases come from the United States Courts of Appeals of the various circuits. In state systems, the highest court of appeals—often called the Supreme Court—is the court of last resort, and it generally hears cases from that state's intermediate appellate courts. The United States Supreme Court can also hear appeals from state courts of last resort, but only if the issue is a matter of federal law. For example, the Court may hear an appeal in order to determine whether a state court has interpreted a law in a way that may have conflicted with the United States Constitution.

Most courts of last resort are not merely courts of error; that is, they do not take cases simply because one party claims that there was an error of law in a lower court decision. For example, Rule 10 of the Rules of the Supreme Court of the United States explicitly says that "[a] petition for a writ of certiorari [the main method for gaining access to the Court] is rarely granted when the asserted error consists of erroneous factual findings or the misapplication of a properly stated rule of law." Instead, a court of last resort takes cases in order to resolve pressing issues, and it may refuse to take cases unless or until it believes that its intervention is necessary.[3] Two factors make it more likely that the United States Supreme Court, for instance, will grant a petition for a writ of certiorari. First, the Court frequently grants certiorari if it believes that a state court or a lower federal court of appeals is misinterpreting or misapplying the Court's jurisprudence. Second, and more commonly, the Court will grant certiorari when two or more courts are in conflict over an interpretation of the federal Constitution, or when courts are in conflict over a question of federal law.[4]

[handwritten margin note: when USSC grants writ of certiorari]

---

[3] The Rules of Practice of the Ohio Supreme Court, for example, describe eight different kinds of cases that the court may hear, including "Appeals of Right." Ohio Sup. Ct. Prac. R. 5.01. The court also hears "Jurisdictional Appeals," which are discretionary and require a supporting memorandum that must contain "[a] thorough explanation of why a substantial constitutional question is involved, why the case is of public or great general interest, or, in a felony case, why leave to appeal should be granted." Ohio Sup. Ct. Prac. R. 5.02(A), 7.02 (C) (2).

[4] *See generally* U.S. Sup. Ct. R. 10.

Interestingly, the Court does not always grant certiorari immediately when either of these factors is present. It is not uncommon for the Court to let a conflict simmer for a few years, with different lower courts writing decisions either way. The Court may use this method purposefully, to benefit from the analysis and reasoning of several different lower courts. By allowing several opinions to be written on a subject, the Court can assess several different resolutions and analyses of the same issue.

Perhaps for these reasons, the Court attaches no precedential value to the denial of a petition for a writ of certiorari. That is, a denial of certiorari does *not* indicate that the Court approves of the decision below. Rather, it means only that the Court did not believe, for whatever reason, that it was an issue that was worthy of its review *at that time.*

2.2
JURISDICTION IN INTERMEDIATE COURTS OF APPEALS

The rules are somewhat different in intermediate courts of appeals. Generally, state and federal intermediate courts of appeals will hear any appeal of a final order if the appellant has met specified procedural guidelines.[5] The United States Courts of Appeals have jurisdiction over appeals from all final decisions of the United States District Courts.[6] The courts of appeals also have jurisdiction to hear appeals from a variety of other judicial and quasi-judicial bodies, including, for example, appeals to enforce or challenge orders of the National Labor Relations Board.[7]

Federal intermediate courts of appeals may decide cases without oral argument. Although, according to the rules, oral argument is presumed, a three-judge panel can vote unanimously that oral argument is unnecessary in a given case for any of the following three reasons:

1. The appeal is frivolous.
2. The dispositive issue or issues have been authoritatively decided.

---

[5] *See, e.g.,* Ohio R. App. P. tit. II, R. 3; Fed. R. App. P. 3. Appeals of certain criminal appeals may have to meet different standards. Interlocutory appeals are governed by the guidelines in 28 U.S.C. §1292. *See also Mohawk Indus. v. Carpenter,* 558 U.S. 100, 109 (2009) (interlocutory decisions adverse to attorney-client privilege do not qualify for immediate appeal); *Coopers & Lybrand v. Livesay,* 437 U.S. 463, 475 (1978) (describing court discretion). Of course, states may have different rules as to various kinds of appeals. *E.g., Commonwealth v. Harris,* 32 A.3d 243, 250 (Penn. 2011) (allowing interlocutory appeals of orders that would reveal privileged information, and noting that "Pennsylvania law permits interlocutory appeals by permission, but under a somewhat different standard than the federal system").

[6] 28 U.S.C. §1291.

[7] 29 U.S.C. §160(e), (f).

3. The facts and legal arguments are adequately presented in the briefs and record, and the decisional process would not be significantly aided by oral argument.[8]

What this rule means in practice is that a large percentage of cases are assigned to the so-called summary docket, and many of those are decided based on memoranda submitted by law clerks and staff attorneys who have reviewed the party briefs. The courts' statistics indicate that in the year ending March 31, 2012, more than 75 percent of the appeals terminated on the merits were decided without oral argument.[9] When cases are on the summary docket, some judges make their decisions based on staff memoranda alone; they may not read the briefs in full at all. The practical brief writer will presume that oral argument will not be granted, and will write a brief that can persuade a law clerk as well as a judge.

2.3
APPELLATE STANDARDS OF REVIEW

Whether an appellate court is an intermediate court of appeals or a court of last resort, whether it hears an appeal as of right or as a matter of discretion, it agrees only to *review* the decision below. Hearing an appeal does not mean that the court will retry the case. Instead of observing the examination and cross-examination of witnesses, hearing opening and closing arguments, and seeing the attorneys present various evidentiary exhibits all over again, the court *reviews* important evidence (whether findings of fact, testimony, or exhibits) and the attorneys' written arguments—in the form of briefs to the court—about the significance of that evidence. During the oral argument on appeal (if any), the court questions the attorneys about the sufficiency of the evidence, the significance of the arguments, or the impact of a holding one way or the other. The court then decides whether to affirm, to reverse, to reverse and remand, or to vacate the decision below.

When reviewing the decision of any lower court, the court—explicitly or implicitly—applies a certain appellate standard of review to that decision. The *appellate standard of review*[10] is a label that a reviewing court puts

---

[8] Fed. R. App. P. 34(a)(2).

[9] Federal Judicial Center, *U.S. Courts of Appeals: Appeals Commenced, Terminated, and Pending, by Circuit (Excludes Federal Circuit)*, http://www.uscourts.gov/Viewer.aspx?doc=/uscourts/Statistics/FederalJudicialCaseloadStatistics/2012/tables/B01Mar12.pdf (last visited Oct. 28, 2013). *See also* Patricia M. Wald, *19 Tips from 19 Years on the Appellate Bench*, 1 J. App. Prac. & Proc. 7, 9 (1999) (estimating that 60 percent of cases nationwide are decided without oral argument).

[10] For the sake of clarity, I use the label *appellate standards of review* to refer to these standards. However, as noted below, many courts use the label *standard of review* to refer to appellate standards of review, motion standards of review, and government action standards of review.

on the level of **deference** it gives to the findings of the court below. The appellate standard of review tells the court how "wrong" the lower court has to be before it will be reversed.

The appellate standard of review that the court chooses to apply depends on which aspect of the case is under review: an evidentiary ruling, a finding of fact, a legal ruling, or some other type of decision. Some decisions can be reversed simply if the reviewing court disagrees with the lower court. Others can be reversed only if the reviewing court can identify a serious error on the part of the court below. Generally, courts give high deference to decisions about facts—that is, they are loathe to upset a finding of fact—and low deference to conclusions of law. Because the particular appellate standard of review can significantly affect the arguments that you make to the court, you should consider this issue early in your research process and decide what standard the court is likely to apply to the decision that you seek to have reversed or hope to have affirmed.

2.3.1
PURPOSE AND MEANING OF APPELLATE STANDARDS OF REVIEW

Various public policies support the competing appellate standards of review.[11] Appellate courts use a low deference appellate standard of review for decisions about the law because they believe that those who must use the law benefit from uniformity.[12] Low deference standards give reviewing courts an opportunity to create a consistent body of law, which may be particularly important for issues of constitutional rights.[13] In fact, when a constitutional issue is involved, courts may decide to substitute the low deference de novo standard for a higher deference standard that might normally be appropriate for a given issue.[14]

A high-deference appellate standard of review promotes judicial economy and finality of certain types of decisions. A high-deference standard is also based on the premise that the trial court is in the best position to understand evidence. Particularly in the case of witness testimony, a trial court judge or jury has an opportunity that the court of appeals doesn't have. The judge or jury can observe the witnesses' demeanor, their tone of voice, and their body language, and use its best judgment based on those intangibles when it makes findings of fact.

[11] For an interesting discussion of the policies behind certain appellate standards of review, see Michael R. Bosse, *Standards of Review: The Meaning of Words*, 49 Me. L. Rev. 367, 374-84 (1997).
[12] *See, e.g., Cooper Indus., Inc. v. Leatherman Tool Group, Inc.*, 532 U.S. 424, 436 (2001); *Ornelas v. United States*, 517 U.S. 690, 698 (1996).
[13] *See generally* Bosse, *supra* note 11, at 383, 397.
[14] *See, e.g., Cooper Indus., Inc. v. Leatherman Tool Group, Inc.*, 532 U.S. 424, 434 (2001) (Court used de novo standard to review a district court determination of the constitutionality of a punitive damages award).

Although many advocates ignore the standard after articulating it, the appellate standard of review is really the context within which the entire argument rests. Because there is often no controversy about which standard applies, however, some litigators are lulled into complacency on this subject and may miss fertile ground for legal argument.[15]

As a practical lawyer, you should devote serious attention to the standard of review early in the research process in order to determine the role it will play in your case. The discussion that follows describes the most significant appellate standards of review, using the labels most commonly used in federal courts. Although, of course, you must rely on research rather than a textbook to provide support for any standard of review argument, state courts often apply standards that are similar to the federal standards.

a. Clearly Erroneous

A **clearly erroneous** standard applies to findings of facts. Rule 52(a) of the Federal Rules of Civil Procedure provides: "Findings of Fact, whether based on oral or documentary evidence, must not be set aside unless clearly erroneous, and the reviewing court must give due regard to the trial court's opportunity to judge the witnesses' credibility." This standard reflects the attitude that the fact finder is often in the best position to observe the presentation of the facts. The United States Supreme Court has commented on the importance of the trial judge's opportunities:

> The rationale for deference to the original finder of fact is not limited to the superiority of the trial judge's position to make determinations of credibility. The trial judge's major role is the determination of fact, and with experience in fulfilling that role comes expertise. . . . [T]he trial on the merits should be "the 'main event' . . . rather than a 'tryout on the road.'" . . . When findings are based on determinations regarding the credibility of witnesses, Rule 52(a) demands even greater deference to the trial court's findings; for only the trial judge can be aware of the variations in

---

[15] The United States Supreme Court frequently addresses standard of review issues. *See, e.g., Brown v. Plata,* 131 S. Ct. 1910, 1932 (2011) (deciding appropriate standard of review of a three-judge district court opinion deciding legal and factual issues relating to prison overcrowding); *Metro. Life Ins. Co. v. Glenn,* 554 U.S. 105, 111 (2008) (analyzing appropriate standards of review in ERISA appeals); *Gall v. United States,* 552 U.S. 38, 46 (2007) (analyzing use of the abuse of discretion standard of review in sentencing decisions); *Cooper Indus., Inc. v. Leatherman Tool Group, Inc.,* 532 U.S. 424, 434 (2001) (finding that de novo review, rather than abuse of discretion, was appropriate standard of review for district court determination of the constitutionality of a punitive damages award); *Ornelas v. United States,* 517 U.S. 690 (1996) (holding that determinations of "reasonable suspicion" and "probable cause" should be reviewed de novo by appellate courts). *See generally* Bosse, *supra* note 11, at 374-84 (discussing *Ornelas*), and Kelly Kunsch, *Standard of Review (State and Federal): A Primer,* 18 Seattle U. L. Rev. 11, 25 (1994).

demeanor and tone of voice that bear so heavily on the listener's under-standing of and belief in what is said.[16]

Courts often note that a court should find clear error only when its review of the record leads to "a definite and firm conviction" that the court has committed a mistake.[17] The clearly erroneous standard is a high hurdle for an advocate to overcome. The Seventh Circuit has used a pisca-torial metaphor to explain the standard's meaning:

(handwritten note: high standard)

> To be clearly erroneous, a decision must strike us as more than just maybe or probably wrong; it must, as one member of this court recently stated during oral argument, strike us as wrong with the force of a five-week-old, unrefrigerated dead fish.[18]

Although not all courts use such vivid language to describe their reactions, all courts are extremely hesitant to overturn findings of fact.[19]

b. De Novo

Because most decisions that come before appellate courts are based on questions of law, the most commonly applied standard is the **de novo** standard. The de novo standard is a low-deference standard—or, more aptly, a no-deference standard—that applies when courts are reviewing the meaning or application of the controlling law. De novo review is sometimes referred to as "plenary review" because it allows the court to give a full, or plenary, review to the findings below. When courts apply the de novo standard, they look at the legal questions as if no one had yet decided them, giving no deference to legal findings made below. When this standard is applied, the reviewing court is willing to substitute its judgment for that of the trial court or the intermediate court of appeals.

Courts apply the de novo standard not only to questions of law, but also, in most cases, to mixed questions of law and fact.[20] A mixed question

---

[16] *Anderson v. City of Bessemer City*, 470 U.S. 564, 574, 575 (1985).

[17] *E.g., United States v. U.S. Gypsum Co.*, 333 U.S. 364, 395 (1948); *Brown v. Plata*, 131 S. Ct. 1910, 1930 (2011); *J. L. v. Mercer Island Sch. Dist.*, 592 F.3d 938, 949 (9th Cir. 2010).

[18] *Parts & Elec. Motors, Inc. v. Sterling Elec. Inc.*, 866 F.2d 228, 233 (7th Cir. 1988).

[19] Note that all federal (and most state) jury findings, which may be hard to separate into distinct questions of law and fact, are usually reviewed under the "substantial evidence" standard per the Seventh Amendment to the United States Constitution, which provides that "no fact tried by a jury shall be otherwise re-examined in any Court of the United States, than according to the rules of the common law." Those "rules of the common law" generally provide that such a finding must have only a "reasonable basis in the law" and have "warrant in the record." *NLRB v. Hearst Publications*, 322 U.S. 111, 131 (1944). Commentators have noted that courts are extremely reluctant to find that there is not "substantial evidence" to support a jury finding. Kunsch, *supra* note 15, at 43. *See also United States v. Ellefson*, 419 F.3d 859, 862-63 (8th Cir. 2005) ("We may reverse a jury's verdict only if 'no reasonable jury could have found the accused guilty beyond a reasonable doubt.'") (citation omitted). *See also United States v. Boria*, 592 F.3d 476, 480 (Fed. Cir. 2010).

[20] *Brown v. Plata*, 131 S. Ct. 1910, 1932 (2011) (applying a deferential standard to a mixed question of law and fact because, in the Court's opinion, "the mix weigh[ed] heavily on the 'fact' side" (citations omitted)).

of law and fact is often characterized as a question about whether certain agreed-upon facts meet a legal standard. In *Ornelas v. United States*, for example, the United States Supreme Court decided that de novo was an appropriate appellate standard of review when it reviewed a trial court's determination as to whether a police officer indeed had probable cause based on the undisputed facts.[21] The Court justifies the de novo standard in mixed question situations, as it does when it reviews other questions of law, with the goal of unifying precedent and stabilizing legal principles.[22]

If the de novo standard applies, the legal findings of the courts below have *no weight* other than their intrinsic validity. Some novice legal writers make the mistake of citing to the decision under review in order to justify a conclusion that they want the appellate court to accept. It is certainly appropriate to argue that the decision below is correct, but you must support that assertion with citations to authorities other than the decision under review.

c. Abuse of Discretion

The **abuse of discretion** standard is typically used to review discretionary decisions such as a judge's procedural rulings during a trial. These decisions might include decisions on nondispositive motions, objections, admissibility of evidence, or general conduct issues.[23] Commentators have noted that language such as "the court may" or "for good cause" are often predictors of an abuse of discretion standard of review.[24] Like the clearly erroneous standard, this standard presumes some expertise on the part of the trial court judge. Some judges see the standard in the same light as the clearly erroneous standard. For example, the United States Court of Appeals for the First Circuit has noted that, as to evidentiary rulings, "[o]nly rarely—and in extraordinarily compelling circumstances—will we, from the vista of a cold appellate record, reverse a district court's on-the-spot judgment concerning the relative weighing of probative value and unfair effect."[25]

d. Other Appellate Standards

Review of administrative agency decisions is governed by the Administrative Procedure Act, which provides at 5 U.S.C. §706 that

---

[21] *Ornelas*, 517 U.S. at 695.

[22] *See generally Ornelas*, 517 U.S. at 697; *United States v. Arvizu*, 534 U.S. 266, 275 (2002).

[23] *See, e.g.,* Kunsch, *supra* note 15, at 34-35.

[24] Kunsch, *supra* note 15, at 35 (citing Maurice Rosenberg, *Judicial Discretion of the Trial Court, Viewed from Above*, 22 Syracuse L. Rev. 635, 655 (1971)). *See also In re Terrorist Bombings of U.S. Embassies in E. Afr. v. Odeh*, 552 F.3d 93, 135 (2d Cir. 2008) (noting use of phrase "the court may" in rule of criminal procedure as signal that abuse of discretion is appropriate standard of review).

[25] *Freeman v. Package Mach. Co.*, 865 F.2d 1331, 1340 (1st Cir. 1988).

reviewing courts should "set aside" agency "actions, findings, or conclusions" that are **"arbitrary, capricious, an abuse of discretion**, or otherwise not in accordance with law." When an agency holds a formal hearing
that creates a record, the reviewing court may set aside agency decisions
only when they are **"unsupported by substantial evidence.**"[26]

2.3.2
IDENTIFYING THE APPROPRIATE APPELLATE STANDARD OF REVIEW

Of course, knowing the standards is only the first step. You must then
decide which standard or standards apply in your case. Some issues are
obviously questions of fact (e.g., Did the defendant hit the victim? Did
the officer ask a certain question of the defendant?), while others are obviously questions of law (e.g., Did the court apply the correct legal standard?
Is a supervisor an "employer" within the meaning of the statute?). Mixed
questions are more difficult to identify; courts generally identify a mixed
question of law and fact as one that is based on how a legal principle
applies to established or agreed-upon facts.

Using one standard over another—for example, a clearly erroneous
appellate standard of review rather than a de novo standard—can lead to a
vastly different review of the same case. Accordingly, you should study the
record below carefully. Identify the decisions, rulings, or findings that are
at the crux of your client's case. First, identify who made the ruling. The
standard of review depends on whether the decision maker was a judge, a
jury, or an administrative body. Second, focus on what kind of decision was
made. If it was a ruling on an evidentiary matter, the abuse of discretion
standard will probably apply. If it was a finding of fact, the court will apply
the clearly erroneous standard. If, as is most likely, it was a decision of law,
the court will apply a de novo standard. If you are arguing to a court of last
resort, you may look to the court of appeals decision to see what appellate
standard of review that court applied. If no standard is mentioned in the
decision (and the standard is often not mentioned), the court probably
applied a de novo standard. Of course, if appropriate, you may decide to
argue that the lower court applied the wrong standard of review.[27]

If you are in doubt as to the appropriate standard of review for the
legal issue your case presents, do a little focused research. You may find
precedent as to the standard of review for the narrow legal issue in your

[26] *See, e.g.,* Kunsch, *supra* note 15, at 40-41; *see also, e.g., Dawson Farms v. Risk Mgmt. Agency*,
698 F.3d 1079, 1083 (8th Cir. 2012).
[27] *See generally Cooper Indus.*, 532 U.S. at 434 (noting that court below erred when applying an
abuse of discretion standard rather than the de novo standard); *Ornelas*, 517 U.S. at 698-99 (noting that court below erred when it applied a deferential appellate standard of review).

case. In addition to conducting primary research, you may find second-ary sources helpful. Many practice manuals are geared to attorneys who practice within the courts of a specific jurisdiction; some of these manu-als address appellate standards of review as they apply to particular legal issues.[28]

Although the appellate standard of review is usually not controversial, at times it is at the heart of the appellate decision.[29] If the standard of review in your case is de novo, it will have almost no impact on your argu-ment. You will address the standard of review—either in the introductory section or in a separate, labeled section—and then you will spend the rest of the argument discussing the appropriate legal standards and how the appellate court should apply those standards.

If your case could or should be reviewed under a more deferential standard, however, that standard will have a significant impact on your argument. Even if the court you are writing to asks for the standard to be announced in a separate section, you must still incorporate it into your argument. For example, if the clearly erroneous standard applies, your argument must identify the particular finding of fact that you assert to be clearly erroneous, and cite to the record. Then, you must show how the evidence indicates that the finding was clearly erroneous, and show how the erroneous finding changed the outcome of the case. Alternatively, if you must assert that the judge abused his or her discretion, you must identify the particular decision the judge made in error, use appropriate authorities to explain why it was wrong, and specify why and how the erroneous decision changed the outcome of the case.

As you must with any legal argument, make appellate standard of review arguments honestly. Do not create an appellate standard of review issue where none exists. If the standard genuinely makes a difference in the case, however, you can and should use it to demonstrate the justice of the result you seek.

2.3.3
FORMAT CONSIDERATIONS

During recent years, many courts have begun using their local rules to ask for a separate statement of the appellate standard of review. The Pennsylvania Rules of Appellate Procedure, for example, require that a

---

[28] *See, e.g., Anderson's Sixth Circuit Federal Practice Manual* ch. 7 (Matthew-Bender & Co., Inc. 2011) (also available at LexisNexis.com),

[29] For an interesting discussion of using policy concerns to drive the discussion of appellate standard of review, *see* Bosse, *supra* note 11, at 374 et seq. If the appropriate appellate standard of review is controversial, you can and should justify your argument with references to policies served by choosing the standard you favor. See Section 5.1.2 in this text for guidance on present-ing rule-choice arguments.

statement of "both the scope of review and the standard of review" appear in the appellant's brief, "separately and distinctly entitled," between sections containing the "order or other determination in question" and the "[s]tatement of the questions involved."[30] Similarly, the local rules of the Third Circuit require that "the statement of the standard or scope of review for each issue on appeal" should appear "under a separate heading placed before the discussion of the issue."[31] The Rules of Court for the Kansas Supreme Court require that within the Appellant's Brief, "[e]ach issue shall begin with citation to the appropriate standard of appellate review and a reference to the specific location in the record on appeal where the issue was raised and ruled upon."[32] If the local rules do not demand a separate statement, the standard should usually be included in introductory material within the argument. No matter what method is used, you should cite to authority for the standard of review, just as you would for any legal proposition.

In most situations, the statement of the appellate standard of review requires no more than a paragraph. As noted previously, however, if the standard is controversial or if it is otherwise significant to your argument, it should be treated like any other major issue, with appropriate point headings and text used to make the point. This method should be used even if the local rules require a separate, formal statement of the standard.

2.4
"PLEADING STANDARDS" OR STANDARDS OF REVIEW IN MOTION BRIEFS

Many courts use the term *standard of review* to describe the standards used to decide some trial-level motions.[33] Some courts use the term *legal*

---

[30] Pa. R. of App. Proc. 2111(a).

[31] 3d Cir. LAR [Local Appellate Rule] 28.1(b).

[32] Kan. Sup. Ct. R. 6.02(e). Of course, the appellee's brief should reflect any disagreement as to the appropriate standard of review. *See, e.g.,* Kan. Sup. Ct. R. 6.03(d) ("Each issue shall begin with citation to the appropriate standard of appellate review; appellee shall either concur in appellant's citation to the standard of appellate review or cite additional authority.").

[33] *E.g., Fin. Res. Network, Inc. v. Brown & Brown, Inc.,* 754 F. Supp. 2d 128, 134 (D. Mass. 2010) (noting "the different legal standard of review that applies to a summary judgment motion as opposed to a motion to dismiss") (citations omitted); *Butler v. Schapiro,* 839 F. Supp. 2d 252, 254 (D.D.C. 2012) (using as a section heading, "Standard of Review for a Motion to Dismiss"). *See also, e.g.,* David F. Herr, Roger S. Haydock & Jeffrey W. Stempel, *Motion Practice* (5th ed., Aspen 2009), for detailed information on motion practice in litigation.

standard or *pleading standard,* which is perhaps the more accurate term.[34] The term *standard of review* is less accurate in this situation because the trial court cannot be said to be *re-*viewing anything: The motion to the trial court represents the first time that any court has viewed the legal argument. Unlike appellate standards of review, motion standards of review do not ask a court to apply a particular level of deference to the actions of another decision maker. Nevertheless, courts frequently use the phrase *standard of review* in this context.

Many motions address routine matters such as requests for extension of time or for discovery. These motions may require little more than a request for action accompanied by the citation to a statute or rule. Other motions, however, may require formal briefing that is similar to the briefing done for appellate courts. Like appellate briefs, motion briefs may be the sole basis for decision: Trial courts frequently decide motions based on the briefs alone, without oral argument.[35] The standard of review is particularly important for motions like the motion to dismiss (Fed. R. Civ. P. 12(b)(6)) and the motion for summary judgment (Fed. R. Civ. P. 56(c)).[36] These so-called dispositive motions can "dispose" of a case, at least temporarily, and thus present an important opportunity for advocacy.[37]

The standards of review for dispositive motions are based on the trial court's competing needs to allow access to courts on the one hand and to use judicial resources efficiently and prevent frivolous lawsuits on the other. Counsel, in contrast, may use motion practice strategically, to educate the court as to the issues the case presents, or to narrow the factual or legal issues in dispute.[38] Whatever your purpose in filing a dispositive

---

[34] *E.g., F.D.I.C. ex rel. Wheatland Bank v. Spangler,* 836 F. Supp. 2d 778, 784 (N.D. Ill. 2011) (using the heading "Legal Standard for Rule 12(b)(6) Motions to Dismiss"); *Ashcroft v. Iqbal,* 556 U.S. 662, 684 (2009) (Court noted, in reference to standards governing motions to dismiss, that "[o]ur decision in *Twombly* expounded the pleading standard for 'all civil actions,' *ibid.,* and it applies to antitrust and discrimination suits alike"). Note that courts often use the term *pleading standard* to refer specifically to standards relevant to Rule 8. *E.g., Giraud v. Bd. of Educ., Newburgh Enlarged City Sch. Dist.,* 12-CV-1842 ER, 2013 WL 3776242 (S.D.N.Y. July 17, 2013) (noting that, in order to "satisfy the pleading standard set forth in Rule 8 and survive a motion to dismiss, 'a complaint must contain sufficient factual matter . . . to state a claim to relief that is plausible on its face'") (citations and internal punctuation omitted).

[35] *See* Herr, Haydock & Stempel, *supra* note 33, at §5.02. *See also* Loc. Civ. & Crim. R. U.S. Dist. Ct. S. Dist. Ohio §III, R. 7.1 (noting presumption that motions will be decided without oral argument and that counsel must apply to the court for permission to present an oral argument on a motion).

[36] Of course, these are not the only kinds of motions that require briefing or that are decided based upon so-called standards of review. *See, e.g., Bryanton v. Johnson,* 902 F. Supp. 2d 983, 993 (E.D. Mich. 2012) (using both "standard of review" and "legal standard" to describe the standard for ruling on a motion for a preliminary injunction).

[37] Unlike other motions, dispositive motions may dispose of the case by creating a final appealable order. *See, e.g.,* Herr, Haydock & Stempel, *supra* note 33, at §4.03 (detailing the differences between motion practice and appellate advocacy).

[38] Motions for summary judgment or partial summary judgment may often be used strategically in this way. *E.g.,* Herr, Haydock & Stempel, *supra* note 33, at §16.02 (discussing when to use motions for partial summary judgment).

motion—or any motion—it is important to know and use the appropriate motion standard of review. The sections below discuss the standards of review for two of the most common dispositive motions and address general methods for using standards of review in motion briefs.

2.4.1
MOTIONS TO DISMISS

A motion to dismiss for failure to state a claim upon which relief can be granted is filed in lieu of answering the complaint, pursuant to Rule 12(b)(6). In general terms, this kind of motion can be granted for either of two reasons: the law does not reach the facts, or the facts do not reach the law. That is, a court may grant a motion to dismiss if (1) the law does not support the type of claim made or (2) the facts pled in the complaint do not indicate that the plaintiff can establish facts that would entitle him or her to relief. The court must take the factual allegations in the complaint as true,[39] but this standard does not apply to legal conclusions.

Two hypothetical Title VII cases can help to illustrate these reasons for dismissing a complaint. Title VII provides that "employers" may not terminate an employee based on race, sex, religion, or other factors. The statute defines an *employer* as someone who employs more than 15 employees. The plaintiff must establish that the employer had knowledge of the protected status at the time of the termination.

First, if a plaintiff filed a Title VII action even though he or she worked for a company with only ten employees, the company would probably file a motion to dismiss. The court would not analyze whether the allegations of discrimination were valid or invalid. Instead, it would consider whether the law reaches the facts by asking, "even if these allegations are true, can this plaintiff recover against this defendant under this statute?" The plaintiff in this example could never recover against this defendant under Title VII, because the law does not support this type of claim: Title VII does not apply to employers with fewer than 15 employees. Accordingly, the court would grant the motion to dismiss.

In another case, a plaintiff might file a Title VII claim and allege that he was terminated based on his religion. Suppose that the complaint merely claimed that he had been fired because of his religion (a legal conclusion) but did not allege facts that indicated that the defendant employer had knowledge of the plaintiff's religion. Again, the defendant would probably file a motion to dismiss. The court would consider whether the facts reach the law by evaluating the facts pled in the complaint, asking whether the plaintiff had alleged facts that were sufficient to plausibly allow that

---

[39] *E.g., Bell Atlantic Corp. v. Twombly,* 550 U.S. 544, 555 (2007).

plaintiff to establish the foundational fact that defendant knew the plaintiff's religion at the time of the termination.

In general, the standard for a motion to dismiss tries to balance the needs of plaintiffs, of defendants, and of the judicial system. The plaintiff need not specify every detail of his or her claim, but the complaint must give the defendant fair notice and must contain either direct or indirect allegations as to all of the claim's material elements. Federal courts generally refer to two twenty-first century cases from the United States Supreme Court when analyzing motions to dismiss.

In 2007, the United States Supreme Court decided *Bell Atlantic v. Twombly,* 550 U.S. 544 (2007). In that case, a somewhat complex antitrust cause of action, the Court arguably made the plaintiffs' job a little more difficult. The Court seemed to require more than mere notice pleading, holding that while "a complaint attacked by a Rule 12(b)(6) motion to dismiss does not need detailed factual allegations . . . a plaintiff's obligation to provide the 'grounds' of his 'entitle[ment] to relief' requires more than labels and conclusions, and a formulaic recitation of the elements of a cause of action will not do." *Id.* at 555 (citations omitted). The Court noted that "[f]actual allegations must be enough to raise a right to relief above the speculative level" but that "the assumption" is "that all the allegations in the complaint are true." *Id.* (citations omitted). A complaint must include factual allegations that make its legal allegations not merely "conceivable," but "plausible." *Id.* at 570.

Two years later, the Court decided a post-9/11 anti-discrimination case, *Ashcroft v. Iqbal,* 556 U.S. 662 (2009). The Court reaffirmed its decision in *Twombly* and articulated a standard that it called "context-specific" and rooted in "judicial experience and common sense":

> [A] court considering a motion to dismiss can choose to begin by identifying pleadings that, because they are no more than conclusions, are not entitled to the assumption of truth. While legal conclusions can provide the framework of a complaint, they must be supported by factual allegations. When there are well-pleaded factual allegations, a court should assume their veracity and then determine whether they plausibly give rise to an entitlement to relief.[40]

Although the Court took care to say that a "plausibility" requirement is "not akin to a probability requirement," *id.* at 1949, some commentators are concerned that this standard puts too much of a burden on plaintiffs, arguing that many plaintiffs will be unable to craft a "plausible" complaint without discovery.[41] In fact, in 2009, the "Notice Pleading Restoration

---

[40] *Ashcroft v. Iqbal,* 556 U.S. 662, 679 (2009) (citation omitted).
[41] Edward A. Hartnett, *Taming* Twombly, *Even After* Iqbal, 158 U. Pa. L. Rev. 473, 474 (2010).

Act" was introduced in Congress to restore the pre-*Twombly* standard of review.[42] Currently, however, the new standards are the law.

Accordingly, the careful pleader will be sure to make the complaint's allegations as fact-specific as possible. Even after *Twombly* and *Iqbal*, courts will construe the factual allegations as true. But if the court can be convinced that the plaintiff cannot plausibly establish a set of facts that will entitle him or her to relief—either because the law does not apply to that set of facts or because the set of facts alleged is too speculative, incomplete, or implausible—the court will dismiss the complaint before trial, and often before significant discovery has occurred.

2.4.2
MOTIONS FOR SUMMARY JUDGMENT

The standard of review for a motion for summary judgment is more complicated than the standard for a motion to dismiss. Like a motion to dismiss, a motion for summary judgment may be granted or denied based on issues of fact, issues of law, or both. The plain language of Federal Rule of Civil Procedure 56(c) indicates that the motion should be granted when the evidence shows that there is "no genuine issue as to any material fact" *and* "the moving party is entitled to a judgment as a matter of law." In 1986, however, the United States Supreme Court decided three summary judgment cases that created some initial controversy regarding the standard of review for a motion for summary judgment.[43] The guidelines from these cases, which many state courts have adopted, indicate that a motion for summary judgment requires the nonmoving party to produce substantial evidence on any issue for which that party bears the burden of production at trial.[44] Perhaps obviously, the motion for summary judgment is usually filed after discovery has begun, and sometimes after substantial discovery has been completed. In the alternative, some attorneys use this type of motion to force the other party to bring forth evidence, moving discovery in a particular direction.

Many complaints allege more than one cause of action, and some may be overly optimistic as to the plaintiff's chances of success on some of these causes of action. Defense counsel may file a motion for summary judgment that forces the plaintiff to produce sufficient evidence to support one or more of the allegations. In other cases, a defendant may file a motion for summary judgment supported by its own evidence to counter

---

[42] *Id.* at note 7.

[43] *Anderson v. Liberty Lobby, Inc.*, 477 U.S. 242 (1986); *Celotex Corp. v. Catrett*, 477 U.S. 317 (1986); *Matsushita Elec. Indus. Co. v. Zenith Radio Corp.*, 475 U.S. 574 (1986). *See generally* Herr, Haydock & Stempel, *supra* note 33, at §16.01.

[44] *Celotex v. Catrett*, 477 U.S. 317, 322-23 (1986). *See also Thomas v. Kidani*, 267 P.3d 1230, 1235 (Hawai'i 2011); *Wing v. Anchor Media, Ltd. of Tex.*, 570 N.E.2d 1095 (Ohio 1991).

one or more of the plaintiff's causes of action. A defendant may use this tactic in hopes of forcing a plaintiff to reveal that it has no evidence to support certain allegations, leading the court to grant summary judgment to defendant as to those allegations.

If you analogize the adversary nature of the trial to a poker game, defense counsel may use a motion for summary judgment to call for a "showdown," — in other words, "show me what evidence you have." In other cases, a motion for summary judgment could be translated as "read 'em and weep" — in other words, "look at the evidence I have; I bet you don't have enough evidence to match it." This technique may force the court to find in defendant's favor or to call an issue into question.

When arguing a motion for summary judgment, be sure to research both how your jurisdiction articulates the standard of review for this type of motion and the relevant burdens of proof for each underlying cause of action.

2.4.3
IDENTIFYING THE APPROPRIATE MOTION STANDARD OF REVIEW

With appellate standards of review, a few set standards apply to the many different kinds of decisions that can be reviewed. Motion standards of review, in contrast, are often specific to a particular motion.[45] As with appellate standards of review, the language of the standard may be similar in both state and federal courts, but you should consult the appropriate rules and authorities in the relevant jurisdiction.

Because motion standards of review tend to be motion-specific, identifying the appropriate motion standard of review is usually a more mechanical process than identifying the appellate standard of review. If the motion is mentioned specifically in the civil or criminal rules, that is the place to start, but not end, your research. In addition to consulting the appropriate rules, you should conduct focused research to identify cases in which the relevant courts have applied the standard. Some of these courts may have elaborated on the meaning of the standard, and this "judicial gloss" may have become a part of the standard of review.

---

[45] There may be some overlap of motion standards of review. For example, under Ohio law, Ohio Rule of Civil Procedure 50 regulates both motions for a directed verdict and motions for judgment notwithstanding the verdict, and the two motions share the same standard of review: "The court must issue a directed verdict when, 'after construing the evidence most strongly in favor of the party against whom the motion is directed, [the court] finds that upon any determinative issue reasonable minds could come to but one conclusion upon the evidence submitted and that conclusion is adverse to such party.' Civ. R. 50(A)(4). This is the same legal standard applied to motions for judgment notwithstanding the verdict ⁒ . . . and tests the legal sufficiency of the evidence." *Berry v. Lupica*, 965 N.E.2d 318, 322 (Ohio Ct. App. 2011) (citation omitted).

As with any legal research, when researching motion standards of review, you should try to identify cases that are recent, on point, in the relevant jurisdiction, and from the highest court possible. On occasion, a particularly germinal case will become "the" case to cite for the boilerplate version of the motion standard of review.[46] When the motion standard and its application are both uncontroversial, it is fine to cite a germinal case for the standard. If either the standard or its application is in controversy, however, you should both update and focus your research. Furthermore, be sure to conduct fundamental research to verify that the germinal standard is still valid. Even in 2010, some attorneys have (mistakenly) continued to cite *Conley v. Gibson* as the standard for a motion to dismiss, despite the fact that it was all but overruled for this purpose in 2007.

2.4.4
INCORPORATING MOTION STANDARDS INTO YOUR ARGUMENT

Because motion standards of review are often not controversial, some writers think that they need not articulate the standard or that they may articulate it without citing authority for it. On the contrary, the motion standard of review is the context in which your entire argument takes place, so you must both articulate the standard and cite to meaningful authority for it.[47] If you are arguing in favor of a motion to dismiss, for example, your underlying reason for the request is the language of the standard of review: The court should grant the motion because the plaintiff has not pleaded a set of facts that plausibly give rise to an entitlement to relief. Your argument may focus on case facts and relevant statutes, but it all comes back to the requirements articulated in the motion standard of review.

In most situations, you can briefly state the boilerplate language from the standard and cite to appropriate authority (whether the standard comes from a rule, from case law, or from both). With a motion to dismiss, this straightforward use of the standard would be appropriate when, for example, the plaintiff has alleged that the defendant has violated a statute, and the defendant argues that the statute does not apply to the

---

[46] For example, in the past, federal courts deciding motions to dismiss under Fed. R. Civ. P. Rule 12(b)(6) frequently cited a 1957 case, *Conley v. Gibson*, 355 U.S. 41 (1957). It seems that citations to *Conley* have been replaced by citations to both *Bell Atlantic Corp. v. Twombly*, 550 U.S. 544 (2007), and *Ashcroft v. Iqbal*, 556 U.S. 662, 678 (2009). In a six-month period in 2013, for example, 753 district court cases cited *Twombly* but not *Iqbal*, 805 cited *Iqbal* but not *Twombly*, and almost 7,000 opinions cited both *Twombly* and *Iqbal*.

[47] Because most states have enacted state civil rules using language almost identical to federal Rule 12(b)(6) and other federal rules, some students writing briefs to a state court will mistakenly cite to the federal rule or to federal cases articulating the standard. Be sure you are citing authority from the appropriate jurisdiction.

situation. Thus, the focus of the argument would not be the factual question of whether particular facts plausibly exist or have been appropriately included in the complaint, but rather the legal question of whether the statutory language applies to a particular set of facts.

Even in this straightforward situation, however, you should still connect the standard of review to your argument. You may not see much connection between the standard of review for a motion to dismiss and the argument that, for example, supervisors cannot be held individually liable for sexual harassment under Title VII of the Civil Rights Act of 1964. But if you think about it, you will realize that the *reason* the plaintiff's complaint does not plausibly give rise to an entitlement to relief is that Title VII does not allow supervisors to be held individually liable. Thus, even if the facts seem to "plausibly" describe a Title VII violation, Title VII does not allow a plaintiff relief from a supervisor.

You can make the standard of review connection explicit in at least two places: in the roadmap or umbrella paragraphs in which you first articulate the standard, and in your conclusion. Your conclusion will be less effective if you say simply, e.g., "Because supervisors cannot be held individually liable under Title VII, this court should grant Defendant Kobacker's motion to dismiss." Instead, you can explicitly connect the standard of review to your argument by saying, "Title VII does not impose individual liability on supervisors. Therefore, plaintiff has not alleged a set of facts that plausibly give rise to an entitlement to relief against Defendant Kobacker under Title VII, and this court should grant the motion to dismiss."

In the alternative, you may face a situation that allows or requires you to present more in-depth arguments on the application of the motion standard of review. You may wish to argue that the complaint should be dismissed because the facts in the complaint raise a "possibility" of relief rather than a "plausible" "entitlement to relief." In a motion for summary judgment, you may wish to note that the plaintiff has the burden of proof as to the cause of action and argue that it should bring forth evidence in support of one or more of the complaint's allegations. If you are arguing against a motion for summary judgment on an issue for which the moving party had the burden of proof, you may argue that your opponent has not brought forth sufficient evidence. Thus, you may need to expand your standard of review discussion by quoting and citing language from court decisions that explain when the requirements for the motion standard of review have been met.

In the situations noted above—just as with the clearly erroneous and the abuse of discretion appellate standards—the standard will enter into your argument more directly. If you are arguing that the complaint contains only a "formulaic recitation" of the legal conclusions without sufficient facts and that it should therefore be dismissed, the reader will expect you to quote and cite the relevant portions of the complaint, and to cite and discuss appropriate authority to explain why the allegations are insufficient. If the burden of proof issue is significant to your summary judgment motion, you must discuss the specific burden(s) of proof for the relevant cause(s) of action, citing and discussing authority as appropriate. You may wish, for example, to frame your argument by stating that your opponent has "failed to present substantial evidence that would support a favorable verdict by a reasonable jury,"[48] and then explain why the evidence is insufficient, using relevant authority as appropriate.

As these examples show, a motion standard of review can be just as significant as an appellate standard of review. Whenever you file a motion that requires a brief, be sure that you understand the appropriate motion standard of review. Although you may often start your research in the court rules that govern the motion, be sure to go beyond that boilerplate to determine how your jurisdiction uses and applies that standard. Be sure to tie your legal argument to the standard in some way, even if the standard is not controversial. When either the standard or how it applies *is* controversial, however, the motion standard of review becomes an important legal rule that governs your case, and it should be analyzed, explained, and applied as thoroughly as any other important legal rule.

2.5
AVOIDING CONFUSION

Unfortunately, courts do not always use the term *standard of review* precisely. I have used the phrase *appellate standard of review* to refer to standards that appellate courts apply to their review of lower court decisions, and *motion standard of review* to refer to standards that courts use when deciding particular motions. Courts, however, often use the bare phrase *standard of review*[49] to mean either or both of these things—and to mean other things. Besides its use to refer to appellate and motion standards of review, courts commonly use the phrase *standard of review* in at least one other context: to describe the level of scrutiny that a court may use to review the constitutionality of a state statute or other government action.

Understanding how "government action standards of review" work, and how all three uses of the term may be relevant in a single case, can help you to master the concept of standards of review.

---

[48] Herr, Haydock & Stempel, *supra* note 33, at §16.01[K].
[49] As noted above, courts may use the phrase *legal standard* or *pleading standard* to refer to a motion standard of review.

2.5.1
GOVERNMENT ACTION STANDARDS OF REVIEW

Courts usually use the phrase *standard of review* to describe the standard that a court will use to review the constitutionality of a state statute or other government action. Some actions will be reviewed under a "strict scrutiny" standard, some under a "heightened scrutiny" standard, and others under a "rational basis" standard.[50] Although these phrases all describe *standards* that are used to *review,* they are not the same thing as appellate standards *of* review. Thinking in terms of "deference," which is so crucial to appellate standards of review, may be helpful. When the court is asked to review the constitutionality of a state statute or other government action, it is deciding whether to defer to the decision of a state legislature or other government actor. The government action standard of review tells it how closely to scrutinize the government actor's decision when conducting its review.

All types of courts, from the trial court on up through the United States Supreme Court, may use a strict scrutiny, heightened scrutiny, or rational basis standard to review the constitutionality of a government action.

2.5.2
MULTIPLE STANDARDS OF REVIEW IN THE SAME CASE

One way to gain a clearer understanding of different standards of review is to identify which standards are used in which courts, and how multiple standards may occur in one case.

Motion standards of review and government action standards of review can be applied in trial courts, courts of appeals, and courts of last resort. Appellate standards of review can be applied only in courts of appeals and courts of last resort. It is not unusual, in fact, for an appellate court to apply all three types of standards in the same case.[51]

For example, a trial court may grant a motion for summary judgment in a case in which the issue was the constitutionality of a state action. That trial court would have used a motion standard of review and a government action standard of review. The appellate court reviewing that case must

---

[50] *E.g., Dragovich v. U.S. Dept. of Treasury,* 872 F. Supp. 2d 944, 950 (N.D. Cal. 2012) (referring to "rational basis standard of review"); *DynaLantic Corp. v. U.S. Dept. of Def.,* 885 F. Supp. 2d 237, 272 (D.D.C. 2012) (referring to "strict scrutiny standard of review").

[51] *E.g., Windsor v. United States,* 699 F.3d 169, 176, 181 (2d Cir. 2012) (applying de novo standard of review to review a decision granting summary judgment to plaintiff and deciding to apply heightened scrutiny to determine whether taxation statute unconstitutionally denied spousal deduction to surviving spouse of same-sex marriage), *aff'd,* 133 S. Ct. 2675 (2013); *Selevan v. N.Y. Thruway Auth.,* 584 F.3d 82, 88 (2d Cir. 2009) (using a de novo standard to analyze whether a trial court correctly chose to use the rational basis standard as part of its decision to grant a motion to dismiss against plaintiffs who had claimed, among other things, an equal protection violation).

use the appropriate (1) appellate standard of review to analyze whether the trial court properly applied the (2) motion standard of review and used the correct (3) government action standard of review. Because the appellate standard in that situation would almost certainly be de novo, the appellate court would, in essence, reapply both the motion standard of review and the government action standard of review as part of its de novo review of the decision below.

Although the use of the same term for three different meanings may be confusing, keep the distinguishing factors in mind: (1) Trial courts may not use appellate standards of review. *Only courts of appeals and courts of last resort* may use appellate standards of review when they review *lower court decisions*. (2) *Any* court (trial or appellate) may use a *motion* standard of review to decide, or to review the validity of a decision on, a *motion*. (3) *Any* court (trial or appellate) may use a *government action* standard of review to review *actions by governmental entities* or to review the validity of a court's decision about the government action. The chart below will help you to understand these three different standards.

TYPE OF STANDARD OF REVIEW:	MOTION STANDARD OF REVIEW[50]	GOVERNMENT ACTION STANDARD OF REVIEW	APPELLATE STANDARD OF REVIEW
Type of court that may use this standard:	Trial court Intermediate court of appeals Court of last resort	Trial court Intermediate court of appeals Court of last resort	Intermediate court of appeals Court of last resort
Example(s) of this type of standard:	Whether the facts alleged plausibly give rise to an entitlement to relief	Strict scrutiny Heightened scrutiny Rational basis	De novo Clearly erroneous Abuse of discretion
What the court uses this standard to decide:	Whether it's appropriate to grant or deny a **motion**	Whether certain **government action** is constitutional	Whether to affirm, reverse, or vacate a **decision** of a court below
Whose decision the court is being asked to defer to:	N/A	The decision of a **government actor**	The decision of a **lower court**

[50] As noted above, courts also use the terms *legal standard* and *pleading standard*.

2.6
SUMMARY

The type of court that hears your case and the standard of review that the court applies can each make a significant difference in the way that you structure your arguments. Even if the applicable standard is not controversial, you must keep that standard in mind as you conduct your research and write your brief. Be sure to update your research so that you are confident about the standard itself and its judicial gloss. In your brief, be sure to connect the standard explicitly to the legal or factual conclusions that you ask the court to accept. If the standard raises substantive or factual issues, you may well need to address those issues in depth within your argument.

It is likely that most of the appellate cases you argue will be reviewed under a de novo standard. However, do not make this decision on automatic pilot. Carefully consider the record, the issues, and the relevant appellate standards of review so that you can make an informed decision about which standard applies to your case.

BEFORE YOU WRITE

Naturally, you would not expect to be able to receive a brief-writing assignment and immediately begin to draft the brief. Nor should you expect that you can immediately go online or to the library and begin your legal research. Just as you plan before you write by conducting legal research and by outlining, you must also plan before you begin your formal legal research. The first step is to become familiar with the facts of the case and the issues that the case presents. Next, decide what questions you need to answer and what types of authorities are best suited to provide those answers. Remember that you need not always restrict your research to cases and statutes. Sometimes, your argument can be enhanced by reference to "extra-legal" authorities.

3.1
CREATING AN ABSTRACT OF THE RECORD

The first thing you should do as you prepare to write a brief is to get to know the case to which you have been assigned. If you are preparing a motion brief, it is likely that you were with the case from its inception. If you are preparing an appellate brief, you may also have worked on the case from the initial pleadings onward. Sometimes, however, both in law school and in practice, you may arrive on the scene a little later. When that happens, your job is to get to know the facts and the procedure as if they had happened to you. Thus, you should carefully study the "record" of the case. The record can consist of many different elements, depending on the stage of litigation and on the case itself. If you are filing a motion to dismiss, for example, the only "record" you may have is the complaint. If you are filing a motion for summary judgment, the record may include not only pleadings, but also affidavits, depositions, answers to interrogatories, and written admissions or stipulations of fact. If you are writing an appellate brief, the record will also include the decision(s) below, and it may include transcripts of trial testimony, reproductions of exhibits or other evidence offered at trial, and other items.

possible items of "record"

Because appellate records can be so voluminous, many appellate courts either require or allow what is often called a *joint appendix,* prepared by the petitioner and perhaps supplemented by the respondent. The joint appendix is a printed document that includes record elements that one or both of the parties would like the appellate court to have before it while the court is making its decision. Technically, the joint appendix does not take the place of the *record*; the court may always refer to the complete record if it wishes. As a practical matter, however, it is reasonable to think that judges would prefer not to have to consult the full record when reviewing decisions below. Thus, you should certainly plan the joint appendix and, later, write the brief, as if the joint appendix is the entire universe of factual information to which the judges will refer.

The joint appendix always contains certain procedural information; it also contains information that one or both of the parties believe is relevant to the appeal. United States Supreme Court Rule 26.2 specifies how the parties should collaborate to compile the joint appendix. Rule 26.1 describes the categories of material that should be included in the joint appendix:

elements of joint appendix

> The joint appendix shall contain: (1) the relevant docket entries in all the courts below; (2) any relevant pleadings, jury instructions, findings, conclusions, or opinions; (3) the judgment, order, or decision under review; and (4) any other parts of the record that the parties particularly wish to bring to the Court's attention.

Rule 26.1 also provides that "[a]ny of the foregoing items already reproduced in a petition for a writ of certiorari [or in another document submitted to the court] need not be reproduced again in the joint appendix." As a practical matter, the joint appendix is often relatively short because the appendix to the petition for the writ of certiorari contained much or all of the needed information. Combined, these appendices usually contain the complete text of any decisions below and may contain excerpts of trial testimony, excerpts of other documents submitted into evidence (e.g., depositions), or reproductions of exhibits used in the case. The selected materials provide the court access to sufficient knowledge about the case without forcing the judges to wade through an enormous record.[1]

When filing an appeal in a court other than the United States Supreme Court, you should consult the relevant rules of procedure and local rules to see what requirements exist regarding the "record on appeal," as it is often known.[2] If you are at the intermediate level, you may be assembling the record on appeal as you work on the brief. If you are arguing to a court of last resort, you may be able to start from an excerpted record that was created for the intermediate court.

Whether the record is a joint appendix, a "raw" record and opinions below, or just pleadings and affidavits, your job at this early stage of the writing process is to identify the important facts of the case. One of the best ways to organize this process is to create an abstract of the record. An *abstract* in this sense is a referenced summary of the information con- *abstract, defined* tained in the record. The purpose of an abstract is to help the lawyer—or whoever is working on the case—to easily find important information from the record throughout the writing process.

Reading the record materials carefully a few times and creating a good abstract will enable you to learn more about your case now and to find important record information later, while you are conducting legal research or writing the brief.

Like conducting legal research, preparing an abstract is often a recursive process. It is difficult to understand the significance of the case's facts until you know what law applies to the case, but it's difficult to identify the relevant law until you know the facts. Therefore, as preparation for creating an abstract, read over the lower court opinions or the pleadings *process* first to familiarize yourself with the major issues that the case presents. Then, read through any other materials two or three times. You may wish to abstract information as you go through it each time, or you may wish

---

[1] Although the joint appendix is usually not the complete record, courts may use the term *record* to refer to information from the joint appendix or from the appendix to the petition for the writ of certiorari. *E.g., Horne v. Flores*, 557 U.S. 433, 470 (2009) ("The record contains no factual findings or evidence that any school district other than Nogales failed (much less continues to fail) to provide equal educational opportunities to ELL students. See App. to Pet. for Cert. in No. 08-294, pp. 177a-178a."); *Herring v. United States*, 555 U.S. 135, 153 (2009) ("[T]he record indicates that there is no electronic connection between the warrant database of the Dale County Sheriff's Department and that of the County Circuit Clerk's office, which is located in the basement of the same building. App. 39-40, 43, 45").

[2] *E.g.*, Fed. R. App. Proc. 10 (describing requirements for the "Record on Appeal"); Fl. R. App. Proc. 9.200 (describing the contents of "the record" in various categories of cases).

to wait until you have read the documents through once before you begin to abstract the details that you think are important.

Your method may differ if you are working on an appellate brief as opposed to a motion brief. If you are working on an appellate brief, be sure to abstract the information and arguments contained in the decisions below. Furthermore, when reviewing an appellate record, note that you may need to distinguish between the court's findings of fact and the information that was merely offered into evidence in the trial court. Consider precisely what decisions of the court are being appealed and be sure to record significant information about each one. If you are working on a motion to dismiss or a motion for summary judgment, consider the standard of review. If you are writing a brief in opposition to a motion for summary judgment, for example, you may be arguing that you have provided evidence sufficient to establish your claim as to one of your causes of action. In that situation, when reviewing the record, you would consider your client's burden of proof as to the relevant issues and be sure to review carefully any information in the record relevant to those issues.

To create the actual abstract, make a chart—either on paper or on a word processor—and summarize the important information found in each part of the record or joint appendix as you read through it. Here are some examples of things to look for and to record:

1. Page cites for positive facts, testimony, and other evidence
2. Page cites for negative facts, testimony, and other evidence
3. Page cites for segments of the appendix (e.g., each separate pleading or other type of document) (if a formal joint appendix has been created, this information may appear in its table of contents)
4. Page cites for evidence that establishes needed elements of the crime or cause of action
5. Page cites for findings of fact in the opinions below
6. Page cites for legal findings in the opinions below
7. Page cites for major arguments that each side has made below
8. Page cites for concessions that either side has made below (e.g., in pleadings or in stipulations)
9. Page cites for information that may support any policy arguments you plan to make
10. Page cites for any information you think is important, even if you are not yet sure why it is important[3]

A section of an abstract of the joint appendix in the case of *Adolph Coors Co. v. Bentsen* (later decided as *Rubin v. Coors Brewing Co.*, 514 U.S. 476 (1995)) might look like the example that follows. In that case, counsel for Coors was arguing that the First Amendment allowed beer manufacturers

---

[3] *See* Michael R. Fontham, Michael Vitiello & David W. Miller, *Persuasive Written and Oral Advocacy in Trial and Appellate Courts* §§11.6, 11.7 (2d ed., Aspen 2007).

to print on beer labels the percentage of alcohol in the beer and that therefore the prohibition-era regulation that forbade this information was unconstitutional. The joint appendix was over 350 pages long, and it contained excerpts of various depositions as well as photographic reproductions of several trial exhibits.

In the excerpts below (from two different parts of the abstract), the attorney has recorded the page number from the joint appendix in the left-hand column. In the right-hand column, the attorney has described the information that can be found on that page. Notice the comments in brackets: They illustrate what an attorney for Coors might write as a way of using the process of creating the abstract to think about potential arguments in the case. As noted above, you will understand the legal significance of the facts better after you have conducted legal research. Do not, however, neglect to record the thoughts that occur to you as you create the abstract. They may yield creative arguments or ideas that would not occur to you after you have been "biased" by your knowledge of what courts usually do with cases like that of your client.

Analyze BEFORE reading other cases to prevent biases

The attorney can use the abstract to ease the process of writing the brief. First, the attorney can scan through the abstract to find references to information that might be helpful. Furthermore, when the attorney recalls facts that need to be quoted or cited in the brief, he or she can use the abstract to quickly find the appropriate page in the joint appendix or opinion below and retrieve specific language, citations, or other information to include in the brief itself.

Excerpts from Abstract

PAGE #	INFORMATION
135	First page of deposition of Timothy Ambler, alcohol mktg. expert from England
139-40	Testimony re: mandatory disclosure of alcohol on beer labels in Britain and the European Community [Any precedent for following international precedent?]
* * *	* * *
284	Plaintiff's Exh. 3A—Chart showing alcohol % by weight of various beers [Use to show low range of variation among most beers?]
289	U.S. Dept. of HHS, Inspector General's Survey on Youth and Alcohol: "Do they know what they're drinking?"
294	Survey findings: "2/3 students can't distinguish alcoholic beverages from nonalcoholic beverages" [Use to show public benefit of putting alcohol percentage on the label?]

In these days of digital recordkeeping, you may find that some or all of the record materials are available in digital form. In that situation, it may be wise to create links to the full text of the record while creating the abstract. But be sure that you still take the time to include relevant quotations and paraphrases in the abstract itself. Do not let the ease of switching to full text make you skip the important step of reading and rereading the complete record and creating a careful summary of the information, as well as creating a record of your thoughts as you review the record.

Creating an abstract may be time-consuming, but it can actually save time in the long run. The process of creating an abstract helps you get to know the realities of your case and lets you rely on recorded information instead of memory. During brief-writing, a good abstract makes it easier for you to support your fact statement and your arguments with vital citations to the record. When you prepare for oral argument, you can use your abstract to study the crucial facts, so that you can refer the court to specific record pages as needed.

3.2
PLANNING YOUR RESEARCH

3.2.1
BEGIN AT THE BEGINNING: DECIDE WHAT QUESTIONS YOU NEED TO ANSWER

Effective legal research begins before you go to the library or access the Web. Of course, when you write a brief, you should follow the same research methods that are relevant to any type of legal research. Be thorough. Take good notes. Be sure to check the validity of your authorities. This section will address some basic methods of legal research and some methods that are particularly appropriate to researching briefs. A good method to use before starting to research any legal issue is to analyze the facts that you have at hand and begin to identify possible search words and possible legally significant categories.[4] Then, create "research questions" based on what you know about the case so far.

Like all statements of legal issues, your research questions should be focused on how the relevant law applies to the legally significant facts. A popular structure for these questions is the so-called Under-Does-When structure.[5] The "under" part of the question identifies the law that governs

---

[4] *See, e.g.* Mary Barnard Ray & Jill J. Ramsfield, *Legal Writing: Getting It Right and Getting It Written* 359-63 (5th ed. Thomson Reuters 2010).

[5] *See, e.g., id.* at 323-24; Laurel Currie Oates & Anne M. Enquist, *The Legal Writing Handbook* §7.4.2 (4th ed., Aspen 2006). Although your research questions may be similar in format to questions presented, you should not expect that the research questions will be identical to the formal question presented.

the legal issue; the "does" part identifies the narrow, yes-or-no legal question that you are trying to answer (whether it is about liability, guilt, or some other legal status or form of legal responsibility); and the "when" part identifies the legally significant facts that relate to the legal issue. Thus, a format for the research question is "Under [relevant law], does [legal status] exist when [legally significant facts] exist?"[6]

Let's presume that you are conducting research on the *Coors* case. From reading the decisions below and the joint appendix, you know that this case is about the constitutionality of a federal statute that prohibits printing alcohol content information on beer labels. If that were all you knew, you'd have a pretty broad "under" clause:

Under the United States Constitution . . .

But of course, when you created the abstract, you read the lower court decisions, and so you know that this is a First Amendment case and that the issue is not a matter of political speech but of commercial speech. Thus, the "under" clause can be a little more focused:

Under the First Amendment's freedom of speech provisions as they pertain to commercial speech . . .

Does = Y/N question

The "does" part of the research question refers to the legal question that your research will answer. In this part of the question, you ask a yes-or-no question—which may or may not begin with the word *does*—that asks whether a certain legal condition has been met or whether a certain legal status exists. This part of the question often focuses on the legal question that the case is about, as in the following example:

Is 27 U.S.C. §205(e)(2) constitutional when . . .

Of course, your reading of the arguments in the lower courts might lead you to address more narrow questions related to the commercial speech test, and thus you might try to articulate questions that reflect your current understanding of that test and of the relevant arguments, as in the following examples:

Does prohibiting the printing of alcohol content information on a beer label sufficiently advance the government's interest in preventing strength wars when . . .

Does prohibiting the printing of alcohol content information on a beer label directly advance the government's interest in preventing consumers from having misleading information when . . .

---

[6]Note also that the narrow question may begin with something other than *does,* and that the section about the facts may begin with *include* rather than *when.* For example, you may ask, "Under relevant law, does legal status include legally significant facts?" Or "Under relevant law, can a party establish legal status when legally significant facts exist?"

These core questions help you to focus your research by forcing you to articulate the narrow questions that your research is designed to answer.

In the "when" part of the question, you list the legally significant facts that you (or your opponent) will use to demonstrate that the legal issue should be resolved in a certain way. One caveat about the "facts" part of the research question—what is a "fact" in a legal question may vary from case to case. In many cases, the facts are "real-world" facts that describe behavior or relationships (such as "when the officer did X," or "when the employment contract specified employment at will"). In a statutory analysis case like *Coors*, however, some (or perhaps all) of the facts may consist of the language or requirements of the statute. For example, if the "does" element had asked merely "is 27 U.S.C. §205(e)(2) constitutional?" then the "when" element should at least describe what the statute requires, as in the following example:

> **when the statute prohibits beer manufacturers from printing alcohol content information on their beer labels**

If the "does" section had been more detailed, the "when" section might be written as follows, based on your predictions as to which arguments the Court would find to be most important:

> **when there is no evidence of strength wars in states or countries in which alcohol content information is allowed to be printed on beer labels**

> **when it is now possible to accurately measure alcohol content in beer and thus the statute is preventing publication of truthful information**

These details may or may not be important later; right now they are useful in planning the research for the case.

Of course, in a case in which statutory language is not at issue, the questions would be different. For example, in *State v. Knowles*, 569 N.W.2d 601 (Iowa 1997), the issue was the constitutionality of the behavior of an officer who conducted a complete search of a vehicle stopped for a traffic violation. In that situation, the "when" part of the question could have more real-world details about the parties in the case, as in this example:

> **when the officer had no indication that the defendant had broken any law other than a traffic law before he initiated the search of the defendant's car**

The "when" part of the question helps to focus your research because it makes it easier for you to recognize relevant authorities that are similar to your client's case. The more familiar you are with the legally significant facts, the more quickly you can identify relevant cases and statutes.

Putting all of the pieces together, here are three sample research questions for the *Coors* case. The first question could be used alone, while the second and third questions might reveal two different aspects of the case, and thus could be used together:

> Under the First Amendment's freedom of speech provisions as they pertain to commercial speech, is 27 U.S.C. §205(e)(2) constitutional when the statute prohibits beer manufacturers from printing alcohol content information on their beer labels?

> Under the First Amendment's freedom of speech provisions as they pertain to commercial speech, does prohibiting the printing of alcohol content information on a beer label sufficiently advance the government's interest in preventing strength wars when there is no evidence of strength wars in states or countries in which alcohol content information is allowed to be printed on beer labels?

> Under the First Amendment's freedom of speech provisions as they pertain to commercial speech, does prohibiting the printing of alcohol content information on a beer label directly advance the government's interest in preventing consumers from having misleading information when it is now possible to accurately measure alcohol content in beer and thus the statute is preventing publication of truthful information?

A complete sample question for *Knowles v. Iowa* might look like this:

> Under the Fourth Amendment's search and seizure limitations, does a police officer have the authority to conduct a complete vehicle search of a car that has been stopped for a traffic violation, when the officer had no indication that the defendant had broken any law other than a traffic law before he initiated the search of the defendant's car?

One more caveat. At this early stage of the writing process, don't worry about perfect form or perfection in any way. The important thing is to get some information down in a useful format.

3.2.2
BROADENING YOUR HORIZONS (YOU *CAN* COMPARE APPLES AND ORANGES)

After you have formulated your research questions, you should take two more steps before you begin researching your specific legal issues. First, evaluate your level of ignorance about the case and do any needed background reading. Second, decide what you're looking for. What are your "ideal" authorities and your "practical" authorities? That is, if you could invent an ideal authority, what would it be? On the other hand, if the ideal authority isn't out there (and it probably isn't), you should decide what types of authorities would be useful in your client's case.

These steps are important because the problem many people have with legal research is not that they can't *find* relevant authorities, it's that they don't *recognize* relevant authorities when they see them. Even people who can eventually recognize relevant authorities often don't recognize them during the initial phase of their research. Perhaps because they don't know enough about the relevant law, they are looking for a case that is the perfect match, and they ignore every authority that is not identical, factually and in every other way. After they realize that they're not going to find the ideal case, they have to retrace their steps to pick up those imperfect authorities that now look a lot better.

Many researchers are able to recognize those valid but imperfect authorities the first time through if they have completed background reading and used their general knowledge about the area of law (whether preexisting or newfound) to help them identify both ideal and practical authorities. To decide what kind of background reading is necessary, consult the "under" clause of any research questions you have drafted to evaluate your level of ignorance. If you have written "under Section 23's limitation provisions," you are pretty well focused on the narrow legal issues. If you are familiar with those provisions and the law governing those provisions, then you do not need to do any background reading before trying to identify what you are looking for. If you are unfamiliar with the statute or the cases governing it, however, you can use narrow search terms to find some worthwhile background reading.

If your "under" clauses are even broader, with such phrases as "under the First Amendment" or "under state and federal employment law," you are obviously pretty unfamiliar with the narrow legal issue that your case presents. In that situation, go to secondary sources first. Do some general background reading by conducting Internet research, by looking for relevant encyclopedia entries, or by reading American Law Reports or law review articles.

Although a search for law review articles in an online database may generate a high number of "hits," remember that unlike case names, law review titles instantly reveal their legal significance. Spending ten minutes scanning through a hundred or more titles may result in finding a title that is exactly on point. Conducting this kind of background reading can help you recognize valid authorities both by teaching you the key terms relevant to your client's legal issues and by giving you a broader understanding of relevant categories of facts and authorities in a particular area of law.

Once you have identified or acquired the needed background information, tentatively identify ideal and practical authorities. Identifying ideal authority is simple: It would be great to find a mandatory authority that dictates a decision in your favor, whether that authority is a statute, a constitutional provision, or an on-point case. Finding your ideal authority may be difficult, because the United States Supreme Court and other courts of last resort frequently take up issues that they haven't decided before. Even if you are writing to a trial court, however, you should also consider what nonideal or practical authorities would support your argument and be acceptable to the court.

To identify practical authorities, broaden your horizons. If your client is a nun who was bitten by an aardvark, don't pass by a case about an antelope that bit a priest. That is, instead of looking at the narrow facts of your case, look for legally significant categories that you can use to characterize the parties, events, or issues in your case and that will help you recognize potentially relevant authorities.

3.2.3
THE ABSTRACTION LADDER

Many legal writers use a theoretical device called the *abstraction ladder* to help them identify relevant categories. The abstraction ladder is based on the concept that everything in the world can be thought of at various levels of abstraction or concreteness. Labeling case facts at different levels of abstraction can help writers and readers understand legally significant similarities and distinctions that might not be obvious at first glance.

First, let's define our terms. The word *abstract* has several meanings and is sometimes hard for people to understand. It is used earlier in this chapter to talk about a written summary of the information in the record or joint appendix. The meaning of *abstract* in the abstraction ladder has perhaps a more familiar definition. In this sense, art is abstract if two people could see different things in the same painting. A word is abstract if two people could perceive two (or more) different meanings from the same word.

For example, if someone asked you what you did before you came in to school or work this morning, you might answer, somewhat abstractly, "I ate." Different people might conjure up different mental images of what kind of food you had from your rather abstract reply. You might be a little less abstract and say, "I had breakfast." Even with this description, some people might picture yogurt, while others would think of bacon and eggs. Or you could be a little more concrete and say, "I had some cereal." Or even more concrete and say, "I had some Cheerios." Or you might be even more concrete and say, "I had one and one quarter cups of multigrain Cheerios and three-quarters of a cup of skim milk." Thus, the words you use to describe something can be placed on a ladder between the extremes of "most abstract" and "most concrete." You might think of the ladder growing wider as it grows taller; the more abstract something is, the more other things share the same rung.

Moving in the other direction, from most concrete to most abstract, you can think of a cow by thinking of Bossy, a particular cow. Or you can be a little more abstract and think of a Holstein. Or you can be a little more abstract and just think of cows in general. Or you could move up the abstraction ladder—or several abstraction ladders—and think of farm animals, or mammals, or farm property, or assets, or wealth. At the top of this (and every) abstraction ladder, you can think of a cow as a "thing."[7]

This concept is important to legal analysis because abstract reasoning helps lawyers to identify analogous authorities. Once you recognize that facts and issues can be put into broader, more abstract categories, you may be better able to see legal similarities between your client's case and relevant authorities. Very frequently, the tension in a legal argument is about whether a rule applies to a broad category that includes a certain person, thing, or event, or whether the rule applies to a narrower group that excludes a certain person, thing, or event. You can use the abstraction ladder to identify both legal and factual categories that may be significant to your argument.

3.2.4
USING THE ABSTRACTION LADDER IN LEGAL RESEARCH

The good news is that if you move high enough up the abstraction ladder, you can almost always identify some connection between two sets of facts. For example, you could analogize a cow to a horse because they are both farm animals. Or you could analogize a cow to a wheat field because they are both income-producing property for farmers. You could even analogize a cow to a tractor because they are both farm property. Or you could analogize a cow to a pet dog because both are mammals.

The bad news is that after asking whether there is an analogy, you must then ask whether the analogy is legally significant. For example, if a rule governs licensing of pet dogs and cats, that rule probably will not apply to cows on a dairy farm, even though cows, dogs, and cats are all mammals. If, however, a common law rule governed additives to cow feed, you might be able to argue that this rule also should apply to fertilizers on wheat fields because both cow feed and wheat field fertilizer may affect food that consumers purchase. One hint about using the abstraction ladder: Try to go up (i.e., to a more abstract level) only as far as you need to go to find a legally significant analogy and no farther. For example, a goat and a cow are both mammals, but their more legally significant connection in a given case could well be lower on the abstraction ladder: They are both animals that produce milk that may be sold for human consumption.

Thus, before you start researching, look at your case and at your research question(s) and decide what types of authorities you're looking for. If you were researching the *Coors* case, for example, you should plan what to do if you don't find any cases dealing with regulation of beer labels. Going up

---

[7] S. I. Hayakawa, *Language in Thought and Action* 155 (4th ed., Harcourt, Brace, Jovanovich 1978) (discussing the abstraction ladder in general and the cow example in particular).

the abstraction ladder, you might look for regulations about labels of any kind. Or going up farther, you might look for regulations about any kind of advertising.

But "any kind of advertising" might be too broad a concept. What is significant about beer advertising as opposed to the general definition of advertising? One obvious answer is that there are lots of restrictions on beer—as one of my students put it, it's a vice that the government regulates. Thinking in terms of "vices" that the government regulated would broaden your horizons to looking for cases about regulation of advertising about liquor, gambling, smoking, or pornography because they are all legal activities subject to significant governmental regulation ("vices").

Broadening your horizons in this way can make the research process easier because you will be more attuned to the cases that are relevant and helpful even though they are not 100 percent on point. By being more practical about the potential results of your research, you will be more likely to recognize relevant authorities.

3.2.5
IDENTIFYING A THEME FOR YOUR ARGUMENT

As you think broadly about the issues that your case presents, it is a good idea to identify a potential theme or themes for your argument. The theme may develop or change as you continue the research and writing process, but identifying at least a tentative theme early in your research can help to direct your research as well. A theme is particularly important when arguing issues for which no mandatory authority governs the outcome, or when arguing to a court of last resort. If counsel on two sides of a case present legal arguments that are equally plausible from a logical or legal viewpoint, an effective theme may help to carry the day.

A good theme is a statement about the law, the facts, or about how the law and facts intersect, and it is a statement that is true even in the face of your opponent's best argument. Good themes are often policy-based for this reason; although two interpretations of a statute may not be able to coexist, two competing policies often can. When courts must choose between two competing interpretations of the law, they often do so by identifying (explicitly or implicitly) which of two competing policy arguments is more important *in this situation*. The court's decision does not negate the validity of the "losing" theme or policy argument; it merely decides that in this particular circumstance, another policy is more important.

To identify a theme, try to think both broadly and specifically about what your case is about, and try to identify a policy that supports the result you seek. For example, if your client is arguing that a state statute that promises a "safe" workplace entitles him to an injunction banning

[handwritten margin note: Theme, defined]

[handwritten margin note: how to identify a theme]

smoking in and around his office building, possible themes include the importance of protecting nonsmokers from secondhand smoke, of protecting the health of workers, or of protecting and promoting public health. In contrast, your opponent might choose as a theme the importance of respecting the autonomy of private employers to make decisions regarding legal activities within the workplace. If both sides present legal arguments of similar validity, the policies behind each theme may help the court to make its decision.

A theme can affect how you write your brief, but it can also help to make your legal research more effective. In the injunction case noted previously, both sides would research the safe workplace statute and its interpreting decisions, as well as authorities relevant to injunctive relief. Going up the abstraction ladder, both sides could research workplace issues in general, and workplace safety issues in particular. Counsel for the employee, however, might spend some time identifying authorities that show the importance of protecting worker health or public health, or the laws and regulations that govern secondhand smoke. Counsel for the employer would try to identify other situations in which legislatures or courts have given employers the autonomy to make workplace decisions that were unpopular with some employees.

Do not close yourself off to other ideas when trying to choose a theme; you may well change your mind as your research and writing progress. By starting to think about possible themes now, however, you make it more likely that you will find authorities that help you to build arguments around your theme.

3.2.6
IDENTIFYING VALID AUTHORITY

When you are writing a brief to a court, you are trying to convince it to do something. On a basic level, your argument consists of assertions that will convince the court to decide in your favor—if it agrees with those assertions. The court will be much more likely to agree with your assertions if it believes in the validity of the authorities you cite as support for your assertions.

The "validity" of each authority depends on several factors. When you are deciding what authorities to cite, realize that most judges are not interested in breaking new ground or making new law: They are interested in not getting reversed. Thus, part of your job is to reassure them that the result you seek is consistent with the mandatory authorities that govern their jurisdiction. Every time your brief includes a cite to an authority that is not mandatory, the judge (or the clerk) who is reading the brief may be thinking, "Why should I care about this?" If you are writing to a court of last resort, like the United States Supreme Court, realize that—even though that court has the power to make new law—its first instinct is to look to its own decisions for authority rather than to lower court authorities. If you are writing to a trial court or to an intermediate court of appeals, its first instinct is to look to decisions of the court or courts that have the authority to reverse its decisions.

This principle does not mean that you should ignore nonmandatory authorities; rather, it indicates that you should *first* identify any mandatory authorities because they will have more validity than nonmandatory authorities. The more valid the authorities you cite, the more weight the authority will have with the court. Nonmandatory authorities can persuade, but because they have less weight, you should be sure that your reader knows why he or she should care about the authority. For example, you may be able to use nonmandatory authorities to show how various courts have applied a particular rule from the mandatory authority, particularly if the lower court decisions are more on point than the decisions of the mandatory authority.

Because each case is decided based on the facts and issues unique to it, the validity of an authority can vary depending on both the court you are arguing to and the facts of the case before the court. Therefore, when assessing the validity of authorities during your research, consider the relevance of the facts, the legal issues, and the source of the authority.

a. Relevant Facts

First, consider what types of facts might be relevant, and look for authorities that relate to those types of facts. Remember that research is recursive; you may not know what facts are legally significant until after you have completed some of your research. Keep an open mind, and revisit your facts frequently (e.g., by reviewing your abstract of the record). Some cases with similar facts will be easy to recognize, but be sure to consider the different levels of similarity. This is where the lessons of the abstraction ladder become important: Thinking about your facts at various levels of abstraction can help you to recognize facts from other cases whose relevance is not apparent. If your client is seeking to ban smoking in the workplace, for example, you should not limit your research to cases in which plaintiffs tried to ban smoking in the workplace. You might look for cases dealing with other types of toxic fumes in the workplace, other types of dangers in the workplace, or other situations in which an employee tried to enforce public health laws (or other laws) in the workplace.

As noted above, you may have to broaden your concept of what a "fact" is. Many law students think of facts as events that involve human beings—the details of a contract negotiation, a car accident, or a termination of employment. In a statutory construction case, however, the language of a statute can be a "fact" that is significant to your argument. Likewise, the way that particular language within a statute operates can also be a "fact"—or a category of facts—that you need to be aware of so that you can look for similar categories of facts when you conduct your research. For example, if you are arguing that the word "employer" in the Family and Medical Leave Act includes "supervisors" as well as the entity-employer, it may be a legally significant fact that Congress used the terms "employer," "person," and other words in particular ways within certain provisions of the Act. A relevant category of facts in this case could be the way that the legislature used words in the statute. Accordingly, you might find relevant cases that discussed how Congress used a variety of words in a variety of contexts. You may miss the significance of these facts if you limit the concept of "facts" to your client's behavior in the workplace and the conversations the supervisor had with your client before the termination.

b. Relevant Legal Issues

Second, consider what types of legal issues might be relevant. Obviously, when choosing authority cases, the more on point the issue, the better. If your issue involves the meaning of a federal statute, for example, cases interpreting the statute would certainly be relevant. But you might also consider looking for cases that have interpreted other statutes that either use similar (or identical) language or govern similar legal problems or categories of legal problems. If your client has sued under the Americans with Disabilities Act, for example, you might search for cases interpreting similar aspects of Title VII. Likewise, if your client is being accused of wrongfully discharging an employee in violation of a contract, other categories of wrongful discharge cases can be helpful as well. Furthermore, if your case has several possible sub-issues, authorities that address a sub-issue might be highly relevant for that sub-issue even though they might not be relevant to every issue in your case. For example, if you are analyzing a torts issue, a case addressing foreseeability might be relevant to your case even if the particular tort at issue in that case is irrelevant. Even a case addressing foreseeability in a context other than torts could be significant.

c. Relevant Sources

i. Legal Sources

Finally, consider what types of sources might be relevant. The most obvious source for legal authority is a court of law, but some courts will have more validity with the reviewing court. Thus, if you are writing to an Indiana Court of Appeals, opinions of the Indiana Supreme Court would have high relevance. The obvious rule is that mandatory authorities from the relevant jurisdiction will have the most validity with a court.

If there is no mandatory authority exactly on point, however, find out how close the mandatory court has come to addressing the relevant issue and build your argument on those authorities. If the mandatory jurisdiction has not yet considered the precise legal issue in your case, or if nonmandatory decisions are much more on point than any mandatory decisions, you may wish to go beyond cases from the mandatory court. When you decide to include citations to nonmandatory authorities, you can increase the validity of those authorities if you tie them to mandatory authorities or to rules from mandatory authorities.

Thus, if you find that there are few opinions addressing the issue in your case, and none that are on point, first find the opinions in your "mandatory court" that are most on point. If you also wish to cite to a nonmandatory authority, begin your discussion of that issue by citing to the mandatory authority. Citing a nonmandatory authority is sort of like bringing an uninvited guest to a small party. You might bring an uninvited guest under some circumstances, but (a) you would almost always explain those circumstances to the host, and (b) you would rarely send the uninvited guest in first, or unescorted. Instead, you would go in first and explain why you are bringing the uninvited guest.

Likewise, you should cite the mandatory authority first; only then should you cite the nonmandatory authorities, noting perhaps that the courts in those cases are applying the mandatory rule or (for cases from other jurisdictions) are applying rules that are consistent with or very similar to the mandatory rule. Although, of course, the court is not obligated to follow these cases, you can lay groundwork that will help the court to find the authorities valid.[8]

Some noncourt authorities can also be valid. If you are asking a court to decide on the meaning of federal legislation, the opinion of a federal agency would be relevant if that agency was involved in drafting regulations, enforcing the legislation, or suing to have the legislation enforced. If the area of law is particularly novel, you may have difficulty finding on-point cases or other authorities. In that situation, consider whether any law review articles have been written on the subject. Although most courts would rather rely on cases in which courts have considered the impact that their decisions would have on real-life parties, they may refer to law reviews when case authorities are few or inadequate.[9] If you can cite to a prestigious professor from a prestigious law school, so much the better, but most courts are more interested in the writer's expertise,[10] or the legal

---

[8] *E.g., Vallies v. Sky Bank*, 591 F.3d 152, 154 (3d Cir. 2009) (affirming decision of district court that "follow[ed] persuasive authority from our sister courts of appeals").

[9] *See generally* Deborah J. Merritt & Melanie Putnam, *Symposium on the Trends in Legal Citations and Scholarship: Judges and Scholars: Do Courts and Scholarly Journals Cite the Same Law Review Articles?*, 71 Chi.-Kent. L. Rev. 871 (1996).

[10] In a 2011 case on election technology, for example, the Texas Supreme Court cited an election law expert several times as it discussed the particulars of DRE voting machines, and the constitutional implications of that technology. *Andrade v. NAACP of Austin*, 345 S.W.3d 1, 4 (Tex. 2011) (citing Daniel P. Tokaji, *The Paperless Chase: Electronic Voting and Democratic Values*, 73 Fordham L. Rev. 1711, 1724 (2005)).

analysis that the article presents, than in the pedigree of its author or of the journal.[11]

ii. "Extra-Legal" Sources

And don't limit your research to traditional legal sources. If your case concerns an issue of public significance—and many cases argued to courts of last resort fit that definition—you may want to give the court information that will help it understand how this issue affects the public, not just the parties that are before the court.[12] Although traditionally courts are restricted in their use of information to facts that have been admitted into evidence, in recent years courts have shown more and more willingness to consider "extra-legal" or "legislative facts."[13] Generally, courts consider adjudicative facts outside the record by taking "judicial notice" of those facts, under Federal Rule of Evidence 201. When considering legislative facts, in contrast, courts can go beyond the record to understand the broad factual context of the issues in a particular case.[14]

For example, suppose you are representing the state in a Fourth Amendment case about the constitutionality of a state law that gives police officers the authority to order all passengers out of a vehicle at a traffic stop. If you are counsel for the state, you might be making a policy argument that the court should find the law constitutional because it will promote officer safety. To support that argument, you could look for statistics about the dangers that police officers face when conducting traffic stops, noting how often passengers in the stopped vehicles became violent or caused other problems. These authorities might persuade the court to agree with your assertion that traffic stops are dangerous situations for police officers, and thus make it more likely to decide that the state law is a valid exercise of police power.

In the *Coors Brewing* case discussed above, one reason the government gave for banning alcohol percentages on beer labels was its fear that consumers, especially young consumers, would base their beer-purchasing choices on the percentage of alcohol in the beer. One of the parties might cite a reputable study that analyzed beer-buying patterns of young people in states or countries in which alcohol percentages were already on the label. The conclusion of that study might convince the court that alcohol percentages on beer labels either helped or hindered consumers' abilities to make good choices when purchasing beer. That conclusion in turn might affect the court's decision in the case.

[11] Merritt & Putnam, *supra* note 9, at 890-92.

[12] *See generally* Ellie Margolis, *Beyond Brandeis: Exploring the Uses of Non-legal Materials in Appellate Briefs*, 34 U.S.F. L. Rev. 197 (2000).

[13] *Id.* at 199 (citations omitted).

[14] *See generally* Coleen M. Barger, *On the Internet, Nobody Knows You're a Judge: Appellate Courts' Use of Internet Materials*, 4 J. App. Prac. & Proc. 417 (2002).

Of course, many of these extra-legal facts could be submitted into evidence at the trial court, but trials are usually focused on the individual parties. Often, arguments about the broad impact of the case become significant only at the appellate level. Just as with legal authorities, extra-legal authorities will be more or less valid depending on the source. The reputation of the source, whether a newspaper article or a university study, will doubtless have an impact on the court's attitude toward the validity of the information from that source. Therefore, when deciding whether to use extra-legal information, consider the source carefully.

iii. Internet Sources

The advent of the Internet is changing the way that lawyers and judges find and use legal authorities.[15] Internet research can be an effective way to bring yourself up to speed on an area of law. Be careful, however, when deciding whether to cite Internet materials in a brief. Certainly, valid authorities do not lose validity simply because they can also be found on the Internet; similarly, however, nonvalid authorities do not become valid simply because they can be called up on the computer screen of an attorney or a judge. In addition, the ever-changing content online can affect judges' impressions of the validity of certain source material. If a judge goes to a link within a brief and does not find the cited material, he or she may question the credibility of the source, the attorney, or both. Thus, attorneys conducting legal research on the Internet should keep both validity and accessibility in mind.

There are numerous resources available on the Internet that have a high degree of validity. Many of the extra-legal sources mentioned above may also be found on the Internet. Numerous government agencies have Web pages that contain reports, research studies, or other information that courts would find useful and reliable. On the other hand, an on-point assertion from a random blog may carry little weight.[16] If the Internet simply makes it easier for you to gain access to a report that would have required a trip to the library or to the state capital in days of yore, then the source may well be worth citing. If, in contrast, the source has come into existence because of the Internet, you may wish to be more circumspect. The most important consideration is the validity of the source.[17]

---

[15] *See id.* at 420-22.

[16] Of course, the correct legal standard is often "it depends," and Internet research is no different. Some blogs contain reasoned analysis that is more akin to that found in law reviews. As with law review articles, a blog may be an appropriate citation for a developing legal issue. For example, a judge in the District of North Dakota cited a law professor's blog in 2011, noting that the particular blog cited was "[a]nother source that courts have found persuasive." *United States v. Peterson*, 774 F. Supp. 2d 1024, 1033 (D.N.D. 2011) (referring to Professor Douglas A. Berman's Sentencing Law and Policy blog).

[17] For excellent advice on using the Internet to conduct effective legal research, consult Laurel Currie Oates & Anne Enquist, *Just Research* (2d ed., Aspen 2009).

The fact that Web pages are constantly updated makes them a wonderful research tool, but it can also hurt accessibility for those trying to access "old" citations. One scholar has labeled as "link rot" the persistent problem of links that lead the researcher to defunct Web sites.[18] Two authors studied the 430 links included in Supreme Court opinions issued from 1995 to 2010 and found that 29 percent of them were invalid.[19] Thus, whenever you include a Web citation in a brief, be sure to print a copy of the material; you should also attach a copy to your brief to make sure that the court has access to the information.[20] In addition, you may wish to copy the source to your hard drive, to a word processing file, or to both. In these ways, you make sure that the resource is preserved, should you or the court need to find it at a later date.

Assessing the possible relevance of the facts, the legal issues, and the sources of the authorities you plan to cite can help you to predict which authorities the court will find more valid, and to decide where and how to concentrate your research.

3.3
EXECUTING YOUR RESEARCH PLAN

If you are working on a motion brief, your research questions will be crucial components of your research plan. Whether you are writing a motion brief or an appellate brief, however, your research questions can help to guide your research. As noted above, the "under" clause can be a signal as to how much background research you need to conduct. The "does" clause can help you to focus your research by reminding you of the particular legal question that you are trying to answer.

Once you have a basic understanding of how your jurisdiction treats this particular area of law, step back for a moment and take a look at the big picture. Although your main goal is to identify support for your arguments, an effective research plan can also help you to discover new arguments. You may wish to use particular research methods when researching a statutory issue, when writing to a court of last resort, or when deciding how to use mandatory versus nonmandatory authorities.

A particular word of advice to those who are accustomed to using electronic search engines such as Google: Many law students begin law school

---

[18] Howard A. Denemark, *The Death of Law Reviews Has Been Predicted: What Might Be Lost When the Last Law Review Shuts Down?*, 27 Seton Hall L. Rev. 1, 32 n. 77 (1996) (cited in Barger, *supra* note 14, at 438 n. 67).

[19] Raizel Liebler & June Liebert, *Something Rotten in the State of Legal Citation: The Life Span of a United States Supreme Court Citation Containing an Internet Link* (1996-2010), 15 Yale J.L. & Tech. 273, 307 (2013).

[20] Be sure to check the court's local rules to see if they specifically address Internet citations.

feeling as though they are accomplished researchers because they have spent much of their lives using computer systems to find answers to questions both large and small. Recognize, however, that the questions you are asking in legal research are usually more complex, and they therefore require more time and careful attention when searching for an answer. If you use Google or another search engine to ask a simple question with a definite answer, you are likely to get dozens or hundreds of "hits." If you scan the first half-dozen or so of those hits and find that they agree with each other, you would be sensible to stop researching and be satisfied with the answer you have received. In legal research, however, you are often asking a more complex question, and you will often ask questions that could have more than one answer. If you have an expectation that the answer will bubble to the surface after your first query, you may be misled as to the state of the law or become frustrated in your research, thinking that something is wrong because you can't find an argument as easily as expected. Recognize that effective legal research may require you to review dozens of cases (and to update those cases in a variety of ways) before you are able to identify the authorities that govern your particular issues.

This is not to say that you *cannot* use Google or other nonlegal search engines to assist you in your research. Just realize that legal research requires more thoroughness and more patience than the nonlegal searches you may have conducted in the past. If you have not yet become proficient in conducting Boolean, or "terms and connectors" research, now is a good time to do so. These searches allow you to find legal sources with more precision.[21]

3.3.1
RESEARCHING STATUTORY ISSUES

If your case presents an issue of statutory or constitutional construction, you should conduct some research in the text or online versions of the United States Code Annotated or the United States Code Service (or the relevant state court code collections). Note that for some resources, it is easier and faster to use the hard-copy version to survey a wide array of authorities that have cited the relevant statute or constitutional provision. In addition, remember that courts are interested in hearing about interpretations of similar statutes, or even different statutes that use similar phrases or clauses.

For example, if your case involves the federal Age Discrimination in Employment Act, you might look for similar language in Title VII of the

---

[21] Take the time to learn the benefits and limitations of the various search engines that you use. As of this writing, Lexis and Westlaw generally allow more precision in researching, but this difference may fade as Google and other search engines update their capabilities.

Civil Rights Act of 1964, which deals with sex and race discrimination, or in the Americans with Disabilities Act, which deals with discrimination against people with disabilities. If your analysis focuses on the meaning of a particular word or phrase in the statute, try using one or more words from the phrase as a search term, and search in a United States Code database to see if you can find any other statutes with the same or similar language. You may then be able to use authorities that interpret those other statutes when making your arguments.

Re understanding of meaning of statutes

When looking for authority on the meaning of statutes, consider the three branches of government. First, the executive—has this statute been interpreted by a relevant federal agency? If so, then the court may defer to the agency's interpretation under the *Chevron* rule.[22] Second, consider the legislative branch: Is there any relevant legislative history? (Keep in mind, however, that courts sometimes refuse to consider legislative history.) Finally, and often most importantly, consider the judicial branch: Has a relevant court interpreted this language or analogous language? When you look for interpretations from all three points of view, you may discover analysis that will help you argue that your interpretation is the correct one.

3.3.2
WRITING TO COURTS OF LAST RESORT

If you are writing to the United States Supreme Court or a state court of last resort, some well-worn research paths can be fruitful. First, review the authorities cited in the lower court opinions; you may well use some or all of them in your brief. Likewise, Shepardizing those authorities may lead you to other relevant authorities. You may also discover, however, that the lower court did not consider some of the arguments that may be most effective for your client. Often, the arguments that end up winning the case at the appellate level either were not considered or were considered and rejected by the lower court.

Consider, too, that the lower courts may have been persuaded by authorities that would not persuade a court of last resort. For example, if at the intermediate appellate level you were arguing to a court of appeals, you (or the attorney then working on the case) might have used on-point authorities from that court or from other courts of appeals. When you must write a brief on that same issue to the court of last resort, you should do more research to see how that court has addressed this issue or at least how close the court has come to addressing that issue. In this way, you

---

[22] *See Chevron U.S.A., Inc. v. Natural Resources Defense Council, Inc.*, 467 U.S. 837, 842-44 (1984) (holding that courts must defer to a federal agency interpretation of an ambiguous statute if it is based on a "permissible construction" of the statute). Note that federal agencies sometimes interpret statutes in documents other than formal rulings.

may discover a variety of authorities that were not explored in the lower courts. Therefore, although you can begin your research with the authorities cited by the court being appealed, those authorities should be only a starting point.

Consider three cases that may or may not be representative. In *Florida v. Jardines,* 133 S. Ct. 1409 (2013), the United States Supreme Court cited approximately 41 cases in its opinion. Thirty of those cases were United States Supreme Court decisions. The Florida Supreme Court, whose opinion the Court affirmed, cited about 95 cases, 45 of which were Supreme Court cases. *Jardines v. State,* 73 So. 3d 34 (Fla. 2011) *cert. granted in part,* 132 S. Ct. 995 (2012), and *aff'd,* 133 S. Ct. 1409 (2013). Only ten of the 95 cases cited in the Florida Supreme Court were also cited in the United States Supreme Court. In *Florida v. Harris,* 133 S. Ct. 1050 (2013), the United States Supreme Court cited only nine cases (other than prior history decisions), all of them United States Supreme Court decisions. That Court reversed a decision of the Florida Supreme Court: *Harris v. State,* 71 So. 3d 756, 759 (Fla. 2011), *as revised on denial of reh'g* (Sept. 22, 2011), *rev'd,* 133 S. Ct. 1050 (2013) and *opinion withdrawn,* SC08-1871, 2013 WL 5476903 (Fla. Oct. 3, 2013). The Florida Supreme Court opinion in *Harris* cited about 47 cases; 20 of these were decisions of the United States Supreme Court. Only five authoritative cases were cited in both the Florida Supreme Court and United States Supreme Court opinions.

Finally, in *United States v. Stevens,* 559 U.S. 460 (2010), the United States Supreme Court cited approximately 44 cases. All of these cases were United States Supreme Court decisions. The United States Court of Appeals for the Third Circuit, whose opinion the Court affirmed, cited approximately 58 cases, of which 42 were United States Supreme Court decisions. *United States v. Stevens,* 533 F.3d 218, 221 (3d Cir. 2008), *aff'd,* 559 U.S. 460 (2010). Eighteen of the 44 cases cited in the Supreme Court decision had also been cited in the opinion being reviewed.

These illustrations provide at least two guideposts: First, although the United States Supreme Court prefers its own decisions, it is willing to consider others. Second, the Supreme Court is likely to consider cases beyond those discussed in the lower courts. Thus, when writing a brief to a court of last resort, carefully consider any decisions from that court that were cited by the lower court(s). If there are other decisions cited—e.g., decisions of relevant courts of appeals—read those decisions and see if *those decisions* cite to the court of last resort. If you want to use the rules or holdings from those lower court decisions, you may be able to find a high court "hook" in the decisions themselves. If you cannot find any high court authority in those decisions and you still want to use the legal principles, use your research skills (and your abstract reasoning) to search for high court decisions that govern the same or similar points. Once again, this is not to say that you must restrict your case citations to mandatory cases when writing to a court of last resort. Nonmandatory cases will be seen as more valid, however, if the writer can connect them to a mandatory rule. The next section addresses methods for pulling arguments from nonmandatory authorities.

3.3.3
HARVESTING ARGUMENTS FROM NONMANDATORY AUTHORITIES

If you are writing to a trial court, you need to know first whether a mandatory authority governs the issue directly. If you are writing to a court of last resort, or if there are no mandatory authorities that are directly on point, you may need to look beyond mandatory authorities. First, if you are in a state court or in a federal court other than the Supreme Court, you should determine whether your jurisdiction is within the mainstream. If your jurisdiction is within the mainstream, and the mainstream is on your side, your arguments will be pretty much laid out for you. If, in contrast, your jurisdiction is the first to tackle a new interpretation of the law, or a new cause of action entirely, one side or the other may be able to argue that it is now time to return to the old way of doing things. If all or most of your sister jurisdictions have made a jurisprudential change, one side can argue that it is time for this jurisdiction to make the change as well.

Whether you are arguing to a trial court, an intermediate court of appeals, or a court of last resort, you need to decide whether to cite nonmandatory, or even nonjurisdictional, authorities. If your jurisdiction is within the mainstream and if authorities within your jurisdiction are sufficiently on point to answer your legal question, there may be no need to cite authorities outside of that jurisdiction. If your jurisdiction is out of the mainstream or if there are no authorities that are directly on point, you may want to consult nonmandatory or nonjurisdictional authorities as well.

If you have not already done so, now is a good time to identify "foundational search terms": These are unique statute numbers or legal phrases that always pull up on-point authorities. They may pull up other authorities as well; I call them *foundational* search terms because they include the fundamental, or foundational, legal terms that are relevant to a particular legal issue. Often, you will discover foundational search terms as part of your research, so don't be surprised if you can't identify them until well into your research. For example, if you were arguing that an employer should ban smoking in the workplace, you would discover the term *safe workplace* in a relevant statute. Both the statute number and the term *safe workplace* could be good *foundational search terms*. A Boolean search that looked for the statute number *or* the term *safe workplace* would be a broad search, but if you limit it to the mandatory authority database,[23] you would be sure to find every case in which the court of last resort in your jurisdiction addressed the issue of safe workplaces.

Search the foundational search terms in your mandatory database to make sure you have the most recent word on how the court of last resort has interpreted the crucial word, phrase, or statute at issue. You should review each relevant case from within the last few years to make sure that you are up to date on the mandatory authority. In addition, you should find the most recent cases in your jurisdiction to have addressed the issue in any way, even if they were not decided by the court of last resort. If your search pulls up too many hits, try using the *when* clause from your research question to help you to identify fact-based search terms to add to your search, which will help you discover the authorities that are most on point. In the smoke-in-the-workplace case, for example, you could add "cigarette or tobacco or smoking or smoke or fumes" to narrow your search.

use "When" language to ① *develop* × *search terms*

If there are relevant authorities in your jurisdiction but no authorities that are sufficiently on point, plug your fact-based foundational search into databases outside your jurisdiction. In this way you may be able to discover any cases that are on point as to issues and facts and that can therefore serve as persuasive authority. Although these cases would be a *source* of an argument rather than an authority for it,[24] courts often find on-point authorities to be helpful guideposts, even when they are not mandatory.

Furthermore, you may be able to "harvest" effective arguments from nonmandatory authorities both within and outside your jurisdiction. When I refer to *harvesting* an argument, I am suggesting that you use the raw materials from an argument or an analysis and then figure out how to *make* that same argument to your court. Harvesting an argument from a nonmandatory or nonjurisdictional authority is a very different thing than *citing* an argument from such an authority. When you harvest an argument, you let nonmandatory or nonjurisdictional sources help to direct your research.

Suppose, for example, that you are arguing that the Americans with Disabilities Act (ADA) forbids your client's employer from requiring her to submit to medical testing. You are arguing the case in a motion brief in a circuit that has no mandatory authority governing the issue. The statutory section at issue, 42 U.S.C. §12112(d)(4)(A), provides:

---

[23] For example, Lexis and Westlaw have search techniques that would allow you to limit your search to just the highest court in the particular jurisdiction.

[24] Chapter Six explains the difference between "sources" and "authorities."

Prohibited examinations and inquiries

A covered entity shall not require a medical examination and shall not make inquiries of an employee as to whether such employee is an individual with a disability or as to the nature or severity of the disability, unless such examination or inquiry is shown to be job-related and consistent with business necessity.

You are arguing that the term *employee* in this section means "any employee," while your opponent is arguing that the term means only "qualified individuals with disabilities." In your research, you discover a case from a nonmandatory authority that looks at the ways that the terms *employee* and *qualified individual with a disability* are used throughout the statute. That court alludes to statutory and regulatory language that supports your conclusion:

A plaintiff need not prove that he or she has a disability unknown to his or her employer in order to challenge a medical inquiry or examination under 42 U.S.C. §12112(d)(4)(A). In contrast to other parts of the ADA, the statutory language does not refer to qualified individuals with disabilities, but instead merely to "employees." 42 U.S.C. §12112(d)(4)(A).

McGuffin v. Bernard, 444 F. Supp. 2d 455, 472 (S.D. Ohio 2009).[25]

A writer who merely *cited* that nonjurisdictional case as authority would not use it effectively:

▽ BAD EXAMPLE

The United States District Court for the Southern District of Ohio has observed that the term "employee" in 42 U.S.C. §12122(d)(4)(A) must refer to all employees and not just to those employees who are qualified individuals with disabilities. McGuffin v. Bernard, 444 F. Supp. 2d 455, 472 (S.D. Ohio 2009). It noted that Congress had used the phrase "qualified individual with disabilities" in other sections of the ADA and could have done so in §12122(d)(4)(A) if it so desired. Id. Therefore, when the ADA forbids medical inquiries directed to "an employee," the term must mean . . .

To harvest the argument effectively, the writer should let the nonmandatory source direct further research. The writer should notice that the court based its analysis—at least implicitly—on a governing rule that says that when Congress uses the same term in more than one section of a statute, the term should be interpreted consistently, and when Congress chooses a different term, it must have intended the term to mean something different. This observation should lead the writer to conduct research to find an appropriate rule in the mandatory jurisdiction. But that is not enough. It

---

[25] The language from this fictional case is adapted from *Lee v. City of Columbus,* 644 F. Supp. 2d 1000, 1011 (S.D. Ohio 2009).

would be ineffective to merely cite the mandatory rule and state the same conclusory analysis. Instead, the writer should also research the language of the statute and figure out how best to apply the rule regarding consistent interpretation of terms to the "fact" of the statutory language:[26]

⚠ GOOD EXAMPLE

When Congress uses one term in one part of a statute and a different term in another, this court should assume that different meanings were intended. <u>Cucilich Industries v. Perek</u>, 599 F.3d 947, 955 (18th Cir. 2009). In <u>Cucilich Industries</u>, the Eighteenth Circuit analyzed the Carriage of Goods by Rail Act and noted that "Congress chose to use different terms in [the Act] when referring to the 'shipper' in conjunction with other parties, on the one hand, and the 'shipper' alone, on the other." <u>Id</u>. at 956. Accordingly, the court refused to interpret the term "shipper" in one clause in the same way that it interpreted the phrase "shipper, receiver, or holder of bill of lading." <u>Id</u>. at 958.

When Congress chose to use the term "employee" in 42 U.S.C. §12112(d)(4)(A) of the ADA, it did so in order to refer to all "employees" of the employing entity, and the term should not be interpreted to mean "qualified individual with a disability." The terms "employee" and "qualified individual" are defined separately in the Act, at §§12111(4) and 12111(8), respectively. Section 12114(c) specifies limits that can be imposed on "employees," while other sections speak specifically to qualified individuals with a disability. Section 12122(b)(5)(A), for example, notes that discrimination against a "qualified individual on the basis of disability" includes not making reasonable accommodations for "an otherwise qualified individual with a disability." Similarly, §12112(b)(5)(B) forbids denying employment in certain circumstances to "an otherwise qualified individual with a disability." Accordingly . . .

Notice that the writer has gone beyond the conclusory statement from the *McGuffin* case. That decision merely referred to "other parts of the ADA" that mentioned "qualified individuals with a disability." As part of harvesting the argument, the writer took a cue from that conclusory language and read the ADA so that he or she was able to quote and cite the specific provisions that mentioned "qualified individuals with a disability" as opposed to "employees."

Accordingly, one way to "harvest" an argument is to (1) unpack a relevant legal conclusion from a nonmandatory source, (2) conduct research to find a mandatory rule that would lead to that conclusion, (3) articulate

[26]The example mentions fictional case law that is adapted from *Sosa v. Alvarez-Machain*, 542 U.S. 692, 712 (2004), and *APL Co. Pte v. UK Aerosols Ltd.*, 582 F.3d 947, 952 (9th Cir. 2009).

that mandatory rule and explain it appropriately, and (4) apply that rule completely and effectively to the appropriate facts in your client's case.[27]

If you believe that the court you are writing to would find the non-mandatory source to be meaningful, you could include a "see also" citation to that authority, but you should not presume that one is appropriate. In the alternative, if the area of law were novel or the facts or legal issues in the nonmandatory cases were particularly relevant, the writer might follow the citations to the mandatory authorities with a discussion of the nonmandatory authority, perhaps beginning the discussion by noting, "This is just the approach taken by the Fifteenth Circuit in a very similar case. . . ."

To sum up, when designing and executing your research plan, think ahead, but be ready to explore new leads as you learn more about your case and its issues.

3.4
THE LEGAL WRITER AS DIGITAL READER

If you are like most twenty-first-century law students, you are accustomed to conducting legal research on a tablet, laptop, or desktop computer. Thus, it is likely that you first start to read most of your research resources in digital rather than hard-copy form. The easy availability of digital documents has been a boon to legal researchers. When I was in law school, in the early 1980s, I could conduct legal research only in a law library. Research databases were in their infancy, and one research computer served the entire student body (which was fine, since we hardly used it). Thus, I conducted virtually all of my research by using book-based finding tools, and then going to the appropriate shelf in the library to find the law review, case reporter, or other text that I wanted. I read many cases in books; if I decided a case was significant to my research, I would pay to make a copy of it so I would be able to mark up the text and take the copy home with me.

I tell you this story not just to evoke your pity (wait till I tell you about using a typewriter to write!) but to illustrate what a physical act research used to be. Researchers had to use their whole bodies. They used their hands and arms to pull books off shelves, and they had to walk around the library to find the books that they needed. These activities certainly had

---

[27] Of course, it is vitally important to note that plagiarism rules vary greatly in academic settings and in litigation settings in practice. In an academic setting, if you "harvest" an argument from an authority, you should always note the source of the argument. When writing litigation materials in an academic setting, the best course might be to drop a footnote and indicate the nonmandatory source of the argument. Some teachers might give you permission to remove the citation, but presume that you should include the citation unless instructed otherwise.

time and place restrictions. But there were benefits, too. When we had to go to one set of shelves to find cases in the F. Supp. reporters, and another set of shelves to find the cases in the F.2d reporters, the constant reinforcement taught us—without any conscious effort on our part—that F. Supp. published only federal district court opinions and F.2d published only federal circuit cases. When we had to flip through the pages of a case to find a pinpoint cite, we could easily notice—due to the reader-friendly printing techniques—when we passed from the majority opinion to a concurrence or a dissent.[28]

These obvious benefits are not the only physical benefits of the hard-copy research process. Scholars who study digital reading have seen that readers of digital text interact differently with the text than do readers of hard-copy text. We might believe that we read only with our eyes, or maybe our eyes and our brains, but scientists are realizing that the physical dimension plays a real role in the reading process. When we read a hard-copy text, the physicality of the document helps to give us more of a sense of the whole document, and of the relationships between and among the various pieces of information within that document.[29] The smaller the screen, the harder it is for us to develop a spatial relationship with the text; this lack of a spatial relationship may inhibit our immediate comprehension,[30] and, more importantly, our learning and long-term memory regarding the text.

Other studies show that digital readers are more likely skim and scan through the document than to read it from beginning to end, and are less likely to read longer excerpts. The skimming and scanning process, obviously, is less likely to promote comprehension and full engagement with the text. The ability to jump from one keyword to another is an obvious benefit of digital reading, but it inhibits learning and comprehension if it changes our behavior by turning readers into skimmers.

Perhaps most obviously, the digital reader faces constant temptation to abandon the relevant document and to go to another document. Hot links within the document may lead to another document and then another, until the reader is unable to remember (or retrieve) the original text. When we face a roadblock in either research or thinking, we may

---

[28] I have nagged legal database publishers for years that they should use shading, colors, marginal markers, or some other signal to make clear to all readers whether case text is a part of majority, concurrence, dissent, or plurality opinion.

[29] Anne Mangen, Bente R. Walgermo & Kolbjorn Bronnick, *Reading Linear Texts on Paper versus Computer Screen: Effects on Reading Comprehension*, 58 Intl. J. Educ. Research 61-68 (2013). "Readers in the paper condition had immediate access to the text in its entirety. This access is, moreover, built on both visual and tactile cues: the reader can see as well as tactilely feel the spatial extension and physical dimensions of the text, as the material substrate of paper provides physical, tactile, spatiotemporally fixed cues to the length of the text." *Id.* at 66 (citations omitted).

[30] *Id.* at 61-68 (reporting results of a study showing that "subjects in the print condition scored significantly higher on the comprehension tests than those in the screen condition," *id.* at 65).

be tempted to abandon our research, or "take a break," and look at other tabs or icons readily available on our screens. Likewise, the dings of new e-mails or Facebook notices call to us even when our research is going well.

I am not suggesting that we should all abandon all digital reading. We should, however, be aware of its limits and take steps to combat them. We can absorb the content from digital documents, but we may have to expend extra energy to do so. To make sure that we are comprehending context, we may want to scan a table of contents, if one is available, or strive to take notes (either on or off the screen) that provide context cues. Many research databases make it easy for writers to insert pop-up notes, and planning to write those notes may encourage us to engage with the text and discourage skimming. Similarly, consciously noting how long a case or article is—either by scanning through the document or by noting a page length that is provided in the document—may help us to subconsciously place the information into a physical context (such as beginning, middle, or end).

Furthermore, when we have the choice to read the article as a .pdf rather than by scrolling, we should do so, especially if we can fit the page to the screen size. Many studies show that scrolling through the text affects comprehension and recall because the information has no permanent physical location.[31] It is common for readers to "picture" information by recalling where it was on a page, or on the two-page presentation common in hard-copy books.[32] Likewise, consider the size of the screen on the device you are using to read the document: the smaller the screen, the harder you have to work to put information into context. Your smartphone will allow you to read cases anywhere, but the benefit of accessibility may impose costs in comprehension.

Thus, when conducting your research, take steps to help you focus your attention. Set timers or use other methods to encourage you to stay with one document for a specific period of time. Read .pdfs or use other hard-page imitations to improve your spatial relationship with your documents. Finally, if you are having a particularly difficult time with a document, or if you know that a document is particularly crucial, spend the toner to print it out. Your brain—and your clients—may be glad that you did.

---

[31] *Id.* at 61-68. "If texts are longer than a page, scrolling and the lack of spatiotemporal markers of the digital texts to aid memory and reading comprehension might impede reader performance." *Id.* at 67.

[32] *Id.* at 61-68. "Evidence suggests that readers often recall where in a text some particular piece of information appeared (e.g., toward the upper right corner or at the bottom of the page)." *Id.* at 65-66 (citations omitted).

3.5
KNOWING WHEN TO STOP

Most lawyers have a hard time ending their research, perhaps because they don't want to start writing. Researching is fun, and you don't have to make any hard decisions; if you think a case or other authority may be useful, you store it or print it and keep on going. Of course, printing is not research; you must actually read and analyze the sources you have found. For some writers, research is like dating and writing is like marriage: With research, you hope that if you keep looking, you'll find the perfect match right around the next corner. With writing, you just have to take what you have and try to work it out.

Accordingly, when doing your research, you should consciously decide when to stop. No matter how diligent your research, your writing will probably reveal some gaps that need to be filled. Don't try to fill those gaps *before* you start writing. Instead, let the writing reveal the gaps to you and help to direct your follow-up research. Think in terms of a partial stop and a full stop. You should come to a partial stop when you have followed a good research plan, you have updated your authorities,[33] and you are not finding anything new—you keep encountering again and again those almost-relevant cases that you've rejected once or twice before.

You can come to a partial stop when you have achieved four goals: (1) you understand the general area of law and how the relevant courts apply it in cases similar to your client's case; (2) you understand whether your jurisdiction is in the mainstream or is an outlier as to the relevant legal issues; (3) you have found the most recent cases that address the issue in any way from (a) the court of last resort in your jurisdiction, and (b) any court in your jurisdiction; and (4) if appropriate, you have identified relevant cases or other sources from nonmandatory courts or jurisdictions.

[handwritten: 4 Goals to achieve]

As you review these authorities and begin to outline and write your argument, you may decide that some of them are not worth citing. The process of reading and analyzing them, however, can help you to understand your case and to identify valid arguments. Conversely, as you write, you may discover new avenues that you wish to explore, and you can make tactical research strikes to grab cases or other authorities to support the points that come up. Some writers continue these tactical strikes until they are stopped by an outside force: a court-imposed due date.

---

[33] Of course, you should update your authorities frequently during the research process, right up until the day you file your brief, and again as you prepare your oral argument.

3.6
SUMMARY

To write an effective brief, you must follow an effective research plan; you need to know your case thoroughly and plan your research accordingly. Before you research, get to know the facts of your client's case by abstracting any record materials. Identify the questions that your research must answer, and be realistic about the types of authorities you can expect to find. When assessing the validity of authorities, use the abstraction ladder to identify those that address analogous facts and issues. Weigh the validity of the source of the authority, and be willing to look beyond legal authorities. Be certain to update your authorities and to get a complete picture of the relevant area of law, including nonmandatory authorities. When appropriate, do relevant follow-up research so that you can "harvest" effective arguments from nonmandatory authorities. When conducting your research, be mindful about the technology you use: Focus your attention, and use methods that promote engagement with the texts that you read.

Finally, be practical about the percentage of your available time that you spend on researching. Set a deadline for research that allows you sufficient time to work on the actual writing of your brief. The process of writing the brief will often reveal gaps in your research; by giving yourself time to write, you create opportunities for finding any research gaps.

FACING THE BLANK PAGE

The hardest thing about writing is writing. Writing is harder than researching before you write, and it's harder than revising after you've written. But to use the research, and to have something to revise, you must actually write a draft of your document at some point.

Two techniques can make it easier for you to face the blank page: (1) deciding on some sort of structure before you begin to write, and (2) using "private memos," which are a way to record your concerns about problems with the draft as you write it. A third thing that can make it easier to face the blank page is facing the fears that often lead to procrastination.

4.1
FINDING STRUCTURE

At this stage, you should have a stack of authorities that you plan to use in support of your client's case. Now, you must make the move from that stack of paper to some sort of an outline. Effective legal arguments are usually best organized around issues, rules, and arguments rather than around authority cases. The court's major concern is not whether the cases you have found are analogous to your client's case. Instead, the court wants to know the issues that your case presents, the rules that govern those issues, and how those rules should apply to your case. Of course, you will probably use cases to illustrate or explain the rules that you identify, but the *rules*, rather than the cases, should be the focus of your analysis.

When trying to identify the rules that you want to use to structure your argument, it may help you to think of possible categories of arguments. Since legal arguments are typically based on authority, you may try to develop your arguments based on the categories of authority, as noted in Chapter Three: case law, constitutions and statutes, regulations, or extra-legal authority. Since these different types of authority may interact within one argument, however, you may wish to think of categories from a different perspective. Wilson Huhn has identified five different types of arguments: text, precedent, intent, policy, and tradition.[1]

If the rules that govern your case are well established, and you must argue how those rules apply, you can structure your argument around those established rules.[2] If your case is not governed by well-established rules, or if you are struggling to discover or articulate[3] the relevant rules, you can use both research and brainstorming techniques to help you discover your structure. Furthermore, remember that some of your rules may be policy-based rules, and that those policy-based rules can help you to structure your argument. Once you have identified the issues, rules, and policies that are relevant to your argument, you can create a working outline.

4.1.1
USING EXISTING RULES AND THE "PHRASE-THAT-PAYS" TO STRUCTURE YOUR ARGUMENT

If your argument is based in whole or in part on well-established statutory or common law rules, you can structure your argument by looking for each rule's "key terms,"[4] or, as I call them, the "phrases-that-pay." I use this term to label the word or phrase that is the focus of controversy about whether or how a rule applies. You can use phrases-that-pay as an effective organizing principle: By focusing on one "phrase-that-pays" within each subsection of the document, you ensure that you are focusing on one issue or sub-issue at a time, and you make it easier for the court to

---

[1] Wilson Huhn, *The Five Types of Legal Argument* 13 (2d ed., Carolina Academic Press 2008). Huhn's text analyzes how to identify these arguments, how to create arguments, and how to attack arguments.

[2] *See, e.g.*, Linda H. Edwards, *Legal Writing: Process, Analysis, and Organization* chs. 2-6 (5th ed., Wolters Kluwer 2010); Richard K. Neumann, Jr. & Kristen Konrad Tiscione, *Legal Reasoning and Legal Writing* ch. 2 (7th ed., Wolters Kluwer 2013).

[3] See Chapter Five for guidance on using inductive reasoning to find rules.

[4] *See, e.g.*, Laurel Currie Oates & Anne M. Enquist, *The Legal Writing Handbook* §§22.3.2 (5th ed., Wolters Kluwer 2010).

understand your argument. Thus, if one or more of your legal issues is governed by well-established rules, you can begin to structure your argument by reviewing those rules and identifying the phrases-that-pay that are in controversy in your case.

You can often identify phrases-that-pay by turning your rule into an if-then statement.[5] An "if-then" rule says, in essence, "if a certain condition exists, then a certain legal status results." The phrase-that-pays is almost always the "condition" that you are trying to prove the existence (or nonexistence) of. Thus, look for the phrases-that-pay in the "if" clause; that clause usually contains the narrow point that the writer is trying to explain or prove. For example, the petitioner in *Minnesota v. Carter* might write a rule within its brief as follows:

> **While a person's home is, for most purposes, a place where he expects privacy, activities that are exposed "to the 'plain view' of outsiders are not protected" under the Fourth Amendment. Katz v. United States, 389 U.S. 347, 361 (1967) (Harlan, J., concurring).**

The same rule stated as an if-then statement would read:

> **IF a person exposes activities to the plain view of outsiders, THEN those activities are not protected against observation by the Fourth Amendment's search and seizure limitations.**

This writer is arguing, at least in part, that the defendant's activities occurred within the plain view of police officers. Thus, "in plain view" is the phrase-that-pays.

Sometimes, one rule will have more than one phrase-that-pays in controversy. To determine if this is true for a particular rule, consider both how courts have interpreted the rule and how the rule relates to a particular set of facts. For instance, in the previous example, the respondents might argue that they did not "expose" their activities to "outsiders," even if the activities were technically within plain view. Some courts might conduct a separate analysis of what exactly it means to "expose" activities; they might also address who is considered an "outsider" for purposes of the plain-view doctrine. If the courts have conducted these separate analyses, it would be easy to divide the argument on this rule into three parts: (1) whether the activities were "exposed," (2) whether the activities were in "plain view," and (3) whether the activities were exposed to "outsiders." On the other hand, if the courts have not addressed these issues separately, but have presumed that all activities in plain view are exposed to

---

[5] Note that you should not necessarily articulate your rule as an if-then statement in the argument itself; this technique is merely a method for identifying the phrases-that-pay.

outsiders, it might not be worthwhile to address these issues separately.[6] The courts' analysis is usually a good starting point.

Whether your rule comes from a statute or the common law, you may find that you can discover the true phrases-that-pay only after further research. Sometimes a term in controversy has one or more layers of judicial gloss, so that the actual phrase-that-pays is one or two layers away from the phrase-that-pays in the rule itself. For example, 28 U.S.C. §1332 gives federal district courts "diversity jurisdiction" over certain lawsuits between "citizens of different states." If you did not conduct further research, you might presume that you had to focus your analysis on the meaning of the term *citizen* as it applies to your client and his or her opponent. If you did conduct further research, however, you would discover that the courts define *citizenship*—for purposes of §1332—as "domicile." Furthermore, the courts explain that establishing a domicile requires that "a person must be physically present in the state and must have either the intention to make his home there indefinitely or the absence of an intention to make his home elsewhere."[7] Upon looking at the cases addressing this rule, you see that courts analyze "physical presence," "intent" to make a home in a state, or both, when determining whether the standard is met.

An often-reliable test for the true phrase-that-pays is to identify the term that courts connect—or "apply"—to the facts of the case. In a diversity case, for example, the court might connect the concept of "citizenship" to "domicile," and "domicile" to "intent." If the court connects case facts to the terms "physical presence" and "intent" ("Mr. Guillen[8] was physically present in Illinois through much of the relevant time period, and stated at a press conference his intent to remain"), you can be pretty confident that for the rule determining diversity of citizenship, the phrases-that-pay are "physical presence" and "intent to make a home there indefinitely or the absence of an intent to make a home elsewhere."

When deciding what points to argue in your brief, however, you must do more than identify the phrases-that-pay that exist within a rule; you must decide which phrases-that-pay are at issue. For example, you may have a diversity situation where a party to a case is obviously "physically present," but where there is some controversy as to whether he or she has the requisite "intent" to make a home in the state. In that situation, you

---

[6] Of course, you may decide that courts should be analyzing issues that they have not analyzed in the past. See Section 5.1.2(c), "Using Inductive Reasoning to Find and Articulate Legal Rules."

[7] *E.g., Deasy v. Louisville & Jefferson County Metropolitan Sewer Dist.*, 47 Fed. Appx. 726, 728 (6th Cir. 2002) (court-designated unpublished decision).

[8] The occasional use of names associated with the Chicago White Sox—the 2005 Major League Baseball World Champions—is purely honorific. The cases and fact scenarios are fictional, and the author does not mean to imply that these baseball stars are or should be involved in any sort of litigation.

would acknowledge that there is no controversy as to physical presence and focus your argument on establishing intent. Chapter Five discusses how best to include uncontroversial issues within the argument.

Thus, you must look both to your case facts and to the courts' analyses to identify the phrases-that-pay that are relevant to your argument: (1) determine what words or phrases the courts focus on when they apply law to facts in their analysis of the relevant issue(s); (2) determine how those words or phrases relate to the rule or statute at issue (are the words part of the rule, part of the courts' definition of terms in the rule, or part of the courts' explanation of how the rule applies?); finally, (3) determine which phrases-that-pay are at issue in your client's case.

When writing, you must be sure to clarify how the phrases-that-pay relate to each other and to the relevant statutes or common law rules. Once you have analyzed all of the applicable rules, identified their phrases-that-pay, and determined which phrases-that-pay are in controversy in your case, you can begin to draft a working outline of your argument.

4.1.2
USING YOUR RESEARCH TO HELP YOU STRUCTURE YOUR ARGUMENT

A second method of identifying argument structure is to use your research. Look at that stack of authorities. Each one of those authorities made it into the "chosen" pile because it appeared to support some aspect of your argument. Some authorities may support more than one, or even several, aspects of your argument. Ideally, you will have used an organized note-taking system as you reviewed each authority. For cases, for example, you may have recorded procedural information such as court and date, and substantive information such as issue(s), facts, holding, and reasoning. Now you can review those notes, and the authorities themselves, and look for organizing principles for your argument.

One way to identify organizing principles is to identify argument points you can get from each authority. To do this, look at each authority and write out the ways in which the authority relates to or supports your argument. These points may be rules or policies[9] that the court would need to consider in order to decide the case, or assertions that the court would have to agree with to decide the case in your favor.

This is a brainstorming technique, so don't worry about making the statements in perfect rule format, or even in formal language. Just use some method to list the holding(s) or other information from the authority that made you think the authority would be helpful to your argument, recording the source for each item. As you proceed through your authorities, you

---

[9] Section 4.1.3 will help you to identify policy-based rules.

may discover that you have already written down the same assertion or a similar one from a different source. If that's the case, simply add the new source to that item, perhaps noting the difference in a parenthetical. You may also have some assertions in mind that you can't tie to a particular source at the moment; be sure to write those down as well.

Although many good writers compose at the computer keyboard, the computer may not be the best place to use this method. You may want to write the assertions on index cards so that you can shuffle them around later. You may want to write them on a big piece of paper so you can think about how the statements from one authority connect to the statements from another authority, perhaps drawing arrows to make the connections more obvious to yourself.

Let's use the case of *Miller v. Albright*, 523 U.S. 420 (1998), for an example. The petitioner in *Miller* was the foreign-born daughter of a United States serviceman. The daughter wanted to become a United States citizen based on her status as the daughter of a United States citizen, but her parents had never married. Section 1409(a) of 8 U.S.C. imposed strict requirements for citizenship on foreign-born children of unmarried citizen fathers and foreign mothers. Because it imposed almost no requirements for citizenship on foreign-born children of unmarried citizen mothers and foreign fathers, the daughter sued to have the statute declared unconstitutional.

Let's presume that you are researching *Miller v. Albright* on behalf of the petitioner, and you have reached a "partial stop" in your research. You have before you a stack of authorities that (you think) support your argument. You might come up with the following list of assertions that you believe the court has to agree with to decide in your favor:

List of points that court must agree with:[10]

1. Court should reverse decision below.
2. Statute is unconstitutional.
3. Statute discriminates on the basis of gender.

   McGuffin v. Podesednik
   Patel v. Yoder

4. Court should scrutinize statutes that discriminate based on gender under intermediate level of scrutiny.

   Reinsdorf v. Williams
   Ifeduba v. Coleman ("heightened" scrutiny)
   Crede v. State ("something less than strict scrutiny")
   Restrepo v. Rowand
   Blum v. Vizcaino

[10] Cases listed are fictional.

5. Statute fails the intermediate scrutiny test.

   Restrepo v. Rowand
   Blum v. Vizcaino
   Zawierucha v. Vanita Public Schools

6. Statute is even unconstitutional under rational basis-type scrutiny.

   Kelly v. City of Chicago
   Yeary v. Brooks

7. Court should not defer to Congress even though this is an immigration law.

   United States v. Shaheen
   United States v. Pelehach
   United States v. Chu

8. The statute is not substantially related to the achievement of the government's objective.

   Zawierucha v. Vanita Public Schools
   Restrepo v. Rowand

9. There is not an "exceedingly persuasive justification" for the distinction between the children of the two types of parents.

   Reinsdorf v. Williams
   Ifeduba v. Coleman
   Crede v. State

10. It is not rational to distinguish between children of United States citizen fathers and children of United States citizen mothers.

    Kelly v. City of Chicago
    Yeary v. Brooks

11. Stopping gender discrimination and "illegitimacy" discrimination is more important than allowing Congress control over immigration.

    United States v. Pelehach
    United States v. Chu

12. Someone who is a child of a United States citizen is not an "immigrant" and so a statute that regulates such a person is not an immigration statute.

    United States v. Shaheen

13. Biological parent-child relationships are important.

    Garcia v. Department of Social Services
    Indiana v. Buehrle

14. A statute that applies differently to citizens of different genders can be upheld only if it passes a significant level of scrutiny.

    Ifeduba v. Coleman
    Crede v. State

Restrepo v. Rowand
Blum v. Vizcaino

After making the list, try to identify relationships between and among the points. For example, points 1 and 2 are really two sides of the same coin: If the statute is unconstitutional, the decision below must be reversed. Some of the points may be repetitive of other points, and so they can be eliminated, or the two repetitive points can be synthesized into one point, for example, points 4 and 14. Some points may be parts or subparts of other points, and so they should be grouped accordingly, for example, points 5, 8, and 9. Some points may be threshold issues, so you may decide that they should be addressed first.

If you have listed these points on index cards, you might try moving the cards around to identify the relationships between and among the points. You might stack the cards that seem to make the same point. If you have listed these points on a piece of paper, you might try drawing lines or circles to connect related points, or to identify a hierarchy among the assertions.[11] Once you have figured out, even tentatively, how the points relate to each other, you are ready to draft an outline.

4.1.3
USING POLICY-BASED RULES IN YOUR ARGUMENT

Another method of creating an outline of your argument—or points to be included in your outline—is to identify relevant policy arguments. Legal writing is based on rules, and usually rules provide the best structure for legal analysis. Some writers, however, focus so much on the structure that the rules provide that they miss important policy arguments.

Policy arguments are based on a special kind of rule called a public policy. In law, *public policy* is defined roughly as a societal rule about how people should behave or how institutions should function in our society.[12] Even when policies remain the same, laws may change as human attitudes change or as scientific knowledge changes. For example, over the past 30 years, laws about smoking in public places have changed based on (1) the public policy or societal belief that one person should not cause harm to another and (2) the scientific knowledge about the harms of second-hand smoke. In many legal arguments, the policy arguments are implicit in the more formal legal rules that apply to the issues in the case, and they need not be addressed separately. Sometimes, however, the court will be more likely to agree with your ultimate conclusion if it can also be

---

[11] *See, e.g.,* Elizabeth Fajans & Mary R. Falk, *Comments Worth Making: Supervising Scholarly Writing in Law School,* 46 J. Legal Educ. 342 (1996).

[12] *See generally* Ellie Margolis, *Closing the Floodgates: Making Persuasive Policy Arguments in Appellate Briefs,* 62 Mont. L. Rev. 59, 70 (2001).

convinced—or reminded—of the importance of a policy that underlies your argument.

In a Fourth Amendment case, for example, you might include a separate point addressing either the importance of protecting police officers from dangers of police work (and therefore the need to allow police officers wide latitude in their work) or the importance of the right to privacy (and therefore the need to limit the abilities of police officers to invade that privacy).

In an argument based on the *Miller v. Albright* case, counsel representing Miller might make a separate argument based on the notion that parent-child relationships are fundamental and must be promoted, no matter when that relationship is formed. In addition or in the alternative, counsel could argue that children should not suffer adverse consequences because of the acts or status of their parents. Courts might have made these points as part of their reasoning in cases that were being cited to support relevant rules. In that situation, these arguments could be incorporated into other arguments. If your on-point cases don't contain these points, you might want to incorporate them into your argument separately, not connected to rational basis or intermediate scrutiny arguments. If the court agreed with either of these policy-based assertions, it might be more willing to apply intermediate scrutiny or to hold that the statute violates the rational basis test.

Even if you make a policy argument separately from more traditional legal arguments, you need not treat policy arguments differently. You may, but you are not required to, label them as "public policy" or "policy" arguments (e.g., you need not say, "For reasons of public policy, this court should . . ."). Furthermore, policy arguments can and should be supported by references to outside authorities.[13] Although policy arguments might be more likely to include citations to extra-legal sources,[14] whenever possible, you should include citations to and analysis of cases in which courts referenced certain policies when deciding similar legal issues.

For example, the writer of the *Miller v. Albright* brief might attack the validity of the statutory requirement that the connection between the parent and the child must be formed before the child's twenty-first birthday. As a separate point heading, the writer might assert that "the Court should not put a time limit on parent-child relationships," and could support that point by citing cases in which courts have articulated the importance of parent-child relationships, especially cases in which the importance of that relationship was legally significant. These cases might include adoption cases, termination of parental rights cases, child support enforcement

---

[13] *Id.* at 66.

[14] For example, if you are arguing that traffic stops are dangerous for police officers, you might cite to statistical information about how frequently police officers are injured in the course of conducting traffic stops.

cases, prison visitation cases, and more. Similarly, counsel for Miller might look to case authority to support an argument that "children should not suffer adverse consequences for the acts or status of their parents" by looking to cases involving the right of a child born out of wedlock to inherit from a parent who dies intestate or to cases involving the right to a free education for children of illegal immigrant parents.

You may have started thinking about policy arguments as you tried to identify a theme for your argument. At this stage, you should make sure that the outline of your argument reflects your theme. As part of that step, note whether policy arguments that support your theme are worth addressing as separate points in your argument and whether there are authorities that would be useful support for these arguments. Not every brief needs a separate policy argument; as noted previously, policy arguments are often implicit in legal arguments. But when drafting a working outline, you may wish to tentatively identify policy arguments that could be incorporated into your argument.

4.1.4
USING A REVERSE ROADMAP TO STRUCTURE YOUR ARGUMENT

Another method of identifying structure is to create an outline in paragraph form. Start with the ultimate point that you want the court to agree with, and then ask yourself what point or points the court must agree with to agree with *that* point, moving in reverse until you are at the smallest part of any test you might ask a court to apply. This method is more complicated because as you write the reverse roadmap paragraph, you must already have in mind some relationships between and among your points. The method might result in several branching paragraphs rather than just one. For example, if you were working on *Miller v. Albright*, the case described previously, part of your reverse roadmap outline might look like this:

> This court should reverse the decision below. In order to decide to reverse, it has to agree that 1409 is unconstitutional.
>
> In order to agree that 1409 is unconstitutional, the court either has to agree that 1409 violates the intermediate scrutiny test or that it violates the rational basis test.
>
> In order to agree that 1409 violates the intermediate scrutiny test, the court first has to agree that the intermediate scrutiny test applies. In order to agree that the intermediate scrutiny test applies, the court has to agree that the statute discriminates on the basis of gender.
>
> The court would also have to agree that this is not an immigration statute, so the court doesn't have to defer to Congress and therefore

apply an easier test, OR it has to agree that even if the statute is an immigration statute, the fact that it discriminates on the basis of gender is more significant.

Now, in order to agree that the statute *fails* the intermediate scrutiny test, the court has to agree both that there's no substantial relationship between the discrimination in the statute and the achievement of the government's goals *and* that there's no exceedingly persuasive justification for the statute.

In order to agree that it violates the rational basis test, the court first has to agree that this test is the correct test to apply, which means that the court thinks that immigration law is more important than gender law. In order to agree that 1409 violates the rational basis test, it first has to agree that Congress had no rational reason for the law.

It might help the court to agree that 1409 is unconstitutional if it agrees that biological parent-child relationships are important, or that reuniting parents and children is important, or that children should not suffer adverse consequences for the acts of their parents or the status of their parents.

As with the "list of assertions" method, this method might be more effective with pen and paper than with a computer. If you want to pick up a paragraph and move it around or draw lines connecting two or more paragraphs with each other, you may be better off with hard copy than digital copy. A reverse roadmap outline might be complete enough to let you start writing, or it may be a method you can combine with other methods to help you draft a working outline.

4.1.5
THE WORKING OUTLINE

After you have used some method or methods to identify the major rules, policies, and assertions that control your argument, you should analyze how they relate to each other and draft a working outline that shows those relationships as you currently understand them. If you were researching the *Miller v. Albright* case, you might come up with a working outline like the one below. (Note that these headings are not in perfect "point heading" form.)

Working Outline

I. This court should reverse because 1409 is unconstitutional.
    A. This court should apply an intermediate scrutiny test.
       1. The statute discriminates on the basis of gender.
       2. This is not an immigration statute, so no special deference to Congress is needed.
       3. Even if it is an immigration statute, fighting gender discrimination and "illegitimacy" discrimination trumps immigration.

    B. This statute fails the intermediate scrutiny test.
       1. There's no substantial relationship between the discrimination in the statute and the achievement of the government's goals.
       2. There's no exceedingly persuasive justification for the statute.
    C. Even if this court applies the rational basis-type test, the statute still fails because there's no rational relationship between encouraging ties between parents and children and requiring a father to establish ties in a different way than mothers do.
    D. This court has always promoted the maintenance of family relationships.

Of course, this outline is not carved in stone. As you write, you may discover that some arguments are incomplete, while others are not worth making. You may discover that some sections of your outline need to be divided into two subsections, or that others are not worthy of a full discussion.[15] As with the research questions, your goal is not perfection; it's to create an outline that is complete enough to get you started on your writing.

If *any* type of prewriting outline is too difficult for you, you may want to try writing *before* you outline. Keep your paragraphs to a reasonable length, and then, after you have written your argument, use the advice in Chapter Ten to write an effective topic sentence for each paragraph. Those topic sentences will reveal the main points you have made and the order in which you have made them. You can then use the topic sentences to evaluate the relationships among your points and to plan your large-scale organization, perhaps using some of the techniques noted in this chapter.

4.2
USING "PRIVATE MEMOS" TO QUIET YOUR INNER DEMONS AND PREVENT WRITER'S BLOCK

Even if you have created a good outline, you may still face writer's block at this stage of the process if you worry so much about avoiding mistakes that you are afraid to write a word. As Ray and Ramsfield have noted, a crisis can result when the "id" of creativity bumps into the "superego" of criticism.[16] As we write, we hear a critical voice yammering away inside our heads, asking, "What about the res ipsa issue? Do I have enough cases

---

[15] See Chapter Five for a discussion of how to decide when to provide a complete analysis of an issue versus when to provide something less complete.

[16] *See* Mary Barnard Ray & Jill J. Ramsfield, *Legal Writing: Getting It Right and Getting It Written* 212 (2d ed., West 1993).

on this point? Shouldn't that second issue come before this one?" and so on. The writer freezes, and writing comes to a stop.

Hearing your critical voice is not a bad thing in itself. After all, writing is a method of thinking and of learning. While you write, you may discover aspects of your case that you hadn't noticed before, new avenues of research, and even whole arguments that didn't occur to you while you were researching or outlining. That's why it's important to leave yourself enough time to write. Consistent with the discussion in Chapter One about the cognitivist school of writing theory, presume that your first couple of drafts will be "thinking drafts" or "learning drafts" that will teach you a lot about your case.

If you stop writing every time your critical voice reminds you of something, however, you may never finish a draft. Instead, allow yourself to write an imperfect first draft, and record the questions or criticisms that occur to you. Instead of freezing up, use a method called "private memos."[17] As the critical voices chatter in your head, drop a footnote and write down what those voices are saying: "Do I need more research here?" "Should I talk about the other issue first?" In this way, you can silence your critical voices by preserving the concerns they represent, but you avoid writer's block because you don't interrupt your writing process. Plan to review your private memo footnotes during the rewriting stage of your writing process. You may find some points were irrelevant after all; on the other hand, some of the private memos may lead you to new and more effective arguments.

Although of course you must delete your private memos before you submit your brief to a court, they may be helpful reading for your teacher or supervisor. You can use these private memos as a way to ask for specific guidance on a problem or to make sure that your teacher or supervisor notices a particular concern that you have. Few people who review writing can notice every problem on every draft. Students can use private memos to draw attention to particular concerns.

4.3
FACING PROCRASTINATION

One more thing may interfere with your ability to write your argument: procrastination. I write about procrastination from the position of an expert—I have years of experience with it. Some of you may have experience with it, too. Procrastination probably has as many causes as

---

[17] *See* Mary Kate Kearney & Mary Beth Beazley, *Teaching Students How to "Think Like Lawyers": Integrating Socratic Method with the Writing Process*, 64 Temp. L. Rev. 885, 894-97 (1991).

there are stars in the sky.[18] I believe, however, that much procrastination is driven by three kinds of fear: fear of commitment, fear of failure, and fear of pain. The sections below describe some methods for dealing with each of these fears.

4.3.1
FEAR OF COMMITMENT

I noted earlier that research is like dating and writing is like marriage, and one of the fears that inhibits writers is a fear of commitment. Just as marriage forces you to commit to one person, writing forces you to commit to a particular writing decision. By committing to one organizational structure, you foreclose the option to choose all the other possible structures out there. By committing to a particular set of cases and other authorities, you shut off the chance to find the one perfect case that would transform your work-a-day brief into the "perfect" brief of your dreams. The psychologist Dan Ariely has observed that one of the ways in which human beings are "predictably irrational" is that we try to keep all of our options open as long as possible, even when doing so creates other problems.[19]

The sad thing is that procrastinating instead of writing almost certainly hurts your ability to create the best possible brief. If you write a draft early in your writing process, you will have time to review and revise your document, increasing the chances that you will write a better brief. If you postpone writing due to fear of commitment, however, you increase the chances that the first draft will be the only draft, making each commitment even more final, and thus, even more difficult. Furthermore, because procrastination usually leaves you with little or no time to revise, the brief will likely not be good work, much less your best work.

If fear of commitment is a problem for you, focus on using private memos as you write. If you are concerned about committing to any particular writing choice, drop a private memo footnote to yourself to articulate your concern and preserve the other options you were considering. The private memo will help to quiet your fear of commitment by reminding you that this is not a "final" commitment and by giving you a way to identify the places where you want to consider other options. Furthermore, the private memos can direct at least part of your revision process by focusing your attention on particular aspects of the draft.

---

[18] Although this section of the text talks about *avoiding* procrastination, I *recommend* procrastinating just a little bit so that you can take the time to read this excellent article: David A. Rasch & Meehan Rasch, *Overcoming Writer's Block and Procrastination for Attorneys, Law Students, and Law Professors*, 43 N.M. L. Rev. 193 (2013).

[19] Dan Ariely, *Predictably Irrational* 183 et seq. (1 Exp. Rev. Ed., Harper Perennial 2010). *See* pp. 139-66 for discussion of procrastination specifically.

4.3.2
FEAR OF FAILURE

Fear of failure is a cousin of fear of commitment. Many of us fear putting words to paper because we feel that we are inadequate writers and that we can never write anything that is worthy of turning in to a teacher, supervisor, or judge.[20] By putting off writing, we postpone the moment that others discover that we have been faking out people all along, and that we are not the good students or effective lawyers that people may think that we are. Conversely, if we fail because we did not try, we may be able to console ourselves that we have controlled the circumstances under which we failed, and convince ourselves that we had the ability to succeed, if only we had tried. The procrastinating behavior thus allows us to maintain a (tenuous) hold on a superior self-image.

Another irrational fear may lurk behind the fear of failure. If we fear that we are unable to *learn*, failure on an early draft means that we will fail on the final draft as well. For if we are unable to learn, there is nothing that a teacher or supervisor can do to help us to improve that "failed" first attempt, and so the bad first draft means that we are doomed to a bad final draft. Carol Dweck, a Stanford psychologist, describes people who believe they cannot learn as having a "fixed mindset."[21] These people believe that intelligence is fixed and limited, and if you can't pick up knowledge or a skill immediately, you will never be able to do so. Those with a "growth mindset," in contrast, understand that intelligence is malleable and that, if they work at it, they can increase their intelligence and learn new skills. Sadly, those with a fixed mindset are often resistant to guidance that will help them to learn, because they believe that such learning is impossible. Happily, however, you can overcome the fear of being unable to learn. Having a fixed mindset is not a fixed state of being; you can learn to have a growth mindset.

To move to a growth mindset, realize that if you were smart enough to get into law school (or smart enough to graduate from law school), you are smart enough to learn to write, and to learn how to analyze even sophisticated legal issues. You can trust me on this; I have been teaching for 30 years, and I have seen students just like you accomplish these goals. But they didn't do it all on the first day, or on the first draft. The ones who made the most improvement tried hard on every draft, and they saw critiques not as insults, but as opportunities. They focused more on learning the skills than on the grade they would earn. The best tonic

---

[20] *E.g.*, Rasch & Rasch, *supra* note 18, at 199, 207-08.
[21] Carol S. Dweck, *Mindset: The New Psychology of Success* 11 (Ballantine Bks. 2006) (defining a fixed mindset) (cited in Carrie Sperling & Susan Shapcott, *Fixing Students' Fixed Mindsets: Paving the Way for Meaningful Assessment*, 18 Legal Writing: J. Legal Writing Inst. 39, 45 (2012)). To learn more about mindset, see Carol Dweck, *Mindset*, http://mindsetonline.com/ (last visited Jan. 15, 2014).

for fear of failure is to write early. Work on producing a draft that reflects your current capabilities, so that the learning can begin. As noted above, starting writing earlier rather than later increases the chances of success on the project as a whole. If we fear criticism from supervisors or teachers, we might try road-testing our ideas by talking them out with friends (if allowed by academic misconduct policies) or by speaking directly with the teacher or supervisor who will be judging our work.[22] It is unrealistic, of course, to expect that someone can pre-approve every aspect of our writing, but by getting early feedback on some of our ideas, we can reassure ourselves that our work will meet with some approval.

Another way to deal with fear of failure is to embrace the prospect of writing a bad draft. If we write a bad draft well before the deadline, we need not fear failure because we will know that we have time to turn that failure around. The writer Anne Lamott specifically advocates writing what she calls "shitty first drafts."[23] Doing so can reduce your anxiety: If *you* know the draft is a bad one, you are still maintaining control over the product, and you can even agree with those who might criticize it. Using private memos can help this process as well: When you experience fear or doubt about a particular aspect of your writing, record your concerns, and be as specific as possible. For example, "I need more research on the X issue. Are there any more cases addressing second part of test?" "This sentence doesn't make sense. I'm trying to say that the defendant's refusal to come to an agreement was legally significant." The private memos can help your fear of failure by allowing you to acknowledge areas where you need guidance; it can help your revision process by targeting the aspects of the draft that need the most work.

4.3.3
FEAR OF PAIN

As noted in an earlier chapter, writing is a series of decisions. When you write a brief, or any analytical document, you have to decide which issues to address and which to ignore. You must decide what authorities to cite and how to organize your discussion of issues. At the micro level, you must decide how to write each sentence, choosing which words to use and which sentence structures to arrange those words in. You must decide whether it is permissible to end a sentence with a preposition, whether you can split infinitives, and whether to use the Oxford comma.

---

[22] *See* Rasch & Rasch, *supra* note 18, at 220, 237. Although Rasch & Rasch do not discuss mindset, they note that "[o]thers' perceptive minds offer a storehouse of information, and you can benefit from knowing what they think is good, or not so good, about your work. . . . You will be more willing and less threatened to hear tough but true words about your legal writing if you believe those words will help you write better." *Id.* at 237.

[23] Anne Lamott, *Bird by Bird: Some Instructions on Writing and Life* 22 (Anchor 1995).

Facing so many decisions can be overwhelming, and many writers choose the pleasure of procrastination over the pain of decision. Good writing requires focused attention, and in our current culture, distraction and inattention seem to reap all of the rewards. We may start writing with all good intentions, but when we reach a difficult decision, we may feel almost a compulsion to stop writing. As Rasch and Rasch tell us, "[we] can easily be derailed from writing by the compelling and ubiquitous siren songs of e-mail, the Internet, parties, conversation, television, hot baths, the refrigerator, or the compulsion to scrub tile grout with a toothbrush."[24] Furthermore, many distractions are readily available, either on our computer—which, ironically, we must use in order to complete the writing project—or on a smartphone that is probably in a nearby pocket or purse.

It is true that we will feel pain if we put off our writing decisions for too long—we will fail the course, lose the case, or damage our academic or professional reputation. These "pains," however, are in the future, and they are abstract, potential pains rather than concrete, immediate pains.[25] Most of us are much more likely to react to immediate, definite, concrete realities than to future, abstract, possible realities.[26]

Fighting pain-based procrastination requires finding methods for imposing self-discipline. You may succeed by drafting a careful schedule and then sticking to it. (Take care, however, that you do not resort to refining the schedule as a new means of procrastination.) Checking off items on the schedule may provide enough satisfaction that you stop procrastinating to give yourself the pleasure of checking off more items.

If making a schedule does not work, try to determine whether you are more motivated by rewards or punishments, or by some combination of the two. You may succeed if you find a way to reward performance and reduce distractions. It might be a good idea to give a friend your phone—or your Facebook password—with instructions not to give it back until you have completed a certain number of pages. Certain apps can shut off electronic distractions for a set time period. In this way you are motivated to go through the pain of writing in order to reap the reward of reuniting with your favorite distractions.

If devising rewards does not work, try to find ways to impose an alternate "pain" that is immediate, and that is worse than the pain of writing. Ideally, you should use this method as a way to force yourself to create an early draft; for most lawyers, the pain that will result if you fail to finish any draft at all should be enough to force you to create some sort of work product by the *final* deadline. But your goal here is to write a draft early enough to allow time for revision. Even if your teachers require interim

---

[24] Rasch & Rasch, *supra* note 18, at 200.
[25] *Id.* at 230.
[26] *E.g., id.*

drafts, you will do better if you allow time for writing and revision before your interim due date.

I have used (and recommend) a method advised by Richard Thaler, one of the authors of the book *Nudge*, which addresses behavioral economics and human decision making. To motivate a new faculty member at Thaler's school, Thaler asked the faculty member to give Thaler a series of $100 checks, dated for a series of self-imposed deadlines for a writing project. If the professor did not meet any deadline, Thaler would deposit that check. Thaler promised that he would use any deposited money to host a party to which the faculty member would not be invited. The faculty member met all of the deadlines.[27] Another version of this method can be found on the Web site Stickk.com, which was founded by other behavioral economists.[28] I tried this method on my own by giving a friend a check written out to a nonprofit organization whose goals I despise. If I did not meet my deadline, he was allowed to mail the check, and I was confident that he would do so. By writing the check, I created the possibility of present "pain" that was worse than the pain of writing. I did not want to give that organization money; perhaps worse, I did not want to get on that organization's mailing list. Having that concrete, present pain before me helped focus my attention in a way that promising myself a cookie just didn't achieve.

You may not want to write a check, but if procrastination hinders your progress, set up some sort of consequence for not creating an early draft. For example, instead of giving your phone to a friend to avoid distractions, you may want to give your friend the right to take your phone overnight (or longer) if you fail to meet an interim deadline. Most of us are so emotionally attached to our phones that the prospect of losing access to the phone might be more painful than losing money, and it might provide just the motivation you need to crank out an interim draft.

Perhaps you are one of the lucky few who eat your Brussels sprouts first, and who never have trouble with procrastination. If so, reading this section might have made you grateful that you don't have this problem. If you are a procrastinator, realize that you are not alone, and that just as you can learn to write, you can learn to defeat procrastination.

---

[27] Cass R. Sunstein & Richard J. Thaler, *Nudge: Improving Decisions About Health, Wealth, and Happiness* 46 (Yale Univ. Press, 2008).

[28] *See id.* at 232 (discussing the use of "commitment contracts" on Stickk.com).

4.4
SUMMARY

You will be able to draft your argument much more effectively if you take the time to create a working outline for the argument. Use legal rules and their phrases-that-pay, policy-based rules, and other assertions to help you recognize the points that you want to make in your argument. While drafting the argument, be ready to recognize and record any private memo questions that you have about your research, your organization, or other aspects of your argument. If procrastination is an issue for you, try to identify its specific causes, and identify techniques that will best help you to finish a draft.

Chapter Five

ONE PIECE AT A TIME: DRAFTING THE ARGUMENT

5.1

USING AN ANALYTICAL FORMULA

Two kinds of formulas can help you draft your argument. The first formula is the formula of assertions and arguments that you create to answer the questions that your case presents. Chapter Four was meant to help you craft that formula, to decide how to structure your analysis of the issues and assertions relevant to your argument. That formula is unique to this set of facts and issues in this jurisdiction at this time; you might be able to reuse certain elements in the formula, but it is doubtful you would ever write another brief with that identical set of assertions and arguments. It is for one-time-use only.

The second kind of formula that can help you draft your argument is far from unique: It can be recycled forever, for as many times as you need it. Similar formulas go by their various acronyms, including CREAC, IREAC, and CRuPAC. As will be explained here, in this book, it is called CREXAC, and it can be used whenever you use a "unit of discourse" to analyze a legal point. As George Gopen has noted, a "unit of discourse" is "anything in prose that has a beginning and an end: a phrase, clause, sentence, paragraph, section, [or] subsection."[1] In analytical writing, then, a "CREXAC unit of discourse" refers to a section or subsection in which you use legal analysis to prove the truth or validity of a legal assertion.

CREXAC is adapted from a syllogistic formula that many first-year law students learn as a method of organizing legal analysis. The acronym for that formula is "IRAC," and it stands for Issue-Rule-Application-Conclusion. IRAC and similar formulas can be helpful because they can serve as heuristics that guide writers to answer vital questions about their arguments. Your outline has identified the issues that you think the court needs to address. For each of those issues, you must answer four questions, questions that IRAC alone won't answer:

1. What rule governs this issue?
2. What does this rule mean?
3. How should this rule be applied (or not applied) in this case?
4. What impact does that application have on the court's decision in this case?

We can illustrate how we need to adapt IRAC by beginning with a familiar syllogism:

Issue:	Is Socrates mortal?
Rule:	All human beings are mortal.
Application:	Socrates is a man.
Conclusion:	Socrates is mortal.

You may notice a problem in this syllogism. The rule application (the minor premise) must be connected to the rule (the major premise), but that connection is not obvious in this example. So we move beyond the

---

[1] George D. Gopen, *Let the Buyer in the Ordinary Course of Business Beware: Suggestions for Revising the Prose of the Uniform Commercial Code*, 54 U. Chi. L. Rev. 1178, 1185 (1987).

syllogism to create a formula that asks the writer to explain what the rule means in this context:

Issue:	Is Socrates mortal?
Rule:	All human beings are mortal.
Explanation:	Men and women are human beings.
Application:	Socrates is a man.
Conclusion:	Socrates is mortal.

The rule explanation makes it easier to show the reader how the rule about mortality connects to the facts about Socrates. Admittedly, rule explanation gets more complicated when we get beyond the question of simple mortality. Nevertheless, the formula remains the same, with two minor adaptations for advocacy writing. Instead of beginning the argument by stating the legal issue as a question, we state it as an assertion, or a conclusion. We change the second "conclusion" to "Connection-Conclusion" to distinguish it from the first conclusion, and to remind us that, at the end of the formula (and thus at the end of each CREXAC unit of discourse), we should connect our analysis to the point we are making in that section of the argument, and sometimes to the overall thesis. Therefore, our formula changes from IRAC to CREXAC, and it now looks like this:

[handwritten margin note: connection conclusion]

Conclusion:	Socrates is mortal.
Rule:	All human beings are mortal.
Explanation:	Men and women are human beings.
Application:	Socrates is a man.
Connection-Conclusion:	Socrates is mortal.

[handwritten margin note: CREXAC]

Thus, for each point you need to prove in your argument, you should write a CREXAC unit of discourse, or "a CREXAC." As will be discussed in Section 5.2 below, you will provide less detailed analysis (or sometimes none at all) for points that are essential but that do not need to be proved in the same depth.

Some writers have a hard time understanding the CREXAC formula. They may try to make the whole argument section one long CREXAC, or they can't decide which elements are worthy of a CREXAC analysis and which elements are not. At this stage of the writing process, let your outline dictate your structure. Presume that you need to write a CREXAC unit of discourse for each point in your outline. Writing up the analysis will teach you about the point, and you may discover that some points are not controversial (and so do not need a CREXAC analysis), while other points are more complex than you realized (and thus may need to be divided into two or more CREXACs). See Illustration 5.1 for a guideline you can use to identify where you need to supply a CREXAC analysis within your argument. Each element of the CREXAC formula is explained more fully below.

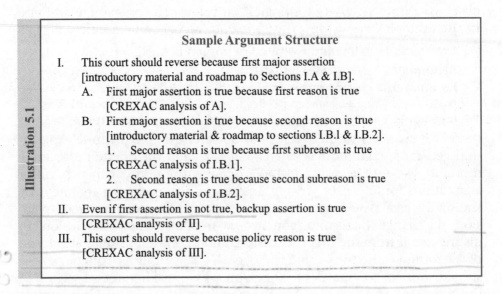

Illustration 5.1

Sample Argument Structure

I.   This court should reverse because first major assertion
      [introductory material and roadmap to Sections I.A & I.B].
      A.   First major assertion is true because first reason is true
            [CREXAC analysis of A].
      B.   First major assertion is true because second reason is true
            [introductory material & roadmap to sections I.B.1 & I.B.2].
            1.   Second reason is true because first subreason is true
                  [CREXAC analysis of I.B.1].
            2.   Second reason is true because second subreason is true
                  [CREXAC analysis of I.B.2].
II.   Even if first assertion is not true, backup assertion is true
      [CREXAC analysis of II].
III. This court should reverse because policy reason is true
      [CREXAC analysis of III].

5.1.1
STATE YOUR ISSUE AS A CONCLUSION

In the first "conclusion" element of the formula, the writer articulates the specific issue that is being addressed, or articulates the problem (or part or subpart of the problem) that is being "solved" in this section of the document. The writer could articulate an issue from *Miller v. Albright*, 523 U.S. 420 (1998), for example, by stating affirmatively what the issue is:

> **Under the intermediate scrutiny test, the first issue that must be decided is whether 8 U.S.C. §1409(a) is "substantially related" to the achievement of the government's objective.**

Although this method effectively tells the court the issue (and is preferable to neglecting to articulate the issue at all), it is not the best choice in a brief to a court because it is not argumentative. Generally, in persuasive writing, you should make your arguments as if they are the only reasonable resolution to the issues before the court. Therefore, it is often best to state your issues as conclusions:

> **8 U.S.C. §1409(a) is not "substantially related" to the achievement of the government's objective because it is unconstitutionally overinclusive.**

If your issue is more complicated, the conclusion may be longer than just a simple sentence. You may need to provide legal or factual context to help the reader to understand how the conclusion fits into your argument. In *Minnesota v. Carter*, 525 U.S. 83 (1998), for example, the Court was asked to determine whether an officer violated the Fourth Amendment when he observed criminal activity through the window of a basement apartment. In the example below, the writer provides factual context before using a conclusory statement to articulate the issue:

> **Because Thielen was located outside the curtilage of the apartment, he was free to observe any scene in plain view. Respondents' activities within the apartment were in plain view from Thielen's lawful vantage point. Thus, Thielen's observation violated no reasonable expectation of privacy and did not constitute a Fourth Amendment search.**

By stating your issue as a conclusion, you begin to focus your reader not only on the issue that you will be addressing in that section of the argument, but also on the result that your analysis of the issue will reveal.

Will My Writing Be Boring If I Use the Same Formula in Each Section?

The CREXAC formula does not provide one rubric that governs the whole argument section. CREXAC provides a rubric that can be used over and over again, any time a writer has some point to explain or prove. The argument section itself will be organized according to the unique issues and sub-issues that the case presents. CREXAC can be used, however, as a formula for your analysis of each significant issue and sub-issue within that argument. Some writers worry that their writing will be boring or overpredictable if they follow a formula like CREXAC in each section of a document. This worry is unfounded for a couple of reasons.

First, CREXAC does not tell you *what to say*. Instead, it recommends a particular *organization* for the information that readers traditionally need when analyzing legal issues. Most legal readers want to know the rule first, then understand the rule's meaning, and then see how it applies to the facts. Most judges want a simple organization; they don't want to have to struggle to find a rule that a writer "creatively" saved for the end of his or her analysis of a legal issue.

The second reason not to worry is related to the first. CREXAC is only an organizational structure. With no extra effort on your part, each section of your argument will vary from the section before according to the *substance* of the argument itself and the particular demands of the issue. Every issue needs a rule, but sometimes the rule is a simple quote from a statute, while at other times it is a common law rule, and at other times it is a cluster of rules that end on the particular rule that governs the narrow legal issue that is the focus of that section of the document. Similarly, the explanation of the rule and application of the rule to the facts will also vary from issue to issue.

Even if CREXAC is not the most perfect organization for the analysis of a particular legal issue or sub-issue, it will probably still be an effective organization. Thus, it is probably most practical for an attorney to assume a CREXAC organization rather than to spend precious time trying to determine what is the "best" structure for analyzing a legal issue.

Whatever organizational method you use, the elements of CREXAC provide a good checklist. In every section of the argument, the reader will always need to know the issue you're addressing, the rule that governs the issue, what the rule means, how it applies in this case, and how that application connects to your argument.

5.1.2
PROVIDE THE RULE

After you have focused the reader's attention on the issue being addressed, you should articulate the rule that governs the issue. First, let's define our terms. A rule essentially says that "if a certain condition exists, then a certain legal status results." For example:

> **If you are a human being [certain condition], then you are mortal [legal status].**

> **If you have a duty, breach a duty, and cause compensable harm [certain condition], then you are liable in negligence [legal status].**

Most rules in a brief will not be stated in "if-then" terminology. However, using the if-then structure can help you to test the rules that you include in your brief.

If your rule comes from a statute or a well-established common law test, stating the rule may be simple. Stating the rule can be more complicated, however, if there is controversy about which rule applies, or if you must use inductive reasoning to "find" your rule.

a. Stating Established Rules

You may state the rule in a variety of ways. If the rule is derived from a statute or other enacted law, you may simply quote the pertinent language, as in this example:

> **26 U.S.C. §5861(d) provides that "[i]t shall be unlawful for any person to receive or possess a firearm which is not registered to him in the National Firearms Registration Transfer Record."**

Similarly, if the rule is a well-accepted common law rule derived from a well-known authority, you may simply articulate the rule in its familiar language:

> **While a person's home is, for most purposes, a place where he expects privacy, activities that are exposed "to the 'plain view' of outsiders are**

not protected" under the Fourth Amendment. <u>Katz v. United States</u>, 389 U.S. 347, 361 (1967) (Harlan, J., concurring).

If your case is more complex, stating one rule may not give the reader enough context. Some writers articulate the rule that governs a narrow situation by providing a <u>"rule cluster"</u> that <u>starts with a well-accepted general rule and moves to the more narrow rule that is the focus of that section of the argument</u>.[2] The following example is from the argument section of *Minnesota v. Carter*, a Fourth Amendment case. This section of the argument is focused on the narrow issue of whether the alleged intrusion by the government agents constituted a "search." Notice how the writer moves the reader from the general rule—the Fourth Amendment—to the narrow rule at issue, which will be the focus of this section of the argument (which, by the way, will include two subsections):

> The Fourth Amendment to the United States Constitution guarantees "[t]he right of the people to be secure in their persons, houses, papers, and effects, against unreasonable searches and seizures." U.S. Const. amend. IV. A search occurs only when governmental agents intrude upon an area in which a person has a reasonable expectation of privacy. <u>California v. Ciraolo</u>, 476 U.S. 207, 212 (1986). This Court will find that a Fourth Amendment search occurred only if two factors exist: (1) the location from which the observation occurred was within a complainant's zone of privacy, and (2) the government agents used extraordinary measures to accomplish the observation. <u>See id</u>. at 213.

Thus, although the paragraph lists three rules, the writer is focusing the reader's attention only on the last rule in the list.

b. Choosing Among Two or More Rules

Some issues are governed by well-established rules, and the court needs to decide only how, or whether, a particular rule applies to the facts of the case. <u>Sometimes, however, a major debate between you and your opponent in the case is a debate as to which of two or more rules the court should apply to the situation.</u> If you have to convince the court to choose the rule that you want, as opposed to the rule that your opponent wants, <u>you must include a section in your argument devoted to proving that</u> "your" rule is the best rule to apply. Of course, that "rule-choice" argument <u>must be based on a rule</u>, as well.

If a court has chosen a particular rule to apply to a situation, it has done so because it has decided that the case has certain factors or raises

---

[2] A rule cluster is appropriate when, as here, the existence and applicability of these related rules is not controversial. The discussion in Section 5.2 of "Tell" issues is relevant here, because you are telling the reader what the rule is and that it is relevant in the given case. A rule cluster may also function as part of an argument's "backstory," as discussed in Chapter Ten.

certain issues that the chosen rule best addresses. You might think of the basic format for a rule-choice rule as follows: "If [factors or issues] exist, then [application of designated rule] results."

Sometimes, courts state the "rule-choice rule" explicitly. For example, everyone who has taken a constitutional law course knows that when courts have to decide whether a certain governmental action is constitutional, they have at least three choices. They can apply the "strict scrutiny test" (which they apply when certain fundamental rights are implicated or the rights of a suspect class are affected); they can apply the "intermediate or heightened scrutiny test" (which they apply in a variety of situations, including situations in which laws make gender-based distinctions); or they can apply the "rational basis test" (which they apply when a law does not affect fundamental rights or make questionable distinctions). Thus, if your case is about the constitutionality of a governmental action, you and your opponent might disagree as to whether the court should apply the rational basis test or the strict scrutiny test. In that situation, your first order of business is to argue about which rule applies, using the "rule-choice rule" that governs strict scrutiny and rational basis. For example, if you believed that strict scrutiny was appropriate, that section of your argument could be based on the following "rule-choice rule":

> **If a statute makes distinctions based on suspect classifications, then the strict scrutiny test applies.**

Of course, even if a rule-choice rule exists, you should use a CREXAC unit of discourse to prove how it applies only if the choice of rule is in controversy. If both sides agree that the strict scrutiny test applies, for example, then the brief need not establish this fact through a CREXAC analysis. The writer can simply introduce the "strict scrutiny" section by telling the reader the rule-choice rule and stating that it results in the use of strict scrutiny before moving on to a CREXAC analysis of the strict scrutiny test itself.

Thus, if the choice of rule is not controversial, a typical argument would have one section devoted to the rule, focusing on how it should apply in the current case. If the choice of rule *is* controversial, however, the writer may need to include as many as three sections of the argument that address the rule-choice issue in some way. For example, in the first section, the writer might argue that the rule-choice rule requires that the preferred rule be applied. In the second section, the writer could argue that his or her client wins when the preferred rule is applied. In the third section, the writer could argue that his or her client wins even if the nonpreferred rule is applied. (Of course, if the result of applying the nonpreferred rule is uncontroversial, it need not be argued.)

If there are two or more competing rules and the courts have not yet labeled the "rule-choice rule," your job is to find and articulate that rule. You can "find" the rule by reasoning inductively from one or more cases in which a court has made the rule-choice decision. The section that follows explains how to use inductive reasoning to find and articulate legal rules.

c. Using Inductive Reasoning to Find and Articulate Legal Rules

As many a frustrated first-year law student can attest, courts sometimes decide cases without explicitly articulating the rule that they are applying. Furthermore, sometimes the rule that they are applying can be accurately stated more narrowly or more broadly. If the cases that are analogous to your case do not contain a clear rule, or if the applicable rule as it is currently envisioned would dictate a bad result for your client, you may have to "induce" a rule. Using inductive reasoning is appropriate for finding rules of all types, not just rule-choice rules.

It is not accurate to say that you are labeling a "new" rule when you use inductive reasoning. The rule was there all along; inductive reasoning simply lets you recognize it, label it, and present it more effectively to the court.

When you use inductive reasoning to find a rule, you are trying to read between the lines of court opinions, to notice patterns that always or never predict certain results, or results that occur *only* when certain patterns are present. Authors of law review articles might observe these patterns in a vacuum, but you have a head start because you know the type of pattern you are looking for. In an advocacy document, inductive reasoning frequently begins when you distinguish your case from the cases that apparently apply.

For example, in the case *Ohio v. Robinette*, 519 U.S. 33 (1996), the issue was the constitutionality of an officer's request to conduct a drug search of a car that had been stopped for speeding. The government argued that the defendant had been free to refuse the officer's request, and so his consent was voluntary and constitutional. Many of the relevant cases addressing consent searches involved officers stopping people in airports and asking for permission to search for contraband. One student, writing a brief on behalf of Robinette, noticed a distinguishing factor between Robinette's case and the so-called airport cases, and she used that distinction to help her to induce a more precise rule. The paragraphs below show her thinking as she moves from noticing the distinguishing factor (the way in which the police-citizen encounter began) to articulating a new rule:

> There are two types of situations in which police request consent to search—those in which the police-citizen encounter begins consensually, and those in which the police-citizen encounter begins by an assertion of legal authority. When police-citizen encounters begin consensually, courts will find the consent request valid if there was nothing in the record to suggest "that the [citizen] had any objective reason to believe that she *was not free* to end the conversation [with

the officers] . . . and proceed on her way," <u>United States v. Mendenhall</u>, 446 U.S. 544, 555 (1980) (emphasis added). On the other hand, when police request consent to search after a police-citizen encounter that began with an assertion of legal authority, the Court should use a different test, and should analyze when the defendant would have an objective reason to believe that he or she *became free* to end the conversation and proceed on his or her way. Because Newsome and Robinette's encounter began with an assertion of legal authority, and because there was no clear end to this assertion of legal authority despite Newsome's return of Robinette's license, this Court should apply the totality of the circumstances test to this case.

Courts use the totality of the circumstances test to ascertain when police behavior rises to the level of a detention. <u>See</u> <u>Florida v. Bostick</u>, 501 U.S. 429, 434 (1991) ("[t]he encounter [between an officer and a citizen] will not trigger Fourth Amendment scrutiny unless it *loses its consensual nature*") (emphasis added). Courts have failed to note, however, that when a police-citizen encounter already involves legitimate force over that citizen, an inquiry as to when the encounter "rises" to the level of a detention is inapposite. . . .

. . . Thus, when a police-citizen encounter begins with the police officer's assertion of legal authority over the citizen, a subsequent request to search is part of a "consensual encounter" only if the citizen has objective knowledge either (a) that the legal detention has ended, or (b) that he or she is free to refuse consent to search.

Note that this analysis is not focused on the reader; the writer is using the process of writing to figure out, or induce, the underlying legal rule. This is an example of the "cognitive" stage of legal writing. When moving from the cognitive stage to the "social perspective" stage—the stage in which you take your readers' needs into account—be sure to revise your writing with the readers' needs in mind. Regarding the example above, the writer should remember that legal readers expect to hear about the rule as soon as they learn about the legal issue. The writer discovered her rule only after reviewing several cases and considering carefully how to draw lines between those cases and her case. When presenting this argument to the reader, however, she should place the newly induced rule early in the argument:

> Because the encounter between Robinette and Officer Newsome began with an assertion of police authority—and because Robinette never knew that the assertion of police authority had ended—cases in which this court analyzes "consensual encounters" are inapposite. When a police-citizen encounter begins with the police officer's assertion of legal authority over the citizen, a subsequent request to search is part of a "consensual encounter" only if the citizen has objective knowledge either (a) that the legal detention has ended, or (b) that he or she is free to refuse consent to search. <u>See</u> <u>Florida v.</u>

Bostick, 501 U.S. 429, 434 (1991); United States v. Mendenhall, 446 U.S. 544, 555 (1980).

However you find your rule, be sure to state it explicitly early within the appropriate section of the argument. In this way, you satisfy the reader's expectations and allow him or her to understand your analysis more easily.

5.1.3
EXPLAIN THE RULE

After you have articulated the rule, you must provide your reader with any needed explanation of the rule. Before you explain the rule, however, you must decide which part of the rule you are focusing on in the particular subsection of your argument. Usually, controversies about whether or how a rule applies will focus on certain words or phrases that are at the heart of the controversy regarding that rule. As noted in Chapter Four, you can refer to each controversial word or phrase as a "key term" or a "phrase-that-pays." By focusing on one phrase-that-pays within each subsection of the document, you ensure that you are focusing on one issue or sub-issue at a time. Thus, after you have articulated your rule, scrutinize that rule and decide what words or phrases constitute the phrase-that-pays for that section of the document.

Identifying a phrase-that-pays for each section of your document is important because it helps you to focus your writing: Once you have identified the phrase-that-pays, you can test the analysis in each section of the formula to make sure that it relates somehow to that phrase-that-pays. In the explanation section, for example, you should define the phrase-that-pays, explain its meaning, or show how it has been interpreted in earlier cases.

After you have identified the phrase-that-pays, you should use the "rule explanation" to explain the phrase-that-pays in appropriate detail. Doing so helps the reader to understand how the rule works. In persuasive documents like briefs, it is usually useful to end the rule explanation by providing a "rule summary." The rule summary nails down exactly what you want the reader to take from the rule explanation, and it prepares the reader for the rule application.

a.   Deciding How Much Rule Explanation Is Needed

When deciding how much explanation to provide for the phrase-that-pays in any particular section of your argument, consider two questions: (1) How ambiguous is the language of the phrase-that-pays? (2) How controversial is the application of the phrase-that-pays to the facts of this case? The more ambiguous and controversial the phrase-that-pays is, the more detailed your explanation should be.

Presumably, all of the issues analyzed in a brief will be controversial; if they were not controversial, they would not need to be analyzed.[3] When a phrase-that-pays is ambiguous, controversial, or both, you should "explain" its meaning, usually by illustrating how it has been applied in one or more authority cases. In the example below, the writer is arguing that an officer's behavior did not violate the Fourth Amendment because the observed activities were in plain view. The writer explains the rule by showing how the concept of "plain view"—the phrase-that-pays—has been interpreted in other cases. Notice how the writer has used the phrase-that-pays (in small capital letters in this example) in each paragraph to help the reader understand how the paragraph connects to the analysis of the legal issue:

2. No Fourth Amendment search occurred because the apartment interior was in PLAIN VIEW from the officer's lawful vantage point.

Because Thielen was located outside the curtilage of the apartment, he was free to observe any scene in PLAIN VIEW. Respondents' activities within the apartment were in PLAIN VIEW from Thielen's lawful vantage point. Thus, Thielen's observation violated no reasonable expectation of privacy and did not constitute a Fourth Amendment search. **1**

The Fourth Amendment protection of the home "has never been extended to require law enforcement officers to shield their eyes when passing by a home on public thoroughfares." California v. Ciraolo, 476 U.S. 207, 213 (1985). While a person's home is, for most purposes, a place where he expects privacy, activities "that he exposes to the 'PLAIN VIEW' of outsiders are not protected." Katz v. United States, 389 U.S. 347, 361 (1967) (Harlan, J., concurring). **2**

3 Illegal activities in PLAIN VIEW from outside the curtilage are not protected even if the police observation is specifically directed at identifying illegal activity. United States v. Dunn, 480 U.S. 294 (1987) (holding that an officer's observation into a barn was not a Fourth Amendment search, and stressing it was irrelevant that the observation was motivated by a law enforcement purpose); Ciraolo, 476 U.S. at 212, 213. In Ciraolo, the defendant was growing marijuana in a 15-by-25 foot plot in his backyard. He surrounded the yard with a 6-foot outer fence and a 10-foot inner fence. Id. at 209. Officers flew over the defendant's house in a private airplane and readily identified the illegal plants using only the naked eye. Id. The government in Ciraolo argued that the observation was analogous to looking through a knothole or an opening in a fence: "If there is an opening, the police may look." Id. at 220. This Court agreed with the government, holding that the observation was not a Fourth Amendment search. Id. The airspace was outside the curtilage of the apartment, and the Court

1 Note statement of conclusion here.

2 Note statement of rule here.
3 Note that the rule explanation begins here.

[3] See discussion below and in Chapter Ten (regarding legal backstory and roadmaps) for examples of how to deal with issues that are not controversial, but that must be included in the analysis in some way because they are necessary elements of a statute, test, or other legal rule.

reasoned that the scene would have been in PLAIN VIEW **to any member of the public flying in the same airspace. Thus, the officers had violated no reasonable expectation of privacy.** Id. **at 213-14.**

The length of your explanation will vary depending on how abstract and/or controversial the rule is. Probably the best way to fully illustrate the meaning of a rule is to use at least one authority that illustrates what the rule does mean in the context of acts that are similar (or nearly similar) to the facts at bar, and at least one authority that illustrates what the rule does *not* mean in the context of facts that are similar to the facts at bar.[4] In the previous example, if the writer had found a case in which the court had held that certain activities in a home were *not within* plain view, the reader would have a fuller understanding of why this case must fall within the definition.

Illustrating what the phrase-that-pays means and does not mean sets the boundaries of the phrase-that-pays, and gives the application of law to facts more validity. Chapter Six includes a discussion of how to use authority cases effectively in your explanation section.

b. Writing the "Rule Summary"

After you have shown the reader how courts have applied the phrase-that-pays in the past (or explained the rule in some other way), your reader should have a good idea about how the rule operates. Because a brief is a persuasive document, however, you may want to be sure that the reader understands the rule the same way you do. Thus, it is almost always effective to end your rule explanation with a brief "rule summary" that drives home what you were trying to teach the reader with the rule explanation.[5] In the rule summary, you should *not* merely restate the rule as you articulated it in the beginning of the argument. The following, for instance, would be an ineffective rule summary for the example above:

▽ BAD EXAMPLE OF RULE SUMMARY

Thus, while a person's home is a place where he expects privacy, activities exposed to the plain view of outsiders are not protected.

This rule summary merely restates the original rule. Instead, you should consider the facet of the rule that you were trying to expose or to emphasize, and make that aspect of the rule the focus of the rule summary. In the example above, for instance, the writer was trying to emphasize that any vantage point outside the house—even one as unusual as an airplane—is a legal vantage point for purposes of the plain view doctrine. She might,

---

[4] *See also, e.g.,* Laurel Currie Oates & Anne M. Enquist, *The Legal Writing Handbook* §12.8.4 (5th ed., Aspen 2010).

[5] I am grateful to my colleague, Monte Smith, who developed and introduced me to this concept.

therefore, write a rule summary that focuses on the vantage point of the viewer rather than on the bald statement of the plain view doctrine:

▲ GOOD EXAMPLE OF RULE SUMMARY

> **Accordingly, the vantage point of the viewer is crucial to the plain view determination: If the viewer sees the activities from a lawful vantage point, the viewer is not violating Fourth Amendment rights.**

The good example above is essentially a generic rule summary, appropriate for a writer using an educational writing style for the brief. Some writers might want to make the rule summary more argumentative, and focus explicitly on what they want the court to find, or on the burden that one side or the other must carry in this case:

▲ GOOD EXAMPLES OF RULE SUMMARY

> **Thus, the only way that this Court can find that petitioner violated the plain view doctrine is if it finds that a public area outside the window of a garden apartment is part of the curtilage of the building.**

> **Thus, the only way that respondents can establish that petitioner violated the plain view doctrine is if they can show that Officer Thielen observed respondents' activities from an unlawful vantage point. Respondents cannot meet this burden.**

The rule summary helps the writer to lay a strong foundation for the rule application. The writer can use the phrase-that-pays, and perhaps crucial facts, to create an expectation in the reader that the writer has an easy task, or that the writer's opponent has a difficult task. The writer can then fulfill that expectation in the rule application.

A rule summary may not be needed if your rule explanation is relatively short and straightforward. I advise, however, that you routinely draft a rule summary. If you decide that it appears overly repetitive, you can delete it. If, however, your rule explanation has advanced a more nuanced understanding of the rule, a rule summary can help the rule explanation have a greater impact.

5.1.4
APPLY THE RULE TO THE FACTS

After you have articulated the rule and explained it as needed, it's time to apply the rule to the facts (some legal writers say "applying the facts to the rule" to mean the same thing). In this step of your analysis, you are trying to show the reader how the phrase-that-pays intersects with the facts. How do the required elements or factors exist (or not exist) in your case? You should never substitute synonyms for the phrase-that-pays in any section, but particularly not in the application section.

Brief writers face a few challenges when applying law to facts. First, some brief writers mistakenly substitute analogies for application of law to facts. Second, some do not exploit the foundation that they have laid in the rule summary. Third, for issues that are "pure" questions of law—and courts of last resort often analyze questions of law—the facts may seem to be irrelevant. Finally, when analyzing statutory interpretation issues, the writers may believe that they don't have any real "facts." This section will address each of these challenges in turn.

a. Apply Rules, Not Cases

Begin the application section of your analysis by stating affirmatively how the rule does or does not apply to the facts. Essentially, you begin your application by saying "Phrase-that-pays equals (or does not equal) our case facts." If your case is not controversial, a short passage might be enough:

> **In this case, Mr. Burglar was "committing a trespass or other criminal offense" when he was bitten. Mr. Burglar was convicted of the crime of burglary in connection with the events of January 8. Burglary is considered a "criminal offense" under Ohio Revised Code §111.1111.**

This writer showed the reader how the rule and its explanation intersected with the client's facts by explaining that burglary "equals" a "criminal offense" under Ohio Revised Code §111.1111.

Do *not* begin the application by drawing analogies; analogies may support the application of law to facts, but they do not substitute for it. Thus, this sentence would usually not be an effective way to begin rule application:

▽ INEFFECTIVE BEGINNING TO RULE APPLICATION SECTION

> **Like the police officers in <u>Dunn</u>, Officer Thielen viewed the illegal activities from a legal vantage point.**

Instead, begin with a direct statement that connects the phrase-that-pays to the client's case. If the issue is at all controversial, you should be sure to provide details about the record facts[6] that support your assertion about how the law applies to the facts, as in this example (the phrase-that-pays, "plain view," is in small capital letters for emphasis):

△ MORE EFFECTIVE BEGINNING TO RULE APPLICATION

> **In the case at bar, Officer Thielen merely observed a scene that was in PLAIN VIEW from his lawful vantage point. The area in which Officer Thielen stood was outside the curtilage of the apartment.**

---

[6] Be sure to cite to the record so that the court can verify each referenced fact. Rules about and methods for citing to the case record are discussed in Chapter Nine.

While standing outside the curtilage, the officer PLAINLY VIEWED Respondents' unlawful activities. <u>See</u> Record E-2. While Officer Thielen did go to the common area outside the apartment window in response to the report from the informant, <u>see</u> Record G-11, his motivation is irrelevant. The illegal activity was in PLAIN VIEW regardless of Officer Thielen's motivation.

You may expand your application section, if needed, by drawing analogies between your client's case and the cases that you cited for authority in your explanation section:

⚐ EFFECTIVE CONTINUATION OF RULE APPLICATION

Like the officers in <u>Ciraolo</u>, who did not need to shield their eyes from what could be seen while traveling in public airways, Officer Thielen did not need to refrain from viewing what could be seen from the public area outside Thompson's window.

Drawing analogies or distinctions is not always necessary; sometimes the application of the rule to the facts alone will be sufficient to make your point. When appropriate, however, analogizing and distinguishing relevant authorities can help to cement the reader's understanding of how a rule operates and of how it does or does not apply to your client's case.

b. Explicitly Connect the Rule Application to the Rule Summary

As noted above, the rule summary should lay a foundation for the rule application by telling the reader what the rule means and why you will succeed—or your opponent will fail—in justifying a particular result. The best way to exploit the rule summary is to echo language from that summary at the very beginning of the rule application. Thus, the following combination of rule summary and rule application is not effective:

⚐ INEFFECTIVE TRANSITION FROM RULE SUMMARY TO RULE APPLICATION

Thus, the only way that respondents can establish that petitioners violated the plain view doctrine is if they can show that Officer Thielen observed respondents' activities from an unlawful vantage point. Respondents cannot meet this burden. **①**

② When Officer Thielen arrived at the scene, he was approached by a neighbor of the respondents, who told him what he had observed through respondents' window. . . .

① The rule summary ends here.

② The rule application begins here.

This transition is ineffective because it does not echo concepts from the rule summary. The only language it echoes is Officer Thielen's name, and that is insufficient to make the connection explicit. This example does a better job of making the connection:

▲ MORE EFFECTIVE TRANSITION FROM RULE SUMMARY TO RULE APPLICATION

> Thus, the only way that respondents can establish that petition-
> ers violated the plain view doctrine is if they can show that Officer
> Thielen observed respondents' activities from an unlawful vantage
> point. Respondents cannot meet this burden. **1**
>
> **2** In the case at bar, Officer Thielen merely observed a scene that was
> in plain view from his lawful vantage point. The area in which Officer
> Thielen stood was outside the curtilage of the apartment. . . .

1 The rule summary ends here.

2 The rule application begins here.

This example is more effective because it uses the phrase-that-pays, "plain view," and the term *lawful vantage point*, which is a crucial concept in the rule summary. By using these concepts in both the rule summary and the first sentence of the rule application, the writer makes it easier for the reader to make the connection between the rule explanation and the rule application.

c. Facts Are Relevant to Questions of Law

A legal question, or question of law, is a question about what the law should mean or how it should be interpreted. Should the law regulate all dog owners or only owners of dangerous dogs? Should the law govern- ing "employers" include supervisors within the meaning of "employer"? Questions of fact, in contrast, ask whether the law should apply to a par- ticular situation. Is a dog "dangerous" if it bites any person who tries to pet it? Is a person a "supervisor" if she is in charge of drawing up work sched- ules for all of the people in her section, but does not have the authority to hire and fire?

Even legal questions, however, are decided in a factual context. There is the hypothetical factual context of noting what will happen to certain categories of people and things if the case is decided one way or another, and there is the concrete factual context of noting what will happen to the parties in this particular case. Your application may focus on the broader legal question, but you may also want to include references to your case facts as a concrete "for instance" that shows a real-life result.

In *Miller v. Albright*, for example, a student writing for Ms. Miller argued that 8 U.S.C. §1409 used an unconstitutionally overinclusive gen- der stereotype to deny foreign-born children of citizen fathers rights that are awarded automatically to foreign-born children of citizen mothers. In one section, the student argued that the gender-based distinction was not "substantially related" to the government's objective of conditioning citizenship on close family ties. When he applied the law to the facts, he spoke both generally about the statute and specifically about Ms. Miller and her father:

⚠ GOOD EXAMPLE OF RULE APPLICATION

The gender discrimination in §1409(a) is not substantially related to the government's legitimate goal of conditioning citizenship on close family ties. Of course, §1409(a) will certainly prevent citizenship from flowing to some children who do not deserve it. The fatal flaw in §1409(a), though, is that it is overinclusive. Section 1409(a)'s various hurdles exclude from citizenship those children—like Ms. Miller—who are deserving of citizenship under the standards of the statute due to their close family ties with their United States citizen parents.

❶ This paragraph speaks generally about the statute.

❶ The degree to which §1409(a) is overinclusive is a function of the degree to which the assumptions underlying §1409(a) are invalid. Thus, because the assumptions underlying §1409(a)—that paternity is hard to establish reliably and that women and men are destined to occupy different roles—are substantially incorrect, the use of these irrebuttable stereotypes is not substantially related to the government's objective.

❷ This paragraph speaks generally about the statute.

❷ The gender stereotypes underlying §1409(a) are the very sort of archaic generalizations that modern equal protection jurisprudence seeks to eradicate. This court has repeatedly recognized that the government "must not rely on overbroad generalizations about the different talents, capacities, or preferences of males and females." Virginia, 518 U.S. at 533 (citations omitted); see also Califano v. Goldfarb, 430 U.S. 188, 223-24 (1977). If we as a society have learned anything about gender in the twenty years since Fiallo was decided, it is that women and men may not be conclusively pigeon-holed solely on the basis of their gender.

❸ This paragraph speaks specifically about the impact of the statute on the client and on people like the client.

❸ The facts of this case support this rather obvious conclusion. Ms. Miller is twenty-seven years old. Although she is not a minor, and although she neither needs nor receives the financial support of her father, she and Mr. Miller have a close family relationship. By the terms of the stereotype underlying §1409(a), all men—including Mr. Miller—irrebuttably do not form close family relationships with their adult "illegitimate" children. To uphold the rationality of this irrebuttable stereotype is to deny the existence of Mr. Miller and those other men who, for whatever reason, form relationships with their children later in life. To uphold the validity of this irrebuttable stereotype is to deny reality. This Court should reject the validity of this irrebuttable stereotype and acknowledge that there is no substantial relationship between the use of the stereotype and the government's goal of fostering close family relationships.

Note how the writer refers to his client, Ms. Miller, in the first paragraph, and how the last paragraph uses concrete details from the case to show the court the impact its decision will have in a specific case. Not every legal issue will need such a lengthy application section or such a detailed description of the client's facts. A good writer, however, will look for opportunities to use client facts to make abstract legal principles vivid.

d. Sometimes Statutory Language Is a Fact

Another challenge that many student writers face when writing the application section is the problem of "no facts." If you are analyzing a statutory interpretation issue, it may seem to you that there are no facts—there is only the statute itself. Many students think of the term *facts* as referring only to tangible events, like a car accident, or a murder, or even an interrogation. For a statutory interpretation issue, however, the word *facts* refers less often to events and more often to realities like the statutory language at issue, other relevant statutory language, or the statute's legislative history. One guideline: If a rule speaks in terms of human or corporate behavior, it is likely that it applies to human or corporate events, and that's where you should look for the relevant facts. In contrast, if a rule speaks in terms of legislative behavior, it is likely that it applies to legislative events—such as the language of a statute—and that is where you should look for the relevant facts.

For example, a student writer who is arguing that Title VII's use of the word "employer" does not allow individual liability for supervisors could have several CREXAC units of discourse focused on rules of statutory interpretation. One section might be focused on the rule that words in a statute should be read consistently throughout the whole statute. She would explain that rule by showing how other relevant courts had read terms consistently in statutes. In the application section, it would be meaningless to talk about the "events" of alleged sexual harassment at the center of the lawsuit. Rather, she must focus on how the term at issue, "employer," was used in the statute as a whole, and how that use demands a particular interpretation in this case:

⚠ GOOD EXAMPLE OF RULE APPLICATION

> The use of the word "employer" in other sections of Title VII demonstrates that Congress did not intend that individual supervisors like Kirkby could be held liable. In §2000e-8(c), the act provides that "every employer is responsible for the execution, retention and preservation of certain employment records." Section 2000e-10 states that "every employer shall post and keep posted in conspicuous places pertinent provisions of the subchapter." Interpretation of §2000e(b) requires the court to read the word "employer" consistently throughout the act. See Holloway, 526 U.S. at 9. It is unlikely that Congress intended to impose such administrative duties on individuals in supervisory positions. It is far more reasonable to conclude that the word "employer" as used in §§2000e(b), 2000e-8(c), and 2000e-10 was intended to apply to employer-entities only.

This does not mean that event-based facts are always irrelevant to statutory interpretation questions. As they can with other legal questions, event-based facts may provide helpful illustrations of how the legal policies at issue play out in concrete situations. Writers should be aware, however, that with statutory interpretation questions, they must think about the concept of "facts" more broadly: They are applying the rule of a canon of interpretation to the fact of the existing statutory language.

5.1.5
MAKE THE CONNECTION

After you have applied the rule to the facts, you should connect the application to your argument by articulating a connection-conclusion. You may not need to begin a new paragraph if the application has been brief and the connection-conclusion is straightforward. For example,

> **Therefore, because Mr. Burglar was committing a burglary when he was bitten, Ms. Restrepo cannot be held liable for Burglar's injuries under Ohio Revised Code §111.1111.**

Stating a connection-conclusion explicitly at the end of your CREXAC analysis is an important part of the formula. Even though you stated a conclusion at the beginning of your analysis, the connection-conclusion at the end of the analysis serves a different purpose. It makes the reader aware of your conclusion, yes, but it also tells the reader that your analysis of this part of the discussion is finished and that you will soon be moving on to another point.

Furthermore, as its name implies, the connection-conclusion shows the reader how this part of the analysis fits into, or connects with, the argument as a whole. If a section of your argument is about a dispositive point, the connection-conclusion should make the connection between that point and the ultimate result you seek. At the very least, you should connect your analysis of the phrase-that-pays (in small capital letters in the following example) to the point that was at issue in that section of the argument:

> **Activities that Respondents exposed to the PLAIN VIEW of outsiders were not protected by the Fourth Amendment. Because Respondents' activities within the apartment were in PLAIN VIEW from Thielen's lawful vantage point, Thielen's observation violated no reasonable expectation of privacy.**

This connection-conclusion connects the writer's point about the phrase-that-pays—"plain view"—to the point of the section, which is whether the respondents had a reasonable expectation of privacy.

5.2
WHEN NOT TO PROVIDE A CREXAC ANALYSIS

The first part of this chapter addressed how to complete a relatively thorough analysis of a legal issue. But not every issue needs a CREXAC unit of discourse. If an issue does not need the full treatment of a CREXAC, you must decide how much space, if any, to devote to the issue. As with most legal questions, an appropriate answer is "it depends." Some issues that would be controversial in one case will be obvious in another, and the depth of your analysis must change accordingly. Illustration 5.2 shows four labels you can use to describe how much discussion to include for each issue or sub-issue: Ignore, Tell, Clarify (CRAC), or Prove (CREXAC):

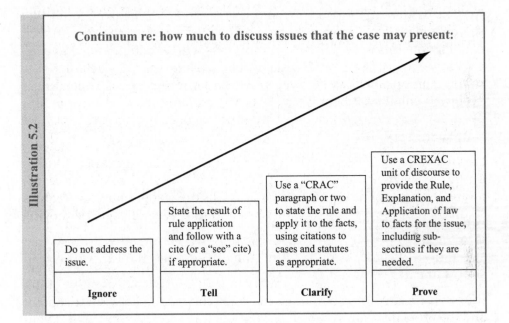

Illustration 5.2

Continuum re: how much to discuss issues that the case may present:

Ignore	Tell	Clarify	Prove
Do not address the issue.	State the result of rule application and follow with a cite (or a "see" cite) if appropriate.	Use a "CRAC" paragraph or two to state the rule and apply it to the facts, using citations to cases and statutes as appropriate.	Use a CREXAC unit of discourse to provide the Rule, Explanation, and Application of law to facts for the issue, including sub-sections if they are needed.

5.2.1
IGNORE ISSUES

Some issues are obviously *not* relevant to the analysis. Others are relevant to the analysis, but are so obviously not controversial that the reader does not need you to spend even one sentence discussing the issue. These are *Ignore issues,* that is, they are issues that you can *ignore* in your written legal analysis.

For example, suppose that the statute forbidding drunk driving in your state contains this language:

> Any person who operates any vehicle, streetcar, or trackless trolley within this state, may not, while operating the vehicle, streetcar, or trackless trolley, be under the influence of alcohol, a drug of abuse, or a combination of them, as specified in section B of this statute.

Let us presume that you work for the state prosecutor, and you have brought charges against a defendant who was arrested while sitting in the driver's seat of her car, a Chevy Impala, parked on the side of a highway. She admitted that she drank four beers earlier that evening, and sobriety tests showed an illegal level of alcohol in her blood. In order to establish that she violated the statute, you would have to prove the following elements (words signaling elements are underlined):

> Defendant is a <u>person</u> who was <u>operating</u> a <u>vehicle</u> while <u>under the influence of alcohol</u>.

In your written analysis, you would not spend any time explaining that the defendant, as a human being, is a "person" under the statute. You could ignore this issue. Likewise, in this case, you would not expend even a sentence to say "a Chevy Impala, an automobile, is a 'vehicle' under the statute." In another case, however, whether the person was operating a "vehicle" might well be at issue. In 2009, an Ohio man was arrested for operating a motorized barstool while intoxicated. In that situation, the state should not treat the "vehicle" element as an Ignore issue.

Thus, if an element is so obviously met that there could be no doubt in your reader's mind that it is satisfied in this case, you should ignore it. Do not, however, let yourself be lulled into a false belief that an issue is not controversial. For example, you might believe that "operating" a vehicle is the same as driving and presume that someone sitting in a parked car is not legally operating the car. Research, however, might well reveal that "operation" includes sitting behind the driver's seat in a car whose gearshift is in park.[7]

5.2.2
TELL ISSUES

As its name implies, a writer includes a *Tell issue* in legal analysis by *telling* the outcome of application of law to facts and then citing to authority. There are two kinds of Tell issues. The first kind is an issue that is relevant but is not controversial. The second kind of Tell issue is an issue that could have been controversial, but that has been removed from controversy by some outside means, such as a party's concession.

For example, suppose that your client, Sam Bell, is a young man who was injured while intoxicated after "hell night" activities at his fraternity. A hometown friend, Marvin Kobacker, had taken him from a supervised "drunk room" at the fraternity and later left him alone in an off-campus apartment, where he fell and injured himself. You are wondering whether Mr. Kobacker is liable to Mr. Bell.

A common law rule in your jurisdiction provides that "a person assumes a duty of care if he or she takes charge of a person who is helpless." You

---

[7] *See, e.g., State v. Cyr*, 967 A.2d 32, 40 (Conn. 2009).

look at the rule and realize that two phrases-that-pay are "take charge" and "helpless." Upon doing the research, you discover that there are several factors to analyze when determining whether someone "took charge" of another person. Likewise, there are several ways to prove that a person is "helpless." At first blush, it might seem that you need to complete two separate CREXAC units of discourse. One case from the highest court in your jurisdiction, however, states unequivocally that a person who is intoxicated is "helpless" under this standard. In this situation, Mr. Bell was unequivocally intoxicated. Thus, this required element is without controversy in your case, and you can treat it as a Tell issue:

> In Vanita, a person assumes a duty of care if he or she "takes charge" of a person who is "helpless." <u>Jenkins v. Diamond</u>, 101 N.E.2d 104, 109 (Van. 2007). An intoxicated person is considered helpless. <u>Id</u>. at 111.

The second kind of Tell issue is one that has been removed from the controversy in some way. In a First Amendment challenge to a statute, for example, a court will use strict scrutiny to analyze a content-based restriction, while it will use a lower level of scrutiny to analyze a content-neutral restriction. If you and your opponent disagree as to whether the restriction at issue is a content-based restriction, you would probably need to use a CREXAC unit of discourse to argue that the statute does or does not impose a content-based restriction. However, if your opponent has conceded the issue—perhaps in a brief or in an oral argument to a lower court—you may treat the issue as a Tell issue, citing authority if possible:

> As the petitioner concedes, the statute at issue criminalizes speech based on its content. Pet'r Br. At 16. Accordingly, this court should apply the strict scrutiny test when analyzing its validity. <u>Cornelius v. NAACP Legal Defense & Ed. Fund, Inc.</u>, 473 U.S. 788, 800 (1985).

Tell issues can arise in different contexts, but they are most commonly found in two places in the brief: As is discussed in Chapter Ten, they can arise in introductory material; when you are providing context for your argument as a whole, you may need to address one or more Tell issues to provide context and clear away the uncontroversial points. Second, they can arise when you are articulating the rule, either as part of a rule cluster or as an uncontroversial but significant facet of a governing rule.

5.2.3
CLARIFY OR CRAC ISSUES

A *Clarify issue* is similar to a Tell issue, but it is an issue that is a shade more complex. The term *Clarify* signals that the issue needs a bit more detail in order for the reader to understand either why the issue is not controversial or why the issue is not relevant.

For example, presume that your client, Old Testament Publishers, is an employer with eight full-time employees. A plaintiff has filed a suit under both state and federal age discrimination statutes. The federal statute applies only to employers with "twenty or more employees for each working day in each of twenty or more calendar weeks in the current or preceding calendar year." In a memorandum in support of a motion to dismiss, you could conceivably treat the applicability of the federal statute as a Tell issue:

> **Because Old Testament Publishers has only eight employees, the federal Age Discrimination in Employment Act does not apply. 29 U.S.C. §630(b) (defining "employer" as having "twenty or more" employees).**

On the other hand, if your client were an ice cream parlor in a tourist town, its employee count might take a little more time to make clear, because its employee count is not stable throughout the year. In that situation, the applicability of the statute would be a little more complicated, and you should treat the issue as a Clarify issue:

> **Mr. Zawierucha cannot bring a cause of action under the federal Age Discrimination in Employment Act. The Act applies only to employers with "twenty or more employees for each working day in each of twenty or more calendar weeks in the current or preceding calendar year." 29 U.S.C. §630(b). Admittedly, Ice Cream Dreams sometimes employs more than twenty people. During this calendar year, it has employed twenty or more people during ten calendar weeks. For the preceding year, it employed twenty or more people during twelve calendar weeks. Because it has never employed more than twenty employees for "twenty or more calendar weeks" in a calendar year, however, Mr. Zawierucha will be unable to bring a cause of action using this statute, and this court should accordingly dismiss Count IV of his complaint.**

You might think of a Clarify issue as a CRAC issue, since it requires you to state a Conclusion, state the Rule, Apply the rule, and provide a Connection-conclusion.

It is difficult to give an exact formula for distinguishing between Tell issues and Clarify issues. You may presume that "more is always better," but that is not always true. You will needlessly annoy some readers by giving a paragraph of analysis where a sentence plus citation will suffice. As you gain more experience in written legal analysis (and experience with various readers), you will develop your own sense of judgment as to the appropriate depth for your analysis. In the meantime, there are a few factors you can consider. For example, is the language in the rule abstract or highly technical? The harder the rule is to understand on its own, the more likely it is that your reader will benefit from a Clarify analysis. Is the connection between the law and the facts complex enough that you want to take the reader by the hand to make sure that the connection is evident? Are you writing about an area of law with which the court may be unfamiliar? If so, it may be worth the extra sentence or two to clarify the outcome of the issue.

5.2.4
PROVE OR CREXAC ISSUES

Now we have come full circle. I use the word *Prove* to describe the kind of analysis provided in a CREXAC unity of discourse—the most in-depth type of legal analysis.[8] An issue is a *Prove* or *CREXAC issue* if (1) the issue concerns a required element of the analysis, and (2) the issue is controversial.

After you have analyzed the kinds of issues that your case presents, you should take another look at your working outline. Decide whether each issue listed is an Ignore, Tell, Clarify, or Prove issue, and mark each as appropriate. Consider whether you have omitted any issues that should be in your outline. You can leave an Ignore issue out of your outline, but you should list Tell issues, perhaps parenthetically, to make sure that you include them in your analysis.

5.3
DEALING WITH YOUR OPPONENT'S ARGUMENTS

A common dilemma for brief writers is whether and how to address their opponent's arguments. Some advocates believe that acknowledging the existence of an opponent's argument in any way is a sign of weakness that should be avoided. These writers may hope that their opponents will present only a weak case or that the court will not notice the gap. Judge Hamilton of the Fourth Circuit notes that the best briefs "[address] head-on the opponent's best responsive argument, best supporting case law or statutory authority, and, if at issue, the opponent's listing of contrary evidence."[9] If these authorities are missing, the judge may draw negative conclusions, as Judge Parker of the Second Circuit observes:

> I would also like to recommend that all advocates distinguish contrary authority, even in their opening brief. If there is bad precedent out there for your case, you can assume your adversary will cite it to us, or we will independently find it. If the first time I see an adverse case is in

[8] In their text, Professors Neumann and Tiscione use the term *rule proof* in much the same way that this text uses the term *rule explanation*. Richard K. Neumann, Jr. & Kristen Konrad Tiscione, *Legal Reasoning and Legal Writing* ch. 12 (7th ed., Aspen 2013).
[9] Clyde H. Hamilton, *Effective Appellate Brief Writing*, 50 S.C. L. Rev. 581, 582 (1999).

the answering brief, then my initial reaction is that the appellant does not have a good explanation as to why that case is inapposite. While a response in the reply brief may dispel this initial impression, it may not. Therefore, by failing to mention contrary precedent in the opening brief, the advocate makes that precedent more weighty than it perhaps should be.[10]

Professor Kathryn Stanchi has analyzed the growing body of social science research that has investigated the impact of including negative information in various rhetorical situations.[11] Professor Stanchi concludes that, beyond following the ethical requirement to address directly contradictory authority,[12] attorneys must be very careful when deciding whether and how to bring up negative arguments.

Addressing negative authorities is a part of addressing your opponent's arguments, but it is not the only part. After you have crafted your working outline, make a list of what you consider to be your opponent's most likely arguments.[13] For each argument, you may need to make three determinations. First, you should identify the precise area of disagreement. Second, determine whether your argument as currently constructed contains any material that contradicts the particular argument. If it does not, your third step is to determine whether and how to introduce contradictory material.

First, determine the exact locus of the disagreement. The heart of the familiar CREXAC formula—Rule, Explanation, and Application—can help you to do so. Perhaps you and your opponent disagree as to the particular rule that must be applied. In that circumstance, you may have to add one or more sections to your argument, using a "rule choice" analysis as described in Section 5.1.2(b).

For another issue, you may agree as to which rule should be applied but disagree as to what that rule means, perhaps because you disagree

---

[10] Fred I. Parker, *Foreword: Appellate Advocacy and Practice in the Second Circuit*, 64 Brook. L. Rev. 457, 463-64 (1998).

[11] Kathryn M. Stanchi, *Playing with Fire: The Science of Confronting Adverse Material in Legal Advocacy*, 60 Rutgers L. Rev. 381 (2008). The article, which is well worth reading, notes that "the decision to volunteer negative information depends on a complicated algorithm" that measures several overlapping factors. *Id.* at 433.

[12] Rule 3.3(a)(2) of the ABA Model Rules of Professional Conduct provides that an advocate may not "fail to disclose" legal authority in the "controlling jurisdiction" that the lawyer knows is "directly adverse" to the client's position, unless opposing counsel has disclosed it. http://www.americanbar.org/groups/professional_responsibility/publications/model_rules_of_professional_conduct/rule_3_3_candor_toward_the_tribunal.html (last accessed April 13, 2014). The American Bar Association notes that these rules "serve as models for the ethics rules of most states." http://www.americanbar.org/groups/professional_responsibility/publications/model_rules_of_professional_conduct.html (last accessed April 13, 2014).

[13] Professor Stanchi warns against bringing up negative arguments pre-emptively unless you are fairly certain that your opponent will actually bring them up. Stanchi, *supra* note 11, at 427, 428. Of course, if you are a respondent, an appellee, or a party opposing the motion, you may be able to consult an actual brief to determine what those arguments are. Admittedly, this option is not always available in a law school setting.

about which authorities best illustrate how that rule should operate. In that circumstance, the explanation section of a particular unit of discourse argument may be longer because you may need to address not only the significance of cases that you believe best illustrate how the rule operates but also cases that your opponent might proffer. You should take care to address what the authorities do *not* mean or do *not* say, and to justify your decisions. You should not make your opponent's arguments, as in this example:

▽ BAD EXAMPLE

The Respondent may argue that the <u>McGuffin</u> case applies here. Respondent may argue that <u>McGuffin</u> stands for proposition that . . .

Instead of spending valuable time on the opponent's actual argument, make your position as to that argument evident from the beginning. If you are writing a responsive brief or are otherwise certain that your opponent will be making a certain point or bringing up a certain authority, you may wish to tie the authority to your opponent, as in this example:

△ GOOD EXAMPLE

Any argument by Respondent that <u>McGuffin</u> applies here is inapposite. The <u>McGuffin</u> court never addressed . . .

This type of argument has risks, particularly if you are writing the opening brief.[14] In the alternative, you can simply attack the negative authority. This type of argument is a method of portraying yourself as an educator.[15] For the court's benefit, you are describing the cases that are relevant and those that are not relevant:

△ GOOD EXAMPLE

<u>McGuffin</u> does not apply here for two reasons. First. . . .

Depending on the amount of detail needed, you may want to devote a paragraph or even a point-heading section[16] to the principle that a case or a series of cases is inapposite.

Finally, as to some issues, you and your opponent may agree as to what the rule is and to what it means, but disagree as to how it applies. In that

---

[14] *See generally* Stanchi, *supra* note 11, at 424-27 (discussing when and how to volunteer negative information).

[15] Commentators have referred to this educational style as the "scholarly" style. Stanchi, *supra* note 11, at 391 (citing James F. Stratman, *Investigating Persuasive Processes in Legal Discourse in Real Time: Cognitive Biases and Rhetorical Strategy in Appeal Court Briefs*, 17 Discourse Processes 1, 8-10 (1994)).

[16] In this situation, you may want to mentally substitute the word "Evidence" for the "Explanation" part of CREXAC. Your assertion that a certain line of cases is inapposite would be your "rule," and in the place of the "Explanation," you would provide evidence for the truth of that assertion by discussing the cases and describing how they do not provide the support that your opponent might suggest.

situation, your rule application section would need to be longer because you would need to provide more detail as to the significance of certain facts that promote your point of view and the insignificance of facts that your opponent might use to promote his or her argument.

Your second step is to determine if your opponent is making or may make an argument that you cannot address within the confines of your argument as it is currently structured. Look at each of the opponent arguments on your list and determine whether your argument contains contradictory analysis. Sometimes the analysis may be indirectly contradictory: Two rules are mutually exclusive, and your argument does the best possible job of explaining why and how a particular rule applies in your case. At other times, your argument may directly contradict your opponent; instead of just saying that rule A applies, you will argue that rule B does not apply, or argue that even if it does apply, it does not result in a finding for your opponent.

You may, however, identify opponent arguments that you have not addressed directly or indirectly, and you must decide whether to do so. If you have no effective response to an issue, it may be better to leave it out of your argument[17] and focus on making your strong arguments as effectively as possible. For other issues, you may decide to make a direct attack on your opponent's point of view.

This kind of argument may be less likely to be rule based. Instead, you may be making a direct assertion that your opponent's argument misinterprets the law or the facts. Instead of *explaining* the meaning of a rule by illustrating how it has been applied in the past, you will, in a way, be providing *evidence* for the truth of your assertion about your opponent's argument. For example, you may be arguing that a particular interpretation of a statute is wrong. The evidence to support that assertion could be legislative (e.g., discussing legislative history or statutory language), judicial (describing on-point cases from appropriate jurisdictions), or empirical (citing studies that support the thesis behind the assertion).

Thus, depending on your assertion, your "evidence" may come from the record, from extra-legal sources, or, as in most CREXAC arguments, from relevant authorities that have applied a particular rule. For example, if you are arguing that a court misinterpreted a rule or a line of cases, your evidence for that assertion would likely consist of a correct analysis of those cases, perhaps showing how other courts had applied that rule. When making arguments of this type, choose your words carefully. If you are petitioner, it may be tempting to attack the lower court for its holding. It might be more tactful and more fruitful, however, to characterize your attack as an attack on the assertion behind the holding rather than on the court that made the holding. Thus, instead of saying, e.g., "The

---

[17] Stanchi, *supra* note 11, at 383.

Eighteenth Circuit erred when it found that the Mousse Statute applied here," it might be better to say, e.g., "Arguments that the Mousse Statute applies are inappropriate."

I close this section with two warnings about dealing with your opponent's arguments. First, addressing negative authorities almost never means that you should begin your argument by addressing negative authorities. Professor Stanchi's research shows that "it is clear that beginning with refutation decreases persuasive value."[18] Second, addressing negative arguments or authorities does not require you to attack opposing counsel or the courts below.[19] Instead of questioning the integrity or intelligence of opposing counsel, note a possibly tenuous connection and then refute it—e.g., "Although this statute, admittedly, governs some types of employment relationships, it is inapposite here. The statute's language . . . ." You increase your credibility when you accord appropriate respect to your opponents and the judiciary.

5.4
SUMMARY

By using the CREXAC formula to analyze every controversial element in your argument, you give the court the information it needs to understand the validity of each element of your argument. An important part of your job as an advocate is to identify which issues need a full CREXAC analysis and which issues should be addressed more succinctly or summarily. Furthermore, you must be sure that, whenever possible, your argument addresses your opponent's best points. Your goal is to write a brief that addresses—in appropriate depth—both the strengths of your arguments and the weaknesses of your opponent's arguments. The more effectively you do so, the more you increase the chances that the court will understand why the law demands the result that you seek.

[18] *Id.* at 397.
[19] *Id.* at 410 (citing Stratman, at 44).

Chapter Six

PRACTICE POINTERS: USING CASE AUTHORITY EFFECTIVELY

One of your brief's most important jobs is showing the court that the law that supports your argument is valid and that the law that supports your opponent's argument is either invalid or not on point. The previous chapter addressed how to discuss your opponent's arguments. This chapter addresses how to include case authority—the authority used most frequently in briefs—in the most effective way possible.

To use authorities most effectively, you must keep both your reader and your user in mind: The brief should include enough information about the case authorities cited so that any reader can understand their significance. In addition, it must include citations in a way that allows them to be found easily by the user, who may be trying to find the relevant authorities so that he or she can review them and assess their validity.

The practical brief writer should assume, however, that none of his or her readers will read anything other than the brief itself before deciding the case. Admittedly, at least the judge who writes the opinion, or his or her law clerk, will probably look up each cited case and review it to test whether it adequately supports your argument. Some readers may conduct additional research to further test the validity of the parties' arguments. Because the audience for an appellate brief includes all of the judges who will be voting, however, and because not every judge will have time to consult outside authorities, your brief should include enough information to be useful to those who want to go beyond it, but to be understandable and credible to those who do not.

With these concerns in mind, brief writers need to pay attention to several different aspects of using case authority: (1) they must provide the reader with an appropriate amount of information about the cases they do cite; (2) they must use quotations effectively; (3) they must use language precisely when they are analogizing and distinguishing cases; (4) they must use unpublished decisions properly; and (5) they must use citations in a way that makes it easy for the judge or the judge's clerk to verify the validity of the rules and authorities in the argument.

6.1
PROVIDING APPROPRIATE DETAIL IN CASE DESCRIPTIONS

Analyzing authority cases is an essential part of effective written advocacy. Many legal writers neglect this important task, presuming wrongly that citations alone provide adequate support for the assertions in the brief. They seem to have the mistaken impression that judges have all of the needed law at their mental fingertips and that the brief writer needs only to allude to some of the relevant authorities, drop in some favorite quotations, or provide a string cite of the cases that might have some bearing on the case at bar—certainly the judge and the clerks can fill in the rest. Most readers, however, need more information than the citation can give.

I gladly agree with the premise that judges are extremely intelligent and very knowledgeable about the law. However, there is a difference between a judge's general knowledge and the specific knowledge that is needed to decide a case intelligently. Most judges know and understand the general rules that apply to commonly encountered legal issues. This means that you do not need to discuss the British practice of writs of assistance in the colonies when arguing a Fourth Amendment case or cite to *Marbury v. Madison* if you are asking the court to declare a statute unconstitutional.

Having the general knowledge to understand what rules mean and how they apply does *not* suggest, however, that all judges know the particular details of every case that you cite, or why and how each is relevant to your legal argument.

When you cite a case in a brief, it will most likely be for one of two reasons. You may be using the case to provide "rule authority"; that is, you are citing the case to provide authority for the existence of a rule. More likely, however, you are citing the case as "illustrative authority"; that is, you believe that the case effectively illustrates how the rule has been or should be applied. While the depth of your case description may vary depending on whether it is being used as a rule authority or an illustrative authority, you should almost always provide some description for each case you cite. As a former deputy solicitor general has noted, "[e]very case that is worth citing . . . is worth discussing sufficiently to show why it is particularly on point or sheds analogous light on the question at hand."[1]

The question remains, what is "sufficient" discussion? In most situations, if you are citing a case, the reader should be able to glean four elements from your case description. Notice that I say that the reader should be able to *glean* these four elements. I am not saying that you must devote a sentence to each of these elements or even that you must state each one directly. Your decisions as to which elements to state directly and which to leave unstated will depend, as do most decisions, on the context in which the case descriptions appear.

With that warning, here are the elements:

(1) **The issue.** Be sure that the reader can identify which of the case's many issues and sub-issues you are using the case to illustrate. You should also provide the legal context in which the court analyzed that issue, *if it is different from the context of the case at bar or the cases under discussion in that section of your argument.* If you will be analogizing or distinguishing the case based on some particular facet of the legal issue, be sure to provide sufficient detail so that the reader can understand that facet of the issue.

(2) **The disposition.** Make clear how the court disposed of that narrow issue and, if relevant, how it disposed of the entire case.

(3) **The facts.** Include enough of the legally significant facts for the reader to understand how the court applied the law to reach its holding on the issue and how the case is analogous to the case at bar. If you wish to draw an analogy to these facts or to distinguish your case based on its facts, provide more detail.

---

[1] James vanR. Springer, *Symposium on Supreme Court Advocacy: Some Suggestions on Preparing Briefs on the Merits in the Supreme Court of the United States*, 33 Cath. U. L. Rev. 593, 601 (1984). (The author was a deputy solicitor general of the United States from 1968 to 1971.)

(4) **The reasoning.** Include enough information to give the reader a basic understanding of why the court decided the issue before it in the way that it did. If either the case or the reasoning behind the court's decision is significant, provide more detail.

When writing a case description, you should presume that you need to include all four of these elements. Admittedly, on some occasions, it may be appropriate to include only three rather than four of the elements. At times, the facts may be omitted in a section devoted to an issue of law, particularly in a situation in which the writer cites two or more cases with similar fact situations. Likewise, when an argument turns on a question of fact, it may be permissible to omit a court's reasoning. When in doubt, however, include all four elements. Note that including these four elements in a case description is not all that the effective brief writer must do. To ensure that the brief is effective, you must be sure that your case description is as succinct as possible; you must use verb tenses accurately; you must choose when to use parenthetical case descriptions instead of textual ones, and to do so effectively and appropriately; and you must be certain that the case description is accurate.

6.1.1
MAKING CASE DESCRIPTIONS AS SUCCINCT AS POSSIBLE

Including the issue, the holding, the facts, and the reasoning in a case description may seem to require a long description. Actually, all four of these elements can often be conveyed in a parenthetical description, and they can certainly be conveyed in a textual description of two sentences. Of course, if the relevant aspect of the case is complex or particularly significant, or if the argument is controversial, your case description will be lengthier.

There are two keys to succinct case descriptions. The first key is focus. You must understand the focus of the argument you are currently making and make sure that the case description has that same focus. The second key is efficient use of language. Too many case descriptions begin with a wasted sentence that does little more than announce that the case exists. Use your subjects and verbs with care to convey the most information in the fewest words.

a. Focus
The case descriptions below are from a discussion about the illegality of gender-based classifications in a brief written in support of the petitioner's argument in *Miller v. Albright*, 523 U.S. 420 (1998). Notice how they efficiently include each of the necessary case description elements (signaled by a number after each of the elements appears):

⚠ GOOD EXAMPLE

As noted previously, the <u>Virginia</u> Court discredited **2** governmental justifications for gender-based classifications **1** as to state-supported military schools **3** because the justifications were based on overbroad generalizations about the different capabilities of men and women. **4** 518 U.S. at 533. The <u>J.E.B.</u> Court also categorically rejected **2** such broad assumptions about men and women's relative capabilities **4** when it struck down **2** a state's use of gender-based peremptory challenges to exclude all men from a jury. **1** & **3** 511 U.S. at 138-40.

1 Issue
2 Disposition
3 Facts
4 Reasoning

One method you can use to test the focus of your case descriptions is to look for the phrase-that-pays for that section of the document. If your case description includes the phrase-that-pays, chances are good that you have at least focused the description on the right legal issue. For example, in the previous example, the phrase-that-pays "gender-based classifications" appears in both case descriptions. In the following example, from the "plain view" argument discussed in Chapter Five, the brief writer discusses cases in which the Court allowed or disallowed certain searches based on whether the officers were looking at things that were in "plain view." Note how the brief writer took care to connect the phrase-that-pays, "plain view," to each of the two case descriptions (the phrase-that-pays is in small capital letters):

⚠ GOOD EXAMPLE

Illegal activities in PLAIN VIEW from outside the curtilage are not protected even if the police observation is specifically directed at identifying illegal activity. <u>United States v. Dunn</u>, 480 U.S. 294 (1987) (finding that an officer's PLAIN VIEW observation into a barn **3** was not a Fourth Amendment search **1** & **2** , even though the observation was motivated by a law enforcement purpose **3**); <u>Ciraolo</u>, 476 U.S. at 212, 213. In <u>Ciraolo</u>, the defendant was growing marijuana in a 15-by-25 foot plot in his backyard. He surrounded the yard with a 6-foot outer fence and a 10-foot inner fence. **3** <u>Id</u>. at 209. Officers flew over the defendant's house in a private airplane and readily identified the illegal plants using only the naked eye. **3** <u>Id</u>.

1 Issue
2 Disposition
3 Facts
4 Reasoning

The government in <u>Ciraolo</u> argued that the observation was analogous to looking through a knothole or an opening in a fence: "If there is an opening, the police may look." <u>Id</u>. at 220. This Court agreed with the government, holding that the officers violated no expectation of privacy and that the observation was not a Fourth Amendment search. **1** & **2** <u>Id</u>. at 215. The airspace was outside the curtilage of the apartment, and the Court reasoned that the scene would have been in PLAIN VIEW to any member of the public flying in the same airspace. **4** <u>Id</u>. at 213-14.

If the court has not been thoughtful enough to use the phrase-that-pays that you have identified for that section of the argument, you can make the connection yourself, as long as you do it honestly. If you do make the connection yourself, be sure to justify the connection in the way you describe the case, or with language that you quote. The word *apparently* is often helpful when describing a connection that is implicit rather than explicit, as in this description of a court's reasoning in a fictional case:

GOOD EXAMPLE

> The court apparently believed that the search was justified by the fact that the defendant was smoking marijuana in PLAIN VIEW of the arresting officer, because it noted that "police officers need not turn away when they encounter illegal behavior right under their noses." <u>Ohio v. McGuffin</u>, 101 U.S. 101, 103 (2013).

When trying to decide how much detail to give the reader, first assess how you are using the case. If you are using the case as rule authority and plan to discuss it in depth in your explanation section, you may give only a "naked cite." On the other hand, you may be using a case as rule authority only because it is from a court of mandatory jurisdiction or it is well known as the source of a particular rule, rather than because of its relevance to your client's case. (Presumably, you plan to use other cases to illustrate the rule.) If that is the situation, you should provide a parenthetical description, as shown above with the writer's use of the *Dunn* case.

A last word about focus: in your casebook courses, you may have been trained to write case briefs that identify the main point of the case, or the point that the case "stands for" in the development of a legal rule. In advocacy, in contrast, your case descriptions must focus on the *relevant* issue, disposition, etc., even if it is not the main point that the court addressed.

b. Using Language Effectively

Even when using a textual case description or when you must give the reader more detail, do not make your case description needlessly long. Provide only the information that the reader needs about each of the four elements. The description of the *Ciraolo* case above is somewhat lengthy, but its length is concentrated in the facts and the reasoning. The plain view issue is fact specific, and thus the details about cases in which plain view was or was not established were particularly important in that case.

In many case descriptions, writers run into trouble in the first sentence. One way to avoid this trouble is to concentrate on the subject-verb combination. The first sentence you write about a case should tell the reader something that the court did or something about why the court did what it did. It should *not* tell the reader what the case *involved, regarded,* or *concerned,* or what the court *addressed, considered, examined,* or *dealt with.* Notice how the first sentence in the following case description wastes the reader's (scarce) time and energy:

▽ BAD EXAMPLE

In **J.E.B. v. T.B.**, 511 U.S. 127 (1994), this Court examined the issue of sex discrimination in the selection of jurors.

This description tells the reader that the court examined an issue, but leaves the reader in suspense as to what happened as a result of the examination. Suspense is the enemy of good legal writing. Instead of saying only that the court "examined" the issue, the writer should say something about a court's ultimate ruling or, if relevant, a particular finding in the case. Verbs such as *held* and *found* are more likely to get your reader to the point of the case:

△ GOOD EXAMPLE

In 1994, this Court held that sex-based ① peremptory challenges ③ violate ② jurors' rights to equal protection. ① **J.E.B. v. T.B.**, 511 U.S. 127, 138-40 (1994).

① Issue
② Disposition
③ Facts

The bad example told the reader only the issue that the court addressed in *J.E.B.* The good example, on the other hand, tells the reader the issue, the legally significant facts, and the disposition of the issue. The writer can add any needed reasoning in a second sentence.[2]

c. Verb Tense in Case Descriptions

Many writers get confused as to the appropriate verb tense when describing cases. This confusion results when courts mix legal rules that are currently in force—properly stated in the present tense—with case facts, findings, and holdings—properly stated in some form of the past tense.[3]

Within a case description, use an appropriate form of past tense to describe events that happened before the case began as well as events that happened in the case. The court's holdings as to specific parties should also be described using the past tense:

△ GOOD EXAMPLES

The plaintiff claimed that the defendant had assaulted him.
The advertisement had not specified the need for a college education.
Defendant had sought outside counsel before deciding to terminate the plaintiff.
The plaintiff alleged . . .
The defendant argued . . .

---

[2] For information on avoiding wordiness generally, see Anne Enquist & Laurel Currie Oates, *Just Writing: Grammar, Punctuation, and Style for the Legal Writer* §6.2 (4th ed., Aspen 2013).

[3] A detailed discussion of the sequence of tenses is beyond the scope of this book; for an excellent explanation of how verb tenses are used in legal writing, see Enquist & Oates, *supra* note 2, at §§8.3, 10.1.2.

> The court found . . .
> The court reasoned . . .
> The court held that Officer Thielen had violated the Fourth Amendment when he observed the defendants through a gap in a window blind.

When you are stating a general rule that the court articulated, however, use the past tense only to describe the court's action, and use the present tense for the rule itself:

◭ GOOD EXAMPLE

> The Court held that police officers do not violate the Fourth Amendment when they are able to observe criminal activity from a lawful vantage point without the aid of special equipment.

The correct verb tense may not make or break your argument, but using the wrong verb tense distracts the reader at best. At worst, it confuses the reader and slows down his or her comprehension.

6.1.2
WRITING AND USING EFFECTIVE PARENTHETICAL DESCRIPTIONS

Parenthetical case descriptions are a useful alternative to in-text, or textual, case descriptions. "Parentheticals" can save both space and the reader's time, but the writer must be careful to remember the principles of focus and completeness. Incomplete parentheticals tend to be ineffective because they give the reader only a snippet of information. Often, unfortunately, the snippet does not contain enough information to make the case useful to the reader, who must decide whether the cited case provides authority for a ruling in the case at bar:

▽ BAD EXAMPLE

> See generally Virginia, 518 U.S. at 533 (plaintiff challenged gender-based classifications in state-run military schools); J.E.B. v. T.B., 511 U.S. at 138-40 (male juror questioned sex-based peremptory challenge).

These parentheticals tell the reader something about the issue (gender-based classifications) and the facts (the classifications occurred in a military school and in peremptory challenges to jury selection), but they do not tell the reader how the court resolved the issue or why the court resolved it the way it did. This type of snippet parenthetical may be effective, but only if the surrounding text—usually the text before the citation—supplies sufficient context. For a parenthetical to be effective, either the parenthetical alone *or* the parenthetical and the preceding text will give the reader information about at least three, and preferably four, of the required elements: the issue, the disposition, the facts, and the reasoning. In the first example below, the text before the citations provides the disposition, the issue, and the reasoning; the parentheticals, therefore, need include only the legally significant facts. In the second example, in contrast, which has no introductory text, the parenthetical includes all four elements:

⚠ GOOD EXAMPLES

> Courts have justified striking down **2** a variety of gender-based classifications **1** when those classifications were based on "overbroad generalizations about the different capabilities of men and women." **4** See, e.g., <u>Virginia</u>, 518 U.S. at 533 (single-sex state-run military schools) **3**; <u>J.E.B. v. T.B.</u>, 511 U.S. at 138-40 (gender-based peremptory challenges in jury selection). **3**

> **1** Issue
> **2** Disposition
> **3** Facts
> **4** Reasoning

> <u>J.E.B. v. T.B.</u>, 511 U.S. 127, 138-40 (1994) ("categorically" rejecting broad assumptions about capabilities of men and women **4** to strike down **2** sex-based **1** peremptory challenges **3**).

As with textual descriptions, using language effectively and focusing on the phrase-that-pays can help to make parenthetical descriptions more useful.

Knowing how to write effective parenthetical case descriptions is important, but the writer must also know *when* to use a parenthetical description. Deciding when to use a textual or a parenthetical description for a cited case is really a question about how much detail to provide. If little detail is needed, as when you are citing to a case only for rule authority, you can easily use a parenthetical description. Ultimately, your decision will be based on the answers to two questions: (1) How is the case significant to your argument? (2) What information does the reader need to have to understand the case's significance? The more significant an authority case is, and the more important it is for the reader to understand its facts and reasoning, the more detail you need to provide *in your argument.* If the issue or the authority case is more straightforward, on the other hand, you can provide a shorter textual description *or* a parenthetical description. Note that you should generally *not* provide both a parenthetical and a textual description for the same case. You may appropriately have a sentence with introductory text that precedes a citation with a parenthetical description. Generally, however, if you need more than a sentence of introductory text, you should use a textual description rather than a parenthetical one. Likewise, it is usually not appropriate to follow a parenthetical case description with further textual description of a case.

As noted in Chapter Five, the ideal explanation section within each unit of discourse in your argument includes at least one case in which a court found that the rule applied to a certain set of facts, and at least one case in which a court found that the rule did *not* apply to a certain different set of facts. In most situations, you will want to provide a textual description of both of those cases. A sensible compromise is to provide one or two more detailed case descriptions, followed up—when needed—by citation to one or more illustrative cases with parenthetical descriptions.

Do not use this method as an excuse to bombard the reader with eight authorities when one would suffice. Cite an additional authority only when it illustrates some aspect of the rule that your previous authorities did not illustrate, or when it proves that the interpretation you are illustrating is well established. (See the discussion about avoiding string cites in Section 6.5.5.)

The following example is an excerpt from a respondent's brief in *Minnesota v. Carter*, 525 U.S. 83 (1998). The brief writer is using four cases to explain the rule that a person has a legitimate expectation of privacy in a location if that person can demonstrate an expectation that his or her activities would be private, and if society will accept that expectation as reasonable. This example shows the "conclusion, rule, explanation" part of the formula. The writer begins by articulating the rule and citing to authority, and follows by stating in a summary fashion how the rule should apply to the client's facts. The writer then proceeds to explain the rule, using the rule authority and other cases. In one of the cases, the Supreme Court found that no legitimate expectation of privacy existed. Some writers seem to think it is dangerous to let the court see any case in which a court ruled "against" their client's interest. Effective writers, however, realize that if a so-called negative case is distinguishable, it can be used very effectively to argue against a particular result. Notice how the writer of this example gives details from the *Rakas* Court's reasoning that he can use to distinguish the defendant in *Rakas* from his clients, who are claiming an expectation of privacy in an apartment that they visited for the purpose of packaging illegal drugs:

GOOD EXAMPLE

A Rule authority that will be used later in this section as illustrative authority and then described in full

B Illustrative authority

1 Issue

2 Disposition

3 Facts

4 Reasoning

This Court has held that people will be recognized as having a legitimate expectation of privacy if they demonstrate an expectation that their activities are treated as private, and if it can be shown that society will find that expectation to be reasonable in a given situation. Katz v. United States, 389 U.S. 347, 361 (1967) (Harlan, J., concurring). **A** In this case, Respondents demonstrated their expectation of privacy when they lowered the blinds to the apartment's window. Society should be prepared to recognize this expectation of privacy in a friend's apartment as reasonable.

This Court has allowed Fourth Amendment protections to extend beyond the home when the defendants have legitimate expectations of privacy **1** and society can accept those expectations as legitimate. See, e.g., Minnesota v. Olson, 495 U.S. 91, 98 (1990). **B** In Olson, this Court held that the unwarranted arrest of defendant, an overnight guest, **3** was an illegal seizure. **2** Id. The Court recognized that overnight guests have a sufficient interest in the privacy of the host's home to be free from unwarranted search and seizure. **4** Id. at 96-97. Furthermore, the defendant's subjective expectation of privacy **1** & **3** was found to be reasonable because society is known to recognize the social custom of staying overnight in another's home: "We will all be hosts and we will all be guests many times in our lives. From either perspective, we think that society recognizes that a houseguest has a legitimate expectation of privacy in his host's home." **4** Id. at 98. The Court specifically noted that it is a "mistaken premise" that a place "must be one's 'home' in order for one to have a legitimate expectation of privacy there." **4** Id. at 96.

1 Issue
2 Disposition
3 Facts
4 Reasoning

Indeed, this Court has consistently found that legitimate expectations of privacy **1** exist outside the home, as long as the circumstances are those in which most people would normally expect to enjoy a feeling of privacy. Olson, 495 U.S. at 96-97. Accordingly, this Court has found that defendants did not have a legitimate expectation of privacy **1** & **2** in the contents of a car in which they were merely passengers, and where they had expressed no expectation of privacy in the areas of the car searched. **3** Rakas v. Illinois, 439 U.S. 128, 148-49 (1978). The Rakas Court specifically refused to make a finding as to whether guests in houses or apartments would be treated similarly, noting that "cars are not to be treated identically with houses or apartments for Fourth Amendment purposes." **4** Id. at 148 (citations omitted). See also Katz v. United States, 389 U.S. 347, 348 (1967) (defendant found to have legitimate expectation of privacy **1** & **2** in conversations in a closed phone booth **3**); McGuffin v. United States, 362 U.S. 257, 265 (1960) (defendant has standing **2** to challenge a search warrant used to arrest him while in a friend's apartment **3**).

The writer highlights the fact that the *Rakas* Court said that houses and apartments should receive special treatment under the Fourth Amendment. The writer can use this point to argue that guests in an apartment, unlike passengers in a car, are entitled to assert an expectation of privacy. Notice that in the parenthetical description of the *McGuffin* case, the issue was implicit: The writer trusts the reader to assume that the *McGuffin* Court was addressing in some way the issue of expectations of privacy, as all of the other cases did. Of course, if the *McGuffin* Court did *not* address that issue, the parenthetical should have made that clear, e.g., "analyzing *res ipsa* issue, court found that . . . ."

6.1.3
ACCURACY IN CASE DESCRIPTIONS

As noted above, an effective case description includes the relevant issue, disposition, facts, and reasoning. It should go without saying that legal writers should not misrepresent any of these elements. Say it I must, however. When I chat with judges and law clerks and quiz them about their legal writing pet peeves, many mention wordiness and poor organization. Almost all of them, however, complain about attorneys who misrepresent the facts or the law. Law clerks describe the many times that they have read in a brief that a case stands for one proposition, only to consult the case and find that it stood for some wholly unrelated point, or worse, that it contradicted the very point the attorney was using the case to make.

So the first thing you need to remember about accuracy is that someone will be checking your work. And don't count on escaping scrutiny if you are submitting a brief to an overworked and understaffed trial court; at the very least, your opponent should be checking the validity of your cited cases.[4] Don't be tempted to misrepresent case law, either through negligence or willfulness. The momentary satisfaction of presenting an argument with a veneer of validity is not worth the cost in reputation and future credibility. Furthermore, you may face sanctions; ABA Model Rule 3.3(a) provides that a lawyer shall not "knowingly make a false statement of fact or law to a tribunal."

Accordingly, let us presume that you are not going to knowingly misrepresent cases; how can you avoid doing so negligently? First, avoid two common shortcuts that often lead to mistakes; second, be careful to avoid characterizing dicta as holdings, particularly when describing certain categories of cases.

One shortcut to avoid is relying on how others have characterized cases. If you read a memo, brief, or court opinion that characterizes a case in a certain way, it is tempting to repeat that characterization yourself.[5] Certainly, you may reason, that attorney or that judge would not have misrepresented the law. Resist the temptation. Take the time to click through to the cited case and to read it for yourself to verify that it says what you think it says. Furthermore, be sure to use Shepard's, Keycite, and BCite, and to conduct further research to verify that the case is still valid law. Even if the judge or attorney did not misrepresent the law, more recent authorities may have changed the validity of that case. Thus, read it and update it yourself; don't rely on the work of others.

Another shortcut to avoid is using a case as authority when you have read only an isolated paragraph or two. Modern computer research can often send legal researchers on a cavalcade of clicking, jumping from one source to another to another, and from one use of a search term to the next. If you are not careful, you can end up citing a dissenting opinion as

---

[4] Admittedly, some lawyers do not take this seemingly obvious step. Take note, and be sure to do so with your own opponents. It is both satisfying and effective to be able to say to a court—in an oral argument, a responding brief, or a reply brief—that the very case that your opponent cites actually hurts rather than helps his or her argument.

[5] Of course, in law school, an academic honor code may forbid you to consult attorney briefs, or to use them without citing them as the source of your analysis. Even if it were permissible to use them without citation, however, you should not rely on their validity.

authority. One reason that this happens is that every paragraph of a case looks the same on a computer screen; if a hotlink or a search term jump takes you to the middle of an opinion, you have no way of immediately telling from that paragraph if you are reading a majority opinion, a concurrence, or a dissent.[6] If you don't take the time to discern the relevant issue, disposition, facts, and reasoning, you may not discover that you are reading something other than the majority opinion.

The second way that writers may negligently misrepresent the law is by failing to distinguish dicta from holdings, especially in what I refer to as *kickback cases.* A kickback case is a case that comes to a court of appeals after the trial court has granted a motion to dismiss or a motion for summary judgment. If the court of appeals reverses and remands the decision, it in essence "kicks it back" to the court below. But a decision to reverse and remand does not necessarily mean that the court made any *findings* as to the merits regarding how the law applies to the facts. In reversing a grant of a motion for summary judgment, the court may be doing no more than finding that a dispute exists as to the material facts. When reversing a grant of a motion to dismiss, the court is merely finding that the pleadings were sufficient to state a claim, not that the pleadings were true or that the plaintiff will necessarily succeed in his or her cause of action. It is particularly important to remember that the standard of review for a motion to dismiss requires a court to presume that a complaint's factual allegations are true. This presumption does *not* mean, however, that the allegations are in fact true or that the plaintiff will be able to establish at trial that they are true.

For example, in a 1991 case,[7] the plaintiffs had alleged that police officers had owed a duty to protect a man made helpless by drunkenness when they interfered with acquaintances who were helping the intoxicated man. These acquaintances left the scene when the officers took control of the situation, the complaint alleged, and the man later fell to his death after the officers ordered him to walk home alone. In granting (and affirming the granting of) defendants' motion to dismiss, the trial court and the court of appeals found that the defendants owed no duty to the plaintiff's decedent under the facts alleged. The state supreme court reversed the decision, noting that the Restatement of Torts provides that a person owes a helpless person a duty of care when he or she "takes charge" of that person and then leaves the person in a worse situation. Accordingly, the court reversed the decision below.

---

[6] As of this writing, no computer databases use color, shading, or another graphic means to signal researchers when they are not reading part of a majority opinion. Even if they do, however, you should never rely on a case without verifying that the language you are relying on is part of the majority opinion.

[7] *Russell v. City of Columbia*, 406 S.E.2d 338 (S.C. 1991).

A careless writer, trying to explain the rule about taking charge of a helpless individual, might misrepresent the court's holding by quoting a partial sentence with a misleading introduction:

▽ BAD EXAMPLE

The court held that "once the police officers took control of the situation and preempted individuals already attempting to aid the petitioner's obviously injured and intoxicated decedent, respondents incurred a duty to follow through and finish what was begun." Russell v. City of Columbia, 406 S.E.2d 338, 339 (S.C. 1991).

The *language* is quoted accurately; the context, however, is not accurate. A law clerk who went to read the decision would find that three words missing from the sentence create a vastly different impression of the case (the emphasis is added):

Petitioner argues that once the police officers took control of the situation and preempted individuals already attempting to aid the petitioner's obviously injured and intoxicated decedent, respondents incurred a duty to follow through and finish what was begun.

The state supreme court did not find that the officers had incurred a duty of care or that the facts were accurate as pleaded. It merely restated the petitioner's argument and found that the complaint was adequate to state a cause of action. In contrast, notice how the writer in this example accurately portrays the disposition of the issue and uses the word "may" to indicate the lack of a legal holding:

△ GOOD EXAMPLE

Persons may incur a duty to a helpless person when they send away others who are rendering aid. Russell v. City of Columbia, 406 S.E.2d 338, 339 (S.C. 1991) (complaint sufficient to state cause of action as to duty when it alleged that officers questioning intoxicated man sent away persons who were trying to help him).

Thus, you can still cite to a kickback case; you must, however, accurately portray the issue and its disposition in any case description.

Accurately describing authority cases is one of the best ways to educate a court about the meaning of the law. You will increase your chances of doing so both effectively and accurately if you make sure to (1) provide sufficient information about the issue, disposition, facts, and reasoning; (2) focus the information on the issue currently under discussion; (3) use language efficiently to avoid unnecessary wordiness; (4) use parenthetical rather than textual descriptions as appropriate for rule authorities or less significant cases; and (5) take care to avoid misrepresenting the cases you cite.

6.2
USING QUOTATIONS EFFECTIVELY IN CASE DESCRIPTIONS

Quotations can be used very effectively to provide proof and support for the brief writer's assertions. When using quotations from cases, however, it's good to keep a couple of points in mind. First of all, you should usually paraphrase rather than quote language from cases. Quotation marks draw the reader's attention, and you want to save that special attention for important statements. Generally, use direct quotations only when you are stating rules or other language at issue, or when you are justifying a conclusion you have drawn about the meaning of an authority. Of course, whether you are quoting or paraphrasing, be sure to provide appropriate citations.[8]

Writers' problems with quotations from cases tend to fall into the two categories of "not enough" and "too much." Some writers drop quotations into their arguments without giving the reader enough information about the case. Without sufficient context, the quotation is meaningless. Other writers give the reader too much quoted language, leaving the reader to complete the writer's job of sifting through the language and sorting out its meaning. Police your writing to avoid these problems.

6.2.1
NOT ENOUGH CONTEXT

Legend has it that Marie Antoinette once said, "Let them eat cake!" If you don't know the context of that remark, she sounds like a pretty nice person. She sounds a lot less friendly, however, once you learn that she supposedly said it while looking down at the peasants in the street who were crying for bread.

Keep Marie in mind when you are tempted to drop a pithy quote from an obscure case into the middle of your rule explanation section. If the judge doesn't know what that court was looking at—i.e., the issue, the rule, and the facts—when it made that statement, he or she can't begin to understand the significance of the quote without looking the case up. And since most judges don't have time to read the cases cited in the briefs, the quote may have a negative impact: The judge will be annoyed at being given insufficient or misleading information.

Thus, when using a quotation from a case, be sure you have provided the reader with the type of context mentioned in Section 6.1. Do not drop a quotation into your argument like a chocolate chip into batter:

---

[8] See Section 6.5.1 for information on when to provide citations.

▼ BAD EXAMPLE

This Court has noted that generalizations "concerning parent-child relations . . . become less acceptable as the age of the child increase[s]." Caban v. Mohammed, 441 U.S. 380, 382 (1979). Thus, the gender-based generalizations in this case are invalid.

An altered quotation with an unaccompanied citation does not fill the court with confidence about the validity of your argument. Instead, include the details that will give context for the quotation:

▲ GOOD EXAMPLE

1 Issue
2 Disposition
3 Facts
4 Reasoning

As far back as 1979, this Court struck down 2 a statute that characterized parent-child relationships between unwed fathers and their children differently from those of unwed mothers. 3 Caban v. Mohammed, 441 U.S. 380, 382 (1979). While conceding that unwed mothers might be closer to their children at birth, the Court stated that the generalization 1 would become "less acceptable as a basis for legislative distinctions" as the age of the child increased. Id. 4

Quotations can also be used effectively in a parenthetical:

As far back as 1979, this Court struck down 2 a statute that characterized parent-child relationships between unwed fathers and their children differently from those of unwed mothers. 3 Caban v. Mohammed, 441 U.S. 380, 382 (1979) (noting that any generalizations 1 would become "less acceptable as a basis for legislative distinctions" as the child grew older) 4.

By making a quotation part of a coherent case description, you make it more likely that the quotation will do the job of convincing the court that the case stands for the proposition you say it does.

6.2.2
TOO MUCH QUOTED LANGUAGE

Some writers are so enamored with the court's language that they are loathe to paraphrase. Instead, they simply provide page after page of excerpted quotes and let the reader determine the significance of the quoted language. "Overquoting" creates two problems. First, the writer is not doing his or her job. The writer is not supposed to provide the raw material to the readers and let them sort out what it all means. The writer's job is to research the law, synthesize the available information, and write up the analysis in a way that allows the reader to understand the situation with a minimum of effort.

The second problem is related to the first. A reader—a judge in this context—who is constantly asked to consume and digest lengthy quotations may lose the thread of the argument. As a practical matter, many readers (including some of the people reading this book) skip long quotations.

Judges who are reading briefs may do so because they know that the quotation says nothing about the case currently before the court; instead, it talks about another case, which must somehow be connected to the current case. Writers who overuse long quotes frequently do so because they have not figured out that connection and thus cannot make the connection within the argument. They compensate by giving the reader background reading that may, with luck and some work, allow the reader to reach the conclusion that the writer espouses. Since the writer, rather than the reader, is supposed to do the work, it is usually ineffective to use lengthy quotations.

The following example is from a student-written brief written in the case of *Chicago v. Morales*, 527 U.S. 41 (1999). In that case, the city of Chicago argued in favor of the constitutionality of a statute that allowed the arrest of people who "loitered" with gang members and who refused to disperse on police order. The writer of the following example apparently wanted the reader to use the quoted language to draw the conclusion that laws that promote "peace and quiet" are constitutional:

▽ BAD EXAMPLE

This Court has provided almost absolute protection to speech of a political nature. **1** In 1969, the Court found the arrest of demonstrators for disorderly conduct3 to be unconstitutional **2** under the First Amendment. **1** & **4** Gregory v. Chicago, 394 U.S. 111, 116 (1969). The Court made this finding in favor of political speech even though the picketers' actions led to a disruption of the peace and quiet of a neighborhood by picketing in front of the mayor's home. **3** Id. at 111. A concurring opinion stressed the lawfulness and peacefulness of the demonstration **3** as well as the petitioners' First Amendment right to engage in that activity. **4** Id. at 121 (Black, J., concurring). However, Justice Black also declared:

1 Issue
2 Disposition
3 Facts
4 Reasoning

> Plainly, however, no mandate in our Constitution leaves States and governmental units powerless to pass laws to protect the public from the kind of boisterous and threatening conduct that disturbs the tranquility of spots selected by the people either for homes, wherein they can escape the hurly-burly of the outside business and political world, or for public and other buildings that require peace and quiet to carry out their functions, such as courts, libraries, schools, and hospitals. **4**

Id. at 118 (Black, J., concurring). Therefore, even if loitering were treated as a fundamental right, Petitioner possesses a significant, legitimate interest in limiting criminal street gang members' right to loiter for no purpose.

Readers who skipped the quote would have no way of knowing where the writer's "therefore" came from. Even readers who read the quote would have to figure out for themselves the significance of the quoted language.

If you are tempted to use a lengthy quotation, try one of two tactics to help ensure that your readers will understand your message.

The first and perhaps most obvious solution is to try to shorten the quote. Start by underlining the language that is most significant to your argument:

> Plainly, however, <u>no mandate in our Constitution</u> leaves States and governmental units powerless to pass laws to protect the public from the kind of boisterous and <u>threatening conduct</u> that <u>disturbs the tran-quility</u> of spots selected by the people either for homes, wherein they can escape the hurly-burly of the outside business and political world, or for public and other buildings that require peace and quiet to carry out their functions, such as courts, libraries, schools, and hospitals.

Then, quote only the underlined material (after removing the underlining), and incorporate a paraphrase of the rest of the quotation into your argument:

⚠ GOOD EXAMPLE

This Court has provided almost absolute protection to speech of a political nature. ① <u>Gregory v. Chicago</u>, 394 U.S. 111, 116 (1969). In <u>Gregory</u>, the Court found the arrest of demonstrators for disorderly conduct ③ to be unconstitutional ② under the First Amendment. ④ <u>Id</u>. The Court made this finding in favor of political speech even though the picketers' actions led to a disruption of the peace and quiet of a neighborhood by picketing in front of the mayor's home. ③ <u>Id</u>. at 111. A concurring opinion stressed the lawfulness and peacefulness of the demonstration ③ as well as the petitioners' First Amendment right to engage in that activity. ④ <u>Id</u>. at 121 (Black, J., concurring). However, Justice Black also declared that "no mandate in our Constitution" prevents states from passing laws that protect the public from "threatening conduct" that "disturbs the tranquility" of homes or certain public buildings. ④ <u>Id</u>. at 118 (Black, J., concurring). Therefore, even if loitering were treated as a fundamental right, Petitioner possesses a significant, legitimate interest in limiting criminal street gang members' right to loiter for no purpose.

① Issue
② Disposition
③ Facts
④ Reasoning

In the alternative, you may determine that the lengthy quote is absolutely necessary for your argument. If this is the case, promote the effectiveness of the quotation by articulating the conclusions you want the reader to draw from it and putting those conclusions into the body of your argument. I recommend using what I refer to as an *NPR Introduction*[9] before the quotation.

---

[9] Previous editions of this text have referred to a "Tom Brokaw Introduction," and a "Katie Couric Introduction," but since they are no longer full-time newscasters, I have changed this label accordingly. As you probably know, "NPR" is an abbreviation for "National Public Radio," which broadcasts programs on public radio stations throughout the country.

An NPR Introduction is an introduction that focuses the reader's attention on the point the writer is using the quotation to prove or establish. I call it that because reporters on NPR and other broadcast outlets constantly introduce little snippets of interviews or public events. In much the same way, a long quote is a little snippet of an opinion or other legal document. Legal writers, unfortunately, often give readers unfocused introductions like, "The Court noted," or, as in the previous illustration, "Justice Black also declared." In contrast, newscasters almost never give introductions like, "The President said," or "The Senator noted." Instead, they give the audience some context and essentially tell them what to listen for when they hear the quoted language.

The illustration below is from a broadcast in which a reporter on *Morning Edition* on NPR excerpted pieces of interviews with people who design video games. The excerpt below focuses on how acceptable subject matter for video games has evolved over the years. Notice how the (italicized) language leading up to the quotation paraphrases the message of the quote to prepare the audience for what is to come:

GOOD EXAMPLE

LARCHUK: Lucas Pope designed the game "Papers, Please." In this game, the player is a border guard working for a fictional communist country. The player is forced to make difficult choices about who can cross the border, all while making barely enough money to help his family survive. *Pope says today's developers have a broad definition of what a videogame can be.*

LUCAS POPE: Like, my generation, or the people who make games now, they grew up with games their whole life. Probably the first generation that did that. So I think it's really natural to like consider that you can have a game about anything.[10]

In the same way, you should prepare your audience for a long quotation by stating the conclusion you want the reader to draw from it:

GOOD EXAMPLE

However, Justice Black also pointed out that governments can prohibit certain behaviors in public places to protect the public:

> Plainly, however, no mandate in our Constitution leaves States and governmental units powerless to pass laws to protect the public from the kind of boisterous and threatening conduct that disturbs the tranquility of spots selected by the people either for homes, wherein they can escape the hurly-burly of the outside business and political world, or for public and other buildings that require peace and quiet

---

[10] *Morning Edition: In Gaming, a Shift from Enemies to Emotions* (Natl. Pub. Radio broadcast Jan. 7, 2014) (transcript available at http://www.npr.org/templates/transcript/transcript.php?storyId=255247261) (last visited on Jan. 11, 2014).

> to carry out their functions, such as courts, libraries, schools, and hospitals.

<u>Id</u>. at 118 (Black, J., concurring). **Therefore, it is possible for municipalities to protect both the Constitution and the peace and quiet of their communities with appropriate legislation.**

Use an NPR Introduction to help the reader to get the most out of lengthy quotations. The focused introduction will encourage the reader to read the quote by directing his or her attention and making it easier to understand the point of the quotation. Even if the reader does skip the quote, the writer has still articulated the point of the quotation in a place that the reader will see it and in a way that the reader can understand.

6.3
USING LANGUAGE PRECISELY WHEN ANALOGIZING AND DISTINGUISHING CASES

Analogizing and distinguishing relevant authority cases can be a vital part of the application sections of your argument. By showing the reader how a case is like or unlike a relevant case, a writer can convince the reader to apply the rule in a way that will achieve the desired result. Note that your application section should not *begin* with the analogy or distinction. Instead, begin with an explicit assertion about how the law applies to the facts (generally, "phrase-that-pays equals or does not equal case facts"). Use the relevant cases to support that assertion. Do not begin your application this way:

▽ BAD EXAMPLE OF BEGINNING OF RULE APPLICATION

This case is like <u>McGuffin</u>.

Instead, begin by telling the reader how the law applies to the facts:

△ GOOD EXAMPLE OF BEGINNING OF RULE APPLICATION

Mr. Pillion had a reasonable expectation of privacy. Like the defendant in <u>McGuffin</u>, . . .

Your case analogies and distinctions will be most effective if they are *precise*. Do not analogize a specific fact to a whole case:

▽ BAD EXAMPLE

Like <u>Robinson</u>, the Defendant here had committed an arrestable offense.

This comparison is inapt because one defendant, by definition, cannot be "like" a whole case. Make your analogy or distinction specific. Compare defendants to defendants, and other actors and things to their specific counterparts in the authority case. These illustrations make the comparisons explicit:

△ GOOD EXAMPLES

In the present case, Respondents, like the defendants in <u>Lewis</u> and <u>Hicks</u>, were present on property for the sole purpose of conducting criminal business.

Like the officer in <u>Lewis</u>, Officer Thielen observed only activities that were a necessary part of Respondents' illegal business. During the entire time Officer Thielen watched the apartment occupants, the occupants did nothing but divide and package cocaine. <u>See</u> Record at E-2, G-14.

Unlike the car at issue in <u>Rakas</u>, an apartment is a private dwelling not normally open to the public view.

These examples also provide details from the client's case that make the analogies vivid. The writer must do more than make the bare statement that "this case is like (or unlike) *McGuffin*" if the reader is to see the connection or the disconnection between the two cases. In the next example, the writer takes care to provide the details that will clarify the distinctions between the two cases:

△ GOOD EXAMPLE

Unlike the defendant in <u>Katz</u>, who argued that he sought privacy by closing the door to his phone booth, Respondents introduced no evidence of conduct that demonstrated an intent to keep their activities private. Though the blinds were drawn, there is no indication that Respondents drew them. <u>See</u> Record at E-2, E-10. On the night in question, Respondents were present in a first-floor apartment that had several windows <u>at</u> ground level. Record G-26. The windows faced a public area that apartment residents and nonresidents frequented. Record G-69, G-70. As darkness fell in early evening, Respondents sat illuminated under a chandelier light at a table directly in front of one of these windows. Record G-13. Only a pane of glass and a set of blinds that featured a series of laths, Record G-50, separated Respondents from the adjacent common area. On the night in question, the blinds, though drawn, had a gap in them; the gap was large enough for a citizen who passed by and an officer who stood a foot or more from the window to view easily the entire illuminated interior scene. Record G-13.

Individuals in Respondents' position would have known and expected that a passerby could look through the gaps in the blinds and see into the illuminated kitchen. Thus, Respondents could not have actually expected that their illegal activities would go unnoticed.

This application is somewhat long, but the details are necessary for the reader to understand how the law applies to the facts. Although analogies and distinctions are not always needed, make sure that when you do include them, you focus them on the specific people or things that you want to compare. Second, make sure that you provide the details that allow the reader to understand both the comparison and the application of law to facts.

6.4
DEALING WITH NONPRECEDENTIAL, OR "UNPUBLISHED," OPINIONS

In recent years, the "publication" and use of unpublished opinions—now more commonly referred to as "nonprecedential opinions"—has become controversial, with some courts forbidding their citation, others allowing them with some restrictions, and one court holding that rules limiting use of unpublished decisions are unconstitutional.[11] Rule 32.1 of the Federal Rules of Appellate Procedure mandates that, as to opinions issued after January 1, 2007, "[a] court may not prohibit or restrict the citation of federal judicial opinions, orders, judgments, or other written dispositions that have been . . . designated as 'unpublished,' 'not for publication,' 'non-precedential,' 'not precedent,' or the like." Because the rules about citation of nonprecedential opinions vary from jurisdiction to jurisdiction,[12] the most important thing to do is to consult both the rules of the jurisdiction and the local rules of the court when deciding whether to cite to them.

All United States Supreme Court opinions are published, as are virtually all opinions of state supreme courts. State and federal trial courts and intermediate appellate courts, however, currently designate a significant percentage of their opinions as nonprecedential or unpublished. Professor Amy Sloan reports that, in 2008, "84% of opinions issued by the federal courts of appeals [were] nonprecedential."[13] Actually, because of the availability of opinions on the Internet and on research services such as Bloomberg, Lexis, and Westlaw, many so-called unpublished decisions are not unpublished in the real sense. Instead, they are decisions that the court has decided to designate as nonprecedential, perhaps because the

---

[11] *Anastasoff v. United States*, 223 F.3d 898, 899 (8th Cir. 2000), *vacated as moot on reh'g en banc*, 235 F.3d 1054 (8th Cir. 2000).

[12] For example, the Minnesota Rules of Civil Appellate Procedure provide that "[u]npublished opinions and order opinions are not precedential except as law of the case, res judicata or collateral estoppel, and may be cited only as provided in Minnesota Statutes, section 480A.08, subd. 3 (1996)." Minn. R. Civ. App. Proc. 136.01(b) (2014).

[13] Amy E. Sloan, *If You Can't Beat 'em, Join 'em: A Pragmatic Approach to Nonprecedential Opinions in the Federal Appellate Courts*, 86 Neb. L. Rev. 895, 898 (2008) (citing Statistics Div., Admin. Office of the U.S. Courts, 2006 Annual Report of the Director: Judicial Business of the United States Courts 52 (2007)).

judges believe that they address routine issues that will not add significantly to the body of law.[14]

The local rules of the various federal appellate courts and of the various state courts treat nonprecedential decisions in a variety of ways. Some courts have promulgated rules that seem to favor the issuance of precedential decisions, while others disfavor their issuance, and still others are silent.[15] Illinois Supreme Court Rule 23, for example, designates categories of appellate court decisions as precedential or nonprecedential, and section (a) of that rule explains which decisions are appropriate for "full opinions":

> The decision of the Appellate Court may be expressed in one of the following forms: a full opinion, a concise written order, or a summary order conforming to the provisions of this rule. All dispositive opinions and orders shall contain the names of the judges who rendered the opinion or order.
>
> (a) Opinions. A case may be disposed of by an opinion only when a majority of the panel deciding the case determines that at least one of the following criteria is satisfied:
>
> (1) the decision establishes a new rule of law or modifies, explains or criticizes an existing rule of law; or
> (2) the decision resolves, creates, or avoids an apparent conflict of authority within the Appellate Court.

Although this rule does not distinguish between "published" and "non-published" decisions, the court's rule designates both kinds of "orders" as nonprecedential. Furthermore, in contrast to the federal rule, this state court rule (at 23(e)) forbids citation of nonprecedential decisions except in limited circumstances:

> (e) **Effect of Orders.**
>
> (1) [A concise written order or a summary order] is not precedential and may not be cited by any party except to support contentions of double jeopardy, *res judicata*, collateral estoppel or law of the case. When cited for these purposes, a copy of the order shall be furnished to all other counsel and the court.

Because a search on the Internet or on Westlaw, Bloomberg, or Lexis may turn up nonprecedential opinions, you must know what the rules are in the court to which you are writing. If you don't know the rules, find out. Check the library or the court's Web site, or call the clerk of the

---

[14] *E.g.*, K. K. DuVivier, *Are Some Words Better Left Unpublished? Precedent and the Role of Unpublished Decisions*, 3 J. App. Prac. & Process 397, 399 (2001).
[15] Sloan, *supra* n.13, at 909-10.

court. If the court does allow citation to nonprecedential opinions, and you cite any in your brief, be sure to attach copies of them as needed to the briefs that you serve on the court and on opposing counsel. Federal Rule of Appellate Procedure 32.1, for example, mandates that a party who cites any federal "written disposition that is not available in a publicly accessible electronic database" must file and serve a copy of the document with the brief or other document submitted to the court. The comments to the rule indicate that "commercial databases" are considered to be "publicly accessible," so any decision available on Lexis, Westlaw, or Bloomberg presumably would not need to be filed.

Nonprecedential opinions require different citation forms. The *ALWD Guide to Legal Citation,* Rule 12.13, for example, describes how to cite nonprecedential opinions that are available only on commercial databases and will never be published in a print reporter. The writer should provide the case name; the docket number (preceded by "No."); its database identifier as shown in the caption; and a court/date parenthetical, with the exact date of decision.

FORMAT OF CITATION TO NONPRECEDENTIAL DECISION AVAILABLE ONLY ON DATABASES

[*Case Name*], No. [Docket Number], [Database Identifier] [pinpoint] ([Court/Exact Date of Decision])

EXAMPLES OF CITATIONS TO NONPRECEDENTIAL DECISION AVAILABLE ONLY ON DATABASES

Radar Rim, Inc. v. CMB Mortg. Servs., Inc., No. 04 C 1945, 2004 U.S. Dist. Lexis 21431, at *1 (N.D. Ill. Oct. 21, 2004).[16]

Particularly if the case is a recent decision, you may decide to provide additional parenthetical material to distinguish a decision that is unpublished because it is so recent from a decision that is unpublished because the court designated it as nonprecedential:

McGuffin v. Coleman, No. LCW25890856 (Fla. 15th Cir. Jun. 13, 2014) (court-designated nonprecedential decision) (copy attached).

In addition or in the alternative, you may want to state explicitly that you are citing to a nonprecedential decision in the text of your argument:

The Ninth District Court of Appeals, in a nonprecedential decision, endorsed just this interpretation in 1992. Restrepo v. McGuffin, No. AB9123561A4 (Ohio App. 9th Dist. Jan. 24, 1992) (copy attached).

Regardless of formal citation rules, some courts may designate a nonprecedential opinion by putting the word "unpublished" in a parenthetical at

---

[16] Association of Legal Writing Directors & Coleen M. Barger, *ALWD Guide to Legal Citation* (5th ed., Aspen 2014). Rule 12.12 addresses methods for citing cases that will be, but are not yet, published in hard copy. Note that the rules in the ALWD Manual produce citations identical to those produced when following the rules in the Bluebook.

the end of the citation.[17] Try to find out about local rules and local customs when deciding whether and how to cite nonprecedential opinions. When citing them, err on the side of giving too much information to avoid violating court rules.

6.5
USING CITATIONS EFFECTIVELY

6.5.1
WHEN TO CITE

The first challenge for many legal writers is figuring out when citations are necessary. Generally, you *must* include a citation at the end of every sentence in which you state a legal proposition, refer to a new authority, or quote or paraphrase information from a court opinion (or other source). One of the few occasions on which you may *omit* a citation is when you have already analyzed an authority and are applying that authority's rule to your case. For example, the statement that "the *McGuffin* rule applies here" does not need a citation in a discussion in which the writer has already introduced and cited *McGuffin*.

Some legal propositions are so basic that they may seem self-evident. If you are asking a court to apply such a legal principle to your client's case, however, you should cite an authority that controls in that court's jurisdiction.

▽ BAD EXAMPLE

It is well known that the Fifth Amendment's protection against compelled self-incrimination applies to the states.

△ GOOD EXAMPLE

The Fifth Amendment's protection against compelled self-incrimination applies to the states through the Fourteenth Amendment's Due Process Clause. See Malloy v. Hogan, 378 U.S. 1, 6 (1964).

Legal writing is referenced writing, and readers expect frequent citation. You can use short citation forms and effective sentence structures to keep your writing readable, but you must include citations whenever you state a legal proposition, refer to an authority for the first time, or quote or paraphrase material from a source. This means that within the rule explanation section, for example, every sentence may have a citation after it.

---

[17] *E.g., State v. Murray*, 271 P.3d 739, 741 (Kan. 2012) (citing *Murray v. State*, No. 91,724, 2005 WL 283604 (Kan. App.) (unpublished opinion), *rev. denied*, 279 Kan. 1007 (2005)).

Many of the citations may be in the *"Id."* form, but the reader will still expect and need citations.

6.5.2
DISTINGUISHING BETWEEN AUTHORITIES AND SOURCES

Although this text, and many legal writers, often refer to all cases, statutes, and the like as "authorities," the reality is that some are only "sources": They contain information that the court may find interesting and relevant, but the source has no *authority* over the court reading the brief. Too many legal writers do not make this distinction, and they annoy and frustrate courts by their imprecise use of citations.

I do not mean to imply that you can cite only to cases, for example, that are written by authoritative courts. Rather, you need to recognize that there are at least three different possible meanings for a citation, some of which may overlap. The citation may mean simply, "I am not the person who first said or thought of this statement." This kind of citation is used to give appropriate credit to the originator of an idea and to avoid charges of plagiarism. A citation may also mean, "Here is the source of the law, facts, or policy I just mentioned, so you can find it if you want." This kind of citation—and its accuracy—is very important for judges and their clerks. Finally, a citation can mean, "This statement is *the law*." This use of citation is very important for the brief-writer because it is used to justify and support legal arguments: In this situation, the writer is citing not merely a source, but an authority.

Unfortunately, the same citation forms are used for all three of these categories of citations, and so brief writers must be sure that their text makes the distinction. If the writer says nothing, the reader's instinct is to presume that a cited statement is authoritative, and the reader may be startled or frustrated when he or she looks at the citation and realizes that the cited case (or other source) is not authoritative.

Writers who quote or paraphrase relevant legal assertions from law review articles and nonmandatory courts must make the necessary distinction by introducing the material with a phrase indicating that an authoritative court did not make the statement. Here are some bad examples from a brief written to a federal district court within the First Circuit:

▽ BAD EXAMPLES

Refusing to allow individual liability for supervisors under Title VII is "manifestly inconsistent" with Title VII's "underlying rationale and primary goals." Tracy L. Gonos, <u>A Policy Analysis of Individual Liability—The Case for Amending Title VII to Hold Individuals Personally Liable for Their Illegal Discriminatory Actions</u>, 2 N.Y.U. J. Legis. & Pub. Poly. 265, 270 (1998-1999).

> With Title VII, Congress intended not only to make discriminatory acts by both employers and their agents actionable, but also to make "those who discriminate"—both employers and their agents—jointly and severally liable for their discriminatory acts. <u>Wyss v. General Dynamics Corp.</u>, 24 F. Supp. 2d 202, 206 (D.R.I. 1998) (citation omitted).

With both of these examples, the statements are relevant legal assertions that are followed by a citation and are not preceded by a qualifier. In both situations, the reader would instinctively presume that the citation provides authority for the validity of the statement, and would be frustrated to see the nonauthoritative citation following the statement. To avoid this problem, simply use qualifying language that reveals that the source is not authoritative. Generally, the best way to do this is to mention or refer to the source; you need not announce to the court that a particular source is not authoritative:

▽ BAD EXAMPLES

> Although not authoritative, a commentator has noted that refusing to allow individual liability for supervisors under Title VII is "manifestly inconsistent" with Title VII's "underlying rationale and primary goals." Tracy L. Gonos, <u>A Policy Analysis of Individual Liability—The Case for Amending Title VII to Hold Individuals Personally Liable for Their Illegal Discriminatory Actions</u>, 2 N.Y.U. J. Legis. & Pub. Poly. 265, 270 (1998-1999).

> A persuasive court has found that Congress intended for Title VII not only to make discriminatory acts by both employers and their agents actionable, but also to make "those who discriminate"—both employers and their agents—jointly and severally liable for their discriminatory acts. <u>Wyss v. General Dynamics Corp.</u>, 24 F. Supp. 2d 202, 206 (D.R.I. 1998) (citation omitted).

The judge or his or her clerk knows that commentators and nonauthoritative courts are only persuasive authority. The best way to make them aware of the nonauthoritative nature of the statement is to succinctly reveal the source in text. If possible, you should also give the court a reason to find value in the statement:

△ GOOD EXAMPLES

> One commentator has argued that refusing to allow individual liability for supervisors under Title VII is "manifestly inconsistent" with Title VII's "underlying rationale and primary goals." Tracy L. Gonos, <u>A Policy Analysis of Individual Liability—The Case for Amending Title VII to Hold Individuals Personally Liable for Their Illegal Discriminatory Actions,</u> 2 N.Y.U. J. Legis. & Pub. Poly. 265, 270 (1998-1999). Title VII's underlying rationale is revealed in Section. . . .

> Another district court in the First Circuit has faced this same issue and agreed that Congress intended to make discriminatory acts by both employers and their agents actionable under Title VII. <u>Wyss v. General Dynamics Corp.</u>, 24 F. Supp. 2d 202, 206 (D.R.I. 1998) (citation omitted). That court further noted that Congress also intended to make "those who discriminate"—both employers and their agents—jointly and severally liable for their discriminatory acts. <u>Id</u>.

In the first example, the writer tries to increase the value of the source by tying its assertion to specific statutory language. In the second example, the writer tells the court why it should care about this nonauthoritative source by stating that the court was addressing the same issue as the issue the court is currently addressing. Admittely, citing to a mandatory authority is almost always preferable. When other citations are necessary, however, the practical brief writer does not try to hide the use of nonmandatory authority, but instead uses effective writing techniques to try to increase the value of nonmandatory sources.

6.5.3
WHERE TO CITE

As noted previously, citations in a brief will sometimes be citations to sources rather than citations to authorities. For this reason, writers should place their citations in text rather than in footnotes in almost all situations. Use footnotes for citations only on rare occasions (e.g., for occasions when a string citation is necessary[18]). Placing citations in text allows readers to identify immediately which citations are and are not authoritative citations. The reader's immediate need to understand a source's validity makes it more important for brief writers to place citations in text than it is for any other kind of legal writer. Only the brief writer has the job of marshaling mandatory and nonmandatory authorities, synthesizing rules from those authorities, applying those rules to facts, and presenting them to a decision maker. The brief writer, much more than the legal commentator or the judge, asks the reader to accept or reject legal arguments based on the authoritativeness of his or her citations. The journal writer, in contrast, may assemble citations from a variety of jurisdictions to posit a theory; the judge derives authority from his or her judicial appointment.[19] The reader of a brief, unlike the reader of a law review article or of an opinion, must reserve judgment about the validity of any legal proposition until the authoritativeness of the citation is known. Putting citations in footnotes needlessly frustrates the reader of a brief.

---

[18] See Section 6.5.5 on how to use string citations appropriately.

[19] This statement is most true about judges who sit on courts of last resort. The opinions of a trial judge or of an intermediate appellate judge, in contrast, may be more likely to be affirmed or reversed depending upon the authoritativeness of cases and other sources that they rely on.

A reader who encounters a brief with citations in footnotes has three choices for deciding what to do, and all of them are bad. First, the reader can presume that the writer is citing an authoritative source. This choice is bad because the reader may be wrong and may overvalue the validity of the writer's argument. Second, the reader can presume that the writer is *not* citing an authoritative source. This choice is bad for the same reason—the reader may be wrong—only this time, the reader will undervalue the validity of the writer's argument. Third, the reader can check each footnote to see if the citation provides an authoritative source or not. Of course, not every footnoted statement will be a legal assertion; the reader will therefore be checking footnotes that do nothing more than provide needed page numbers for quoted or paraphrased statements of fact. These citations could be passed over easily if they were in text, but in a footnote they require the same two "finding actions" that every footnote requires: First, the reader must check the number of the footnote and find the corresponding number at the bottom of the page. Second, the reader must return to the text and find the place where he or she stopped reading.

Although at least one judge prefers that citations appear in footnotes,[20] others say quite pointedly that footnotes interfere with effective reading. Speaking of footnotes in general, former Justice Arthur J. Goldberg praises elimination of all footnotes from judicial opinions in the name of increased readability.[21] Judge Abner Mikva notes that "[i]f footnotes were a rational form of communication, Darwinian selection would have resulted in the eyes being set vertically rather than on an inefficient horizontal plane."[22] More recently, both Judge Posner and Justice Scalia have protested the placement of citations in footnotes.[23] A reader who wants to read a brief responsibly—i.e., understanding the validity of legal assertions—will find footnoted citations just as distracting as any other footnotes.

The practical brief writer will remember the old saw that the only person who likes to be interrupted in the middle of a sentence is a prisoner. Presume that all citations should be incorporated in the text, and make exceptions only rarely.

---

[20] Mark Painter, *The Legal Writer: 40 Rules for the Art of Legal Writing* 47 (2d ed., Jardyce & Jardyce 2003).

[21] Arthur J. Goldberg, *The Rise and Fall (We Hope) of Footnotes*, 69 A.B.A. J. 255, 255 (1983).

[22] Abner Mikva, *Goodbye to Footnotes*, 56 U. Colo. L. Rev. 647, 647 (1985) (quoting Professor Rodell, quoted in Kenneth Lasson, *Scholarship Amok: Excesses in the Pursuit of Truth and Tenure*, 103 Harv. L. Rev. 926, 942 (1990)).

[23] J.H. Huebert, *How to Persuade Judges in the Real World*, 35 Ohio N.U. L. Rev. 829, 831 (2009) (book review of Antonin Scalia & Bryan Garner, *Making Your Case: The Art of Persuading Judges* (2008), which cites Scalia & Garner, at 35, and Richard A. Posner, *Against Footnotes*, 38 Court Rev. 24, 24 (2001)).

6.5.4
USING EFFECTIVE SENTENCE STRUCTURES TO ACCOMMODATE CITATION FORM

Incorporating citations into text is the best way to promote easy identification of the value of your authority. You will help both your reader and your user, however, if you use effective sentence structures to accommodate citations. Many writers instinctively— and wrongly— introduce a new case by beginning a sentence with a long-form citation:

▽ BAD EXAMPLE

In <u>J.E.B. v. T.B.</u>, 511 U.S. 127, 138-40 (1994), this Court held that sex-based peremptory challenges violate jurors' rights to equal protection.

This sentence is difficult to read because the citation takes up a lot of space within the sentence. Furthermore, this structure puts too much emphasis on the citation and not enough emphasis on the substance of the sentence. To solve this problem, some writers mistakenly separate the case name from the rest of the citation:

▽ BAD EXAMPLE

In <u>J.E.B. v. T.B.</u>, this Court held that sex-based peremptory challenges violate jurors' rights to equal protection. 511 U.S. 127, 138-40 (1994).

This "separated long-form" structure is also not optimal. Although some citation rules may condone this separation, it can confuse the reader, who could be expecting a long-form citation because he or she does not recall reading about the case earlier. The best way to write a readable sentence and still use correct citation form is to put the citation in a separate citation sentence:

△ GOOD EXAMPLE

This Court has held that sex-based peremptory challenges violate jurors' rights to equal protection. <u>J.E.B. v. T.B.</u>, 511 U.S. 127, 138-40 (1994).

Thus, instead of focusing the attention in your sentence on the citation, you focus it on the court that took the action or, as in this next example, on the rule itself:

△ GOOD EXAMPLE

Sex-based peremptory challenges violate jurors' rights to equal protection. <u>J.E.B. v. T.B.</u>, 511 U.S. 127, 138-40 (1994).

This structure lets the citation do its work of telling the reader the name of the case, the court, and the year of decision, but keeps it from intruding on the sentence itself. Including a case name alone in your sentence is appropriate only if you have already cited the case in full in that same discussion:

⚠ GOOD EXAMPLE

This Court has held that sex-based peremptory challenges violate jurors' rights to equal protection. J.E.B. v. T.B., 511 U.S. 127, 138-40 (1994). In J.E.B., the Court found peremptory challenges invalid because they were based on broad assumptions about men's and women's relative capabilities. Id.

Thus, structure your sentences so that all citations, and particularly long-form citations, can be placed in their own citation sentences. You can accomplish this goal by keeping the focus on the substance of the cited material rather than on the citation.

6.5.5
AVOIDING STRING CITATIONS

Judges almost uniformly condemn the use of string citations. As Judge Boyce Martin notes, "When I read a lengthy string cite in a brief or slip opinion, I often find that I have lost the gist of the argument after fighting through line after line of gobbledygook."[24] Admittedly, string citations are useful on rare occasions. For example, if you need to illustrate a trend in the law, give a brief overview of a still-developing area of law, or establish that multiple authorities in a variety of jurisdictions have followed or not followed a particular rule, a string citation may be appropriate. Two warnings: First, most cases you write briefs for will not present any of these situations, so presume that you will not need a string cite. Second, the longer the string cite, the less likely it is that anyone will look at it except the unfortunate judge's clerk who has been assigned to review all of the cited cases. You will make more friends if you have fewer string cites.

When a string cite is unavoidable, put as much information as possible into the sentence preceding the string cite. Most readers would have to struggle to pick up any information in phrases and clauses interspersed among the citations. One problem with a string citation is that it inevitably creates a very long sentence, and, psychologically, the reader tries to keep that sentence "going" in his or her brain. A sentence with text and citations interspersed is probably the hardest thing for a reader to read:

▽ BAD EXAMPLE

Several courts of appeals have considered the issue of whether a transient visitor has a legitimate expectation of privacy while within the

---

[24] Boyce F. Martin, Jr., *Judges on Judging: In Defense of Unpublished Opinions*, 60 Ohio St. L.J. 177, 193 (1999).

residence of another, <u>see, e.g.,</u> <u>United States v. Gale</u>, 136 F.3d 192 (D.C. Cir. 1998), and they have considered this issue in a variety of contexts and using a variety of factors in reaching their decisions, including the frequency of rent payments, <u>id</u>. at 193; the lack of an overnight stay, <u>United States v. Maddox</u>, 944 F.2d 1223, 1234 (6th Cir. 1991); the use of another's hotel room, <u>United States v. Carr,</u> 939 F.2d 1442, 1446 (10th Cir. 1991); the lack of evidence of connection to the residence, <u>United States v. Antone</u>, 753 F.2d 1301, 1313 (5th Cir. 1985); and mere presence in a hotel room, <u>United States v. Irizarry</u>, 673 F.2d 554, 558 (1st Cir. 1982).

To make this information easier to digest, write a sentence informing the reader of the significance of the cases, and then end it with a period. Depending on the circumstances, the string citation could be placed in a footnote; even if it is in the text, using this technique will make the citation string easier for the reader to read:

⚠ GOOD EXAMPLE

1 Issue
2 Disposition
3 Facts
4 Reasoning

Several courts of appeals have decided that a transient visitor has no legitimate expectation of privacy 1, 2 while within the residence of another, whether the residence was a home or a hotel room, 3 when the visitor did not have sufficient connection to the residence. 4 <u>See, e.g.,</u> <u>United States v. Gale</u>, 136 F.3d 192, 193 (D.C. Cir. 1998) (current day visitor's one rent payment seven months ago 3 not enough 2 to establish sufficient connection); <u>United States v. Maddox</u>, 944 F.2d 1223, 1234 (6th Cir. 1991) (attendance at drug party without overnight stay 3 does not 2 establish sufficient connection); <u>United States v. Carr</u>, 939 F.2d 1442, 1446 (10th Cir. 1991) (guest in another's hotel room 3 does not 2 have sufficient connection); <u>United States v. Antone</u>, 753 F.2d 1301, 1313 (5th Cir. 1985) (fingerprints on book not enough 2 to establish daytime visitor's 3 connection to residence); <u>United States v. Irizarry</u>, 673 F.2d 554, 558 (1st Cir. 1982) ("mere presence" in hotel room 3 not sufficient 2 to establish connection).

The best solution is one that avoids the string cite entirely. If you are using the string cite to point out the well-established fact that many courts have already agreed with a legal rule, you may be able to use a parenthetical to accomplish the goal of the string cite. Often, one of the most recent cases in a "string" will have addressed the fact that the rule is well established, and may have cited most or all of the other cases. In that situation, you may tell the reader that the cases exist and give him or her access to those cases by citing only the most recent one:

⚠ GOOD EXAMPLE

Since 1978, every Ohio court that has addressed this issue has decided in favor of the employee. <u>See, e.g.,</u> <u>Restrepo v. McGuffin Corp.</u>, 901 N.E.2d 911, 933 (Ohio 2014) (citing cases).

This citation supports an accurate statement—that every Ohio court has decided a certain type of case in a certain way—and it allows the judge or the judge's clerk to find all those decisions if needed by citing to a decision that cites them. Use this method with care. It cannot be used unless the text of your argument accurately reflects what the cited case has said about the list of cases cited. Furthermore, you should not use this method if information from each authority is important to your argument. When this method is appropriate, however, the legal writer is able to simultaneously avoid a string cite and give the reader access to multiple authorities that support his or her argument.

6.5.6
CASES THAT CITE OTHER CASES

A citation dilemma for many legal writers is what to do when citing an excerpt of a case that has quoted another case. Traditionally, writers have been encouraged to cite the original source, as the writer does in the following example:

▼ BAD EXAMPLE

A person possesses a reasonable expectation of privacy, and thus a search occurs when an officer makes an observation from a location within the curtilage of a private home. See Oliver v. United States, 466 U.S. 170, 180 (1984). Curtilage, "the land immediately surrounding and associated with the home," is "the area to which extends the intimate activity associated with the 'sanctity of a man's home and the privacies of life.'" Id. (quoting Boyd v. United States, 116 U.S. 616, 630 (1886)).

Although this guideline may be appropriate for law review articles and other publications, it is not always the best rule for brief writing. In this situation, it is doubtful that the court needs to know about an 1886 case that is the origin of the "sanctity" language.

Of course, a legal writer may need or want to cite the original source to give added credence to a discussion of a case decided by a nonmandatory court. In the example below, from a petitioner's brief in *Minnesota v. Carter*, the writer is discussing a California case that applied *Minnesota v. Olson*, a significant United States Supreme Court case that had been previously cited in that same section of the brief:

▲ GOOD EXAMPLE

In 1992, a California court found that a defendant who moved to suppress items seized at his brother's apartment while the defendant was babysitting there had a legitimate expectation of privacy. People v. Moreno, 3 Cal. Rptr. 2d 66, 70 (Cal. Ct. App. 1992). The court cited Olson and indicated that, "[l]ike 'staying overnight in another's

> home,' babysitting 'is a longstanding social custom that serves func-
> tions recognized as valuable by society."' Id. at 70 (quoting Olson, 495
> U.S. at 98).

If the reviewing court knows that the California court was basing its decision on United States Supreme Court authority, the court may give that
California decision more weight in a brief, especially if the reviewing court
is the United States Supreme Court. Thus, if knowing the origin of the
cited language could affect the Court's understanding or acceptance of
your argument, identify that source. This situation does not occur regularly in legal writing; generally, if the origin of the language is significant,
the writer should go to the original source and cite that authority in addition or instead. It is only when the relationship between the two sources is
significant—as it is when an on-point nonmandatory court applies a rule
from a mandatory court—that the reader is likely to be interested in the
origin of the quoted language.

In most other situations, however, judges looking at the citations supporting an argument want to know only that a valid court made that statement in an analogous case. They usually have little or no interest in the
original source of particular words or phrases. If the cited opinion is a valid
authority for that quote, it matters only that an authoritative court made
the statement in its majority opinion and that the statement is not dicta.
Even if that court misinterpreted the original language, what usually matters is the court's belief that the language was appropriate to apply to the
particular set of facts that was before it. Thus, determine whether your
argument would be more effective if the court you are writing to knew the
original source of the quoted language. If knowing the source would not
improve your argument's effectiveness, you can omit the citation, as long
as you inform the court that you are doing so:

GOOD EXAMPLE

> Curtilage, "the land immediately surrounding and associated with
> the home," is "the area to which extends the intimate activity associ-
> ated with the 'sanctity of a man's home and the privacies of life."' Id.
> (citation omitted).

Substituting the "citation omitted" parenthetical phrase for the full citation will allow those who wish to track the original language the opportunity to do so. Most judges and clerks, however, will be grateful that you
have not cluttered the brief with irrelevant citations.

6.5.7
IMPORTANCE OF PINPOINT CITATIONS

A pinpoint citation is a citation to the specific page on which quoted
or cited language appeared. Some legal writers use the phrases *pin cite*,

pinpoint, or *jump cite* to mean the same thing. You must include pinpoint citations *every time* you cite to a case.

Do not convince yourself that you are citing the case only "generally" and thus do not need to include a citation to the specific page. If you want your readers to be able to verify that the authorities you cite stand for the propositions you say they do, you must make it incredibly easy for them to find the law that is the source of your argument. Remember that the clerk of the judge who is writing the opinion will often be given the task of verifying the truth of the assertions in the briefs. If you do not give pinpoint citations, you may force the clerk to wade through 30- or 40-page opinions, trying to find the legal principle that you said was in there. If you cite a case for its main holding, find the page on which the court articulated that holding: That is the pinpoint page. Even if you are citing to the first page of the opinion (a rare event, since many reporters fill the first page with headnotes and other editorial information), you must still provide a pinpoint citation:

GOOD EXAMPLE

McGuffin v. Restrepo, 101 F.3d 115, 115 (6th Cir. 2015).

Think of the judges and their clerks whenever you are making a citation decision. Whenever you can make it easier for them to understand your argument by putting a little more information into the brief, you should do so.

6.6
SUMMARY

The practical brief writer has a lot to remember when trying to use case authorities effectively. Remembering the needs of the judges and clerks who must use your brief will help you (1) to include all of the authorities that are necessary; (2) to give enough information about those authorities, but not too much; (3) to present that information accurately and in a helpful way; and (4) to cite that information in a way that provides sufficient information without needlessly intruding on the text.

Chapter Seven

SEEING WHAT YOU HAVE WRITTEN

7.1
FOCUSING YOUR REVISION: USING THE SELF-GRADED DRAFT[1]

The etymology of the word *revision* shows that the word means "to see again." You can revise your writing most effectively if you can figure out a way to "see" it more effectively.

After completing a good draft of your document and checking your use of authority, the next step you should take is to check the document's content and large-scale organization. One way to check content, of course, is to review your substance. If you have not yet Shepardized, BCited, and KeyCited your authorities, now is a good time to do so.[2] While reviewing your authorities, you may wish to follow up on any unexplored leads to verify that you have marshaled the best arguments and authorities in your client's favor.

---

[1] Some of the material in this section comes from Mary Beth Beazley, *The Self-Graded Draft: Teaching Students to Revise Using Guided Self-Critique*, 3 Legal Writing 175 (1997).

[2] The best course is not to rely on any one service alone, but to use more than one.

After you have checked the validity of the points you are trying to make, the next step is to review your writing—the way in which you have made those points in your brief. At this stage, you should review the argument for structure, focus, and completeness. Of course, it is often difficult for people to review their own writing because they lack the psychological distance necessary to see what they have actually written, to distinguish between the information on the printed page and the information still "inside their heads." Using an exercise like the "self-graded draft" is one way to combat these difficulties.

Completing a self-graded draft requires you to review your argument and to complete nine fairly simple tasks within each analytical segment of the document. Although you could complete many different types of self-grading tasks, this chapter illustrates the method by describing common analytical requirements and their purposes. Each of the nine tasks should help you with one or more of the areas of structure, focus, and completeness.

The nine tasks require you to use both objective methods (highlighting) and subjective methods (marginal notes) to find and label the elements of the CREXAC formula (Conclusion, Rule, Explanation, Application, Connection-Conclusion) within *each* analytical section of the document.

7.1.1
BACKGROUND

The self-graded draft is an objective, focused critiquing exercise that helps writers avoid the self-delusion that often interferes with self-editing. Essentially, the exercise asks you to find, mark, and evaluate individual elements within each part of your document. The process of finding the elements and of labeling them or highlighting them encourages you to focus your attention on one element of the document at a time. This focus often helps to provide enough psychological distance to allow you to conduct an objective evaluation of your writing and then improve it.

An "objective" or focused critiquing method is particularly helpful in legal writing because of the predictable structure of legal documents and the predictable behavior of legal readers and legal writers. Most legal documents have a set format, and they require analytical elements that are usually found at predictable "intellectual locations" within the format. In a brief, for example, "intellectual locations" would include elements within each CREXAC unit of discourse[3]: the statement of the rule, the explanation of that rule, and the application of the rule to the facts.

---

[3] As noted in Chapter Five, I use the term *CREXAC unit of discourse* to mean a section of your document in which you use legal analysis to prove the truth or validity of an assertion. Thus, introductory material between an "A" heading and a "1" subheading would not be a CREXAC unit of discourse. Chapter Ten gives guidelines about how to write effective introductory material.

Most of us lack focus when we sit down to edit. We may review our writing by reading and rereading the document with no definite goal in mind. We may focus on typographical or grammatical errors, hoping that substantive problems will leap out at us as we read. Essentially, we are reviewing the document and asking ourselves, "Is this okay?"

The self-graded draft addresses this lack of focus by concentrating your attention on various parts of the document and then asking focused questions. For example, instead of looking at a *sentence* and asking yourself "Is this okay?" you will look at the *application of law to facts* within a particular section and ask yourself, "Did I use the phrase-that-pays when I applied law to facts? Did I include all of the legally significant facts?" This improvement in focus often helps to improve your ability to self-edit.

The second, and more difficult, problem self-editors face is that of psychological distance. Many of us find it psychologically impossible to really see what we have written. Those of us who have reviewed our own writing several weeks, months, or years after "polishing" it have had the experience of discovering glaring mistakes, inconsistencies, or other weaknesses. We are aghast; how could we have missed those mistakes? And yet the phenomenon is not that surprising.

When we write, we are, naturally, thinking about our complete message. When we later revise and edit, we see the words we wrote, and these (often inadequate) words remind our short-term memories of the complete message we had in mind when we were writing. The short-term memory then "tells" the brain the complete message, and we presume that the words we wrote contained the message. Actually, the short-term memory often fills in the blanks. The complete message may never have made it into the written word.[4] This phenomenon creates a sort of eclipse of the brain[5]: The short-term memory "passes between" the written document and our brain, "blocking" us from seeing and understanding the words that we actually wrote.

Self-grading can address your brain eclipse by requiring you to look at individual words, sentences, and elements (for example, elements of CREXAC), instead of at the document as a whole. The self-grading exercise does not ask you *whether* you included an element; it asks you to *mark* the very words that comprise the element. This marking forces you to discover for yourself what words and ideas actually made it onto the paper, and what words and ideas are still inside your brain. The self-graded draft does not create the message; it simply helps you to discover whether the document includes the complete message. If part of the message is not written down, you will not be able to find and mark it during the self-grading. In

---

[4] *Cf.* Joseph M. Williams & Joseph Bizup, *Style: Lessons in Clarity and Grace* 39 (11th ed., Pearson Education, Inc. 2014).

[5] I am grateful to Professor Nancy Rapoport for suggesting this term to describe this mental phenomenon.

this way, you will discover what parts of the message are missing, and you will be in a better position to make revision decisions.

In addition to helping you discover what analytical elements are missing, self-grading helps revision simply by focusing your attention. After you have marked the places in the document in which you applied the rule to the facts, for example, you can focus your attention on that aspect of analytical writing and critically review your work.

7.1.2
COMPLETING THE SELF-GRADING

Some writers like to complete their self-grading by working on one unit of discourse at a time, completing their marking of each section's CREXAC before moving on to the next. Others prefer to complete all of the "objective" tasks first because the highlighting that these tasks require may help them with the more subjective tasks. Whichever method you use, you should keep a separate sheet of paper or an empty word processor screen handy so that you can use private memos to note any questions or concerns that arise as you self-grade, record any possible revisions that you find necessary, and write a final comment.

Each of the self-grading tasks is listed below, followed by an explanation of how best to accomplish the task and of how that task can affect the revision process.

7.2
COMMON SELF-GRADING TASKS AND EXPLANATIONS

7.2.1
IDENTIFY THE FOCUS OF EACH CREXAC UNIT OF DISCOURSE

Within each CREXAC unit of discourse, write "focus" in the margin next to the sentence(s) in which you articulate the rule, policy, assertion, or thesis *that is the focus* of that section or subsection. Do *not* write "focus" next to every statement that could be called a rule.

A helpful self-grading task is identifying the point you are focusing on in each CREXAC unit of discourse of your document. Usually, you will be focusing on a rule that governs the issue that you are discussing, but sometimes you may be focusing on a policy, an assertion, or some other thesis. Every section of the document should be focused on *something*; identify the first place in which you articulate that something and mark it in the margin as the "focus" of that section. If you find that you cannot find an explicitly articulated focus in a given section, take a moment and draft a sentence that articulates the section's focus.

Overview of Effective "Self-Grading" Tasks

For each CREXAC unit of discourse:

1. Identify and label the Rule/Focus for that unit of discourse

   (Subjective)

2. Identify the Phrase-That-Pays and highlight it in Pink throughout that unit of discourse

   (Subjective/Objective)

3. Highlight support citations (not record citations) in Green

   (Objective)

4. Identify and label all paragraphs or sections of paragraphs that contain Rule Explanation and mark the Rule Summary

   (Subjective)

5. Highlight the client's facts (not facts from cited cases) in Blue

   (Objective)

6. Identify and label all paragraphs or sections of paragraphs that contain Rule Application

   (Subjective)

7. Identify and label the Connection-Conclusion and highlight it in Yellow

   (Subjective)

For the whole document:

8. Create a "Focus List"

   (Objective)

9. Write Private Memos & a Final Comment

   (Subjective)

7.2.2
IDENTIFY THE PHRASES-THAT-PAY WITHIN EACH CREXAC UNIT OF DISCOURSE

Within the sentence that articulates each focus, identify its phrase-that-pays and highlight that phrase-that-pays in PINK. Highlight each phrase-that-pays wherever it appears throughout its unit of discourse. Note that each CREXAC unit of discourse should have a different phrase-that-pays.

As you find or articulate the focus of each CREXAC unit of discourse, identify the phrase-that-pays that is the focus of your analysis, and highlight that phrase-that-pays wherever it appears within that unit of discourse. Remember that in most briefs, each section will have a different phrase-that-pays because each section will be focused on a different rule, policy, or other thesis. Take some time with this task; it is important to accurately identify the phrase-that-pays.

Usually, you can find the phrase-that-pays by identifying what you are trying to prove in that section. One method for identifying the phrase-that-pays is to manipulate the language of your rule and then analyze that language: (1) mentally restate the rule as an if-then proposition (do *not* presume that rules should be stated as if-then statements in the document itself); then (2) look in the "if" clause to identify what you are trying to prove. That thing that you are proving usually constitutes the main phrase-that-pays.

As noted earlier, an "if-then" rule says, "if Condition exists, then Legal Status or Legal Consequence results." The phrase-that-pays is usually found in the "if" clause; your rule explanation would try to show what the phrase-that-pays means so that, in your application section, you can analyze whether the phrase-that-pays (condition) exists in your client's case. Once you establish that the phrase-that-pays does or does not exist, you can argue in your conclusion section that the legal consequence should or should not result.

For example, if you were writing about whether the victim of a dog bite could recover damages from the owner of the dog, you might have a statutory rule that says, among other things, that the owner cannot be held liable if the victim of the dog bite was committing a trespass or other criminal offense on the dog owner's property at the time of the attack. You could turn that proposition into an "if-then" rule as follows:

> **IF the victim of a dog bite is committing a trespass or other criminal offense on the dog owner's property at the time of the attack, THEN he or she cannot recover damages for any injury or loss.**

Looking in your "if" clause, you see several items that could be the focus of analysis in a legal document. For example, you could be trying to prove (1) that the dog bite victim was *committing a trespass or other criminal offense*, (2) that the dog bite victim was *on the dog owner's property*, or (3) that the trespass or criminal offense was being committed *at the time of the attack*. Your goal is to identify what language of the rule is at issue in the particular section you are focusing on. Let's presume that, in this section, you are trying to prove that a civil trespass is included in the types of trespass described in the statute. Thus, your phrase-that-pays would be "committing a trespass or other criminal offense," and your explanation section would be devoted to establishing the meaning of that phrase.

Finding and highlighting the phrase-that-pays in each CREXAC unit of discourse can help you to evaluate whether your analysis is focused. Ideally, you should see the phrase-that-pays several times within the section. It should appear at least once within each CREXAC-related element that you mark: the focus, the explanation of that focus, the application of that focus to the facts of your client's case, and the connection-conclusion for that unit of discourse. If, after identifying the phrase-that-pays, you have a hard time finding it within the unit of discourse, you should ask yourself why. Perhaps you misidentified the phrase-that-pays. In the alternative, you may have mistakenly used synonyms instead of the phrase-that-pays, which can easily be corrected. Occasionally, "disappearing phrase-that-pays syndrome" is a symptom of an organizational problem: You may have switched your focus to another point without taking the reader along. In that situation, the self-grading process may be telling you that you need to divide one section into two or more. Whatever the reason for problems finding the phrase-that-pays, you may consider revising to correct this problem, and you should note private memo questions for your teacher.

7.2.3
IDENTIFY CITED AUTHORITIES

Highlight each citation (or reference to authority, even if not in a formal citation) in GREEN. Do *not* highlight citations to client facts, even if those facts appeared in the decisions below and thus have formal citations.

After you have identified the phrases-that-pay, a useful task is to highlight all citations to authorities that you have used to support your arguments. Be sure to highlight all kinds of citations: long-form, short-form, and *id.* citations. This task helps you to analyze the completeness of your document. You will review your authorities for quantity (do you have enough support for each point?) and for validity (do you cite at least one mandatory authority in each section? Does each non-mandatory authority have a reason for being included?). You should also review your analysis of each authority (have you provided the reader with enough information about each case?).

7.2.4
IDENTIFY THE EXPLANATION OF EACH FOCUS

Write the word "Explanation" in the margin next to the paragraphs in which you *explained* the focus. Generally, you will be marking paragraphs that contain only pink and green highlights, because in those paragraphs you will be explaining the meaning of the phrase-that-pays according to various authorities. Next, write "RS" next to the sentence(s) at the end of the rule explanation in which you summarize the rule.

Looking for green citations and pink phrases-that-pay should help you to find the explanation within each unit of discourse. Of course, do not presume that every "green and pink paragraph" is an explanation paragraph: You may have green highlights in application paragraphs if you analogized or distinguished authority cases, or, for a statutory interpretation issue, if statutory language is a "fact." Usually, however, looking for pink and green highlights is a good place to start looking for your explanation of the phrase-that-pays; your explanation probably consists of discussions of definitions of the phrase-that-pays, or descriptions of cases in which the phrase-that-pays has been applied in the past in relevant cases. The task of labeling the explanation is another step in evaluating the completeness of your analysis.

As noted in Chapter Five, a "rule summary" is almost always a strong way to end your rule explanation section. Obviously, you can look for the rule summary at the end of the rule explanation, but don't presume it is there. Look to see whether you have a sentence or sentences in which you summarize what the reader has learned about the rule from your rule explanation. You might find the rule summary in sentences that begin with phrases like, "Accordingly, a [petitioner/plaintiff] can [succeed in having case reversed/avoiding dismissal] only when . . . " or "Therefore, [phrase-that-pays means or prohibits . . .]."

7.2.5
IDENTIFY YOUR CLIENT'S FACTS

Within each CREXAC unit of discourse, highlight any references to facts from your client in BLUE. (Remember, if the language of enacted law is at issue, that language may sometimes act as part of your "facts.")

This task is usually relatively simple. By this stage of the writing process, you are very familiar with the facts of your client's situation, and you simply need to highlight them in blue wherever they appear. This task can be complicated if your case involves the analysis of a statute or another legislative provision. In that situation, part of your "facts" may be the language of the provision, for you may be applying a "rule" of statutory interpretation to the "facts" of the provision's language.[6] One important note: Do *not* highlight facts from authority cases that you happen to discuss. Highlight only facts from your client's case.

---

[6] As with any of the self-grading tasks, if you have any problem identifying your facts within a heading section, you may want to drop a private memo note so that you can ask for help if needed.

7.2.6
IDENTIFY THE APPLICATION OF EACH FOCUS TO YOUR CLIENT'S FACTS

Within each CREXAC unit of discourse, write "Application" in the margin next to the paragraphs or portions of paragraphs in which you discuss how the rule/focus for that section applies or does not apply to those facts. Look for paragraphs with both pink highlights (phrases-that-pay) and blue highlights (client facts) when looking for application, but do not presume that every paragraph with pink and blue highlights is an application paragraph.

After you have highlighted all of the facts in blue, write "Application" in the margin next to the sentences or paragraphs in which you applied the law to the facts in that unit of discourse. Looking for paragraphs that contain both blue facts and pink phrases-that-pay should reveal where you applied the law to the facts, and allow you to analyze both the focus and the completeness of this part of your document. Ideally, you will find a sentence that says, in essence, "phrase-that-pays equals [or does not equal] my case facts." Of course, your application will often be much more detailed than this, particularly if the issue is a controversial one.

7.2.7
IDENTIFY THE CONNECTION-CONCLUSION

Within each CREXAC unit of discourse, write "C/C" in the margin next to the sentence in which you explicitly state your "connection-conclusion," that is, your *ending* conclusion for that unit of discourse. Highlight the connection-conclusion in YELLOW. Do *not* highlight any statement that could be characterized as a conclusion (particularly, do not highlight the conclusion at the beginning of the subsection). In the connection-conclusion, you should make explicit how your analysis *connects* to the focus for this unit of discourse and, if appropriate, to your overall thesis.

An easy task is finding and labeling the sentence(s) in each section of your argument in which you state the connection-conclusion for the section (also known as the internal conclusion or the mini-conclusion). Many writers make the common mistake of merely highlighting the last sentence in the unit of discourse. The self-grading will be more effective if you take the time to note whether you have actually included a connection-conclusion. Note whether it contains the phrase-that-pays for the section and whether you have connected the phrase-that-pays to the point heading for that section, or, if appropriate, to your ultimate thesis. For example, in some arguments, winning a particular point may mean that you win the case. Those sections might follow a statement about the conclusion to that section with a statement like, "therefore, the court should reverse" or "therefore, the court should grant the motion to dismiss." If you cannot find an explicit connection-conclusion, take a moment and write one.

7.2.8
CREATE A SEPARATE FOCUS LIST

After you have identified or drafted all of your focuses, block and copy each focus into a separate document in which you list each focus in order of appearance. You can use this list to review your issues and your large-scale organization.

After you have finished the tasks that are focused on individual units of discourse, it is time to look at the document as a whole. First, create·a focus list that records the focus of each CREXAC unit of discourse. The focus list can help you to evaluate the completeness of your document because it will remind you of which points you have discussed. You can check this list against your initial research or your follow-up research to see if you have addressed all of the points that you need to address. The list can also help you to evaluate structure. Note whether you are addressing your most important arguments first and whether you have addressed your arguments in a logical order. Finally, note whether you can link each point to your ultimate thesis.

7.2.9
WRITE A FINAL COMMENT

By now, you should have an idea of some of the areas you want to concentrate on in your revision. List the two or three most important elements or sections that you plan to revise. You may also want to note the areas of your brief that you believe are strongest.

Your final task is to review your entire document and write a final comment. What two or three aspects of your document need the most revision? What elements of the document are particularly effective? Recording this information now, while the impressions are strong in your mind, will help you later as you tackle the important step of revising your document with your reader in mind.

7.3
SUMMARY

Use the self-graded draft exercise to separate yourself from your text so that you can see what is really on the printed page. By looking for specific analytical elements and asking yourself focused questions, you can begin to see your writing through your reader's eyes. Now is the time for you to shift your focus. Your first focus must always be on gaining an understanding of the case: what the facts are, what the relevant rules and authorities are, and how they work together in your argument. Now you must also start to think about how the reader will perceive your argument and, more importantly, how you can craft your argument to increase the reader's understanding of your case.

PROFESSIONALISM: FOLLOWING FORMAT RULES

Although fulfilling your brief's format requirements is a much less intellectually demanding task than writing the argument, it is nonetheless important. Rightly or wrongly, many readers form an impression of your credibility based on whether you conform to the minutiae of court rules. Your willingness to learn and follow rules about document format and filing guidelines tells the court that you are a professional, and that you take court requirements seriously. More significantly, you may suffer sanctions—from having to fix offending portions of the brief to having your case dismissed—for failure to follow certain rules.[1]

Most state and federal courts in the United States are governed by at least two sets of rules. The more significant rules are the rules of procedure that govern all of the courts within a certain jurisdiction, for example, the Federal Rules of Civil Procedure, the Federal Rules of Appellate Procedure, or the Ohio Rules of Appellate Procedure.

Most courts also have so-called local rules that may deal with requirements such as filing requirements, page length, certificates of service, service on opposing parties, citations, and the like. Obeying these rules is crucial to the effective practice of law. In 2010, for example, an Indiana court refused to accept expert affidavits in opposition to a motion because they were filed after the deadline, even though both parties had agreed to an extension of time. Counsel had neglected to file the appropriate motion with the court to request the extension.[2] Similarly, in 2002, the Ninth Circuit dismissed an appeal for failure to comply with certain Federal Rules of Appellate Procedure (FRAP) and with circuit rules.[3] The court noted that "[a]n enormous amount of time is wasted when attorneys fail to provide proper briefs and excerpts of record that should have supplied the court with the materials relevant to the appeal. The FRAP and Ninth Circuit rules are not optional suggestions . . . but *rules* that . . . are entitled to respect, and command compliance."[4]

In addition to expecting counsel to follow local rules, some courts expect counsel to be aware of local practices, the customs and behaviors that are unwritten but practiced by experienced local lawyers. Appellate courts that allow electronic filing may prefer to have counsel file an additional hard copy if the document is lengthy.[5] Trial judges may have "standing orders" that lay out rules for counsel to follow in all trials in front of that particular judge. Taking the time to read a judge's standing order (often posted on the judge's Web site) may provide you with valuable information that will save you time and trouble and help you to make a good impression on the

---

[1] Judith D. Fischer, *Bareheaded and Barefaced Counsel: Courts React to Unprofessionalism in Lawyers' Papers*, 31 Suffolk U. L. Rev. 1, 31 et seq. (1997) (this article also contains several examples of courts' reactions to misstatements of law and facts and other failings). *See also* Judith D. Fischer, *Pleasing the Court: Writing Ethical and Effective Briefs* (Carolina Academic Press 2005).

[2] *Booher v. Sheeram, LLC*, 937 N.E.2d 392, 394 (Ind. Ct. App. 2010), cited in *Above the Law*, "Always Follow the Rules" (Dec. 27, 2013), available at http://abovethelaw.com/tag/booher-v-sheeram-llc/.

[3] *In re O'Brien*, 312 F.3d 1135, 1136 (9th Cir. 2002).

[4] *Id.* at 1137 (citation omitted; emphasis in original).

[5] *E.g.*, King County Local Rule 7(b)(4)(F) (discussing working copies, and requiring paper working copies for documents of 500 pages or more).

court. Whenever you have to file a brief, make sure that you have copies of all of the written rules that apply to documents submitted to that court, and try to find out the local practices and customs by consulting court Web sites, more experienced colleagues, or both.

This chapter explains the format requirements that are common to appellate briefs and motion briefs. For appellate brief requirements, it usually refers to Supreme Court rules; however, most of the requirements listed are common in other appellate courts. For motion brief requirements, it usually refers to federal court rules. Samples of a motion brief and of appellate briefs appear in Appendix C. Of course, you should follow the rules of the court to which you are writing or of your professor.

8.1
LENGTH REQUIREMENTS

Probably the most significant format mistake that lawyers make is to fail to follow required length limits. Unfortunately, some lawyers see an imposed length limit as a sort of challenge, and they turn the limit into a goal. Most courts design their limits to accommodate even complex cases that require lengthy analysis of each issue. Your goal as a writer should be to write enough about each issue to answer the question that issue presents and to give the reader confidence that your answer is correct. Lawyers do not win any points from judges for padding simple arguments, making the same point in two or three different point heading sections, or describing five cases where one would make the point. On the contrary, most judges are grateful to read a brief that makes its points effectively and then stops.[6]

All of this is not to say that you should give the court only a cursory description of your arguments. Presume that your readers are intelligent, but that they are ignorant of the particulars of the case currently before the court. Your brief should give enough details about your case, and about the cases and other authorities that you cite, for the members of the court to understand your analysis without having to resort to other documents. Of course, they might understand things more deeply if they read all of the cases or reviewed the entire record, but your job is not to give them the same in-depth knowledge of the case that you have. Rather, you should perform a cost-benefit analysis vis-à-vis the information that you provide. For example, a brief case description will give the court a reasonable understanding of the authority and will take two or three sentences. A lengthy case description may take two or three paragraphs, but in most situations, it will not provide any more needed insight than a two-or-three sentence description.

---

[6] *See generally* Fischer, *Bareheaded and Barefaced Counsel, supra* note 1, at 27.

Courts may express a length limit as a page limit, a word limit, or both. The Local Rules of King County, Washington, for example, limit motions for summary judgment and supporting memoranda to 24 pages; Rule 32(a)(7) of the Federal Rules of Appellate Procedure limits a principal appellate brief to 30 pages (with certain typeface restrictions) or 14,000 words. Rule 32(a)(7)(C) specifically allows counsel to rely on the "word or line count of the word-processing system used to prepare the brief." The page limits on briefs may vary depending on what category a brief falls into. Briefs on dispositive motions generally have higher page limits; for example, Rule 3.1113(d) of the 2014 California Rules of Court specify that a supporting memorandum for a summary judgment or summary adjudication motion is limited to 20 pages, while memoranda for all other motions are limited to 15 pages.

8.2
TYPEFACES AND MARGINS

Many courts have imposed font size and margin requirements in reaction to lawyers who try to evade length requirements by using smaller margins, smaller fonts, or other techniques. Note that courts may sanction counsel who violate length requirements.[7] In addition to font and length *requirements*, some courts have issued suggestions to help counsel make their briefs easier to read. The Seventh Circuit, for example, has published a "Guideline for Briefs and Other Papers" on its Web site, and it recommends that counsel read a law review article to help improve the typography of documents submitted to the court.[8] If the court to which you are submitting your brief does not specify anything beyond page limits, presume standard margins (one-inch all around) and a standard font size (12-point, nonproportional spacing).

8.3
FILING REQUIREMENTS AND NUMBER OF COPIES

Courts impose very specific filing requirements on brief writers, listing specifics for everything from the method of service to the number of copies filed. Although some requirements may seem overly detailed,

---

[7] *See* Fischer, *Bareheaded and Barefaced Counsel, supra* note 1, at 31-32.

[8] *Requirements and Suggestions for Typography in Briefs and Other Papers* 4, http://www.ca7. uscourts.gov/Rules/type.pdf (last accessed Jan. 22, 2014) (citing Ruth Anne Robbins, *Painting with Print: Incorporating Concepts of Typographic and Layout Design into the Text of Legal Writing Documents*, 2 J. Assn. Legal Writing Dirs. 108 (2004)).

following them helps both the readers and the users of the brief to do their jobs more easily and efficiently. This section explains some categories of common requirements, but be sure to consult jurisdictional rules, local rules, and local practices before filing a brief in a new court.

In the past, all documents were filed in hard copy at the courthouse, and counsel attached a paper certificate of service (discussed below) to certify that he or she had served opposing counsel as appropriate. These days, more and more courts are allowing or even requiring the electronic filing of documents as a substitute for hard-copy delivery. Most courts that do so provide very precise instructions as to method. If you file a brief electronically, make sure that your document survived the trip through cyberspace. The court may provide an electronic receipt that allows you to open your document to check it. Be sure to do so. Do not rely on the receipt itself: Open the document and make sure that the document transmission was successful. Further, the first time you use an electronic filing system for a particular court, plan to file your brief at least 24 hours in advance. Many courts now have midnight filing deadlines. If you put off filing your brief until shortly before the deadline, you will have no one to ask for help if things go wrong. On the other hand, if you file early and have trouble, you will be able to seek help during normal business hours.

As for number of copies, United States Supreme Court Rule 33.1(f) requires that 40 copies of the brief should be filed with the court in most circumstances. It is common for appellate courts to require a large number of copies (if it requires the filing of hard copies) because a panel of judges and their clerks will all need to review the brief. Rule 31.1 of the Third Circuit Local Appellate Rules requires that "each party must file ten (10) paper copies (i.e., an original and nine copies) of each brief with the clerk for the convenience of the court" and serve one paper copy on opposing counsel unless counsel has agreed to electronic filing. Of course, if you are filing a motion brief, you are submitting the brief to a single judge rather than to a panel, so a smaller number of copies may be required.

As noted previously, in some courts, local practice dictates that when attorneys file either appellate or motion briefs, they must file "courtesy copies," "working copies," or "judges' copies" with the court. If a document is filed in hard copy, the "official version" of the document cannot be marked up by a judge or the judge's clerk. Thus, counsel may provide one or more extra copies to speed the court's consideration of the brief. Even when briefs are filed electronically, some courts may require either electronic or hard-copy "working copies."[9]

---

[9] For example, the court Web site for King County, Washington, provides detailed instructions for filing electronic working copies: http://www.kingcounty.gov/courts/Clerk/E-Working%20 Copies.aspx (last accessed Jan. 13, 2014). Note that if court rules do not forbid it, you may wish to file paper working copies to promote ease of reading.

Court rules may also specify particular typefaces or font sizes (to ease reading), the method of binding (to prevent staple injuries), the color of the brief cover (to allow easy retrieval of a particular brief), and the method of service on opposing counsel. Whenever you file a document with a court, make sure that you are following all needed filing requirements. Doing so will impress the court with your professionalism, will avoid sanctions, and may help speed a decision in your case.

8.4
DOCUMENT FORMAT REQUIREMENTS AND SERVICE REQUIREMENTS FOR APPELLATE BRIEFS

The United States Supreme Court rules specify exactly what elements are to be included in every type of brief submitted to it, from a brief petitioning for a writ of certiorari to a petitioner's reply brief on the merits. The Federal Rules of Appellate Procedure and rules of state supreme courts lay out similar guidelines. This section will focus on the document requirements of a petitioner's brief on the merits, which are described in Supreme Court Rule 24.

In practice, the party filing the responsive brief—whether it is an appellee's brief or a respondent's brief—is allowed to omit certain segments of the brief (e.g., the jurisdictional statement, the fact statement, or the opinions below) if he or she agrees with the other party as to that information. In most appellate advocacy courses, however, students on each side of the case are required to complete all segments of the document for pedagogical reasons. Whether in practice or in class, you must learn and follow the local rules.

8.4.1
COVER PAGE

Supreme Court Rule 34.1 lists the elements that must be included on the cover page of the brief, including the docket number of the case, the name of the court in which the case will be heard, the caption of the case, the court of origin of the case, the type of document, and the name of the counsel of record. Similarly, Rule 341(d) of the Illinois Civil Appeals Rules lists the elements that must appear on the cover page of a brief, including the case number, the name of the court that is being appealed to and of the tribunal whose decision is being reviewed, and the name of the case as it appeared in the lower tribunal, with the parties' identities indicating their status in both courts (e.g., "plaintiff-appellant").

8.4.2
ISSUE

Appellate briefs designate the issue or issues before the court with a formal question or questions presented. In many briefs, the question presented may be the fifth or sixth element of the brief; Rule 28 of the Federal Rules of Appellate Procedure places the statement of the issues after the jurisdictional statement and before the statement of the case. In Supreme Court briefs, however, the question presented appears alone on the first page after the cover page. As noted in Supreme Court Rule 24.1(a), the brief may not raise additional questions or change the substance of the questions raised in the petition for the writ of certiorari; however, "the phrasing of the questions presented need not be identical with that in the petition for a writ of certiorari." Note that if your case has multiple questions, you should number the questions. Note also that if you are writing a brief to the United States Supreme Court, the page number of this page should be written in lowercase roman numerals (i.e., the question presented appears on page i), and that this method of pagination continues through the table of authorities (see Section 8.4.5). Arabic numbering of the pages begins with the opinions below (see Section 8.4.6). Consult local rules for pagination guidelines for other appellate briefs; if pagination is not mentioned, you may presume that Arabic pagination is acceptable throughout. Chapter Nine discusses methods for writing an effective question presented.

8.4.3
PARTIES TO THE PROCEEDING

Appellate briefs may require a separate listing of "parties to the proceeding." In many cases, all of the parties to the proceedings have been listed in the caption on the cover page of the brief. In some cases, however, the parties are too numerous to list on the cover page, or the parties have changed since the decision of the case below. In either of these situations, Supreme Court Rule 24.1(b) requires you to include a separate page labeled "Parties to the Proceeding," which (1) lists all parties not listed on the cover sheet and (2) explains any additions to or absences from the parties to the proceeding in the court whose judgment is under review. The *Miller v. Albright* brief in Appendix C contains an example of this requirement. If any of the parties is a company with parent companies or nonwholly owned subsidiaries, you may need to add corporate disclosure information about that company here. Supreme Court Rule 29.6 describes corporate disclosure requirements.

8.4.4
TABLE OF CONTENTS

Supreme Court Rule 24.1(c) requires a table of contents for all briefs that exceed five pages. Generally, the table of contents contains a list of every element of the brief that has a title, from the question(s) presented, the opinions below, the argument *and* its sections that are labeled with point headings, to the conclusion, the certificate of service, and the appendix (if any). The table of contents should list only the first page on which each element appears.

8.4.5
TABLE OF AUTHORITIES

Supreme Court Rule 24.1(c) also requires a table of authorities for all briefs that exceed 1,500 words. Rule 34.2 requires that the table of authorities include "cases alphabetically arranged, constitutional provisions, statutes, treatises, and other materials." Most attorneys use the categories listed in the rule as headings within the table, and some will subdivide any longer categories further. For example, they may group cases into United States Supreme Court cases, United States Circuit Court cases, and so on. This grouping may help the court to assess the brief's authority, but the rules do not require it.

The most important requirement is that the table should note *each* page on which each authority is cited. If an authority is cited so frequently that listing the individual pages would not help the court to find particular discussions of the authority, the table of authorities may note *passim* (Latin for "throughout") instead of listing individual pages. *Passim* is often necessary to refer to a statute that is at issue because the statute may well be referenced on every page of the argument. Take care to use *passim* only when absolutely necessary; it is not an excuse for being too lazy to search through the brief to find the particular pages on which the citations appear.

Word processing programs may have a "Table" function, which will allow you to create a table of authorities more easily. If you use this function, I do not recommend that you *rely* on it. After the table is generated, double-check to be sure that it includes each needed authority and each needed page reference.

8.4.6
OPINIONS BELOW

Supreme Court Rule 24.1(d) requires that the brief writer cite the official and unofficial reports of "the opinions and orders entered in the case by courts and administrative agencies." This section is usually designated "Opinions Below." If official citations exist, the writer must provide them; if the opinions are also (or only) available in the joint appendix or some other document submitted to the court, the writer should make that clear as well—e.g., "The decision of the Second Circuit Court of Appeals is found at 101 F.3d 101 and at page 73 in the Joint Appendix." With this section, the Supreme Court brief writer begins Arabic page numbering with page 1. Some writers reprint the caption of the case before this element; although Rule 24.1 does not specify this requirement, reprinting the caption helps the reader to distinguish between front matter and the body of the brief.[10]

8.4.7
JURISDICTION

In Supreme Court briefs, the jurisdictional statement, required by Rule 24.1(e), is usually rather straightforward. The attorney should include the date on which the judgment being reviewed was entered, the date on which the petition for certiorari was filed, and the date on which the petition was granted. These items are necessary because they show that a final decision has been entered and that the petitioner has followed the necessary procedural steps. The brief should also include the statute or statutes that give the reviewing court the authority to hear this type of appeal.[11]

In cases in other appellate courts, the jurisdictional statement may be more complex. For example, Rule 28(a)(4) of the Federal Rules of Appellate Procedure requires that an appellant's brief include:

> (4) a jurisdictional statement, including:
>   (A) the basis for the district court's or agency's subject-matter jurisdiction, with citations to applicable statutory provisions and stating relevant facts establishing jurisdiction;
>   (B) the basis for the court of appeals' jurisdiction, with citations to applicable statutory provisions and stating relevant facts establishing jurisdiction;
>   (C) the filing dates establishing the timeliness of the appeal or petition for review; and
>   (D) an assertion that the appeal is from a final order or judgment that disposes of all parties' claims, or information establishing the court of appeals' jurisdiction on some other basis.

---

[10] See the sample appellate briefs in Appendix C, at page 1, for an example of this type of internal caption.

[11] See the jurisdictional statement in the sample briefs in Appendix C, and accompanying annotation, for information about the most common relevant statutes.

Jurisdictional issues can be raised for the first time at any point in the proceedings; thus, in practice, be sure that you understand the court's jurisdiction in your client's case.

8.4.8
RELEVANT ENACTED LAW

Rule 24.1(f) requires the attorney to set out— "verbatim with appropriate citation" —the constitutional provisions, treaties, statutes, regulations, and ordinances (in that order) at issue in the case. Thus, this section should include only those statutes or other enacted laws whose language or application is in controversy. This section should not be used to reprint any statute *cited* in the brief. Rather, you should include statutes or other enacted laws only if you are asking the court to interpret or apply them (or not to apply them) in this case. Label this element according to what it contains, e.g., "Relevant Constitutional Provisions" or "Relevant Statutes" or "Relevant Constitutional and Regulatory Provisions."

If only one paragraph of a lengthy statute is in controversy, you can quote only the pertinent part, but be generous: Do not quote merely the sentence at issue. In general, when excerpting enacted law in a section of this type, you should quote at least a paragraph, and be sure to include introductory material that provides sufficient context (e.g., "Section 125 defines 'stevedore,' and provides in pertinent part: . . .").

If printing the entire text of the relevant provisions would take up too much space (more than a page), simply include the citations here and explain that the full text is reprinted in an appendix.[12]

8.4.9
STANDARD OF REVIEW

As you read in Chapter Two, the standard of review is the framework within which the court makes its decision. You must tell the court what standard of review applies to any decision you are asking it to review. The United States Supreme Court does not require that the standard be laid out in a separate section, but some courts are allowing or encouraging this. For example, the United States Court of Appeals for the Third Circuit, in Rule 28.1(b), requires counsel to specifically identify the standard of review:

> (b) The following statements should appear under a separate heading placed before the discussion of the issue: the statement of the standard or scope of review for each issue on appeal, *i.e.,* whether the trial court

---

[12] See Section 8.4.17 for discussion of Supreme Court rule requirements for the appendix.

abused its discretion; whether its fact findings are clearly erroneous; whether it erred in formulating or applying a legal precept, in which case review is plenary; whether, on appeal or petition for review of an agency action, there is substantial evidence in the record as a whole to support the order or decision, or whether the agency's action, findings and conclusions should be held unlawful and set aside for the reasons set forth in 5 U.S.C. §706(2).

The sample appellate briefs in Appendix C place this section before the statement of the case, on the theory that knowing the standard of review may give the reader needed context before he or she begins reading the fact statement. Obviously, you should place the section where the court asks for it; if the court does not ask for it, you could create a separate section for the standard (presuming the court has not forbidden the creation of "extra" sections). In the alternative, you could include the standard in introductory material. If different issues are subject to different standards of review, the introductory material preceding each issue should include the standard for that issue. In contrast, if the same standard applies to all issues, you could include it early in the argument section in your overall introduction (unless court rules require otherwise, as does the excerpt above). Chapter Ten discusses incorporating the standard of review into introductory material; the *Miller v. Albright* brief in Appendix C provides an illustration of this technique.

8.4.10
STATEMENT OF THE CASE

Supreme Court Rule 24.1(g) asks for a "concise statement of the case, setting out the facts material to the consideration of the questions presented." Although writing an effective statement of the case is addressed in Chapter Nine, for now you should keep in mind that the statement usually includes both facts and procedure and always includes citation to the record, the joint appendix, and/or the appendix to the petition for the writ of certiorari.[13]

8.4.11
SUMMARY OF THE ARGUMENT

Writing the summary of the argument is addressed in Chapter Nine. The formal requirements are few, but some are quite particular. Supreme Court Rule 24.1(h) specifically notes that "mere repetition of the headings

---

[13] See the sample briefs in Appendix C for examples of correct citations within the statement of the case.

under which the argument is arranged is not sufficient." If you are arguing in a different appellate court, be sure to consult the local rules, as not all courts have this requirement.

8.4.12
THE ARGUMENT

Much has already been written about the argument; I will simply note here that Rule 24.1(i) asks that the argument exhibit "clearly the points of fact and of law presented and [cite] the authorities and statutes relied on." Some appellate courts may ask counsel to list any relevant authority that goes against counsel's argument. Thus, even though the method of written argument may not vary from court to court, you must still consult local rules about the argument itself.

8.4.13
THE CONCLUSION

The only requirement that the Court imposes on the conclusion, in Rule 24.1(j), is that it "[specify] with particularity the relief the party seeks." At a minimum, your conclusion should tell the court what you want it to do: affirm, reverse, reverse and remand, or vacate the decision below. Be precise when requesting relief. Ask the court to "affirm" or "reverse," not to "uphold" or "overrule" the decision below. Many lawyers write only one sentence as a conclusion, as in this example:

△ GOOD EXAMPLE

For the foregoing reasons, this Court should reverse the decision below.

It can be effective to make the conclusion more specific to your case. Even if you wish to do so, however, you should usually avoid writing a lengthy conclusion. Instead, substitute your best reason(s) for the opening clause, as in this example:

△ GOOD EXAMPLE

Because the First Amendment should never be interpreted in a way that keeps truthful information from consumers, this Court should affirm the decision below.

You will sometimes see flowery language in the conclusion, such as "Counsel for the Petitioner respectfully requests that the Court affirm the decision below." Although this language probably does not hurt counsel, it probably does not help, either. Because the words "respectfully submitted" appear in the signature block, just below the conclusion, there is probably no need to use "respectfully" in the conclusion itself. Indeed, briefs filed by the solicitor general of the United States typically have extremely short conclusions, consisting most often of an extremely short request for relief:

⚠ GOOD EXAMPLES

The judgment of the court of appeals should be reversed.

The judgment of the court of appeals should be affirmed.

Some courts will have little patience for a conclusion that is much longer than a paragraph. Make sure that you are aware of both local rules and local customs in this regard.

8.4.14
SIGNATURE

The rules of the United States Supreme Court do not specifically require that attorneys sign briefs (although certificates of service must be signed). Rule 34.3 requires that the body of every document (i.e., information before any certificate of service or appendix) "shall bear at its close the name of counsel of record."

Although other courts have traditionally required a signature, that practice is changing with the rise of electronic service. The Third Circuit's Local Appellate Rule 46.4 provides that "[a]ll documents, motions and briefs must be signed by an attorney or by a party appearing pro se. Electronically filed documents must be signed with either an electronic signature or 's/typed name.'" Likewise, Local Rule 28.4 specifies that "[e]lectronic briefs may be signed with either an electronically generated signature or 's/ typed name' in the signature location. Counsel's state bar number, if any, and address and phone number must be included with the signature."

Unless rules specify otherwise, you should presume that a handwritten signature is required with a document filed in hard copy. Whether your signature is manual or electronic, you should include the phrase "Respectfully submitted" before the signature line.

8.4.15
CERTIFICATE OF SERVICE

Most courts require that litigants who serve papers on the court also certify that they have served copies of those documents on opposing counsel. In this way, the court ensures that all litigants have copies of all of the documents in the case. Supreme Court Rule 29.2 specifies that "[a]ny document required by these Rules to be served may be served personally, by mail, or by third-party commercial carrier for delivery within 3 calendar days on each party to the proceeding at or before the time of filing." Rule 29.5 specifies that "proof of service . . . shall accompany the document when it is presented to the Clerk for filing and shall be separate from it." The rule specifies several methods of certifying service, including "a certificate of service, reciting the facts and circumstances of service . . . and signed by a member of the Bar of this Court representing the party on whose behalf service is made."

Federal Rule of Appellate Procedure 25 provides that "[u]nless a rule requires service by the clerk, a party must, at or before the time of filing a paper, serve a copy on the other parties to the appeal or review. Service on a party represented by counsel must be made on the party's counsel." Some courts may allow service of opposing counsel after the brief is filed with the court, while others require that counsel file a certificate indicating that such service has already been accomplished.

If you are filing electronically, you may be able to serve your opponent electronically as well. Once again, be sure to consult local rules, as electronic filing has added some wrinkles to the filing process. In some courts, only those who have registered with the court may use electronic filing services. Federal Rule of Appellate Procedure 25(c)(1)(D) provides that service may be made "by electronic means, if the party being served consents in writing." Along those lines, the Third Circuit's Local Appellate Rule 31.1(d) provides that "[a] party who is a Filing User as provided in L.A.R. Misc. 113.4 consents to electronic service of the brief through the court's electronic docketing system (cm/ecf). Service by alternate means must be made on all parties who are not Filing Users. The certificate of service must note what method of service was used for each party served." If your opponent is not able to receive electronic service, in other words, you may need to provide service using more traditional means. Be sure to find out service requirements well in advance of your filing deadline.

In general, the certificate of service should describe how service was accomplished. If you hand-deliver the document to opposing counsel's office, the certificate should say so and list the address. If the brief is filed electronically, the certificate may be filed electronically as well; as always, consult local rules to find out the particulars. The sample briefs in Appendix C contain examples of a certificate of service.

8.4.16
CERTIFICATE OF COMPLIANCE

The certificate of compliance is a fairly new requirement; it seems to serve as a supplement to page-length and word-limit requirements. Modern word processing systems could make it difficult for a court to tell if an attorney has "cheated" a page limit, e.g., by using 11.8 point font instead of 12 point font. A certificate of compliance typically requires an attorney to certify that he or she has complied with particular court rules as to length. (In a law school setting, you may also be asked to certify that you have complied with the honor code.) Although the certificate of compliance is a recent phenomenon, it is being required more frequently.

Federal Rule of Appellate Procedure 32(a)(7) requires that a brief must either comply with a page limit or with a word limit that is verified in a certificate of compliance. Federal Rule of Appellate Procedure 32(a)(7)(C) requires that the certificate must state either the number of words in the brief or the number of lines of monospaced type in the brief. Local rules may add more requirements. Rule 31.1(c) of the Local Appellate Rules of the Third Circuit, for example, requires that counsel must certify consistency between hard-copy and electronic documents and allows for sanctions if an electronic document is infected with a computer virus:

> In addition to the certification of type-volume limitations required by [FRAP] Rule 32(a)(7)(C), and in the same document, counsel must certify that the text of the electronic brief is identical to the text in the paper copies. Counsel must also certify that a virus detection program has been run on the file and that no virus was detected. The certification must specify the version of the virus detection program used. Sanctions may be imposed if a filing contains a computer virus or worm.

Likewise, the United States Supreme Court now requires a Certificate of Compliance for all briefs filed in booklet format (and this has been the typical format). Rule 33.1(h) requires that the certificate state the number of words in the brief (according to the word processing program) and state that the brief complies with the required word limits. One sample brief in Appendix C includes an example of a Certificate of Compliance.

8.4.17
APPENDIX

Few courts have rules that require an appendix for every brief. As noted previously, however, Supreme Court Rule 24.1(f) suggests an appendix when legislation is too lengthy to reprint in the "applicable statutes" section of the brief. If an appendix is necessary, do not simply attach copies of statutes printed from Bloomberg, Lexis, or Westlaw. Instead, retype the statutes in a readable format, or download the text into a word processing system and reformat the text, using typefaces and margins that promote readability.

Local rules and local practice—as well as the particular needs of your brief—will dictate the items that you include in the appendix. In general, you should include any information to which the court may need to refer while it considers the case, and which is not contained in the Joint

Appendix or the Appendix to the Petition for the Writ of Certiorari. For example, you may include unpublished decisions, copies of documents (or segments of documents) that are at issue, and the like.[14] Note that some court rules may require an appendix in certain circumstances; some trial courts require that counsel attach copies of unpublished decisions or of decisions from courts of another jurisdiction.

8.5
DOCUMENT FORMAT REQUIREMENTS AND SERVICE REQUIREMENTS FOR MOTION BRIEFS

Unlike appellate courts, trial courts do not always specify the requirements for motion briefs. Many say only that a "memorandum of points and authorities" must accompany the motion, or that the brief should state "the concise facts, the grounds for the motion and the authorities relied on." In practice, however, counsel filing dispositive motions often submit briefs that closely resemble appellate briefs. This chapter identifies segments that may appear in effective motion briefs, and a sample following this format appears in Appendix C. Note that while pagination rules for appellate briefs often indicate use of small roman numerals on pages containing introductory material, you should paginate a motion brief with Arabic numerals unless court rules designate otherwise.

In practice, the party filing the responsive brief—generally the plaintiff, for a motion brief—may be allowed to omit certain segments of the brief (e.g., the fact statement) if he or she agrees with the other party as to that information. In most law school settings, however, students on each side of the case are required to complete all segments of the document for pedagogical reasons. Whether in practice or in class, you must learn and follow the local rules.

8.5.1
CAPTION

Unlike an appellate brief, a motion brief usually does not require a separate cover page. It will, however, probably require a formal caption that includes the name of the court hearing the case, the parties, their procedural titles, the case's docket number, and the title of the document (e.g., "Memorandum in Support of Defendant Guillen's Motion to Dismiss").

---

[14] *See, e.g.,* Ruggero J. Aldisert, *Winning on Appeal* 84-89 (rev. 1st ed., Natl. Inst. Trial Advoc. 1996); Carole C. Berry, *Effective Appellate Advocacy: Brief Writing and Oral Argument* 107 (3d ed., Thomson/West 2003).

Note that in some courts, counsel must request oral argument within the caption, so it is particularly important to consult local rules in this regard.

8.5.2
ISSUE

Some courts require attorneys who file motion briefs to draft formal questions presented. Others may rely on the motion itself to articulate the issue and require only an "introduction" to the issue in the brief itself. The introduction may appear under a heading just below the caption. Chapter Nine discusses methods for writing both formal questions presented and introductions appropriate for motion briefs.

8.5.3
PARTIES TO THE PROCEEDING

Motion briefs generally do not require a separate listing of parties to the proceeding. Generally, the names of all parties are included in the caption. If your case contains numerous plaintiffs or defendants, consult local rules to see if you can list only the first party, or use "et al." It may be that the rules require all parties to be listed only on the caption of the complaint, and allow counsel to use "et al." (or some other abbreviated listing method) for other documents in the case.

8.5.4
TABLE OF CONTENTS

Typically, motion briefs do not need a table of contents unless they exceed a certain number of pages, which will be designated in court (or classroom) rules. Some courts seem to leave the decision to include a table of contents to the discretion of the attorney. If a table of contents is included, it should list every element of the brief that has a title, e.g., the introduction or question(s) presented, the fact statement, the argument *and* its sections that are labeled with point headings, the conclusion, the certificate of service, and the appendix (if any). The table of contents should list only the first page on which each element appears. Each appellate brief in Appendix C contains a table of contents.

8.5.5
TABLE OF AUTHORITIES

As with the table of contents, a table of authorities is not always required in motion briefs, and deciding whether to include one may be up to the filing attorney. If you are in doubt as to whether a table is required, ask yourself if the table will be helpful to either the reader or the user. If your brief is ten pages or more, you may want to include one to make it easier for the judge, or his or her clerks, to find the sections of your argument that are focused on particular authorities. If you are filing your brief electronically, and you are considering including hot links to the authorities cited, it may be best to do so in a table of authorities rather than in the argument section of the brief. Of course, in practice settings, local custom may be the best guide.

To create the table of authorities, use headings to divide the authorities into relevant categories. The most likely categories are (1) Cases, (2) Constitutional Provisions, (3) Statutes, and (4) Other Materials. Obviously, create extra categories as needed to reflect the authorities that are actually included in your brief. Within each category, list the sources alphabetically (*not* by date). The most important requirement is that the table note *each* page on which each authority is cited. If an authority is cited so frequently that listing the individual pages would not help the court to find particular discussions of the authority, the table of authorities may note *passim* (Latin for "throughout") instead of listing individual pages. *Passim* is often necessary to refer to a statute that is at issue because the statute may well be referenced on every page of the argument. Take care to use *passim* only when absolutely necessary; it is not an excuse for being too lazy to search through the brief to find the particular pages on which the citations appear.

Word processing programs may have a "Table" function that will allow you to create a table of authorities more easily. If you use this function, I do not recommend that you *rely* on it. After the table is generated, double-check to be sure that it includes each needed authority and each needed page reference. To see a sample of a table of authorities, consult any of the appellate briefs in Appendix C.

8.5.6
OPINIONS BELOW

Presume that you do not need this section in your motion brief. You would need to include it only in the unusual circumstance that you are filing a motion in a case with a procedural history that includes relevant written decisions. If citations to these decisions are available, provide them; if the opinions are also (or only) available in record materials, make that clear as well—e.g., "The decision of the Second Circuit Court of Appeals is found at 101 F.3d 101 and at page 73 in the Record." If a decision is not available in a publication or online, you should attach a copy of the decision, and indicate as much in this section: "The June, 2014, decision of the Agency is attached as Appendix I."

8.5.7
JURISDICTION

A jurisdictional statement is rare in a motion brief, and it should be included only if the court specifically requires it or if you believe that some controversy exists as to the court's jurisdiction in your case.

8.5.8
RELEVANT ENACTED LAW

A section that quotes appropriate sections of the relevant enacted law, often labeled "applicable statutes" or the like, can be extremely helpful to a court deciding a dispositive motion. This section is worth including even if the court has not asked for it. This section should include any constitutional provisions, statutes, regulations, and ordinances (in that order) at issue in the case. The section should include only the enacted laws whose language or application is in controversy. It should not be used to reprint any of these items that you *cited* in the brief. Rather, you should include statutes or other enacted laws only if you are asking the court to interpret or apply them (or not to apply them) in this case. Label this element according to what it contains, e.g., "Applicable Constitutional Provisions" or "Applicable Statutes" or "Applicable Constitutional and Regulatory Provisions," or the like.

If only one paragraph of a lengthy statute is in controversy, you can quote only the pertinent part, but be generous: Do not quote merely the sentence at issue. In general, when excerpting enacted law in a section of this type, you should quote at least a paragraph, and be sure to include introductory material that provides sufficient context (e.g., "Section 125 defines 'stevedore,' and provides in pertinent part: . . .").

If printing the entire text of the relevant provisions would take up too much space (more than a page), simply include the citations in this section and explain that the full text is reprinted in an appendix.[15]

8.5.9
STANDARD OF REVIEW *OR* PLEADING STANDARD

As you read in Chapter Two, the standard of review is the framework within which the court makes its decision. You must tell the court what standard of review applies to any decision you are asking it to make. As noted above, courts deciding a motion may refer to this standard as a

---

[15] See Section 8.5.17 for discussion of requirements for the appendix.

"legal standard" or, more accurately, as a "pleading standard." You should use the term that the courts in your jurisdiction use.

Generally, the standard can be dealt with in introductory material, in a somewhat summary fashion. Different issues may be subject to different facets of the standard. For example, in a motion to dismiss, you may be arguing that the complaint fails as to one issue because the facts pled were insufficient, and that it fails as to another issue because the law does not reach the facts of the case. In that situation, you could state the standard within the introductory material preceding each issue, emphasizing the appropriate aspect of the standard and citing to authority as appropriate. Chapter Ten discusses methods for incorporating the standard of review into introductory material; one of the sample briefs in Appendix C provides an illustration of this technique.

8.5.10
STATEMENT OF THE CASE

Writing an effective statement of the case is addressed in Chapter Nine. For now you should keep in mind that the statement usually includes both facts and procedure and always includes citation to the record.[16] Attorneys writing motion briefs do not usually have a formal record available, but you should cite to the pleadings (by paragraph) and to any other documents that you drew the fact statement from (and that the court has before it), including affidavits, depositions, answers to interrogatories, or written admissions or stipulations of fact.

8.5.11
SUMMARY OF THE ARGUMENT

A motion brief only rarely needs a formal summary of the argument; once again, length and local rules are the determining factors. Writing the summary of the argument is addressed in Chapter Nine.

8.5.12
THE ARGUMENT

Much has already been written about the argument; I will simply note here that you should consult local rules to see what limitations exist, if any. Some trial courts specify that counsel should cite only or primarily to courts of the mandatory jurisdiction, and may ask for copies of any

---

[16] See the sample briefs in Appendix C for examples of correct citations within the statement of the case.

nonjurisdictional sources. Some courts may ask counsel to formally list any relevant authority that goes against counsel's argument. If you are writing a memorandum in support of a motion for summary judgment, the court may ask you to list the material facts that you claim are not in dispute, and cite to the pages in the record materials on which each undisputed fact can be found. If the party opposing the motion disagrees that the facts are undisputed, he or she may be required to note, for each disputed fact, the pages in the record that show that a dispute exists. Thus, it is important to consult local rules to make sure that your document meets all requirements.

8.5.13
THE CONCLUSION

At a minimum, your conclusion should tell the court what you want it to do: grant or deny the motion. Many lawyers write only one sentence as a conclusion, as in this example:

> GOOD EXAMPLE
>
> **For the foregoing reasons, this Court should grant the defendant's motion to dismiss.**

Make sure that you are precise when requesting relief: You should ask a court to "grant" or "deny" a motion, not to "uphold" it or "strike it down."

It can sometimes be effective to make the conclusion more specific to your case. Even if you wish to do so, however, you should usually avoid writing a lengthy conclusion. Instead, you might include one sentence that succinctly states your most fundamental points, and then follow with the specific request for relief. In motion briefs, it can be appropriate to incorporate phrases-that-pay from the standard of review into the conclusion, as in this example:

> GOOD EXAMPLE
>
> **Title VII does not impose individual liability on supervisors. Therefore, plaintiff has not alleged facts that plausibly give rise to an entitlement to relief against Defendant Kobacker under Title VII, and this court should grant Defendant Kobacker's motion to dismiss.**

You will sometimes see flowery language in the conclusion, such as "Counsel for the Defendant respectfully requests that the Court grant the motion to dismiss." Although this language probably does not hurt counsel, it probably does not help, either. Because the words "respectfully submitted" typically appear in the signature block, just below the conclusion, there is probably no need to use "respectfully" in the conclusion itself.

8.5.14
SIGNATURE

Presume that you need to sign your document in some way. If the document is filed in paper form, presume that it must contain counsel's original signature in ink.[17] If the document is filed electronically, the court has probably enacted local rules that designate what constitutes an "electronic signature." In some jurisdictions, only those who have pre-registered with the court are allowed to file electronically; accordingly, be sure that you understand the particular requirements of your court well before the filing deadline. Do not presume that the court allows electronic filing. The Maine Rules of Civil Procedure, for example, provide that "[f]ilings by electronic transmission of data . . . or any other method for electronic or internet filing in place of the filing of paper documents required by these rules, is not permitted."[18]

Whether your signature is manual or electronic, be sure you are aware of other requirements. Some courts may require you to include your bar registration number, your address and phone number, your e-mail address, or all of the above. No matter the signature requirements, you should include the phrase "Respectfully submitted" before the signature line.

8.5.15
CERTIFICATE OF SERVICE

Most courts require that litigants who serve papers on the court also certify that they have served copies of those documents on opposing counsel.[19] In this way, the court ensures that all litigants have copies of all of the documents in the case. In general, the certificate should describe how service was accomplished. If you hand deliver the document to opposing counsel's office, the certificate should say so and list the address. If the brief is filed electronically, the certificate may be filed electronically as well; as always, consult local rules to find out the particulars. The sample briefs in Appendix C contain examples of a certificate of service.

---

[17] *E.g.,* Rule 5.1(B)(5), Rules of the United States District Court for the Northern District of Florida, available at http://www.flnd.uscourts.gov/forms/Court%20Rules/local_rules.pdf (last accessed Jan. 25, 2014).

[18] Me. R. Civ. P. 5(k), available at http://www.courts.state.me.us/rules_adminorders/rules/MRCivPONLY1-12.pdf (last accessed Jan. 25, 2014).

[19] *E.g.,* Rules of the United States District Court for the Northern District of Florida, *supra* note 17, at Rule 5.1(D).

8.5.16
CERTIFICATE OF COMPLIANCE

The certificate of compliance is a fairly new requirement; it seems to serve as a supplement to page-length requirements. Modern word processing systems could make it difficult for a court to tell if an attorney has "cheated" a page limit, e.g., by using 11.8-point font instead of 12-point font. A certificate of compliance typically requires an attorney to certify that he or she has complied with particular court rules as to length; as electronic filing becomes more common, courts may add requirements depending on what kinds of problems they encounter with electronically filed documents (e.g., computer viruses, electronic documents that differ from hard-copy documents).[20] (In a law school setting, you may also be asked to certify that you have complied with the honor code.) You should look specifically to see if your court requires this kind of certificate; note that some courts may use this title in other contexts, or use a different title for a similar certificate. One sample brief in Appendix C includes an example of a certificate of compliance.

8.5.17
APPENDIX

Few courts have rules that require an appendix for every brief. As noted previously, however, an appendix may be appropriate when legislation is too lengthy to reprint in the "applicable statutes" section of the brief. If an appendix is necessary, do not simply attach copies of statutes printed from Lexis, Bloomberg, or Westlaw. Instead, retype the statutes in a readable format, or download the text into a word processing system and reformat the text, using typefaces and margins that promote readability.

Local rules and local practice will dictate the items that you include in the appendix. In general, you should include any information to which the court may need to refer while it considers the case, and which it will not have easy access to otherwise. Note that some court rules may *require* an appendix in certain circumstances; some trial courts, for example, may require that counsel attach copies of unpublished decisions or of decisions from courts of another jurisdiction.

---

[20] *See* Rule 31.1(c) of the Local Appellate Rules of the Third Circuit.

8.6
SUMMARY

Format requirements are not intellectually demanding, but they do take time and require attention to detail. Whenever you file a brief, make sure that you have access to all relevant rules and allow yourself time to read, understand, and comply with their requirements.

SPECIAL TEAMS: ISSUE STATEMENTS, STATEMENT OF THE CASE, SUMMARY OF THE ARGUMENT, POINT HEADINGS

9.1 Writing the Issue Statement
    9.1.1 Motion Brief Introductions
    9.1.2 Questions Presented
        a. Elements to Include
        b. Persuasive Questions Presented
        c. Problems to Avoid
            i. Assuming Elements at Issue
            ii. Overlong Questions
        d. Summing Up
9.2 Statements of the Case
    9.2.1 Formal Requirements
    9.2.2 Organizing the Fact Statement
    9.2.3 Making the Fact Statement Persuasive
        a. Positions of Emphasis
        b. Pointillism
        c. Spending the Reader's Time, Saving the Reader's Energy
    9.2.4 Special Considerations for Motion Brief Fact Statements
    9.2.5 Summing Up
9.3 Summary of the Argument
9.4 Point Headings
    9.4.1 Format and Function
    9.4.2 Drafting the Point Headings
    9.4.3 The Relationships Between and Among Point Headings
    9.4.4 The Relationship Between the Point Heading and the Paragraph Immediately Following
    9.4.5 Summing Up
9.5 Summary

In football, coaches organize several different types of practices. The offense and the defense must prepare differently, just as you must prepare a petitioner's brief differently from the way you prepare a respondent's brief, or a memorandum supporting a motion differently from a memorandum in opposition to a motion. Football coaches also have practices for their "special teams," the teams that handle certain types of plays that occur during most games. For example, coaches will hold a separate practice for kickoffs, for kickoff returns, and for the onside kick. Coaches do this because each of these plays presents special situations not part of the regular play of the game, and each has special rules that govern it. Because these situations are opportunities to score points, or at least to create opportunities to score points, time focused on special teams may mean the difference between victory and defeat.

In brief writing, most of the attention goes, properly, to the argument section. But brief writers must pay attention to their "special teams," too. Different rules apply to various sections of the brief, and the writer must bring different skills to bear in these sections. Furthermore, even though most of these sections are not part of the argument per se, they can have an impact on the argument, either by encouraging the reader to reach certain conclusions before reading the argument or by persuading the reader to take a more sympathetic view of the argument. Although advocacy on behalf of a client is not a game, you can use your special teams to help the court to understand your arguments better. In this way, these sections of the document can have a significant impact on the outcome of the case. This chapter will discuss rules and strategies for writing effective issue statements, fact statements, argument summaries, and point headings.

9.1
WRITING THE ISSUE STATEMENT

Judge Patricia Wald of the United States Court of Appeals for the District of Columbia notes that counsel should spend some time on the issue because it "provides the lens through which the judge-reader enters the rest of the brief."[1] For most appellate judges, the issue, or question presented, provides the first image of the case, and each time they consider a new angle of the case by reading a new brief, they gain a new image (or regain an old image) by reading the question presented first. Practical lawyers exploit this opportunity and make sure that the image conveyed in the issue statement is one that they want the court to see.

Writers of motion briefs may articulate the issue in a short paragraph under the heading "Introduction" or "Preliminary Statement." In contrast, writers of appellate briefs, and of some motion briefs, write a formal question presented that crystallizes the issue in one sentence.

9.1.1
MOTION BRIEF INTRODUCTIONS

The introduction in a motion brief presents the issue in its legal and factual context. In the introduction, you should inform the court about the issue or issues before it and about the precise procedural step you are asking it to take. The introduction should be specific, mentioning parties by name, not just by procedural status, and clarifying the issue that is before the court on the motion:

---

[1] Patricia M. Wald, *19 Tips from 19 Years on the Appellate Bench*, 1 J. App. Prac. & Process 7, 12 (1999).

▽ BAD EXAMPLE

This motion arises out of a Title VII action. Defendant has filed a motion to dismiss because the Plaintiff has failed to state a claim upon which relief can be granted under Fed. R. Civ. P. 12(b)(6). This memorandum is filed in support of Defendant's Motion.

This introduction provides bare procedural information in that it tells the court that it is being asked to grant a motion to dismiss a Title VII action. It does not, however, clarify the narrow issue that is before the court, identify facts needed for context, or name the specific grounds for the defendant's motion:

△ GOOD EXAMPLE

This Motion arises out of an action alleging sexual harassment under Title VII, 42 U.S.C. §2000e-2. Plaintiff Lynda Garrett alleges Title VII violations by Defendants Gary Kirkby, her supervisor, and Marvin-Kobacker, their mutual employer. Defendant Gary Kirkby has filed this Motion to Dismiss as to himself alone under Fed. R. Civ. P. 12(b)(6). The Complaint fails to state a claim upon which relief can be granted against Defendant Kirkby because he is a supervisor and cannot be held individually liable as an "employer" under 42 U.S.C. §2000e(b). This Memorandum is filed in support of Mr. Kirkby's Motion.

This introduction tells the reader that this is a sexual harassment case, not just a Title VII case. It reveals that the ground for the motion is the assertion that supervisors cannot be held individually liable as "employers." In addition to providing the factual context that this is a sexual harassment case in the employment context, the introduction reveals that although there are two defendants, only one has filed this motion to dismiss.

The introduction is important in a motion brief because motions frequently address issues that are separate from the merits of the case. By writing a clear introduction, counsel provides needed context to the court that will enable it to better understand the rest of the brief. Although the introduction is not the place for strident argumentation, you can be mildly persuasive in your phrasing.

9.1.2
QUESTIONS PRESENTED

Some motion briefs—and many appellate briefs—use questions presented to articulate the issues before the court. Supreme Court Rule 14.1(a), which governs the questions as they appear in the petition for the writ of certiorari and which is referred to in Rule 24.1(a), requires that each question be "expressed concisely in relation to the circumstances of the case, without unnecessary detail." The rule further requires that the question be "short" and that it "should not be argumentative or repetitive." For briefs on the merits, Supreme Court Rule 24.1(a) requires that the brief contain "the questions presented for review under Rule 14.1(a)." Although this language appears to require that the attorney repeat the exact language of the question(s), the rule later states explicitly that the attorney may rewrite the language:

> The phrasing of the questions presented need not be identical with that in the petition for a writ of certiorari or the jurisdictional statement, but the brief may not raise additional questions or change the substance of the questions already presented in those documents.

Supreme Court Rule 24.1(a). Supreme Court Rule 14.1(a) specifically provides that "[t]he statement of any question presented is deemed to comprise every subsidiary question fairly included therein." Thus, the question presented written to the Court is generally a broad question that addresses the ultimate issues that the Court must consider in order to decide how to dispose of the case. Counsel for either party may decide to rephrase the questions to give the Court what it considers to be a more accurate snapshot of the issue. All questions presented, whether written for a motion brief or an appellate brief, should include certain elements, should be appropriately persuasive, and should avoid certain problems.

a. Elements to Include

Generally, writers should include three elements when writing a question presented: the question itself, expressed as a yes-or-no question; the relevant law; and the legally significant facts. Two formats that writers commonly use are the "under-does-when" format and the "whether" format. The "under-does-when" format essentially asks, "Under relevant law, does a certain legal status exist when these legally significant facts exist?" The "whether" format contains the same elements, but the information can be arranged in a different order: "Whether a certain legal status exists when relevant law governs the situation and these legally significant facts exist?" A "whether" question could also be arranged differently: "Whether a certain fact situation results in a certain legal status under this relevant legal standard?"[2] Here is an example of the same question written once in "under-does-when" format and once in "whether" format:

> **Under the Fourth Amendment's privacy guarantees, does an invitee into a residence have a legitimate expectation of privacy when the**

---

[2] People who are particular about grammar often cringe at the "whether" format because lawyers use it as if it is a complete sentence, even though it is technically a sentence fragment. (If you wanted to use the format correctly from a grammar viewpoint, you would write, "The issue is whether . . ." and end the sentence with a period.) Lawyers, however, have adopted the "whether" format as a valid sentence (using either a question mark or a period) and seem unlikely to change.

invitee's sole purpose for being present is to assist the resident in an illegal activity?

Whether an invitee into a residence has a legitimate expectation of privacy under the Fourth Amendment when the invitee's sole purpose for being present in the residence is to assist the resident in an illegal activity?

Some writers use the question presented to ask a question about a substantive legal issue, essentially asking, "Under relevant law, does a certain legal status exist when these legally significant facts are present?" as in this example:

Under the Fourth Amendment, can a state promote the interest of officer safety by enacting a statute that gives police officers authorization to conduct a search of a motor vehicle when they issue a citation to a person who has committed an offense that allows arrest?

Some appellate brief writers put the legal issue in the context of the decision that the court is being asked to reverse, essentially asking, "Whether the court below was correct when it held that under the relevant law, a certain legal status existed when these legally significant facts were present?" as in this example:

Whether the Iowa Supreme Court correctly held that states can, consistent with the Fourth Amendment, promote the interest of officer safety by enacting a statute that gives police officers authorization to conduct a search of a motor vehicle when they issue a citation to a person who has committed an offense that allows arrest?

Writers of motion briefs do not have this concern, but they may face others. Many motion briefs are focused on legal issues, and motion brief questions presented based on those issues will look almost identical to appellate brief questions presented. Questions about the sufficiency of the pleadings, however, will of necessity be more focused on specifics of the complaint. These questions presented may well include language that focuses the court's attention on the pleading standard (e.g., the standard of review for a motion to dismiss).

The following example shows two questions from a motion brief addressing issues related to Ohio's public policy exception to the employment-at-will doctrine. The doctrine allows a plaintiff to recover damages for a wrongful discharge if he or she can establish four elements. One of the elements is a question of law that requires the plaintiff to establish that a particular public policy will be "jeopardized" by the plaintiff's termination. Another element is a question of fact that requires the plaintiff to prove that the discharge was "caused" by public policy related behavior. Note how the questions differ in focus; in particular, note how the second question includes language relevant to the pleading standard:

⚠ GOOD EXAMPLES

> Under Ohio's public policy exception to the employment-at-will doctrine, which provides that a public policy is "jeopardized" only when relevant statutes do not provide adequate remedies to protect society's interest in the policy, can a plaintiff establish jeopardy when the relevant statutes provide for a series of penalties, beginning with a warning letter and moving on to fines in the thousands of dollars?

> Under Ohio's public policy exception to the employment-at-will doctrine, which provides that causation can be established when an employee is terminated soon after protected behavior by a person who had knowledge of the protected behavior, has a plaintiff pled facts sufficient to raise his right to relief above the speculative level when he alleges that he complained about illegal cigarette smoking to one supervisor and that he was fired by another supervisor five months later?

In addition to deciding how to focus your question, you must also decide how to structure the question. The "whether" structure often moves the core question to the beginning of the question:

> Whether the court below erred when it held that this law applied in this way to the legally significant facts?

or

> Whether legal status exists when these legally significant facts exist and when this law applies?

The "under-does-when" format, on the other hand, puts less emphasis on the core question, putting the law at the beginning. It also allows the writer to shift the legally significant facts to the end of the question, which may help to emphasize positive facts, as in this example:

> Under the Fourth Amendment's privacy guarantees, does an invitee into a residence have a legitimate expectation of privacy when the invitee's sole purpose for being present is to assist the resident in an illegal activity?

When deciding which format to use, consider what information you would like in the positions of emphasis within the question. Generally, the beginning and the end of the question are positions of emphasis, with the end of the question being the strongest position.

b.   Persuasive Questions Presented

When choosing the format and the type of question that you ask, consider which drafting method will allow you to emphasize your point of view. The practical brief writer does more than merely write a question that includes all three of the needed elements. Karl Llewellyn notes the importance of "controlling" the legal issues in a case:

Of course, the first thing that comes up is the issue and the first art is the framing of the issue so that if your framing is accepted the case comes out your way. Got that? Second, you have to capture the issue, because your opponent will be framing an issue very differently. . . . And third, you have to build a technique of phrasing your issue which will not only capture the Court but which will stick your capture into the Court's head so that it can't forget it.[3]

Conventional wisdom has it that the advocate should draft a question so that a "yes" answer is favorable to his or her case. This advice is valid, but following it may not result in a question that grabs the reader's attention and allows the reader to see the case from the advocate's point of view. The better path is to ask yourself how you would describe your client's case in a nutshell. What facts are most important? How would you characterize the issue? Look at the differences between the following two questions. They were written from the opposite sides of *Minnesota v. Carter*, 525 U.S. 83 (1998), a case about the constitutionality of an arrest that was based on an officer's observation of two apparent drug dealers in a colleague's apartment as they "bagged" some drugs for sale:

Under the Fourth Amendment, was the Minnesota Supreme Court correct when it found that Respondents, as social guests, had a reasonable expectation of privacy in the home they were visiting?

Whether the Fourth Amendment gives invitees into a residence a legitimate expectation of privacy while in the residence when their sole purpose for being present is to assist the resident in an illegal activity?

Note that the writer of the first wants the reader to answer "yes," to agree with the assertion that social guests have a reasonable expectation of privacy in the home in which they are visiting. The second is also an effective question, but the drafter of that question has essentially asked the question "do invitees have a legitimate expectation of privacy when they are doing something illegal?" and hopes that the reader will answer "of course not!" By asking the question in this way, the drafter tries to show that the opponent's argument is based on a ridiculous premise. The drafter hopes that the court's dramatic, negative reaction to the question will convince it that the other side is asking for a ridiculous result.

---

[3] Karl N. Llewellyn, *A Lecture on Appellate Advocacy*, 29 U. Chi. L. Rev. 627, 630 (1962), cited in Bryan A. Garner, *The Deep Issue: A New Approach to Framing Legal Questions*, 5 Scribes J. Legal Writing 1, 11 (1994-95).

The writers of both of these questions are trying to influence the Court's image of the case by including what Judge Ruggero Aldisert calls "enthymemes": unspoken premises that support their arguments.[4]

Although the best enthymemes are based on legal premises that any court would agree with, some effective enthymemes can be based on policy premises or even commonsense premises. Some enthymemes are conveyed through the focus of a question on a particular angle of the case, while others may be conveyed merely by the choice of one word over another.

In the first example shown previously, the writer is basing his or her arguments on at least three unstated premises: (1) that the Supreme Court should give some deference to the Minnesota Supreme Court, (2) that "homes" are private places, and (3) that "social guests" have expectations of privacy.

The second example, written from the government's point of view, is based on some opposite premises: (1) that "invitees" have less of an expectation of privacy than "social guests," (2) that "residences" are less private than "homes," and, most importantly, (3) that people who participate in illegal activities have no expectation of privacy. The writer asks whether the opponent's premises are correct, hoping that they are so obviously wrong (as they have been portrayed in the question) that the reader will answer the question with an immediate "of course not!"

If you can base your question on a premise that is both valid and applicable, you can go a long way toward getting the court to agree with your argument before it has even read your first point heading. Often, both sides will have valid and applicable premises on which to base their questions, and so both sides can exploit this technique to emphasize their point of view. When writing the question, remember that readers naturally pay more attention to information that appears in certain natural positions of emphasis—usually beginnings and endings—and try to put your best points in the beginning and especially at the end of the question presented. By planning your question in advance, noting what elements are most important and least important, you can structure your sentence to highlight your best points.

c. Problems to Avoid

i. Assuming Elements at Issue

When writing questions presented, include facts and law that will help the readers to reach the conclusion you want them to reach. Avoid, however, assuming as true an element that is at issue in the case. A question that assumes an element at issue often asks, in essence:

---

[4] *See* Ruggero J. Aldisert, *Winning on Appeal* 142-43 (rev. 1st ed., Natl. Inst. Trial Advoc. 1996).

▽ BAD EXAMPLE

Will this Court find that condition X exists when Appellant has established all of the factors necessary for condition X?

Even though you may firmly believe that all of the factors are there, your question should not assume away elements that your opponent legitimately disputes. Instead, include the facts and the law that you can use to prove that the court should decide in your favor.

For example, in the following question, the writer has assumed that no fundamental right has been violated:

▽ BAD EXAMPLE

Do voter-initiated, state constitutional amendments that prohibit the enactment of legislation desired by an identifiable class comply with the Equal Protection Clause of the Fourteenth Amendment when such amendments do not violate a fundamental right?

Because the other side argued that the amendment *did* violate a fundamental right, the question assumes an element at issue. Instead, the writer should include the facts and law that he or she plans to use to show that no fundamental right has been violated:

△ GOOD EXAMPLE

Do voter-initiated, state constitutional amendments that prohibit the enactment of legislation desired by an identifiable class comply with the Equal Protection Clause of the Fourteenth Amendment when the amendments do not inhibit the right to vote?

This question focuses on the fact that the writer thinks is most important: Whatever else the amendments may do, they do not inhibit the fundamental right to vote.

In the following example, a different version of a question appropriate in *Minnesota v. Carter*, the writer has assumed that the issue of whether the defendant had a "reasonable expectation of privacy" has been met:

▽ BAD EXAMPLE

Whether citizens have a constitutionally protected right to be free from a police officer's covert observation into a private dwelling when that citizen reasonably expected and took measures to ensure that his activities would be shielded from the public's view?

Instead of including the citizen's "reasonable expectation" as a fact, the writer should include the facts that he or she will use to prove that the expectation of privacy was reasonable:

△ GOOD EXAMPLE

Under the Fourth Amendment, does a citizen have a right to be free from a police officer's covert observation into a private dwelling when

the citizen was sitting in a kitchen and the blinds on the windows
had been closed against the public's view?

This question still makes effective use of the enthymemes "citizens have
a right to privacy," "private dwellings are private," and "covert observations violate privacy rights," but it doesn't sabotage itself by assuming the
crucial element at issue.

In addition to violating rules of logic, questions that assume elements
at issue needlessly annoy the judge or justice reading the brief, and fail to
do the job of the question presented: to enlighten the court as to the issue
or issues before it. The Honorable Fred I. Parker of the United States Court
of Appeals for the Second Circuit has noted that questions that assume the
element at issue "serve no useful purpose."[5] Furthermore, he notes, they
may prejudice the judge against an attorney who would write such a use-
less question:

> [A]fter reading such a statement, my natural instinct is to believe the
> actual issue probably involves [some other legal question], which the
> writer of the brief was not nice enough to clearly state for me and has
> instead left me to figure out on my own. I am, therefore, immediately less
> than sanguine about the brief and, consequently, the advocate and his or
> her client. Further, in failing to quickly be able to ascertain what the issues
> are, I may resort to the other brief for help.[6]

Thus, by avoiding the trap of assuming elements at issue, you can both
preserve your credibility with the court and incline the judge or justice to
rely on your brief for a fair analysis of the case.

ii. Overlong Questions

Writers who try a variety of persuasive techniques may also fall into
the trap of writing a question that is too long. Questions that are too
long are not read carefully—if they are read at all—and so any individual
points that the writer may make in the question are lost to the reader, as in
the following question, written by a student for one of the parties in *Rubin
v. Coors Brewing Co.*, 514 U.S. 476 (1995):

▽ BAD EXAMPLE

Should the Supreme Court of the United States affirm both the
District Court and Tenth Circuit Court of Appeals decisions to enjoin
enforcement of that portion of 27 U.S.C. §205(e)(2) and its pertinent
regulation 27 C.F.R. §7.26, which prohibit labeling malt beverages
with their accurately measured and truthful alcoholic content and

---

[5] Fred I. Parker, *Foreword: Appellate Advocacy and Practice in the Second Circuit*, 64 Brook. L. Rev.
457, 461 (1998).
   [6] *Id.*

thus allow the plaintiff and other brewers of malt beverages to better inform the consumers of their products by placing the percentage of alcohol contained in the beverage on the beverage container's label?

This question includes several valid premises—truthful information is good, informing consumers is good, it is legal to give accurate information to people—but the question's length reduces its effectiveness. The following question covers some of the same ground, but more briefly:

◮ GOOD EXAMPLE

Under the First Amendment, is a prohibition against labeling malt beverages with their alcohol content valid when including the content on the label would allow consumers to have access to accurate and truthful alcohol content information?

d. Summing Up

When writing the question presented, strive to control the picture that the court has of your case by deciding what question you want to focus its attention on and by using appropriate writing techniques, including (1) giving the court a complete picture of the issue by including the legal context, the core legal question, and the relevant facts; (2) using appropriate enthymemes in the question; (3) structuring the question to highlight the positive aspects of the question; (4) avoiding assuming elements at issue; and (5) keeping the question to a reasonable length.

9.2
STATEMENTS OF THE CASE

The statement of the case provides the court with information about the procedural life of the case before it, as well as about the relevant facts that led the parties to court. For this reason, it is known familiarly as the statement, the statement of the case, and the fact statement. Some writers of appellate briefs use these last two categories as headings to divide their statement into factual and procedural categories.

Although fact statements for appellate briefs and motion briefs have many common challenges, fact statements for motion briefs present some unique difficulties. The author of an appellate brief often has a well-developed record, with findings of facts articulated by the court below. In contrast, the writer of a motion brief may be working from a complaint or from other documents alleging facts that must be taken as true, even though no court has made formal findings of fact. Nevertheless, both writers of motion briefs and writers of appellate briefs must follow similar formal requirements and can use similar persuasive techniques.

9.2.1
FORMAL REQUIREMENTS

Supreme Court Rule 24.1(g) provides that a brief on the merits for a petitioner or an appellant[7] shall contain

> [a] concise statement of the case, setting out the facts material to the consideration of the questions presented, with appropriate references to the joint appendix, *e.g.*, App. 12, or to the record, *e.g.*, Record 12.

An effective statement of the case will make it unnecessary for the court to resort to the record or the joint appendix, providing a "universe of facts" to which the court can refer. With rare exceptions, the statement should include in sufficient detail any fact even *referenced* in the argument.

In an appellate brief, the statement of the case should include necessary procedural facts and relevant background information in addition to the facts needed for the argument. The advocate should tell the story of the events that gave rise to the litigation and how it progressed through the court system on up to the current hearing. A motion brief, in contrast, usually occurs at a very early stage in the litigation. The writer must provide procedural information as to how the lawsuit began and how it has progressed, but this information is usually not lengthy and is thus not a significant part of the statement.

The statement should also include citations that will allow the reader to verify easily the information cited. In an appellate brief, most of the information will come from a joint appendix or a record, and that information should be cited according to Rule 24.1(a) or the appropriate rule from your jurisdiction. For many Supreme Court cases, the appendix to the petition for the writ of certiorari contains important factual information. This appendix is usually cited along the same lines as the joint appendix, e.g., Pet. App. 12. Information that comes from the lower court opinions in the case (when these are not part of the record materials), as well as any statutes that may be included in the fact statement, should be cited according to appropriate citation rules.

As noted previously, if you are writing a motion brief, you usually will not have a lengthy record to draw on. You should take care, however, to cite precisely to the documents on which you have relied for your information, and to be sure the court has access to those documents as well. If the document has numbered paragraphs, as most complaints do, then cite

---

[7] Supreme Court Rule 24.2 permits respondents and appellees to omit several items from the brief (questions presented, the list of parties to the proceedings, opinions below, jurisdictional statement, statutes involved, and statement of the facts) "unless the respondent or appellee is dissatisfied with their presentation by the opposing party." In most appellate advocacy courses, however, students are required to include all elements of the brief.

to the specific paragraph referred to. For documents without numbered paragraphs, cite to the page number. Thus:

⚠ GOOD EXAMPLE

Mr. Kirkby was the Section Manager responsible for the supervision of the Plaintiff and 25 other administrative personnel. Compl.¶5. According to the Executive Vice-President of the Company, this number of employees was typical for most supervisors at Marvin-Kobacker. Sczesny Aff. at 23.

Citations in the fact statement are vital because many judges will not trust facts without an appropriate citation. Judge Clyde H. Hamilton, of the United States Court of Appeals for the Fourth Circuit, counts missing citations as one of the major problems with fact statements:

> [The importance of] appropriate citations to the appendix . . . cannot be overemphasized. Little else makes my blood boil quicker than reading an appellate brief that lacks appropriate citations to the appendix in the statement of facts and the argument components. Apparently, the parties submitting these briefs are under the serious misimpression that appellate judges have endless hours to spend combing the appendix in an effort to match up scattered pieces of evidence with a party's unreferenced factual assertions.[8]

Thus, it would not be unusual to have a citation at the end of every sentence in a fact statement. Because the use of "*id.*" Is as appropriate for record citations as for any other kind of citation, these multiple citations need not be intrusive.

If this is the first time you are working with a lengthy record, you may be tempted to "treasure hunt" for facts that help your client's case or hurt your opponent's. Hunting for treasure is fine, but be sure you have not found fool's gold: Only formal findings of fact can be cited as such. If you think it would be helpful to cite testimony or other evidence that was not part of the court's factual findings, be sure that you characterize it appropriately.

9.2.2
ORGANIZING THE FACT STATEMENT

A good fact statement begins by providing the reader with the necessary context. Too many writers begin the statement with the first happening in the case's chain of events, as in the following example from a fact statement written in the case of *Rubin v. Coors Brewing Co.*:

---

[8] Clyde H. Hamilton, *Effective Appellate Brief Writing*, 50 S.C. L. Rev. 581, 586 (1999).

▽ BAD EXAMPLE

> **In 1987, Coors Brewing Company submitted an application to the Bureau of Alcohol, Tobacco and Firearms requesting approval for the labels that disclosed the alcohol content of their Coors and Coors Light Beers. App. 60-65.**

Although this sentence makes reference to the controversy—whether beer manufacturers can put alcohol content on their labels—it does not identify the controversy for the reader. The following example provides better context:

△ GOOD EXAMPLE

> **This Court is being asked to affirm a decision of the Ninth Circuit Court of Appeals that found that 27 U.S.C. §§205(e)(2) and 205(f)(2) violate the First Amendment to the United States Constitution. Those provisions prohibit labels or advertisements disclosing the alcohol content of malt beverages unless disclosure is required by state law.**

These two sentences set both the procedural and legal context, and better enable the reader to understand the significance of the rest of the information in the statement.

After providing context, the writer must decide how to organize the rest of the fact statement. Although chronological organization is often favored, sometimes a topical organization is more effective. For example, in *Locke v. Davey*, 540 U.S. 712 (2004), the Court was asked to decide whether a state scholarship program could refuse to grant a scholarship to a student because he was studying for the ministry. The state constitution forbade funding religious education. The writer could combine a chronological organization and a topical organization, beginning with the enactment of the constitution, moving to the creation of the scholarship program, and then ending on the facts leading up to the respondent's challenge. In the alternative, the writer could begin with the respondent being denied a scholarship, and use that denial to set the stage for the other facts.

You may have strategic reasons for choosing or avoiding chronological organization. If causation is at issue, presenting information chronologically may send the implicit message that the events that occurred earlier caused the events that occurred later. If you do *not* want to send that message, present the later events first (using topical headings as needed) and then move back to the earlier events.

When deciding how to organize the fact statement, try to identify a set of topics that you can use as an organizing principle, whether or not you ultimately discuss those topics chronologically. Identifying topics can allow you to create topical headings within the statement; headings are particularly helpful if the statement is long. Although the writer must provide procedural as well as "factual" information, there is no requirement as to where in the fact statement this information must be included. Some writers provide the information about court proceedings immediately after giving context; others progress chronologically from the facts that happened "in the world" to the facts that happened in court. Finally, some writers include internal headings to separate their "statement of the case" (including procedural information) from their "statement of the facts" (for factual information).

9.2.3
MAKING THE FACT STATEMENT PERSUASIVE

Most courts frown on the inclusion of legal arguments in the fact statement. They frown even more on lying, even if by omission, or on stretching the truth in the way that you characterize the facts. You should include all legally significant facts, even those that may hurt your case. Including all relevant facts is important both for moral reasons—your oath as an attorney requires it—and for practical reasons—your opponent will point out that you lied, and you will lose your credibility with the court.[9] Judge Morey L. Sear, of the United States District Court for the Eastern District of Louisiana, notes that "[i]f a lawyer's brief . . . fudges on the content of clear testimony, credibility is immediately destroyed. In my view, credibility is one of the most important virtues a litigator can possess."[10]

Supreme Court Justice Ruth Bader Ginsburg advises that "[a]bove all, a good brief is trustworthy. It states the facts honestly."[11] Judge Parker notes that severe distortions of the facts "will actually make me stop reading the brief and go to the district court's opinion, or even the opposing brief." [12]

Nevertheless, you can use persuasive writing techniques to tell the story from your point of view, to highlight the facts that are in your favor, and to lead the reader to draw honest and favorable conclusions about your client's case.[13]

When drafting the fact statement, remember that your reader will not be a passive recipient of information, dutifully taking in whatever you have put on the page and doing nothing more with it. Most readers—yourself included—are constantly assessing, using inductive and deductive reasoning, leaping to conclusions, and, at times, leaving the text entirely. In the

---

[9] *See, e.g.,* Parker, *supra* note 5, at 462.

[10] Morey L. Sear, *Briefing in the United States District Court for the Eastern District of Louisiana,* 70 Tul. L. Rev. 207, 219 (1995).

[11] Ruth Bader Ginsburg, *Remarks on Appellate Advocacy,* 50 S.C. L. Rev. 567, 568 (1999). *See also* Joel F. Dubina, *How to Litigate Successfully in the United States Court of Appeals for the Eleventh Circuit,* 20 Cumb. L. Rev. 1, 5 (1998/1999); Sarah B. Duncan, *Pursuing Quality: Writing a Helpful Brief,* 30 St. Mary's L.J. 1093, 1101 (1999).

[12] Parker, *supra* note 5, at 462.

[13] For an excellent discussion of persuasive writing techniques in fact statements, *see* Laurel Currie Oates & Anne M. Enquist, *The Legal Writing Handbook* §§17.7, 18.12 (5th ed., Aspen 2010).

argument, you will be announcing your conclusions to the reader and then, ideally, supporting them with your analysis. In the fact statement, on the other hand, you can provide information that the reader can put together to reach a conclusion. If you do it skillfully enough, the reader will have drawn a conclusion in your favor even before reaching the first page of the argument section.

For example, my father, who served in the Coast Guard in the early 1950s, tells this possibly apocryphal story about a captain and his first mate—and at least one episode of drunkenness:

> One day, when the sailors took shore leave, the first mate returned to the ship drunk. The Captain recorded this event, noting, "The first mate was drunk today" in the Captain's log. The first mate has the responsibility for keeping the log when the Captain is off duty, so he soon saw the note. He was furious; he had never been drunk before, he had been off duty when he was drunk, and he was one of a dozen drunken sailors, none of whose drunkenness was recorded in the log. He decided to retaliate. He knew he couldn't lie about the Captain, for the Captain would be seeing the log the very next day. So he wrote the simple truth: "The Captain was sober today."

If you read that log without knowing the details, you would no doubt jump to the conclusion that the Captain was *usually* drunk; thus, it was worth recording the rare occasion when he was sober. Scholars who study narrative theory note that readers who jump to conclusions probably do so due to their conscious or unconscious awareness of "stock stories," or "schemas" that they have been accumulating all of their lives.[14] Because the state of being sober is an unremarkable fact for most people, a reader subconsciously decides that if the mate wrote "the captain was sober today," he must have done so because the captain was usually *not* sober. Narrative reasoning is logical reasoning. It consists of major and minor premises, just as traditional reasoning does. The difference is that the premises are often not included explicitly in the written word; rather, the writer relies on the reader's schemas to provide one or more of the relevant premises.

Some schemas concern presumptions about how people communicate, as in the first mate story, which we can portray in a syllogism as follows:

---

[14] Linda L. Berger, *How Embedded Knowledge Structures Affect Judicial Decision Making: A Rhetorical Analysis of Metaphor, Narrative, and Imagination in Child Custody Disputes,* 18 S. Cal. Interdisc. L.J. 259, 263 (2009) ("We make sense out of new experiences by placing them into categories and cognitive frames called schema or scripts that emerge from prior experience.") (citations omitted). For further discussion of narrative theory and other persuasive writing techniques, see Michael R. Smith, *Advanced Legal Writing: Theories and Strategies in Persuasive Writing* (3d ed., Aspen 2012); Ruth Anne Robbins, Steve Johansen & Ken Chestek, *Your Client's Story: Persuasive Legal Writing* (Aspen 2012).

Issue:	Is the captain usually drunk?
(Unstated) Major premise:	Normal states of being are not worth observing or recording; only unusual behavior should be recorded.
Minor premise:	The first mate recorded the fact that the captain was sober today.
Conclusion:	Therefore, sobriety is not his normal state of being, and the captain must usually be drunk.

If we can assume that the captain was not actually a drunkard, the first mate enlisted his readers and had them tell themselves a lie on his behalf. But even though the mate told the literal truth, he is not innocent of the lie: His knowledge of human thought and behavior no doubt told him how his readers would react, and he wrote his truthful statement conscious of the untruth that would result.[15]

I am not telling you this story so that you will make your readers lie to themselves; rather, I want you to realize that whenever people read, many different thought processes come into play: They use deductive and inductive reasoning, and their own knowledge and prejudices, to fill in details and jump to conclusions. Readers jump to conclusions based not only on information that is included, but also based on information that is not included. For example, while I was in the middle of reading a novel set in and written in the nineteenth century, a new male character was described as "clean-shaven." I suddenly realized that all of the *other* male characters must have had "whiskers." I had pictured them as clean-shaven because that fit with my schema, or default image, of adult males: Presume no facial hair unless told otherwise. The author did not believe that whiskers were worth mentioning, for in her world whiskers were the default mode for adult men.

Although narrative reasoning may rely on schemas about human communication, it may also rely on schemas about human or institutional behavior. For example, you may remember the economic crisis of October 2008. As it happened, my husband and I were in Paris that week, and it was interesting to observe the crisis as it was reported by French newspapers (through my feeble translations) and on CNN International. Whenever I tried to tell the story, however, I could see my listeners shut down as soon as I said, "My husband and I were in Paris, and . . . ." I could almost hear them thinking, "must be nice," and I hypothesize that their thoughts could be put into a syllogism as follows:

---

[15] *See* Steven J. Johansen, *This Is Not the Whole Truth: The Ethics of Telling Stories to Clients*, 38 Ariz. St. L.J. 961, 992 (2006) ("left unchecked . . . [the] deception [of false stories] could be disruptive to our legal system").

Issue:	Do I want to listen to Mary Beth's story?
(Unstated) Major premise:	I don't want to listen to her story if I don't like her.
(Unstated) Major premise:	I don't like rich people.
(Unstated) Major premise:	People who go to Paris are rich.
Minor premise:	Mary Beth and her husband go to Paris.
Conclusion:	Mary Beth is rich; I don't like her; and I don't want to listen to her story.

I found, however, that if I included one or two other details, I got a completely different reaction from my listeners. Sometimes I started the story by saying, "in honor of our twentieth wedding anniversary, my husband and I were in Paris last October." Instead of shutting down, people almost invariably, said, "Aww! Did you have a good time?" And I was able to go on with my story. At other times, I added the detail that we had stayed in the same hotel that I had stayed in when I visited Paris on a backpacking trip in college. This detail also cut off the "must be nice" reaction and enabled me to tell the story (and since I love telling stories, that was very important to me). I hypothesize that adding these details (which were true, by the way) led to schemas that changed the path of my listeners' thoughts:

Issue:	Do I want to listen to Mary Beth's story?
(Unstated) Major premise:	I will listen to her story if I like her.
(Unstated) Major premise:	I don't like rich people.
(Unstated) Major premise:	Trips in honor of anniversaries are special trips that people scrimp and save for.
(Unstated) Major premise:	Hotels that college students stay in are inexpensive.
Minor Premise:	Mary Beth and her husband went to Paris for their anniversary and stayed in a student hotel.
Conclusion:	Mary Beth is not rich, so I like her and will listen to her story.

When you are writing a statement of facts, you are trying to tell a story. Recognize that including certain details may lead your readers to jump to conclusions—or refer to schemas—that may help or hurt your case. Aim to tell the story in a way that is consistent with and promotes your legal argument. As indicated above, readers sometimes jump to conclusions; those conclusions may be factual conclusions or legal ones. For example, if you are trying to persuade your reader that certain activities were or were not within an employee's "scope of employment," you might tell the story in a way that emphasizes the connection between the challenged activities and the job's duties and responsibilities. To the extent that you can get your reader to conclude that the challenged activities were "just part of the job," you have gone a long way to advance your "scope of employment" argument. Storytelling can go beyond appealing just to "pathos," or a reader's emotions. When done well, it can enhance the credibility of the writer (thus appealing to "ethos") and engage the reader's logical thought processes as well ("logos").[16] Upon reading the captain and the first mate story, after all, you used logical reasoning to reach your own understanding of why the first mate wrote "the captain was sober today."

Legal writers can use storytelling method to help their readers understand why certain parties have behaved in particular ways. Professor Ruth Anne Robbins notes that "people respond–instinctively and intuitively" to certain schemas and "character archetypes," and that lawyers should "systematically and deliberately integrate into their storytelling the larger picture of their clients' goals by subtly portraying their individual clients as heroes on a particular life path."[17] Professor Robbins advises against casting the client's opponent (or other antagonist) as a Voldemort-style villain.[18] Instead, she recommends a more benign role: The antagonist is someone who is frustrating the hero, barring him or her from achieving a goal.[19]

You may want to tell your story in terms of a quest.[20] What does your client seek? Rather than thinking in pure procedural terms—that your client wants the court to grant or deny a motion, or to affirm or reverse a decision—think in terms of your theme. In the Coors Beer case, for example, Coors wanted to give its customers truthful information about the percentage of alcohol in its beers, but it was thwarted by an outdated government regulation. The government, in contrast, sought to protect its citizens from harmful binge drinking, and it was thwarted by greedy corporations who wanted to make money by promoting excessive alcohol consumption. In *Miller v. Albright*, the petitioner could have the goal of establishing a relationship with her father, while the government seeks the right to control its borders and to determine who is eligible for automatic citizenship. A more difficult case is the case of an employee who is trying to establish individual liability of supervisors so that she can sue the person who sexually harassed her. Rather than portraying her purely as a victim,[21] the fact statement can show her as someone who wants to

---

[16] *See* Jennifer Sheppard, *Once Upon a Time, Happily Ever After, and in a Galaxy Far, Far Away: Using Narrative to Fill the Cognitive Gap Left Behind by Overreliance on Pure Logic in Appellate Briefs and Motion Memoranda,* 46 Willamette L. Rev. 255, 256 (2009).

[17] Ruth Anne Robbins, *Harry Potter, Ruby Slippers and Merlin: Telling the Client's Story Using the Characters and Paradigm of the Archetypal Hero's Journey,* 29 Seattle U. L. Rev. 767, 768-69 (2006).

[18] *Id.* at 788.

[19] *See id.*

[20] *See id.* at 781-82.

[21] *See id.* at 779-80 (advising against portraying client as a victim).

vindicate herself and prevent future harassment by suing her harasser directly. The defendant, in contrast, could portray himself as someone who wants to be treated as an individual and not as a corporation.

Your fact statement can identify the hero or protagonist (perhaps your client, perhaps a legislature, perhaps the constitution) and the antagonists (perhaps your opponent, or some agent of your opponent).[22] Your protagonist, though, is frustrated; its goal has been thwarted by some outside actor or problem.[23] Seen from this perspective, the antagonist can be a person, a governmental body, or an "absurd" interpretation of a statute. Your client's goal is not merely a particular court decision; rather, the goal is an experience or status *made possible* by the court's decision.

Accordingly, when you are writing your statement of the facts, review your theme and the legal conclusions you want the reader to draw, and consider how those legal conclusions relate to the facts. Recognize conclusions that you might want to lead your readers to, and conclusions you want the reader to avoid. Consider what presumptions, schemas, or "default images," could be relevant to the case generally, and to people like your client or your opponent in particular. For example, has your client had several drug arrests? Could your readers have certain presumptions about police officers or corporate executives that you want to reinforce or rebut? As I did with my Paris story, you might want to add certain details that will lead your readers' thoughts in a good direction.

For example, if you want the court to overturn your client's criminal conviction, it might help the court to decide in your favor if it believes both that your client was treated unfairly and that your client is essentially an innocent person who was in the wrong place at the wrong time (a familiar schema). Your fact statement can include the details that will help the reader reach these conclusions independently. In *Holloway v. United States*, 526 U.S. 1 (1999), for example, counsel for Mr. Holloway had to convince the Court that it should overturn a conviction under the federal carjacking statute. The controversy centered on whether Holloway's participation in the carjacking constituted sufficient "intent to cause death or serious bodily harm." Holloway (petitioner at the Supreme Court) admittedly had been part of the carjackings, and a carjacking is a frightening crime to most people. One (student) counsel for Holloway tried to add details in the facts that would contradict the presumption that someone who would participate in a carjacking would be a violent person, and essentially tried to portray the client as an innocent who was trying to make the best of a bad situation:

---

[22] Kenneth D. Chestek, *The Plot Thickens: Appellate Brief as Story*, 14 Legal Writ. 127, 152-53 (2008) (describing strategies for choosing protagonists and antagonists).

[23] Robbins, *supra* note 17, at 778 (discussing different types of heroes, from the innocent to the warrior).

Vernon Lennon recruited Petitioner to steal cars with him. Record 156. Lennon showed Holloway the revolver that Lennon planned to carry during the commission of the robberies. Apparently, it was Holloway's job to drive the "getaway" car. Id. There is no evidence in the record that Lennon told Holloway that he planned to shoot the victims. Holloway never carried a gun during any of the robberies.

On October 14, 1994, Lennon and Holloway stole a car in Queens. Record 83-84. The car's owner sustained no injuries. The next day, the two men stole a Toyota and a Mercedes-Benz. Record 84. Holloway never even approached the driver of the Toyota; like the first driver, he escaped unharmed. Id. Lennon and Holloway both advanced toward the driver of the Mercedes-Benz, and Lennon produced his gun and threatened to shoot. Record 84. When the driver hesitated momentarily, Holloway stepped in and struck him once, before Lennon could take any action. Id. At this point, the driver surrendered his keys and fled, essentially unharmed. Id.

These details emphasize that Holloway never carried a gun and that none of the victims were shot. In the last incident, Holloway seems to become a legitimate hero; it appears that he prevented Lennon, his accomplice (or perhaps, in this telling, a bullying ringleader), from shooting one of the victims.

After you have considered your theme, the conclusions you want the reader to draw, and the schemas you might want to exploit, make a list of all of the facts that are relevant to your case. You may consult the abstract of the record, the record itself, the lower court decisions, and even the argument to come up with all of the legally (and emotionally) significant facts. (Be certain, of course, not to mischaracterize facts that were offered into evidence and rejected.) Perhaps divide your list into three parts: neutral facts, positive facts, and negative facts. As you tell your story, you can use some or all of the following persuasive techniques to highlight the positive facts and "lowlight" the negative ones.

a. Positions of Emphasis

An easy and effective way to highlight information is to put it into positions of emphasis within the document. Readers subconsciously pay more attention to information that appears before or after a mental or physical break within the document. Thus, both the beginning and the ending of the fact statement are positions of emphasis, as are the beginnings and endings of any heading sections within the facts, and even the first and last sentences of paragraphs.

When writing your fact statement, strive to put your "positive facts" into positions of emphasis. You may even create positions of emphasis by inserting topical headings, by creating paragraph breaks, or by using headings to separate the introduction from the fact statement or the fact statement from the statement of the "case" (i.e., the description of the proceedings below).

b. Pointillism

One way to think about the power of narrative reasoning is to compare it to pointillism, a painting technique developed in the nineteenth century by Georges Seurat. Instead of mixing red and blue paint on his palette to make purple paint, he painted red dots next to blue dots and allowed the viewer's eye to "mix" the color. Legal writers can practice pointillism to try to control the way the reader sees information in the fact statement. If you put certain facts next to certain other facts, the reader's brain may "mix" the information to draw the conclusion that you want. When making your list of facts, try to identify facts that can be paired, either to lead the reader to draw a good conclusion or to prevent the reader from drawing a bad one. For bad facts, use the "buddy system": Make sure that every bad fact that is included in the statement is paired with a good fact that explains (or neutralizes) its presence. Certain negative facts will look better if they are juxtaposed with a good fact, or even a neutral fact that readers can use to explain to themselves why the negative fact occurred or why it is not significant. For example, in the case of *Miller v. Albright*, 523 U.S. 420 (1998), Ms. Miller, who was born in the Philippines, was trying to establish United States citizenship through her relationship with her father, a United States citizen. One reason that had been given for limiting the ability to establish citizenship in this way was the prevention of fraud. Ms. Miller's father had not been listed on her birth certificate, a "bad fact" that needed to be addressed. One writer tried to put that fact into a good context in the following way:

⚠ GOOD EXAMPLE

> **Ms. Miller was born in the Philippines on June 20, 1970. App. 15. Although her birth record did not include her father's name, a voluntary paternity decree issued on July 27, 1992, by a Texas state court established Charlie R. Miller, a United States citizen, as her biological father. Pet App. 37.**

Thus, the reader learns that even though the father's name was not on the birth certificate, he was willing to have paternity established by a voluntary paternity decree. This juxtaposition would encourage readers to conclude that their relationship was a legitimate one and that fraud was not an issue here.

c. Spending the Reader's Time, Saving the Reader's Energy

To make sure that your reader remembers the positive facts in your case, make him or her spend more time and less energy on them. Use several sentences to make a point instead of crowding the information into one sentence.[24] Be as concrete as you can be when describing a positive fact so that the reader doesn't have to figure out what happened. Conversely, when you want to deemphasize a fact, don't spend much time on it, don't go into a lot of detail, and don't use concrete language. For example, in *City of Indianapolis v. Edmond*, 531 U.S. 32 (2000), a case about the constitutionality of drug interdiction roadblocks, counsel for the city of Indianapolis might describe the police procedure succinctly:

> Traffic stops consist of two simple steps: Officers verify the driver's license and registration, and then conduct a quick walk-around of the car with a narcotics-sniffing dog. Record 57a. They conduct a more thorough search *only* if the narcotics dog, plain-view, or plain-smell observation reveals a suspicion of narcotics possession, or if the driver gives explicit consent to search. Record 57a, 53a.

These two rather long sentences give a complete, but not detailed, account. The reader would have to expend energy to identify the details that this brief description implies, and more than likely would not do so. Counsel for the respondent, on the other hand, might describe the police procedure in greater detail:

> Upon entering the checkpoint, an automobile's driver and occupants are subjected to a number of examinations, which are conducted by Indianapolis police officers. Record 57a. First, the officers approach the vehicle, and the driver is asked to produce both a valid driver's license and the registration for the vehicle. Record 57a. After one officer examines and verifies this documentation, other officers scrutinize the vehicle in two ways. First, they use plain-view detection techniques, looking through the vehicle's windows. In addition, they use plain-smell methods, sniffing the air around the car as they walk around it. Both of these techniques are used to determine whether the officers can discover probable cause that would allow them to conduct a more invasive search of the automobile and its occupants. Record 57a. Furthermore, if the officers can persuade the driver to consent to a search, they can conduct an even more extensive search of the vehicle. Record 53a. One other method of search is used during even routine stops: A narcotics detection dog is walked around the exterior of the vehicle, in a final attempt to discover probable cause to search the vehicle for narcotics. Record 57a.

Notice how the writer has unpacked the details to state explicitly information that is implicit in the first example. In the first example, the officers "verify license and registration." These words imply request, retrieval,

[24] *See also* Oates & Enquist, *supra* note 13, at §17.7.6 (discussing "airtime" and detail).

handing over, and inspection; the second example provides these details to create an impression of significant intrusion on the driver and the passengers. The writer provides every detail; the reader does not have to spend any energy figuring out things on his or her own. The numerous sentences, the level of detail, and the word choice all work to create an image of a long, intrusive stop. If the reader believes in minimal police intrusion without probable cause, he or she could be halfway to a favorable conclusion merely after reading the statement of facts, for it will have created a concrete picture in the reader's mind of precisely what a "routine stop" entails.

Of course, as with any persuasive method, use good judgment. If you go overboard in either direction, you will hurt rather than help your argument.

9.2.4
SPECIAL CONSIDERATIONS FOR MOTION BRIEF FACT STATEMENTS

As noted previously, the writer of a motion brief faces some special challenges. If you are writing a brief in support of a motion to dismiss, you may be arguing about a question of law. Nevertheless, you cannot ignore the facts in the complaint, even though they may consist of negative characterizations of your client. The aforementioned techniques for deemphasizing negative facts may be helpful, but you must always balance the desire for persuasion with the need for credibility. If you are too abstract in your description of the underlying facts, the court may distrust you. The following example comes from a defendant's brief in support of a motion to dismiss. The defendant has been charged with sexual harassment and has been accused of numerous instances of unwanted physical contact with the plaintiff. The description here is technically correct, but it would be very ineffective in a motion brief:

▽ BAD EXAMPLE FROM DEFENDANT'S BRIEF

Plaintiff, Lynda Garrett, claims that she experienced gender discrimination during her employment. Compl.¶7.

The court gets only a vague idea of what happened in the case and would be surprised when it reads the plaintiff's version of events:

△ GOOD EXAMPLE FROM PLAINTIFF'S BRIEF

While Ms. Garrett was employed by Marvin-Kobacker, Defendant Kirkby created a hostile work environment for her because of her gender. Compl.¶7. Kirkby continuously made sexual comments both to and about Ms. Garrett. Compl.¶7. On an almost daily basis, Kirkby would ask Ms. Garrett to have intercourse with him, often using vulgar language. Compl.¶7a. Ms. Garrett initially ignored Kirkby's comments and then repeatedly pleaded with him to stop making such comments. Compl.¶7a.

On the other hand, the statements in the complaint are merely allegations, even though they must be taken as true for purposes of the motion. Thus, if you are counsel for the defendant, you should not write your fact statement as if you believe that the statements are true:

▼ BAD EXAMPLE FROM DEFENDANT'S BRIEF

> Plaintiff, Lynda Garrett, experienced a hostile working environment during her employment with Marvin-Kobacker. Compl.¶7. Defendant Kirkby assigned her to an area where she was required to work alone, and he made sexual comments and advances, to which she initially made no response. Compl.¶6. Kirkby touched her in an offensive manner and threatened to fire her if she complained about his behavior. Compl.¶7b.

Instead, put these allegations in the plaintiff's "mouth"; that is, make clear that these are allegations in the complaint:

▲ GOOD EXAMPLE FROM DEFENDANT'S BRIEF

> Plaintiff, Lynda Garrett, claims that she experienced gender discrimination during her employment that created a hostile working environment. Compl.¶7. She alleges that Kirkby assigned her to an area where she was required to work alone. Compl.¶6. Garrett also accuses Kirkby of making sexual comments and advances, to which she initially made no response. Compl.¶6. The complaint alleges that Kirkby touched her in an offensive manner and threatened to fire her if she complained about his behavior. Compl.¶7b.

This paragraph does not hide the fact that the defendant is accused of severe sexual harassment, but it characterizes the allegations as what they are: allegations.

In addition to the controversial facts, there will likely be facts in the complaint that will help the court to understand the arguments, but which both sides agree on. These facts can be stated without labeling them as the allegations of one party or another. Here is an example from the defendant's brief:

▲ GOOD EXAMPLE FROM DEFENDANT'S BRIEF

> Both Kirkby and Garrett were employed by Marvin-Kobacker during the time of the alleged harassment. Compl.¶4. Marvin-Kobacker employs over 200 individuals in its Foster, Rhode Island, location. Compl.¶2.

9.2.5
SUMMING UP

When writing your fact statement, you should (1) decide what conclusions you want the reader to draw after reading the facts and note which presumptions the reader might bring to the fact statement; (2) collect the facts, noting which facts are positive, negative, and neutral vis-à-vis the conclusions you want the reader to draw; (3) organize the facts; (4) make the facts persuasive by exploiting positions of emphasis, context, level of detail, and specificity; (5) take care not to violate ethical or logical rules; and (6) make sure that you cite to the record as needed.

9.3
SUMMARY OF THE ARGUMENT

The summary of the argument follows the statement of the facts, and it signals an abrupt change. Up until this point, the writer has been describing the case, including its issues, the opinions below, and the facts. Now the writer begins to argue.

Supreme Court Rule 24.1(h) provides that the brief must include

> [a] summary of the argument, suitably paragraphed. The summary should be a clear and concise condensation of the argument made in the body of the brief; mere repetition of the headings under which the argument is arranged is not sufficient.

Only lengthy motion briefs require a summary of the argument, but they are required for almost all appellate briefs. In both motion briefs and appellate briefs, the summary of the argument can play two roles. First, the summary can serve as a roadmap to the argument as a whole. The writer should succinctly state the major arguments relied on in the brief, in the order in which they appear in the argument section. Second, the summary can be used to present a "holistic" picture of the case, focusing more on policy and equity than on black-letter law.

Judge Hamilton notes that the summary of the argument is "significant on several levels":

> First, it is the party's first opportunity to put a legal gloss on the facts. Second, it is the party's first opportunity to orient the appellate judges assigned the appeal to the theme of the party's argument. Third, and most importantly, it serves as the party's official opening statement, previewing and summarizing the key legal points the party wants to make in the argument component of the brief.[25]

---

[25] Hamilton, *supra* note 8, at 586-87.

A good summary should grab the reader's attention in its opening paragraph. While the statement of facts should open with a somewhat objective statement of what the case is about, the summary of the argument can be more dramatic, identifying the underlying issues that the case presents. In the case of *Rubin v. Coors Brewing Co.*, for example, counsel for the United States (Rubin) might open the summary with a declarative statement about the result being sought:

BAD EXAMPLE

> Section 205(e)(2) of the Federal Alcohol Administrative Act, prohibiting alcohol content disclosure on malt beverage labels, does not violate the Free Speech Clause of the First Amendment.

While this opening is appropriately argumentative, it doesn't grab the reader's attention. To create a more dramatic opening, counsel might begin the summary by reminding the reader of the original purpose of §205(e)(2). The statute was drafted shortly after Prohibition ended; the government was seeking to prevent strength wars among brewers and to prevent beer drinkers from "forum shopping" for the most powerful beer. Counsel for the United States might bring that purpose up to date by opening the summary of the argument like this:

GOOD EXAMPLE

> Prohibition is not just a time in history that ended 60 years ago. Every day is the end of Prohibition for someone who reaches the legal drinking age.

You can be both more dramatic and more argumentative in the summary than you can in the fact statement. *Miller v. Albright* addressed the citizenship of children born outside of the United States to unmarried United States citizens, when only one of the parents was a citizen. The issue was whether a statute could constitutionally distinguish between children of United States citizen fathers and those of United States citizen mothers. An attorney representing Ms. Miller could have opened the summary of the argument by reminding the Court of the harsh reality of the statute's distinction:

BAD EXAMPLE

> The issue before this Court is whether Congress may use an irrebuttable gender stereotype to impose an arbitrary time limit on the relationship between a father and his daughter.

This opening is not horrible, but it states the issue objectively when it should be arguing. Lopping off the objective opening and making a flat statement of the writer's position creates a much more effective opening sentence:

▲ GOOD EXAMPLE

Congress may not use an irrebuttable gender stereotype to impose an arbitrary time limit on the relationship between a father and his daughter.

I think of a dramatic opening to the summary of the argument as a "boom" opening, because it is meant to make a "noise" in the reader's brain to attract attention. I also believe, however, that not every summary needs to have a boom opening. Sometimes, it can be effective to slow things down and to make the reader think for a moment. In *United States v. Stevens*, for example, the issue was the constitutionality of a federal statute that restricted creation and distribution of certain videos that included depictions of violence between or against animals. The statute was drafted to stop the creation of a category of videos that depicted the murders of puppies and kittens. The statute was challenged as overbroad by Stevens, a filmmaker whose films about pit bulls included some footage of dogfighting, which he opposed.

Stevens could, no doubt, have started his summary of the argument with a boom opening. Instead, he slowed the pace and isolated the disagreement between himself and the government:

> This case is not about dogfighting or animal cruelty. The government and Stevens stand together opposing that. The question here is more fundamental: whether the government can send an individual to jail for up to five years just for making films—films that are not obscene, pornographic, inflammatory, defamatory, or even untruthful. They are controversial. But that is supposed to invigorate, not contract, the First Amendment's protection.[26]

This opening for the summary is effective because it disarms the emotional arguments that focus on animal cruelty and puts the focus on the less emotional—but equally important—issue of First Amendment guarantees.

Once the writer has written an appropriate opening, it is time to concentrate on the rest of the summary. Many writers clog up the summary of the argument with too much detail. This part of the document is meant to provide a *summary*. It should focus more on rules and how they apply than on detailed explanations.

In the excerpt below, from the summary of the argument in a petitioner's brief in *Minnesota v. Carter*, the author summarized a 30-page argument in two pages. The case had two main points. After introducing those points in the opening paragraph, the writer used one paragraph to lay out the first rule, then two paragraphs to apply it, followed by one paragraph

---

[26] *United States v. Stevens*, Respondent's Brief, available at 2009 WL 2191081.

on the second rule, and another paragraph to apply that rule. She ends the summary by telling the Court how she wants it to decide the case:

GOOD EXAMPLE

Respondents did not have a reasonable expectation of privacy when they bagged cocaine in front of a partially covered window in a basement apartment. The Minnesota Supreme Court incorrectly reversed the trial court's denial of Respondents' motion to suppress. First, it erroneously ruled that Respondents had a legitimate expectation of privacy while in another's apartment for the sole purpose of illegally bagging cocaine. Second, it wrongly held that an officer conducted a search when he merely observed criminal activity in plain view from an area outside the apartment's curtilage. **1**

This Court's Fourth Amendment jurisprudence demonstrates that the Minnesota Supreme Court's ruling was erroneous. In order to invoke the Fourth Amendment's protections, an individual must prove that he had a legitimate expectation of privacy. An individual possesses a legitimate expectation of privacy when he demonstrates that he has both a subjective expectation of privacy and an expectation of privacy that society is prepared to view as reasonable. **2**

Respondents were sitting at an illuminated kitchen table facing a window of a ground-floor apartment and packaging cocaine. Respondents should have realized that a passerby could have looked into the apartment and noticed the illegal activity occurring within the apartment. Thus, Respondents can claim no subjective expectation of privacy. **3**

Additionally, any subjective expectation of privacy Respondents possessed is not one that society is prepared to recognize as reasonable in light of longstanding social customs that serve functions recognized as valuable by society. <u>Minnesota v. Olson</u>, 495 U.S. 91, 96-97 (1990). As non-overnight guests, they lacked the connection with the premises that legitimizes an expectation of privacy. Even if shorter-term guests can claim the protection of the Fourth Amendment, only those short-term guests who are present for socially permissible and valuable reasons qualify for Fourth Amendment protection. Respondents were present only to conduct criminal business activities and therefore did not have an expectation of privacy that was reasonable in light of longstanding social customs that serve functions recognized as valuable by society. **4**

Furthermore, even assuming that Respondents are entitled to invoke the Fourth Amendment's protections, no Fourth Amendment search occurred. A search occurs only when governmental agents intrude upon an area in which an individual has a reasonable expectation of privacy. A reasonable expectation of privacy is violated when an officer intrudes upon the home or its curtilage, the area immediately surrounding the home that shares the same private characteristics as the home. Conversely, there is no violation of a reasonable expectation of privacy, and therefore no *search*, when an officer

1 Note how the writer lays out the two issues that the argument, and thus the summary, will address.

2 In this paragraph, the writer lays out the basic rule that governs the first issue, identifying two sub-issues. She does not cite to authority, which is an acceptable convention in the summary of the argument.

3 In this paragraph, the writer connects the facts to her legal conclusion that the Respondents can claim no subjective expectation of privacy.

4 In this paragraph, the writer gives the factual details that show why society is not prepared to recognize Respondents' expectation of privacy as reasonable. These reasons reflect the organization of her argument.

5 In this paragraph,
the writer lays out in
detail the rule that
governs the second
main issue. Again,
she does not cite
to authority other
than the Fourth
Amendment.

6 In this paragraph,
the writer applies
the second rule
to the facts of the
case.

7 In this paragraph,
the writer sums
up the two main
conclusions as
to the issues and
connects those
conclusions to
her assertion that
the Court should
reverse the decision
below.

merely stands outside the curtilage of a residence and observes what is in plain view. **5**

In this case, the officer stood in a publicly accessible common area outside the apartment's curtilage. The officer used only his natural senses to observe what was in plain view. He conducted his observation without physical intrusion, without the use of any device, and in a manner that any member of the public could have employed. The officer's conduct violated no reasonable expectation of privacy and therefore was not a Fourth Amendment search. **6**

For these reasons, this Court should hold that Respondents had no legitimate expectation of privacy in the apartment and that the observations of the officer did not constitute a search. This Court should reverse the Minnesota Supreme Court's judgment. **7**

In most situations, the summary of the argument need not contain numerous citations to authority. Of course, if a case, statute, constitutional provision, or other authority is at issue, it will be mentioned; likewise, if a particular issue is largely controlled by a case or other authority, that authority may be mentioned as well. Usually, however, the focus is on legal principles rather than on the authorities that are the source of those principles.

To summarize, the summary of the argument should (1) signal the writer's theme, (2) signal the writer's major arguments and the order in which those arguments will appear, (3) focus on rules and their application rather than detailed explanations, and (4) avoid most citations to authority.

9.4
POINT HEADINGS

9.4.1
FORMAT AND FUNCTION

Court rules do not give much guidance about point headings. Supreme Court Rule 24.1(h) mentions them in passing, noting that an effective summary of the argument should not merely repeat "the headings under which the argument is arranged." They are rarely mentioned at all in the limited court rules that guide motion briefs, and even then they are mentioned only in reference to related material—for example, the pleading standard that applies to a given section of the argument—and not in reference to the content of the heading itself. Nevertheless, well-drafted point headings can help both the reader and the user get the maximum benefit from the brief.

**Format Requirements for
Point Headings**

Traditionally, major contentions are labeled with roman numerals. Subpoints under roman numerals are labeled with capital letters. Subpoints under uppercase letters are labeled with Arabic numerals. Subpoints under Arabic numerals are labeled with lowercase letters. Thus:

I.
   A.
      1.
         a.
         b.
      2.
   B.
   C.

Conventional wisdom is that you should never have a "I" without a "II," an "A" without a "B," and so on. While this advice is valid (because you cannot divide something into just one section), there is an exception in written advocacy. If your argument relies on one dispositive point, that point can be labeled as a "I" even though there is no "II." (Some writers, in the alternative, simply do not label their main argument with a roman numeral at all.) Note that the *only* exception to this point is at the roman numeral stage. You *must* have at least a "B" heading if you have an "A" heading, a "2" if you have a "1" heading, and so on.

A recent piece in the *Columbia Business Law Review* suggests that brief writers should use so-called scientific numbering, as this text does.[27] Thus:

1.
   1.1
      1.1.1
      1.1.2
   1.2
   1.3
2.
   2.1
   2.2

The reason for this suggestion is that this method of enumeration makes it easier for readers to be aware of their location within the document as a whole.[28] Scientists have found that this awareness is more difficult for those who read documents on computers or other digital devices, since they are not holding a set of pages that would provide a physical signal of their location within the document.[29]

Note that the same subpart advice applies to this type of numbering: You can't divide something into just one part, so if you have a section 2.1, you should also have a

---

[27] Daniel Sockwell, *Writing for the iPad Judge, Announcements*, Colum. Bus. L. Rev. Online (Jan. 14, 2014) (available at http://cblr.columbia.edu/archives/12940) (last accessed April 13, 2014).

[28] *Id.*

[29] *Id.; see also, e.g.,* Ferris Jabr, *The Reading Brain in the Digital Age: The Science of Paper Versus Screens,* Scientific American (Apr. 11, 2013), http://www.scientificamerican.com/article.cfm?id=reading-paper-screens (discussing the physical "rhythm" of reading hard-copy text).

section 2.2. Of course, before using this type of numbering, be certain that it does not violate local rules or entrenched local culture.

Although some traditionalists may use all capital letters for the text of their roman numeral (or main) point headings and underline the next level of point headings, these traditions no longer make sense. They come from the days before word processors; typewriters did not allow much flexibility. Unless court rules require otherwise, you should consider putting *all* headings (both point headings and section headings — e.g., The Summary of the Argument) in **boldfaced type** to increase their visibility and thus help the user to find particular segments of the brief.

Point headings are used as headings and subheadings within the argument section of a brief. They also appear in the table of contents; they are useful there both as a concise summary of major points for the reader and as a tool to help the user find those points. Point headings serve three functions in the body of the argument. First, they give the court easy access to the writer's basic argument. The point headings are thesis statements of the writer's argument in each section and subsection of the brief. Point headings are particularly effective as concise statements of the writer's best points because they occur in a position of emphasis within the document. Anytime the reader takes a break between one segment of a document and another (whether those segments are sentences, paragraphs, or sections) his or her attention peaks. A boldfaced heading spikes the reader's attention and makes it likely that he or she will pay attention to the information in the heading. The writer gains maximum benefit from this position of emphasis when his or her major contentions appear in the headings.

The second function of the point headings is organizational. The point headings help the reader to understand the relationships between and among the different sections of the argument, for example, that these subpoints are part of the argument related to the related main point heading, or that the writer has three main arguments as expressed in roman numerals I, II, and III (or Arabic numbers 1, 2, and 3). On a less substantive but equally important note, the point headings help the user to find the particular argument that he or she wants to read. Often, judges and their clerks do not read through a brief from beginning to end. Even if they do once read the brief straight through, after that initial reading they may use the brief like a reference work, and they will use the point headings to help them to find what they are looking for.

The third function of the point heading is its simplest: The point heading provides a graphic break for the reader between sections of the brief. By inserting a heading or subheading, the writer tells the reader, "You are finished with the previous point, and now you are moving on to the next point." Because reading briefs can be a daunting task, effective use of point headings can help break a long argument up into easy-to-understand (or easier-to-understand) segments. Remember that judges are more likely to be persuaded by briefs that they can easily understand. Therefore, to promote understanding, try not to have more than three or four pages without a point heading or subheading.

At this stage of the writing process, you should have already identified the main assertions you plan to make to convince the court to decide in your favor. When deciding how to arrange these assertions into headings, identify the relationships between and among those assertions. First, group the assertions that are related; second, identify the major assertions. In particular, identify the assertions that are dispositive: That is, if the court agrees with this assertion, it must decide the case in your favor.

When you first try to identify the relationships between and among your headings, your roman numeral, or main, point headings should be only dispositive assertions. This method is the most logical, and it is most likely to display an argument whose main points track the brief's questions presented. Many good attorneys do not follow this advice, however. If a case is complex, with many sub-issues related to the one dispositive assertion, the brief could end up with sub-sub-sub-subheads. In that situation, it would be preferable to eliminate the single dispositive heading and "promote" all of the other headings. Your starting point, however, should always be to identify the points that are dispositive.

9.4.2
DRAFTING THE POINT HEADINGS

A classic point heading is a concise, persuasive statement of
1. either

    a. a conclusion that you want the court to accept **OR**
    b. an action that you want the court to take, **PLUS**

2. the reason that the court should take that action or agree with that assertion.

To draft your point headings, first consult your list of ultimate assertions and identify something you want the court to *do* or something the court must *conclude or agree with* to decide in your client's favor. Next, identify the reasons that support taking those actions or reaching those conclusions. If the reasons are the subparts of an argument, make each reason a separate point heading. If there are no subparts in that section of the document, "add" the reason(s) to the assertion, often with a "because."

For example, this point heading, from a respondent's brief in *Knowles v. Iowa*, 525 U.S. 113 (1998), is based on something the writer wants the court to do:

I.   **This Court should extend the search-incident-to-arrest exception to the Fourth Amendment's warrant requirement to situations in which an officer is issuing a citation in lieu of arrest.**

The same point could be written in a different way, as an assertion that the writer wants the court to agree with:

I.   **The search-incident-to-arrest exception to the Fourth Amendment's warrant requirement should include situations in which an officer is issuing a citation in lieu of arrest.**

The three subheadings below show the reasons that support the writer's assertion:

A.   **The situation contemplated by Iowa Code §805.1(4), where an officer issues a citation in lieu of arrest, presents the same policy concerns as when an actual arrest takes place.**

B.   **The public interests advanced by such a search substantially outweigh the extent to which the search intrudes upon individual privacy rights.**

C.   **Outlawing a warrant exception for a search incident to a citation in lieu of arrest would encourage police officers to arrest more people in order to conduct searches.**

Note, however, that many readers will skip point headings that are more than three lines long, or even more than two lines long. An imperfect short heading that a judge reads is better than a perfect heading that a judge skips because it is too long.

Thus, when space permits, a good point heading should (1) indicate the issue being discussed, (2) indicate your position on the issue, and (3) indicate the basic reason(s) for that position. (If needed, you can eliminate item (3) to keep the heading to a reasonable length.) Accordingly, your point headings should be full sentences, not phrases. They should be statements about how the law applies to the people or entities in your case, not abstract pronouncements about the law generally.[30] As a test, see if you could "recycle" your point heading in another brief on the same point. If so, you probably need to be more specific. In particular, you need to be more specific if your point heading could be used in your opponent's brief. For example, don't write, "The First Amendment protects freedom of speech." Instead write, "Because the First Amendment protects freedom of speech, Mr. Johnson should be allowed to distribute homemade, anonymous leaflets at a public rally."

---

[30] *See, e.g.,* Lynn Bahrych & Marjorie Dick Rombauer, *Legal Writing in a Nutshell* §9.5 (3d ed., West 2003).

9.4.3
THE RELATIONSHIPS BETWEEN AND AMONG POINT HEADINGS

There can be many different types of logical relationships between and among point headings, but four are particularly common. One type of relationship exists when the main heading describes a multipart test and the subheadings discuss each of the parts in turn. For example, this set of point headings for the petitioner in *Miller v. Albright* shows how the writer believes that two parts of the intermediate scrutiny test should be applied:

III. The use of an irrebuttable gender stereotype in 8 U.S.C. § 1409(a) is not "substantially related" to the achievement of the government's objective, and there is no "exceedingly persuasive justification" for the stereotype's use.

    A. 8 U.S.C. §1409(a) is unconstitutionally overinclusive and, therefore, is not "substantially related" to the achievement of the government's objective.

    B. There is no "exceedingly persuasive justification" for the use of an irrebuttable gender stereotype in 8 U.S.C. §1409(a) because less discriminatory methods would achieve the government's objective.

In the second type of relationship, the main heading makes an assertion, and the subheadings provide legal support that may or may not be formal "subparts" of the main assertion. In this excerpt from a petitioner's brief in *Minnesota v. Carter*, note how the four lettered headings make legal arguments that support heading "I." Although they are not all necessary subparts of a "reasonable expectation of privacy" argument, the reader will be more likely to agree with heading "I" if he or she agrees with the lettered subheadings:

1. As temporary business invitees present in another's residence for the sole purpose of packaging drugs, Respondents had no legitimate expectation of privacy.

    A. Respondents failed to meet their burden of proving that they had a legitimate expectation of privacy because they introduced absolutely no evidence regarding their status in Thompson's apartment.

    B. Any subjective expectation Respondents might have had while temporarily in another's home for the sole purpose of conducting illegal business was not one society recognizes as reasonable.

    C. By engaging in criminal acts in a well-lit room, directly in front of a window facing a widely used common area, Respondents exhibited no subjective expectation of privacy.

    D. This Court should maintain its reluctance to expand the class of individuals who may claim a legitimate expectation of privacy and invoke the exclusionary rule.

In the third type of relationship, the main heading makes an assertion, and the subheadings focus on how particular facts support the main assertion:

> 2. Even if the <u>Olson</u> rule extends to non-overnight guests, Respondents' expectation of privacy is unreasonable because they were present only to conduct illegal business that is not valuable to society.
>
>> a. Illegal drug distribution is not a longstanding social custom that serves functions recognized as valuable by society.
>>
>> b. Respondents were present for a purely commercial purpose and were not entitled to the Fourth Amendment protection associated with the home.

The fourth common type of relationship is a relationship between "equal" headings rather than between a main assertion and its subheadings. In this relationship, the headings present alternative arguments, as in this example from a petitioner's brief in *Minnesota v. Carter*:

▲ GOOD EXAMPLE

> 1. The <u>Olson</u> rule dictates that only overnight guests have a connection to a premises that gives rise to a legitimate expectation of privacy.
>
> 2. Even if the Olson rule extends to non-overnight guests, Respondents' expectation of privacy is unreasonable because they were present only to conduct illegal business that is not valuable to society.

Using "even if" language in the second alternative point heading can help the court to understand the relationships between the headings more quickly. Despite the concerns of some students, alternative arguments are perfectly acceptable, as long as the law and the facts could reasonably support both arguments.

9.4.4
THE RELATIONSHIP BETWEEN THE POINT HEADING AND THE PARAGRAPH IMMEDIATELY FOLLOWING

In the paragraph immediately following the point heading, you may have a couple of jobs to do. If you are dividing this heading section into two or more subsections, this paragraph may need to contain legal backstory and perhaps a roadmap (we'll discuss these requirements in Chapter Ten). Even if you are not further dividing this heading section, however, the paragraph after the point heading must tell the reader what the section is about. And it needs to do so even though your point heading should also have accomplished that goal.

Because headings that appear in briefs are complete sentences, it is tempting to treat them as the first sentence of the paragraph that immediately follows. Don't. Remember that you must write for both users and readers. As you know, some *users* will read only the headings, and so each heading must succinctly address the main point of that section. Because some *readers* will skip headings, however, the first sentence in the section should also address that main point. However, that first sentence cannot just repeat the heading word for word, because some readers will read both the heading and the text. As contradictory as it may seem, your writing must accommodate all three of these concerns.

This example treats the heading as if it is the first sentence of the paragraph that follows:

▽ BAD EXAMPLE

D. **This Court should maintain its reluctance to expand the class of individuals who may claim a legitimate expectation of privacy and invoke the exclusionary rule.**

Therefore, the court should reverse the case at bar because . . .

A reader who skipped the heading would have no frame of reference for the word "therefore," and would not have a basis for the inference. As noted above, however, copying the heading word for word is not a good solution to this problem:

▽ BAD EXAMPLE

D. **This Court should maintain its reluctance to expand the class of individuals who may claim a legitimate expectation of privacy and invoke the exclusionary rule.**

This Court should maintain its reluctance to expand the class of individuals who may claim a legitimate expectation of privacy and invoke the exclusionary rule. Therefore, the court should reverse the case at bar because . . .

A reader who read both the heading and the text would find this exact repetition annoying. Instead of repeating the entire heading, follow the heading with a sentence that uses different phrasing but still repeats the same point. Note that not every word needs to be different; you can and should use the phrases-that-pay and other important language in both the heading and the first sentence of the paragraph that follows:

△ GOOD EXAMPLE

D. **This Court should maintain its reluctance to expand the class of individuals who may claim a legitimate expectation of privacy and invoke the exclusionary rule.**

Because the arguments for limiting the use of the exclusionary rule are compelling, this Court should continue its reluctance to expand the

class of persons that may invoke the rule. The Court should reverse the case at bar because doing so recognizes . . .

By taking a few minutes to consider an effective opening sentence to follow your headings, you can make sure that your headings are effective for those who encounter your brief, in whatever manner they encounter it.

9.4.5
SUMMING UP

When drafting your point headings, (1) base the headings on actions you want the court to take or assertions you want the court to accept, (2) make sure that the point headings reflect logical relationships between and among the issues in your case, and (3) make your point headings concrete assertions that incorporate the facts and law at issue in your case.

9.5
SUMMARY

The Issue Statement, the Statement of the Case, the Summary of the Argument, and Point Headings each hold a special place in the brief. The reader and user have different expectations and needs for these elements than they have for the Argument Section.

By writing a good question presented, a brief writer can focus the reader on an issue presented from the client's point of view. A well-written fact statement can lead the reader to draw favorable conclusions even before the reader reaches the argument. An effective argument summary can give the reader a complete picture of the writer's argument, and better prepare the reader to absorb the details presented within the argument itself. Finally, well-written point headings can help the user to find and the reader to understand the writer's arguments. Paying attention to these "special teams" can help a writer to craft a winning brief.

SIX DEGREES OF LEGAL WRITING: MAKING YOUR DOCUMENT READER-FRIENDLY AND USER-FRIENDLY

Chapter Ten

A brief is a functional document, and it functions in different ways at different stages in the decision-making process. As noted earlier, the judges and the clerks who see your brief wear two different hats. As "readers," they move through pages, paragraphs, and sentences sequentially, and they need valid, well-supported legal arguments; a reasonable organizational scheme; and coherent sentence structures. As "users," they scavenge through the document, searching for the point they care about, or trying to figure out what point is being made in a particular sentence, section, or paragraph so they can decide whether to continue reading it. Users need all the things that readers need, but they need something more: Users need finding tools, the signals that announce what is going on in various parts of the document.

If there is an oral argument, the judges may review the brief before the argument to understand how the law and the facts support that argument. After the argument—or if there is no argument—one or more of the judges and clerks may *use* the brief to help them write the opinion. Thus, your audience will have different needs at different times, and your brief must meet these different needs. The first time the brief is reviewed, readers must be able to understand how the different parts of the argument work together to support the conclusion you want the court to reach. Later, users must be able to find particular points and authorities.

Furthermore, your audience will have different needs depending not only on *when* they encounter the brief, but also on *how* they encounter it. Our brains work differently when we are reading digital documents than when we are reading hard copy. Accordingly, you should be sure that your brief will be readable in any format.

When most judges and clerks consult your brief, they will not be reading it the way you might read a favorite novel. Instead, they will be trying to find the parts they care about. As one commentator noted in the *Harvard Law Review* back in 1959, the brief-writer cannot expect the complete and undivided attention of every judge:

> [W]ritten arguments filed with the Court are not documents like law review essays which the author is entitled to expect each of [the] readers to peruse carefully and reflectively from beginning to end. Perhaps the writer of an opinion reads a brief this way. But for other members of the Court these documents necessarily serve a different function than the communication simply of a connected line of thought. They are documents from which busy [people] have to extract the gist in a hurry. . . . Briefs on the merits need not only tell their story to one who takes the time to read all the way through them, but to be so organized that they can be used, like a book of reference, for quick illumination on any particular point of concern.[1]

Because your document will be *used*, not just *read*, it not only must be focused and well organized, but it also must highlight that focus and organization for those who are reading and using the document in both its hard-copy and digital forms.

Even after you have written a complete draft that says what you want it to say, it may still be only a "writer-based" document. That is, it is a document that only the writer can understand and use effectively. At this stage of the writing process, it is time to remember the lessons of the social perspective school of writing theory: Consider the needs of your audience and make your document a "reader-based" and "user-based" document, a document that is written and organized to promote understanding by others, no matter when or how they are encountering the document.

There are various techniques that you can use to make your documents both reader-friendly and user-friendly. First, include explicit connections so that the reader can understand how each part of the argument supports your thesis. Second, through this technique and others, make sure that you provide the reader with context when necessary. Finally, use headings, topic sentences, and other techniques to make sure that the user can easily find information within the document. As you will see, these techniques have substantive as well as organizational benefits to both hard-copy and digital readers.

---

[1] Henry M. Hart, Jr., *The Supreme Court, 1958 Term, Foreword: The Time Chart of the Justices,* 73 Harv. L. Rev. 84, 94 (1959) (cited in James VanR. Springer, *Symposium on Supreme Court Advocacy: Some Suggestions on Preparing Briefs on the Merits in the Supreme Court of the United States,* 33 Cath. U. L. Rev. 593, 593-94 (1984)).

10.1
FIND YOUR "KEVIN BACON"

Several years ago, Craig Fass, Michael Ginelli, and Brian Turtle created the game "Six Degrees of Kevin Bacon." The game is based on the concept at the heart of the 1990 John Guare play, *Six Degrees of Separation*: We are all connected to everyone else in the world through no more than six people. The game's premise is that "Kevin Bacon is the center of the entertainment universe"[2] and that he can be connected to any other actor through no more than six movies. For example:

Oprah Winfrey was in *The Color Purple* with Danny Glover,
Danny Glover was in *Places in the Heart* with Sally Field,
Sally Field was in *Punchline* with Tom Hanks, and
Tom Hanks was in *Apollo 13* with Kevin Bacon.

Now, what does all of this have to do with legal writing? Every legal document should have a "Kevin Bacon" element—something that is the "center of the universe" to which everything else in the document connects. With a well-written legal document, the reader should be able to throw a dart at any sentence in the document and get back to the document's focus just as easily as we moved from Oprah Winfrey to Kevin Bacon in the previous paragraph. When writing a brief, you should decide what the center of your brief's "universe" is: That's your "Kevin Bacon."

In *Minnesota v. Carter*, 525 U.S. 83 (1998), for example, one of the petitioner's dispositive arguments was that people who come to an apartment for the sole purpose of bagging cocaine cannot invoke Fourth Amendment protections. The focus of that brief, as for all petitioners' briefs, would be the assertion that the decision below should be reversed. If we throw a theoretical dart at the brief, we find the assertion that "the respondents were in the apartment solely to conduct commercial activity." The reader could use "Bacon links" to connect that point back to the ultimate assertion this way:

Respondents were in the home only to conduct illegal commercial activity;
Because the activity was an illegal commercial activity, it is not an activity that is recognized as valuable by society;

---

[2] To play the game and learn more about it, visit "The Oracle of Bacon" Web site at http://oracleofbacon.org/ack.php (last accessed Mar. 9, 2014). Brett Tjaden founded the site in 1996; Patrick Reynolds has maintained it since 1999. When I submitted "Oprah Winfrey," I learned that she has a Bacon number of two. (Oprah Winfrey was in *The Princess and the Frog* (2009) with John Goodman; John Goodman was in *Death Sentence* (2007) with Kevin Bacon.) Because a Bacon number of four provides a better teaching tool, I have left my example as is. Kevin Bacon has created a charitable organization that links celebrities to worthy causes; if you wish to contribute or learn more about it, consult http://www.sixdegrees.org/ (last accessed Mar. 10, 2014).

> Because their activity is not recognized as valuable by society, Respondents can have no legitimate expectation of privacy when conducting that activity;
>
> Because Respondents have no legitimate expectation of privacy when conducting that activity, they cannot invoke the Fourth Amendment; and
>
> Because Respondents cannot invoke the Fourth Amendment, this Court must reverse.

Thus, in a brief, the "Bacon links" in the Six Degrees of Legal Writing game are the assertions that you are focusing on in the various sections of your document, and the main focus is your ultimate conclusion. Knowing that the links are there is only half the battle, however. You must make the connections between the links explicit in the text of your brief so that the reader is as aware of the connections as you are.

For example, the following paragraph from a petitioner's brief in *Minnesota v. Carter* does not make the links explicit:

▼ BAD EXAMPLE

Because society does not value the Respondents' illegal business activity, this Court must reverse.

Most readers would not immediately grasp the connection between respondents' illegal business activity and the conclusion that the court must reverse. Instead of making this unmoored statement, the writer should connect the point about illegal business activity to the conclusion that the court must reverse by making the connections explicit:

△ GOOD EXAMPLE

Thus, Respondents, who were conducting a purely commercial activity, were not visitors to a "home" and were not engaging in long-standing social customs that serve functions recognized as valuable by society. While Respondents may have been legitimately in the apartment, in the sense that Thompson permitted their presence, Respondents did not have any legitimate expectation of privacy in the apartment because they were present only to conduct illegal business. Because Respondents' expectation of privacy was not one that society recognizes as reasonable, they cannot claim the Fourth Amendment's protections, and this Court must reverse.

Although the example above shows a connection-conclusion paragraph, an equally important location for making links explicit is in the beginning of a section or subsection. In the illustration below, notice how the writer connects subsection B.2 to subsection B.1 and to the "B" point heading. She then provides a roadmap to the two subpoints to section B. I have included all of the relevant headings so you can see how the writer makes the connections clear:

B. Respondents had no legitimate expectation of privacy because any subjective expectation they might have had while temporarily in another's home for the sole purpose of conducting illegal business was not one society recognizes as reasonable. . . .

1. The <u>Olson</u> rule dictates that only overnight guests have a connection to premises that gives rise to a legitimate expectation of privacy.

2. Even if the <u>Olson</u> rule extends to non-overnight guests, Respondents' expectation of privacy is unreasonable because they were present only to conduct illegal business that is not valuable to society.

     If <u>Olson</u> does not stand for the proposition that only overnight guests may assert a Fourth Amendment challenge, it at least stands for the proposition that only a very limited category of guests may do so. The limited category includes only those guests whose connections to the home give rise to an expectation of privacy that society is prepared to recognize as reasonable. <u>See</u> <u>Olson</u>, 495 U.S. at 95. Respondents failed to demonstrate that their expectation of privacy was one society is prepared to recognize as reasonable.

     The Minnesota Supreme Court found that Respondents demonstrated an expectation of privacy that society is prepared to recognize as reasonable because they were present in the apartment "to conduct a common task." <u>State v. Carter</u>, 569 N.W.2d 169, 176 (Minn. 1997). This Court should reverse the decision of the Minnesota Supreme Court because (1) the distribution of drugs is not a longstanding social custom that serves functions recognized as valuable by society, and (2) Respondents were not "guests" in a home but rather were business invitees on the property for a purely commercial purpose, and therefore lost the Fourth Amendment protection normally associated with the home.

a. Illegal drug distribution is not a longstanding social custom that serves functions recognized as valuable by society.

b. Respondents were present for a purely commercial purpose and were not entitled to the Fourth Amendment protection associated with the home.

When you revise, consider how each section of your document relates to the other sections and to your overall thesis. If the connection is not obvious, see if you can make the connection obvious by adding a sentence or a paragraph in which you make the connection explicit. If you cannot figure out how to connect the point to your overall thesis, consider whether the section really belongs in your argument.

One of the most effective ways to make connections explicit is by repeating significant words and concepts. Just as you repeat the names of the various actors when you play the Kevin Bacon game, you should repeat significant words (often, phrases-that-pay) when making Kevin Bacon connections in your writing. Doing so makes it easy for your reader to understand how your ideas connect to each other.[3]

In connection-conclusions, for example, you should connect the points in each section to the other relevant points and, when necessary, to your overall thesis. By doing so, you save the reader's time and effort and increase his or her understanding of your argument.

10.2
INSTALL A SYMBOLIC TEMPLATE TO HELP YOUR READER AND YOUR USER

When personal computers were new, they came with little plastic templates that fit over the function keys to label the various purposes of the keys and to help users find the correct one. In a brief, you can provide a symbolic template by using headings, roadmap paragraphs, and topic sentences, and by using effective connection-conclusions within each CREXAC unit of discourse. A template of this kind helps in three ways. First, creating the template forces you to break your argument into smaller parts, and this lightens the reader's burden. Second, judges and clerks can use the template to skip the parts of the document they don't need and to find the parts they do need. Likewise, those who are reading the brief digitally will use headings and other signals both as finding tools and for information. Finally, readers will look for connections in the template items so that they can understand how each section of the document relates to the other sections or to your overall thesis, thus increasing their understanding of your arguments.

The template can be created in a four-step process. First, identify or write topic sentences for every paragraph. Second, identify your large-scale organization and insert headings that reveal that large-scale organization. Third, use the headings to create as many roadmap paragraphs as are appropriate. Finally, insert connection-conclusions at the end of each unit of discourse.

---

[3]*E.g.*, Rebekah George Benjamin, *Reconstructing Readability: Recent Developments and Recommendations in the Analysis of Text Difficulty*, 24 Educ. Psychol. Rev. 63, 70 (2012) (noting that where "there are few or no gaps in overlap across sentences, then a text is seamlessly moving from one point of information to another while giving the reader all the help he or she needs to build new knowledge"). *See also* Anne Enquist & Laurel Currie Oates, *Just Writing* 62 (4th ed., Aspen 2013) (recommending "substantive transitions" in which the writer echoes a word or a phrase from a previous sentence, noting that these transitions "[interlock] ideas by creating an overlap of language").

10.2.1
TOPIC SENTENCES

Although most of us learned in grade school that the topic sentence could be the first, second, or last sentence in the paragraph, in legal writing the topic sentence should always come first. Putting the topic sentence first is vital because most legal readers decide whether to read a paragraph based on its first sentence. If the first sentence shows the readers how the paragraph is relevant to the issue under discussion, they will continue. If not, they may skip down to the next paragraph, looking for more relevant information.[4] Furthermore, when your audience is in "user" mode, it may scan the topic sentences, looking for paragraphs that address the point it are interested in.

Topic sentences can also help the legal writer: When well written, they signal the document's organization and can be used to check organizational effectiveness. After you have used the guidelines below to write an effective topic sentence for each paragraph (and verified that each sentence in the paragraph is connected to that topic), you can make a "topic sentence outline" by copying and pasting the first sentence of each paragraph into a new document.

When you review the topic sentence outline, you should see logical groupings: First, you should find several topic sentences relevant to your first point, then several topic sentences relevant to your second point, and so on. To the extent that you find topic sentences that are out of place, decide whether to fix the topic sentence, move the paragraph to a new location, or remove the paragraph from the brief.

Two reminders can help you to write effective topic sentences in a brief. First, whenever possible, use the phrase-that-pays within the topic sentence. Second, focus particular attention on topic sentences for rule explanation paragraphs. Those paragraphs lay the foundation for your argument, and the topic sentences provide an important substantive and persuasive opportunity.

a.   Including the Phrase-That-Pays in Each Topic Sentence

One objective method you can use to check the effectiveness of your topic sentences is to look for the phrase-that-pays. Using the phrase-that-pays in each topic sentence tells the reader that the paragraph is worth reading and that it will provide more information about the word or phrase that is the focus of that section of the document.

---

[4] *See, e.g.,* Geoffrey B. Duggan & Stephen J. Payne, *Skim Reading by Satisficing: Evidence from Eye Tracking,* Proceedings of the SIGCHI Conference on Human Factors in Computing Systems 1141-50, 1147 (2011) (agreeing with a conclusion about eye-tracking studies showing that "skimmers begin every paragraph and continue reading until the rate of information gain drops below a threshold whereupon they skip to the beginning of the next paragraph").

Only rarely is it appropriate to use words other than the phrase-that-pays to show the paragraph's focus on the key topic. In the example below, from a section of a *Minnesota v. Carter* petitioner's brief, the writer was arguing that the respondents did not have an expectation of privacy in the apartment in which they were bagging drugs because they were there only for a commercial purpose, so "commercial purpose" was the phrase-that-pays. In the list of topic sentences below, the words "commercial purpose" or their substitutes are in boldfaced type.

Respondents were not present in a "home," but were on property for a purely **commercial purpose**.

This Court has recognized that **business premises** invite lesser privacy expectations than do residences.

In <u>Lewis</u>, this Court held that a defendant who used his home for the felonious **sale of narcotics** could not claim a violation of any reasonable expectation of privacy when an undercover officer entered the home to purchase marijuana.

Utilizing the same reasoning, the D.C. Circuit held that a visitor who used another's apartment solely to **conduct drug transactions** could not claim Fourth Amendment protection.

In the present case, Respondents, like the defendants in Lewis and <u>Hicks</u>, were present on property for the sole purpose of **conducting criminal business**.

Like the apartments in <u>Lewis</u> and <u>Hicks</u>, the property in the present case had been converted into a **commercial center** to which outsiders were invited for **purposes of transacting unlawful business**.

Thus, Respondents, who were conducting a **purely commercial activity**, were not visitors to a "home" and were not engaging in longstanding social customs that serve functions recognized as valuable by society.

Whenever you substitute synonyms for the phrase-that-pays, you risk confusing and alienating the reader or user. In the example shown here, the reader must do some work to recognize that "business," "sales," and "drug transactions" are all related to the concept of "commercial purposes." Although most people would be able to make this connection with a little extra effort, your argument should not require the reader to *make* any extra effort. *You* should make the extra effort and incorporate the phrase-that-pays into the topic sentence to signal that the paragraph says something meaningful about the phrase-that-pays. In the list that follows, notice how small revisions allow the writer to incorporate the phrase-that-pays:

Respondents were not present in a "home," but were on property for a **purely commercial purpose.**

This Court has recognized that **business premises**, which exist for **commercial** rather than domestic activity, invite lesser privacy expectations than do residences.

In <u>Lewis,</u> this Court held that a defendant who used his home for the **commercial purpose of selling illegal narcotics** could not claim a violation of any reasonable expectation of privacy when an undercover officer entered the home to purchase marijuana.

Utilizing the same reasoning, the D.C. Circuit held that a visitor who used another's apartment solely for the **commercial purpose of conducting drug transactions** could not claim Fourth Amendment protection.

In the present case, Respondents, like the defendants in <u>Lewis</u> and <u>Hicks</u>, were using the property for a **commercial purpose:** They were present on the property for the sole purpose of **conducting criminal business.**

Like the apartments in <u>Lewis</u> and <u>Hicks</u>, the property in the present case had been converted into a **commercial center** to which outsiders were invited for **purposes of transacting unlawful business.**

Thus, Respondents, who were conducting a **purely commercial activity**, were not visitors to a "home" and were not engaging in long-standing social customs that serve functions recognized as valuable by society.

The small amount of work it will take to incorporate the phrase-that-pays is worth the trouble. Using the phrase-that-pays in a topic sentence increases the likelihood that the reader will actually read the paragraph, and that the user will find the paragraph that he or she is looking for. These topic sentences therefore increase the value of your argument by making it easier to read and easier to use.

b. Using Legally Significant Categories in Topic Sentences

Topic sentences can be used effectively in the summary of the argument and the fact statement, but their effectiveness is crucial in the argument section. In particular, the topic sentences in the rule explanation section have a job to do. At a minimum, an effective topic sentence in the rule explanation should tell the reader something about what the phrase-that-pays means, usually by showing how it has been applied in the past. A formula for an effective topic sentence in the explanation might be expressed as:

> Phrase-that-pays is established [or cannot be established] when category of facts or reasoning that reveals a new facet of the phrase-that-pays exists. [<u>Citation to relevant authority</u>.]

Many writers waste the beginning of a rule explanation paragraph with a sentence about the facts of an authority case, as in this example from a brief about *Rubin v. Coors Brewing Co.*, 514 U.S. 476 (1995):

▽ BAD EXAMPLE

> In <u>McGuffin</u>, the owner of a casino gambling operation sued to enjoin enforcement of a restriction on casino advertising. 101 U.S. at 101.

This sentence tells the reader that the paragraph is about the *McGuffin* case. While on some level that may be true, the paragraph is probably really about the *principle* from the *McGuffin* case, and that principle—and its phrase-that-pays—should be the focus of the topic sentence:

△ GOOD EXAMPLE

> State legislatures have more latitude to regulate speech in areas of socially harmful activity. <u>McGuffin</u>, 101 U.S. at 101.

In this way, the writer focuses the reader's attention on the true point of the paragraph: the legislature's ability to "regulate speech," which is the focus of that section of the document. The reader then knows that this paragraph will explain some new facet of the conditions under which states may regulate speech: They have more authority to do so when socially harmful activity is at issue. In the first example, in contrast, the reader knew only that the writer would be talking about the *McGuffin* case.

Being able to identify legally significant categories is an important skill in legal analysis, and you can use it to your advantage in topic sentences. For example, if you are planning to argue that the rule in the case(s) discussed in a particular paragraph should apply in the same way to your client's case, you will want to look for categories—and use language—that makes it easier for the reader to see that connection. In the example above, the writer was advocating for restrictions on beer advertising and wanted to analogize those restrictions to restrictions on casino advertising. Rather than talking about the specifics of casino advertising, she talked categorically about "socially harmful activity." If appropriate, the writer might also find a way to use a word—such as "broad," "general," "wide," or the like—that highlights the breadth of the latitude allowed to state legislatures:

△ GOOD EXAMPLE

> State legislatures have wider latitude to regulate speech in areas of socially harmful activity. <u>McGuffin</u>, 101 U.S. at 101.

The topic sentence connects the concept of the phrase-that-pays—regulating speech—to a legally significant category from an authority case—socially harmful activity. Upon reading this sentence, the reader may instantly realize that drinking beer is a socially harmful activity and decide that state legislatures should have more latitude to regulate it. When the writer later argues this exact point, the reader may accept it more readily, believing that he or she reached it independently.

In contrast, if the writer were arguing *against* limits on beer advertising, she might try to talk about the *McGuffin* case in a way that stressed its differences from the client's case. The restriction on speech was allowed in *McGuffin*, so the writer might first, if appropriate, use language like "only," "narrow," "few," or "limits" to signal that a restriction of this type is unusual. Furthermore, instead of using a category that is easy to connect to beer drinking— "socially harmful activities" —the writer could try to be more specific *or* to identify a category that might not connect so readily to the concept of drinking beer:

GOOD EXAMPLE

> Only on rare occasions—such as when an activity operates within strict geographic parameters—has this court allowed states to regulate advertising-related speech. <u>McGuffin</u>, 101 U.S. at 101.

By categorizing casino gambling as an activity that operates within strict geographic parameters, the writer can lead the reader to distinguish it from beer drinking, which does not. She may then have more success with her argument that her client's situation does not represent one of the rare occasions that call for regulation of speech.

Thus, in the rule explanation section, you can use the topic sentence as a tool to characterize the law in a favorable way. Two caveats: First, be sure that your characterization is fair as well as persuasive. Second, be certain that the case description(s) that follows the topic sentence provides support for the characterization that appears there. (See Chapter Six to review techniques for effective case descriptions.)

Effective topic sentences make it easier for you to check your organization. More importantly, they make it more likely that readers will keep reading and that users will find the paragraphs that they are looking for. Finally, when you review authority cases for analogous or distinguishable categories to use in your topic sentences, you may generate substance for your arguments.

10.2.2
HEADINGS

Effective point headings are discussed in Chapter Nine. I raise them here only as a practical matter. By this stage of the writing process, most writers will have identified where their headings belong and will have begun to draft headings as well. On those unusual occasions when you must churn out a brief without time for revision, however, you might use the template method to help you to turn a stream-of-consciousness draft into a readable document.

Inserting headings is one of the simplest steps a writer can take to improve the brief's effectiveness because headings allow the user to find the most important parts of the document. In an objective document, a heading can be simply a word or phrase that accurately describes the subject of the section or subsection — for example, "Damages," "Breach of duty to provide due care," and the like. Because the writer is usually not pushing one conclusion or another, the headings can be merely objective labels. When writing an argument, however, resist the temptation to take the easy way out: Take the time to draft argumentative point headings.

Argumentative point headings are an important part of your template because they are so highly visible. Further this advantage by choosing highly visible typefaces and styles for your point headings. Boldfaced type is usually an excellent choice, unless local rules forbid it.

You may be told that local rules "require" all capital letters, but be sure to check the rules yourself. Often, local practice has interpreted phrases such as "conspicuous type" to mean "all capital letters."[5] In the examples below, note how much less readable the all-caps heading is:

▽ BAD EXAMPLE

ILLEGAL DRUG DISTRIBUTION IS NOT A LONGSTANDING SOCIAL CUSTOM THAT SERVES INTERESTS RECOGNIZED AS VALUABLE BY SOCIETY.

△ GOOD EXAMPLE

Illegal drug distribution is not a longstanding social custom that serves functions recognized as valuable by society.

Many legal typeface customs evolved during the age of the typewriter. Use of all-caps and underlining were common because boldfaced and italicized fonts did not exist. Judges welcome being able to find new point headings easily as they page through the argument, and boldfaced headings will help them do this. Headings made up of all capital letters are usually difficult to read.[6] Accordingly, you should never use all caps for point headings unless the court requires it.

In addition to typeface concerns, consider placement of your headings as well. Although by now you have probably broken your document

---

[5] *See generally* Mary Beth Beazley, *Hiding in Plain Sight: "Conspicuous Type" Standards in Mandated Communication Statutes forthcoming* J. Legis. (2014) (describing how various courts and legislatures have mandated all capital letters with the phrase "conspicuous type").

[6] *E.g.,* Ralf Herrmann, *How Do We Read Words and How Should We Set Them?* Wayfinding & Typography (June 14, 2011), available at http://opentype.info/blog/2011/06/14/how-do-we-read-words-and-how-should-we-set-them. This essay explains that we can see clearly only a few letters at a time, and that we use our more blurry peripheral vision to pre-read and decipher upcoming letters. It also shows that all-caps letters are indistinguishable when blurry and that use of all-caps lettering therefore slows comprehension.

into sections, on some emergency projects, creating a template may help you to identify appropriate subsections. One way to identify sections and subsections is to consult your topic sentence list. As noted above, in a well-organized document, you should see several paragraphs about one issue, then several paragraphs about the next issue, and so on. When your topic sentences indicate that you have shifted to a new topic, it's time to insert a new heading.

10.2.3
PROVIDING CONTEXT WITH LEGAL BACKSTORY AND A ROADMAP

When one of my daughters was in the fourth grade, she wrote a paper on the Ottawa people. Her teacher told her she had to begin with an introduction, so she wrote, "Hello, here is my paper on the Ottawa people." The introductory material that you provide in a brief to a court is not as simple, but it should be almost as direct.

Professor Linda Edwards has used the term *umbrella paragraphs* to describe the combination of introductory material and roadmap paragraphs that appear—or should appear—at the beginning of most arguments.[7] In introductory material, the writer generally includes any information that is needed to provide context, that is common to all of the subpoints, or that will connect the subpoints to the writer's thesis. Illustration 10.1 shows where the umbrella paragraphs should appear. Generally, any time you break a section down into further subsections, you should provide some sort of introduction and roadmap. Sometimes these items can be combined in one paragraph, while at other times you may need two or three paragraphs. Note that it would be extremely unusual to need more than a page for your umbrella.

Many brief writers mistakenly believe—consciously or subconsciously—that they do not need to provide the court with an introduction within the argument. The court knows the law, they believe, and it can read the

Illustration 10.1

I. **First Major Point**
    [legal backstory relevant to A, B, & C and roadmap foreshadowing A, B, & C]
    A.
    B.
    [legal backstory relevant to 1 & 2 and mini-roadmap foreshadowing 1 & 2]
        1.
        2.
    C.
II. **Second Major Point**
    [legal backstory relevant to A & B and roadmap foreshadowing A & B]
    A.
    B.
III. **Third Major Point**

---

[7] Linda Holdeman Edwards, *Legal Writing: Process, Analysis, and Organization* 69-74, 133-37, 160-61 (5th ed., Aspen 2010).

facts and then figure out how this case fits in the scheme of things. And on one level they are right; the court could figure it out, with enough time. But good legal writing doesn't make readers figure things out: It provides them with the information they need when they need it. And at the beginning of the argument, legal readers need two things: They need to know what's already happened, and they need to know what's coming. You must write the legal backstory to tell them what has already happened, and a roadmap to tell them what's coming.

a.   What's Already Happened: The Legal Backstory

"What's already happened" is not just the facts and the procedure in the case (although certainly, readers do need this information, which you have no doubt supplied in the Fact Statement). I'm talking about what has already happened "in the law." Where did this issue come from? How has it been spending its time? If the law is a seamless web, what part of the web are we looking at right now? Perhaps, rather than thinking of the law as a seamless web, you should think of it as a complicated movie. Thus, the beginning of any argument can be thought of as the middle of the movie. And the court just came in late, sat down next to you, and whispered, "What's happened so far?"

To explain what has happened "so far," you need to provide the legal backstory, as succinctly as possible and with citations as appropriate. By doing so, you provide the reader with vital context for the rest of the argument. If you are saying that the defendant did not have a reasonable expectation of privacy, don't dive into the reasonable expectation of privacy analysis, presuming that the reader knows how it is relevant to the plaintiff's rights. Instead, set the argument in the context of the Fourth Amendment. Likewise, if you are arguing that the public policy exception to the employment-at-will doctrine does not apply, make sure that you tell the reader what the employment-at-will doctrine is. Furthermore, if there is a split in the circuits, don't make the court figure that out five pages later; tell that important detail right away.

Broadly stated, the reader should be able to glean four elements from the legal backstory:

1. **The question that this part of the document is answering.** If you are writing the backstory for the whole argument, you should address the question that the whole document is answering. If you are providing backstory for just one part of the argument, focus on that part alone. In almost every situation, you should state this question as an argumentative declaration, as in, "The plaintiff's complaint should be dismissed because supervisors cannot be held individually liable under Title VII."

2. **The legal rule or standard that is at the root of the issue being addressed in that part of the document.** Many legal arguments are

about the meaning of a particular word or phrase within a constitutional provision, statute, or legal rule. Even when there is a thick layer of judicial gloss on the original rule—as there is, for example, on the First Amendment—you should still note (or quote) the pertinent part of the First Amendment before moving to the concept of, for example, the existence of a chilling effect in a particular case.

3. **How the legal issue in this case (or section of the argument) relates to the rule.** After stating the rule that is at the root of your controversy, move from that rule to the rule or sub-rule currently at issue. The concept of the "rule cluster," which was discussed in Chapter Five, may be appropriate here, as there may be a direct progression from one rule to the next. In contrast, the legal issue in your case may be a subpart of the main rule.

4. **The current status of that issue in the relevant jurisdiction, if needed.** Although this piece of the umbrella is not always needed, for some cases its inclusion is crucial. Most umbrellas will make evident how the rule operates in general. Include more details about the rule's status if there are any controversies about this rule that are relevant to your argument. For example, perhaps you are arguing that the court should allow an exception to a particular rule when circumstance C exists. To identify the current status of the rule, you might point out that the court has previously created exceptions for circumstance A and circumstance B. In addition or in the alternative, there might be a split in the circuits as to the issue. If you are writing to a court other than the United States Supreme Court, it might be appropriate to point out that sister states or sister circuits have adopted a particular rule but that your particular jurisdiction has not yet done so.

Be honest in the legal backstory. For example, if there is a split in the circuits, it might be tempting to point out only that certain other courts have decided the case the same way you want the court to decide this one. Your credibility would suffer, however, when the court reads your opponent's brief and discovers the truth. In contrast, if you begin by laying out the complete backstory, you will do much to help the court and to burnish your own image as an honest dealer.

Note how this writer accurately identifies contrasting authorities in this legal backstory:

⚠ GOOD EXAMPLE

Gary Kirkby cannot be found individually liable as an employer under Title VII. ① Title VII defines an employer as "a person engaged in an industry affecting commerce who has fifteen or more employees . . . and any agent of such a person." 42 U.S.C. §2000e(b) (2001). ② Neither the Supreme Court nor the First Circuit has addressed the specific question of whether a supervisor is an "employer" for purposes of individual liability under Title VII. ③ Morrison v. Carleton Woolen

① This sentence tells the court the question that the document will ultimately answer.

② Here is the legal rule at the root of the issue.

③ This sentence tells how the legal issue in the case relates to the legal rule: the issue is about the meaning of the word "employer" as it relates to supervisors. The sentence also begins to tell the reader the current status of the issue in the relevant jurisdiction: the court has not decided it yet.

4 Here, the writer provides more information about the current status of the legal issue, noting that there is a split in the circuits.

5 Note that, although the writer honestly portrays the split in the circuits, she is appropriately argumentative, ending the paragraph by noting that more of the circuits are on her side. This case is set in the District of Rhode Island; if she were on the other side of the case, she might note that although there is a split in the circuits, courts within the District of Rhode Island are on her side.

1 This sentence tells the reader the question that this part of the document answers. Note how it also shows how this issue connects to the previous issue: these are alternative grounds on which the court can grant the motion.

2 This sentence tells the reader how the issues under discussion (causation in fact and legal cause) relate to the general rule regarding causation, and how they operate in this context in a motion to dismiss.

3 At this point, the writer is shifting from backstory to roadmap.

<u>Mills, Inc.</u>, 108 F.3d 429, 444 (1st Cir. 1997) (declining to consider whether Title VII provides for individual liability); <u>Scarfo v. Cabletron Sys. Inc.</u>, 54 F.3d 931, 951-52 (1st Cir. 1995) (because the law on the point of individual liability has not been decided in the First Circuit, the district court did not commit plain error when it held that a supervisor could be liable).

Differing interpretations of the phrase "and any agent" in the definition of employer have engendered a split in the federal circuits regarding whether Title VII provides for individual liability. E.g., <u>Tomka v. Seiler Corp.</u>, 66 F.3d 1295, 1313 (2d Cir. 1995) (concluding Title VII does not provide for individual liability); <u>Wyss v. General Dynamics Corp.</u>, 24 F. Supp. 2d, 202, 206 (D.R.I. 1998) (finding that individual liability is appropriate under Title VII). **4** The vast majority of circuits deciding this issue have determined that Title VII was intended only to impose vicarious liability on employers. E.g., <u>Tomka</u>, 66 F.3d at 1313. **5**

The backstory for subsections within the argument may be much shorter. Sometimes, the backstory may require nothing more than a sentence. You may need slightly more detail if, for example, you are analyzing a part of a rule that itself has multiple parts. The following example of legal backstory comes from a motion to dismiss a negligence cause of action. In the main backstory, the writer had laid out the four-part test for negligence in the relevant jurisdiction (duty, breach, causation, damages) and then noted that there were two grounds for dismissal: First, the defendant in the case owed no duty to the plaintiff under the circumstances. Second, even if the defendant did owe a duty, the complaint did not plead sufficient facts as to the causation issue. The excerpt below provides the backstory for the causation issue. Because the writer has stated earlier the rule at the root of the case, the backstory here need only refer to it:

Even if this court finds that plaintiff will be able to establish a legal duty, it should dismiss the complaint because the plaintiff will not be able to establish causation. **1** To survive a motion to dismiss as to causation, a complaint must plead sufficient facts for both causation in fact and legal cause. <u>McGuffin v. Restrepo</u>, 426 S.E.2d 802, 804 (Vanita 1993). **2** This complaint has not done so. First **3**

By referring specifically to the causation element (and the legal duty element), the writer has ensured that the reader will be able to understand what rule is at the root of the controversy for this part of the argument. The status of the rule is not controversial, and so the writer merely relates the two parts of her analysis to the causation rule.

Whether your legal backstory is simple or complex, providing it will go a long way toward helping the reader to understand the rest of the argument.

b. What's Coming Next: The Roadmap

Roadmap paragraphs follow the legal backstory. And roadmaps are the opposite of what you whisper to someone who wants to know what's going on in a movie because a good roadmap will be full of spoilers; it will tell the reader exactly what's going to happen in the argument. For purposes of narrative reasoning, roadmaps are important because the backstory has set up a problem: The roadmap literally shows the court how it can solve the problem.[8]

Roadmap paragraphs are important in the template because they help confirm, and sometimes establish, the reader's expectations for the document. A good roadmap will also reveal the writer's position on the points to be addressed in the relevant sections or subsections. By writing an effective roadmap, the writer tells the reader how "far" this part of the document extends—how many points does the writer talk about before stopping? In addition, an effective roadmap lays out the document's large-scale organization by telling the reader the order in which the writer will address the main points. Even a poorly organized document will be easier to understand if the writer has provided a good roadmap.

It is tempting to skip this step, but providing this material makes your brief more effective by reducing the reader's suspense. If the reader sees a "I" heading, followed immediately by an "A" heading, for example, he or she does not know how many subheadings will follow or how the subheadings connect to the writer's main point. By writing a backstory and a roadmap, the writer provides "Bacon links" for the reader so that the connections are obvious.

Although many writers are familiar with the law review style of roadmap paragraphs (e.g., "this article will address three issues"), roadmaps in court documents can and should be more sophisticated. A simple technique is to provide the legal backstory and then use the decision maker's needs as the focus of the roadmap,[9] as in the following example based on *Miller v. Albright*, 523 U.S. 420 (1998):

> I. Section 1409(a) Is an Unconstitutional Denial of Equal Protection as Guaranteed by the Fifth Amendment's Due Process Clause.
>
> The statute at issue in this case, 8 U.S.C. §1409(a), classifies foreign-born children of a United States citizen and a noncitizen into three groups: (a) those whose parents are married, (b) those whose parents are unmarried and who have a United States citizen for a mother, and

---

[8] *See* Kenneth D. Chestek, *The Plot Thickens: Appellate Brief as Story*, 14 Legal Writ. 127, 155-56 (2008) ("The 'road map' paragraphs . . . describe where the legal issues will be encountered in the remainder of the brief. They serve both as 'foreshadowing' of the conflict to raise in the coming pages and as a neat transition to the 'rising action' portion of the plot.").

[9] *See* Laurel Currie Oates & Anne M. Enquist, *The Legal Writing Handbook* §21.2.1 (4th ed., Aspen 2006).

1 Here is the rule—
a statute—that
is the root of the
controversy.

2 Here is
information about
the current status of
the legal rule, i.e.,
how it is currently
being interpreted by
the Court.

3 Here is more
information about
the status of the
legal rule.

(c) those whose parents are unmarried and who have a United States citizen for a father. **1** Children in the first two groups—those whose parents are married and those with a United States citizen mother—are United States citizens by birthright. See 8 U.S.C. §1401(g). Children in the last group—those whose parents are unmarried and who have United States citizen fathers—may receive their fathers' citizenship only after clearing several statutory hurdles. **2**

Even when paternity has been established by "clear and convincing evidence," and even assuming that the father was a United States citizen at the time of the child's birth, a child in this third group will still be denied citizenship unless (a) the father agrees in writing to support that child until age 18, *and* (b) the child is "legitimated" before he or she reaches the age of 18, *or* the father acknowledges paternity before the child reaches the age of 18, *or* the father's paternity is established by adjudication before the child reaches the age of 18. **3**

Section 1409(a) illegally discriminates against children of United States citizens based on the marital status of their parents and on the sex of their citizen parent. For more than 25 years, this Court has consistently applied a heightened scrutiny to state statutes or state constitutional provisions which have classified persons based on gender. See, e.g., J.E.B. v. Alabama, 511 U.S. 127, 140 (1994) (citing cases). Similarly, for almost 20 years, this Court has applied a heightened scrutiny to those state statutes which have classified persons based on their "legitimacy." See, e.g., Pickett v. Brown, 426 U.S. 1, 6-9 (1983) (citing cases). In reviewing federal legislation, this Court has also demanded that Congress satisfy a higher standard than the traditionally deferential one for classifications based on either legitimacy, see id. at 8 (quoting Trimble v. Gordon, 430 U.S. 762, 767 (1977)), or based on gender. See, e.g., Rostker v. Goldberg, 453 U.S. 57, 66-70 (1981). **4**

4 In this paragraph,
the writer is
identifying a
second rule that is
at the root of the
controversy: the
rule about how to
interpret statutes
that discriminate on
th 5 basis of gender.
roadmap.

6 Part two of the
roadmap.

Because of its questionable classifications, §1409(a) should be subjected to a heightened scrutiny despite the great deference normally due congressional authority to enact immigration legislation. **5** Section 1409(a) cannot survive this level of scrutiny because neither its gender-based classifications **6** nor its legitimacy classifications are supported by "exceedingly persuasive" justifications, nor does either classification substantially further an important governmental interest.

This roadmap paragraph does not include enumeration but indicates that the writer will first address which test applies and then address the argument that neither classification within the statute—the classification based on gender nor the classification based on legitimacy—can survive the test. Notice how the roadmap foreshadows the points made under the three subheadings within that section of the document:

> **A. This Court should apply a heightened scrutiny to §1409(a) consistent with the Fifth Amendment's equal protection guarantee.**

B. Section 1409(a) does not survive the heightened scrutiny that this Court has applied to gender-based classifications.

C. Section 1409(a) does not survive the heightened scrutiny that this Court has applied to legitimacy-based classifications.

Some writers provide a roadmap to the entire argument within the summary of the argument. They then provide mini-roadmaps—as the writer in the previous example has done—to each complex section of the document (i.e., each section of the document that has further subparts). The structure of the headings will dictate the structure of the roadmap paragraphs. If there are two main headings, there should be two points in the overall roadmap. If a main heading section contains three subsections with subheadings, then the mini-roadmap that introduces that section should have three points. Do not provide too much detail in a roadmap. For example, if your main roadmap lays out the elements of duty and causation, do not include subparts of the causation issue in the main roadmap; they are properly included in the mini-roadmap to the causation section.

Although the writer in the example above chose not to use enumeration (perhaps because there had been several other sentences with enumeration in the backstory), enumeration almost always makes roadmap paragraphs more effective. The user's eye is drawn to numbers on a page, and it is easy for the reader to see how the points relate to each other. The previous roadmap paragraph could be enumerated with a few simple changes:

> This Court should reverse the decision below for three reasons: (1) because of its questionable classifications, §1409(a) should be subjected to a heightened scrutiny despite the great deference normally due congressional authority to enact immigration legislation; (2) the gender based classifications in §1409(a) cannot survive heightened scrutiny; and (3) the legitimacy-based classifications in §1409(a) cannot survive heightened scrutiny.

Whether you use enumeration or not, your roadmap should be argumentative. An ineffective roadmap will say, in essence, "this court must decide three issues: (1) whether to rule for or against my client as to issue one . . . ." Because you know how you think the court should come out, make that hoped-for result the premise of your roadmap, as in the previous examples, saying in essence: "This Court should rule in favor of my client for three reasons." You should also review your headings and roadmaps to make sure that the roadmaps predict exactly the points you will address and echo language that you will use when you address each point. You should not copy and paste your exact headings into the roadmap, but the roadmap should certainly include words and phrases—particularly phrases-that-pay—that appear in the headings. The roadmap will create expectations in the reader; by using similar language in the roadmap and the headings, you can reassure the reader that you are fulfilling those expectations and make it easier for the user to find needed information.

10.2.4
EXPLICIT CONNECTION-CONCLUSIONS

Just as the headings help the writer to craft any needed roadmap paragraphs, they can also help the writer to check for explicit connection-conclusions. The last paragraph before a new heading is a strong position of emphasis, and stating an explicit connection-conclusion is a good way to exploit that position of emphasis. The writer can easily check for connection-conclusions by looking for each new heading or subheading and then checking the paragraph above that heading; unless it is a roadmap, the paragraph should end on the writer's explicit conclusion as to the point under discussion within that heading or subheading, and it should connect that point as needed to any other points in the argument.

Although some writers end a point heading section by foreshadowing the next issue, this technique is usually not necessary in a document with headings. If making the connection between the points in two sections or subsections is important, try reaching back to the earlier section instead of reaching forward to the later section.

For example, in a subsection about part one of a two-part test, some writers will end the subsection by saying, in essence, "Petitioner meets part one of the test. Next, it will be shown that petitioner meets part two of the test." To use positions of emphasis more effectively, the writer could end the first subsection by saying, "Petitioner meets part one of the test." After an appropriate, persuasive point heading, the next subsection's text can begin by saying, e.g., "In addition to meeting part one of the test, Petitioner also meets part two . . . ." In this way, the writer shows a connection between the two parts of the test, but also exploits the position of emphasis at the end of the first subsection by focusing on the point made in that subsection. This technique can also be useful as a way to support digital readers, who may be jumping to that portion of the document and would otherwise have no context for the information.

The guidelines are slightly different if the point is dispositive, that is, if that point alone can result in a victory for your client. In that situation, you may want to include terms in your connection-conclusion that serve as "Bacon links" to connect the point to your overall thesis and tell the court what it must do:

⚠ GOOD EXAMPLE

Thus, Respondents, who were conducting a purely commercial activity, were not visitors to a "home" and were not engaging in long-standing social customs that serve functions recognized as valuable by society. While Respondents may have been legitimately in the apartment, in the sense that Thompson permitted their presence, Respondents did not have any legitimate expectation of privacy in the apartment because they were present only to conduct illegal business. Because Respondents' expectation of privacy was not one that society recognizes as reasonable, they cannot claim the Fourth Amendment's protections, and this Court must reverse.

If the point is not dispositive, exploit the position of emphasis that a section ending provides to articulate a connection-conclusion that hammers home the point you wish to make in that section.

10.3
WRITING FOR THE DIGITAL READER

Lawyers, perhaps more than those in any other profession, have benefitted from the information revolution. We can now access information almost anywhere, and at almost any time, thanks not only to smartphones, laptops, and tablets, but also to computer research databases and wireless access to those databases. Furthermore, once we have access to the information, we can use a variety of search mechanisms to find words or statute numbers that we are interested in.

But easy access comes with costs as well as benefits, and scientific research is beginning to show that digital readers do not read or comprehend information as effectively as readers of hard-copy documents.[10] At first glance, this result seems surprising. After all, judges and clerks read both digital and paper documents by deciphering the same 26 letters, by using their eyes to read those letters, and by moving their eyes from left to right across the line of text. But it turns out that the medium in which we encounter the written word has an effect on how well we comprehend the information that we read.[11]

First, judges and clerks—like all readers—are reading with more than just their eyes. If they are reading a hard-copy brief, they are aware of

---

[10] *E.g.*, Anne Mangen, Bente R. Walgermo & Kolbjorn Bronnick, *Reading Linear Texts on Paper versus Computer Screen: Effects on Reading Comprehension*, 58 Intl. J. Educ. Research 61-68 (2013). "Subjects who read the texts on paper performed significantly better [on reading comprehension tests] than subjects who read the texts on the computer screen." *Id.* at 65.

[11] Furthermore, the package that gives us those accessible documents—whether it is a desktop, a laptop, a tablet, or an iPhone—also brings with it a host of distractions that can affect our ability to read and retain the information that we read.

the heft of the document, and of where they are within it—the beginning, middle, or end. They have this awareness without making conscious effort, without even glancing around for a page number. In other words, they encounter the information physically as well as visually, and they maintain a subconscious image of the complete document. Even as they focus on one page, one sentence, or one word, they subconsciously imagine the physical context of the words they are reading, often retaining both the location within the document and the location on the page or pair of pages.[12] Because they have this spatial concept of how the pieces of information fit into the document, they can more easily grasp both large- and small-scale organization.

When people read digital documents, in contrast, it is more difficult for them to conceptualize the parts they are not reading. They know that an electronic brief does not exist inside the computer as a physical stack of pages; even if their electronic device simulates the sound of pages turning as they read, they never perceive the physical movement from the beginning of the document to the end: physically, they perceive every page identically. Comprehension suffers even more if they must scroll through the document—a common occurrence—because even that identical physical context is impermanent, as the words rise and fall on the screen.[13]

Accordingly, when reading digital documents, readers and users must work harder to understand the content and organization of the information in the brief. This requirement creates a problem, of course: We can't be sure that our readers will do the extra work. So what should we do?

Alas, we cannot force hard copies into the hands of judges and clerks; digital documents are here to stay. Instead of getting rid of digital documents, we must use writing and presentation techniques that compensate for the hard-copy benefits that are lost in digital documents.[14]

First, use enumeration and headings to provide digital readers with finding tools and signals. As you know from your own behavior as a digital researcher, digital readers may skip around in a document and have little idea where they have landed most recently. Thus, you may want to use the labels on your headings to let them know where they are. Traditional roman/alphabet labels may not be helpful:

---

[12] *See* Mangen et al., *supra* note 10, at 65-66 ("Evidence suggests that readers often recall where in a text some particular piece of information appeared (e.g., toward the upper right corner or at the bottom of the page) . . . . [T]he fixity of text printed on paper supports reader's construction of the spatial representation of the text by providing unequivocal and fixed spatial cues for text memory and recall.") (citations omitted).

[13] *See* Mangen et al., *supra* note 10, at 65 ("Scrolling is known to hamper the process of reading, by imposing a spatial instability which may negatively affect the reader's mental representation of the text and, by implication, comprehension.") (citations omitted).

[14] *See, e.g.,* Robert Dubose, *Writing Appellate Briefs for Tablet Readers*, Appellate Issues (Spring 2012), available at http://www.americanbar.org/content/dam/aba/publications/appellate_issues/2012sprng_ai.authcheckdam.pdf) (last accessed Mar. 11, 2014).

▽ HEADING LABEL THAT IS LESS EFFECTIVE FOR DIGITAL READER

> **B. Plaintiff's complaint has not alleged sufficient facts as to the** *causation* **element.**

This label tells the reader only that he or she has landed at "B," presumably the second subpart of some argument within the document. The label does not reveal, however, whether that "B" is a subpart of argument "I," argument "II," or even argument "IX." By using scientific numbering, however,[15] the writer can signal the argument's approximate location:

△ HEADING LABEL THAT IS MORE EFFECTIVE FOR DIGITAL READER

> **3.2. Plaintiff's complaint has not alleged sufficient facts as to the** *causation* **element.**

Unlike the label on the previous example, this label tells the reader that this argument is the second subpart within the third section of the argument as a whole.

In addition to effective enumeration, of course, you should use effective substantive headings, following the guidelines in Chapter Nine. Make sure you use language that will signal both the issue under discussion and your position on the issue. Likewise, use boldfaced or other contrasting type that will allow users to see your headings as they scroll or scan through your document.

Second, use the "template," phrases-that-pay, and Kevin Bacon connections to provide digital readers with contextual and organizational cues. As you know from reading this chapter, headings are one part of a symbolic "template" that you can install to help provide context for your reader. Headings, topic sentences, and roadmap paragraphs can all provide context and finding tools for digital readers. As noted above, eye-tracking research shows that readers scan the first parts of pages and paragraphs to look for information that is useful to them.[16] You should therefore exploit those locations.

As you know from your own research behaviors, readers often use search terms to lead them to the most significant part of documents. Be sure to use phrases-that-pay appropriately, and to do so in a way that promotes searching and finding. Furthermore, because new headings may draw a digital reader's focus in the same way that the top of a new page does, be sure to place context cues in these high-focus locations. For example, by

---

[15] Daniel Sockwell, *Writing for the iPad Judge, Announcements,* Colum. Bus. L. Rev. Online (Jan. 14, 2014) (available at http://cblr.columbia.edu/archives/12940) (last accessed April 13, 2014).

[16] *E.g.,* Duggan et al., *supra* note 4, at 1146, 1147 (agreeing with a conclusion about eye-tracking studies showing that "skimmers begin every paragraph and continue reading until the rate of information gain drops below a threshold whereupon they skip to the beginning of the next paragraph," and explaining research results showing that "lines towards the top of the page were more likely to be fixated upon than lines towards the bottom of the page").

making explicit Kevin Bacon connections at the beginning of a new section, you can make it easier for the digital reader to understand how the different pieces of your argument fit together.

Finally, be thoughtful in how you choose and use your software. Specific recommendations as to software are beyond the scope of this book (and the expertise of this author). When choosing software, however, be mindful of both court rules and the devices that judges and clerks use to read their briefs. If possible, use software that creates fixed pages; likewise, look for software that sends structural signals to your reader.[17] Some current software, for example, runs a table of contents down the left-hand side of the screen, giving readers context as well as allowing them to move easily from one section of the document to another.

It is tempting to take advantage of all of the bells and whistles that your software offers, but be mindful of the impact of your decisions. Hot links can be useful, for example, but they can also take the reader away from your document and into another document. If that document also has hot links, the reader may soon be many documents away from your well-crafted argument. If you believe that the court would benefit from hot links, it may be better to include them in a table of authorities or an appendix rather than in the body of the argument itself.

Thankfully, hard-copy readers have many of the finding and comprehension needs that digital readers do. Although sensing structure and making connections may be easier for hard-copy readers than for digital readers, you will likely enhance the comprehension of all readers by using these user-friendly techniques.

10.4
SUMMARY

To make your document reader-friendly and user-friendly, first be sure that you understand how the parts of your argument fit together. Then, make sure to show explicitly how the pieces fit together, and make it easy for all readers to find the various sections of your argument. Use roadmaps, headings, topic sentences, and connection-conclusions to show hard-copy and digital readers and users both where each section of the argument is and how each section relates to the whole.

---

[17] *See, e.g.*, Dubose, *supra* note 14 (making recommendations about highlighting structure for digital readers).

Chapter Eleven

EXPLOITING OPPORTUNITIES FOR PERSUASION

11.1
OPPORTUNITIES FOR PERSUASION

In the game of Scrabble, players use letter tiles to spell words in a crossword puzzle pattern on a game board. They score points based on which letter tiles they use: The infrequently used "X" is worth 8 points, while the more common "T" is worth only 1 point. Players earn bonuses, however, if a letter is placed on a special space on the board: Some spaces are "double letter score" or "triple letter score" spaces, which allow the player to double or triple the points of the letter on that square. Even better, some spaces are "double word score" or "triple word score" spaces, which allow the doubling or tripling of the points for the whole word.

When you write a brief, you will "score points" with your reader just based on your "tiles"—the strength of the arguments you make about the law or the facts. In addition, however, there will be opportunities for persuasion that arise at various times as you write the brief. These opportunities for persuasion, like the colored squares on the Scrabble board, allow you to make the most of what you have.

The opportunities for persuasion addressed in this chapter are based on knowledge about how people read and use legal documents. Practical advocates exploit this knowledge and base their writing decisions on it. Every writing decision you make—from which issues to argue, to how you structure your sentences, to what typeface to use—can affect how the reader understands and perceives your argument, or how easily a user is able to find the argument. Some decisions will affect the reader's impressions of you as a credible advocate and a reliable reporter of the law and the facts. Others will affect the user's ability to find the most relevant or important parts of the argument. All must be made with care, and with the reader and user in mind.

11.2
How Not to Persuade

The first and most important point to make is that persuasion is not about lying. There are two reasons not to misstate the facts or the law in your case. The first reason is simply because it is wrong. The ethical canons in every state forbid it. For example, Rule 3.3 of the Illinois Rules of Professional Conduct provides in part:

Rule 3.3 Candor Toward the Tribunal

(a) A lawyer shall not knowingly:

(1) make a false statement of fact or law to a tribunal or fail to correct a false statement of material fact or law previously made to the tribunal by the lawyer;

(2) fail to disclose to the tribunal legal authority in the controlling jurisdiction known to the lawyer to be directly adverse to the position of the client and not disclosed by opposing counsel. . . .

Furthermore, Rule 46(c) of the Federal Rules of Appellate Procedure allows a court of appeals to discipline attorneys for "for failure to comply with any court rule," and the local rules of many courts specifically prohibit misrepresenting the law or the facts. Furthermore, Rule 11(b) of the Federal Rules of Civil Procedure provides that when an attorney presents a motion, a brief, or any other document to a court, the attorney gives several assurances to the court, including the following:

(1) it is not being presented for any improper purpose, such as to harass, cause unnecessary delay, or needlessly increase the cost of litigation; [and]

(2) the claims, defenses, and other legal contentions are warranted by existing law or by a nonfrivolous argument for extending, modifying, or reversing existing law or for establishing new law.

Courts will sanction counsel for misrepresentations of law and of fact.[1]

The second reason not to lie to the court is that it hurts your credibility. After an academic life filled with anonymous grading, many law students forget that the practice of law is not anonymous. Judges remember attorneys who have lied to them, and so an attorney's credibility with the court is a valuable asset. Judge Parker notes that an attorney's clients suffer from the attorney's loss of credibility, because the loss "ultimately . . . inhibits that advocate's ability to persuade."[2] In contrast, if you write a strong, reliable brief, you help not only your current client, but future clients as well. Judge Duncan notes that "a Quality brief—that is, one that is accurate, concise, and logically analyzed and organized . . . not only increases a lawyer's chance of winning an appeal, but (more important in the long run) transforms that lawyer into becoming a permanent friend of the court."[3]

Judge Saufley of the Maine Supreme Judicial Court warns attorneys not to "squander" their credibility:

Do not ever misquote cases or the record. Be absolutely vigilant about such practices in your office. Failure to do so may lose much for your clients and your reputation. It is never worth it.[4]

Another "persuasive" tactic that usually fails is an attack on opposing counsel or the judges in the court(s) below. Because law students do not usually fall into this trap, given their hypothetical cases and clients, law school may be the best time to learn that judges are not persuaded by ad hominem arguments. Judge Pregerson notes that attorneys injure themselves and their clients' cases if they "vilify or belittle [their] opponents. . . .

---

[1] *See generally* Raymond T. Elligett, Jr. & John M. Scheb, *Professional Responsibility of Appellate Advocates*, 1 Fla. Coastal L.J. 101 (1999) (citing cases).

[2] Fred I. Parker, *Appellate Advocacy and Practice in the Second Circuit*, 64 Brook. L. Rev. 457, 462 (1998).

[3] Sarah B. Duncan, *Pursuing Quality: Writing a Helpful Brief*, 30 St. Mary's L.J. 1093, 1101 (1999).

[4] Leigh Ingalls Saufley, *Amphibians and Appellate Courts*, 51 Me. L. Rev. 18, 22 (1999).

A shrill tone in a brief diminishes its persuasive force."[5] Judge Saufley worries that too many attorneys rely on the old adage: "If the law is with you, argue the law; if the facts are with you, argue the facts; if neither is with you, call the other guy names." She points out that name-calling has a negative effect on the brief writer: "As soon as I see an attack of any kind on the other party, opposing counsel, or the trial judge, I begin to discount the merits of the argument."[6] Supreme Court Justice Ruth Bader Ginsburg notes that a "top-quality brief" "scratches put-downs and indignant remarks about one's adversary or the first instance decision-maker" because they will "more likely annoy than make points with the bench."[7] Persuasion is a subtle art. It consists of creating an image of yourself as a competent, credible, helpful, reliable advocate—the kind of person whose brief the court can't wait to read. It also consists of taking advantage of opportunities at every stage of the brief-writing process to highlight your strengths and "low-light" your weaknesses.

11.3
CHOOSING ISSUES RESPONSIBLY

One of the first ways that advocates establish their credibility is by arguing only those issues—and cases—that are worthy of argument. Most law students cannot choose which issues to argue, but they can choose how many arguments to make. Soon, they will be choosing the issues, as well as deciding whether a case or a motion is worth filing or whether an appeal is worth pursuing. You should appeal any case and make any argument that has a credible chance of a positive result, but use good judgment when making those decisions, and remember the busy courts to whom you are arguing. A marginal argument weakens the advocate's present and future credibility; a brief that addresses fewer issues argued well is better than a brief with many issues argued poorly.

Judge Patricia Wald, of the United States Court of Appeals for the District of Columbia Circuit, notes: "Confident counsel should almost always go for broke and rely on their one or two best arguments, abandoning the other 9-10 wish-list entries. . . . The fewer arguments you make the more attention they will get from us in preparing and disposing of

---

[5] Harry Pregerson, *Appellate Brief Writing and Other Transgressions,* 34 UCLA L. Rev. 431, 436 (1986).

[6] Saufley, *supra* note 4, at 23.

[7] Ruth Bader Ginsburg, *Remarks on Appellate Advocacy,* 50 S.C. L. Rev. 567, 568 (1999).

your case."[8] Judge Pierce notes that trial judges make "relatively few mis-takes" and that a brief that asserts a half-dozen or more key points of error may "needlessly divert" the judge's attention from the more compelling grounds, with the result that the court's ability to recognize the validity of any one of the grounds "decreases significantly."[9] Similarly, former Chief Justice Burger has noted that "a brief that raises every colorable issue runs the risk of burying good arguments."[10] Judge Wiener advises that counsel should "[d]ecide which legal arguments are key to resolving the issues of the case in your client's favor," and should "[f]orce" themselves to "omit fringe issues and far-out theories; they will only dull the thrust of your appeal and obscure the potentially winning points."[11] Finally, Judge Parker notes that you do a disservice to your client when you raise too many issues on appeal, noting that if you raise 20 issues and give them all "equal [time]—and therefore, short-shrift," you may fail to convince the court that the district court "committed just one error which justifies some relief for your client."[12]

Thus, when choosing issues and arguments, restrict your brief to those that are best supported by both the law and the facts. Not every error is worthy of appeal, or even of argument. Before arguing about an error in the trial court, identify a causal link between the error and the court's judgment against your client; without that link, the error is irrelevant. Before filing a motion, identify a valid purpose for that motion. While you may sometimes file a motion as a method of narrowing issues rather than in a bona fide attempt to dispose of the whole case, be sure that you are not wasting the court's time. Furthermore, remember that the validity of each individual argument has an impact on the whole brief. Every specious argument chips away at your overall credibility. When all the arguments are legitimate, on the other hand, the stock of the whole brief rises, along with that of counsel.

11.4
EXPLOITING POSITIONS OF EMPHASIS

Within the brief itself, the practical advocate exploits physical positions of emphasis. Your words will have more impact if you place them in

---

[8] Patricia M. Wald, *19 Tips from 19 Years on the Appellate Bench*, 1 J. App. Prac. & Process 7, 11 (1999).

[9] Lawrence W. Pierce, *Appellate Advocacy: Some Reflections from the Bench*, 61 Fordham L. Rev. 829, 835-36 (1993).

[10] *Jones v. Barnes*, 463 U.S. 745, 751-52 (1983).

[11] Jacques L. Wiener, Jr., *Ruminations from the Bench: Brief Writing and Oral Argument in the Fifth Circuit*, 70 Tul. L. Rev. 187, 194 (1995).

[12] Parker, *supra* note 2, at 460.

certain physical locations within the brief. Scientists called psycholinguists have learned that readers pay more attention to certain physical positions in a document. Any time there is extra white space in a document—at the beginning or ending of a paragraph, for example, or more importantly, at the beginning or ending of a document element such as a point heading section, a statement of the case, or a summary of the argument—readers subconsciously pay more attention.[13] Just as Scrabble players angle to put certain letters or words in certain positions on the game board, you should angle to put your strongest arguments and statements in certain positions in your brief.

A reader's attention peaks to varying degrees when reading all titles and headings, as well as when reading the first and last paragraphs in document segments (e.g., the statement of the case, the argument), the first and last paragraphs in point heading sections, and even the first and last sentences in paragraphs. To a lesser degree, information at the beginning or ending of a sentence is also in a position of emphasis,[14] as is a short sentence, particularly when it is placed within a group of longer sentences. Finally, within a sentence itself, the reader pays more attention to the information expressed in the subject-verb combination, with particular emphasis on the verb.[15]

Positions of deemphasis are positions that are away from white space and away from the natural breaks that the reader takes while reading. In other words, "middles": the middle of a point heading section, a paragraph, a document. A series of long sentences slows down comprehension by making the reader work harder to assemble the information in the sentences. Within a sentence, moving information from a verb to a noun, or using passive voice to remove an actor (that is, the person or thing that "verbed"), also deemphasizes information.

Thus, to make your brief more persuasive, focus your attention. Decide (a) what information you want to emphasize and (b) what information you want to deemphasize. Exploit the positions of emphasis by making sure that you fill them with the information that is most important to the case and/or the reader. Lessen the impact of negative information by placing it in positions of deemphasis. The various positions of emphasis present many opportunities for persuasion in your brief.

---

[13] *See generally* Robert P. Charrow & Veda R. Charrow, *Making Legal Language Understandable: A Psycholinguistic Study of Jury Instructions,* 79 Colum. L. Rev. 1306 (1979).

[14] *See, e.g.,* Joseph M. Williams & Gregory G. Colomb, *Style: Lessons in Clarity and Grace* 82-86, 91-94 (10th ed., Longman 2010). *See also* Laurel Currie Oates & Anne M. Enquist, *The Legal Writing Handbook* §§17.7.6(c), 18.12.5, and 24.6.3 (5th ed., Aspen 2010).

[15] This point is now a staple for most legal writing teachers. It was famously articulated by Richard Wydick in a law review article that later became a book: Richard C. Wydick, *Plain English for Lawyers* chs. 3-4 (5th ed., Carolina Academic Press 2005). *See also* Williams & Colomb, *supra* note 14, at Lesson 3. See Section 11.4.4(a) below for specific examples.

11.4.1
PERSUADING WITH LARGE-SCALE ORGANIZATION

To exploit the reader's peak attention at the beginning of the argument section, begin with your best point rather than starting with a weak point and leading up to a strong point. Judge Coleman advises you to "[p]resent your strongest points first to try to capture votes early."[16] When you start your argument with a weak point, your reader may think, "Is this the best they can do?" That bad impression can taint the rest of the argument. On the other hand, when you start your argument with a strong point, the reader's first thought is "This is a good argument," and that impression can carry over to the rest of the points that you make.

One exception to this guideline is a case that could be governed by a threshold issue. If you are arguing a standing or jurisdictional issue in addition to a substantive issue, for example, logic dictates that you should place the substantive issue second. It could be ludicrous to argue for several pages about a legal error as to one of the case's issues, and then move to the point that the court should not be hearing the case at all.

Particularly in a lengthy brief, your last argument is also in a position of emphasis. For example, if you have decided that you must include a desperation argument in your brief, you may *not* want it to be the last thing the court reads. Just as you want to start with a good impression, you also want to leave the court with a good taste in its mouth. Whenever possible, move that weak argument to the second-to-the-last position to help keep your image as a credible, responsible advocate.

11.4.2
PERSUADING WITHIN EACH ISSUE

Exploit natural positions of emphasis within each unit of discourse as well. Make sure that the first paragraph in the section articulates the point you are proving in that section. The CREXAC formula recommends using the first paragraph in the section to state your conclusion as to the issue addressed in that section. Similarly, end the section by using the connection-conclusion to restate your main assertion and connect it to your argument. In this way, your point is driven home in the precise locations where the reader is likely to be paying the most attention.

In general, state your conclusion as if it is the truth, not as if it is one of many possible ways for the court to rule. Do not begin any section of your argument by stating the issue as a question that must be resolved:

---

[16] James H. Coleman, Jr., *Appellate Advocacy and Decisionmaking in State Appellate Courts in the Twenty-First Century,* 28 Seton Hall L. Rev. 1081, 1083 (1998).

▽ BAD EXAMPLE

The next issue turns on whether an officer issuing a citation in lieu of arrest should have the same authority to search as an officer who is placing a suspect under arrest.

Instead, articulate the issue as an assertion:

△ GOOD EXAMPLE

Officers who issue citations in lieu of arrest and officers who actually arrest should have the same authority to search for weapons that might be used against them.

Similarly, do not label your arguments as your arguments. The petitioner should avoid statements like "The Petitioner argues . . . ." If you do this with any argument, you might as well start every argument with that statement, for each argument in the brief is one of the petitioner's arguments. The entire document is labeled as "Brief for the Petitioner," so the court knows that it will be made up of petitioner's arguments. Do not remind the court of your partisan slant by labeling individual arguments within the brief.

Finally, if practical or ethical requirements require you to discuss cases or arguments that do not support your client's case, you may decide to deemphasize them by including them in the middle of a point heading section rather than highlighting them in a separate section. For example, in the excerpt below, the writer of a respondent's brief in *Minnesota v. Carter*, 525 U.S. 83 (1998), is trying to emphasize connections to cases in which the Court found that a privacy right existed and to deemphasize cases in which the privacy right was found not to exist. Notice how the topic sentence (the first sentence in the paragraph) states the rule in a way that is favorable to her clients before the paragraph discusses a case in which the Court found no expectation of privacy:

> **Indeed, this Court has consistently found that legitimate expectations of privacy exist outside the home, as long as the circumstances are those in which most people would normally expect to enjoy a feeling of privacy. <u>Olson</u>, 496 U.S. at 96-97. Accordingly, this Court has found that defendants did not have a legitimate expectation of privacy in the contents of a car in which they were merely passengers, and where they had expressed no expectation of privacy in the areas of the car searched. <u>Rakas v. Illinois</u>, 439 U.S. 128, 148-49 (1978). The <u>Rakas</u> Court specifically refused to make a finding as to whether guests in houses or apartments would be treated similarly, noting that "cars are not to be treated identically with houses or apartments for Fourth Amendment purposes." <u>Id</u>. at 148 (citations omitted).**

Of course, "hiding" a contrary authority in the middle of a paragraph or section will not turn a losing case into a winner. You must also show why the substance of your argument is more effective. Using positions of emphasis and deemphasis simply makes it easier for the reader to see and understand the validity of your points. In the example above, the writer takes care to emphasize the Court's distinction between cars and houses, and ends the paragraph on that point, rather than on the negative point about the passengers' expectations of privacy.

11.4.3
PERSUASIVE PARAGRAPH STRUCTURE

Within the argument, review the topic sentences to make sure that you are not wasting the first sentence in a paragraph on a case citation or a description of authority case facts. Instead, exploit these positions of emphasis by using them to state rules or make favorable assertions about the result you want the court to reach. If you must deal with a negative authority, you may wish to sandwich it between positive assertions. (See Chapter Ten for more information about writing effective topic sentences.)

In addition to considering structure within paragraphs, you can use a short paragraph to create a position of emphasis. Although conventional wisdom frowns on one-sentence paragraphs, one- or two-sentence paragraphs can, on rare occasions, effectively draw attention to a statement. Conversely, you can bury a negative point in a long paragraph to lessen its impact. Take care when using this tactic, however; if the paragraph is so long that it distracts or annoys your reader, you will cancel out any benefit from the persuasive technique.

In this example, the writer applies the law to the facts in one long paragraph that provides the details to establish that respondents did not manifest a subjective expectation of privacy:

BAD EXAMPLE

In the case at bar, both Respondents' behavior and their location within the apartment indicate that they had no actual, subjective expectation of privacy. Respondents manifested at most a hope that no one would observe their unlawful pursuits inside Thompson's apartment. Unlike the defendant in <u>Katz</u>, Respondents introduced no evidence of conduct that demonstrated an intent to keep their activity private. Nothing in the record indicates Respondents took any action to preserve their privacy. Though the blinds were drawn, there is no indication that Respondents drew them. <u>See</u> Record at E-2, E-10. On the night in question, Respondents were present in a first-floor apartment that had several windows at ground level. Record G-26. The windows faced a public area that apartment residents and nonresidents frequented. Record G-69, G-70. As darkness fell in early evening, Respondents sat illuminated under a chandelier light at a table directly in front of one of these windows. Record G-13. Only a pane of glass and a set of blinds that featured a series of laths, Record

G-50, separated Respondents from the adjacent common area. On the night in question, the blinds, though drawn, had a gap in them large enough for a citizen who passed by and an officer who stood a foot or more from the window to view easily the entire illuminated interior scene. Record G-13.

The only difference in the following example is that the writer has provided paragraph breaks to draw attention to the fact that respondents did not take action to preserve their privacy. The white space creates a position of emphasis that highlights not only the one-sentence paragraph, but also the paragraphs around it, particularly the paragraph after the one-sentence paragraph.

◭ GOOD EXAMPLE

In the case at bar, both Respondents' behavior and their location within the apartment indicate that they had no actual, subjective expectation of privacy. Respondents manifested at most a hope that no one would observe their unlawful pursuits inside Thompson's apartment. Unlike the defendant in <u>Katz</u>, Respondents introduced no evidence of conduct that demonstrated an intent to keep their activity private.

Nothing in the record indicates Respondents took any action to preserve their privacy.

Though the blinds were drawn, there is no indication that Respondents drew them. <u>See</u> Record at E-2, E-10. On the night in question, Respondents were present in a first-floor apartment that had several windows at ground level. Record G-26. The windows faced a public area that apartment residents and nonresidents frequented. Record G-69, G-70. As darkness fell in early evening, Respondents sat illuminated under a chandelier light at a table directly in front of one of these windows. Record G-13. Only a pane of glass and a set of blinds that featured a series of laths, Record G-50, separated Respondents from the adjacent common area. On the night in question, the blinds, though drawn, had a gap in them large enough for a citizen who passed by and an officer who stood a foot or more from the window to view easily the entire illuminated interior scene. Record G-13.

As you might imagine, you should use this method sparingly. A one-sentence paragraph is a dramatic technique; if overused, it will lose its drama and annoy the reader.

11.4.4
PERSUADING WITH SENTENCE STRUCTURE

There are many ways that sentence structure can create positions of emphasis; this chapter will address three that most legal writers can conquer. First, by using active voice and strong verbs rather than passive voice and nominalizations, you can focus the reader's attention on subjects and verbs that emphasize actors and actions that support your argument. Second, you can alternate independent and dependent clauses in sentences to emphasize the information in the independent clauses and deemphasize the information in the dependent clauses. Finally, using short sentences in the middle of a series of long sentences can pique the reader's interest.

a. Subject-Verb Combinations

Just as readers pay more attention to information at beginnings and endings of documents and sections, they place subconscious emphasis on the information in the verb position of a sentence. They also subconsciously look for the verb's actor—that is, the noun that is "doing" the action of the verb. You can control what information is in the subject position and the verb position, and where (or whether) you include information about the verb's actor.[17] How you arrange that information will affect how your reader comprehends your message. To take a simple example:

> The dog bit the child.
> The child was bitten by the dog.
> The child was the victim of a dog bite.
> A dog bite occurred.
> A bite occurred.

Most of these sentences could describe a dog bite. In some of the sentences, the reader can instantly understand the complete story. In others, however, the reader has to work harder to get that information; in others, even when working hard, the reader can get only a vague idea of what has happened.

Thus, the way you arrange the information within a sentence can have a big impact on how quickly the reader understands the message. Information arrangement can sometimes have an impact on how the reader feels about the message as well. Take a look at these two versions of a sentence that might appear in a letter from a law school to its students:

> We are increasing your tuition by $5,000 per year.

> A tuition increase of $5,000 will occur.

The first sentence is more likely to make the student angry at the law school administration. Through their use of subjects and verbs, they have taken direct responsibility for the tuition increase. The reader instantly understands the message, and its clarity may intensify the reader's reaction. The second sentence is a more typical example of how to deliver bad news. No one takes responsibility for the dramatic tuition increase; it

---

[17] *See, e.g.,* Williams & Colomb, *supra* note 14, at Lesson 3.

seems to come from the outside. Thus, the clarity that is helpful when easy understanding is beneficial ("the dog bit the child") has quite a different impact on those rare occasions when the writer wants to blunt the impact of the message ("we are increasing your tuition").

Writers can learn a wide variety of techniques to control the clarity of a sentence. Two of the most important are (1) using or avoiding nominalizations, and (2) using or avoiding passive voice.

i. Nominalizations

A nominalization is, quite simply, a verb that has been turned into a noun. Turning a verb into a noun does not violate any rules of grammar, but it does slow down the reader's comprehension of the information in that word. For example, the word *decision* is a nominalization of the verb *decide*. When you move the word *decide* from the verb position into the noun position, you lessen the impact of that verb:

We decided to raise your tuition.

We made a decision that a tuition increase is necessary.

Look at these two different questions presented that describe the actions of a police officer looking into the windows of a basement apartment from a distance of 12 to 14 inches. Notice how nominalizations in one illustration and concrete verbs and other language in the other may change the perception of what the officer did:

> **Under the Fourth Amendment, does an officer's sight observation into a home, made while standing a foot or more from the apartment and peering through gaps in the covered window of the apartment, constitute an unlawful invasion of curtilage?**

> **Under the Fourth Amendment, does an officer invade the curtilage of an apartment house when he stands within inches of the building and looks through a gap in the blinds of a basement apartment?**

Neither sentence is wrong; they are just different ways of conveying the same information, depending on what the writer wants to emphasize.

You can often find nominalizations by looking for words that end in *-ence*, *-ment*, or *-ion*. In the alternative, review your sentences (particularly overlong sentences) and circle just the verbs. When you find sentences in which all of the verbs are weak words without a lot of concrete meaning—e.g., *was*, *is* (or other *to be* verbs), *had*, *made*, *occurred*, *existed*, etc.—look for verbs that are "hidden" in nominalizations in that sentence.

When deciding whether or how to change nominalizations back into verbs, ask yourself whether you want to put more emphasis on the information that you nominalized. The answer may not always be yes. Sometimes, as in the tuition letter example above, you may want to deemphasize certain negative information. Unless that is the case, however, identify your hidden verbs, find the actor that is "verbing" (i.e., doing the action of that verb), and create a stronger, more easily comprehensible sentence.

When looking for nominalizations, you might find a sentence like this:

> **This case is a recognition of the coercion that may happen during an arrest.**

If you circled the verbs in this sentence, you would identify the rather weak verbs *is* and *may happen*. Once you identify the hidden verbs *recognize*, *coerce*, and *arrest*, you can work on making the sentence more clear:

> **In this case, [someone] recognized that [someone] may coerce [someone] when [someone] arrests [someone].**

Revising to avoid nominalizations provides a hidden benefit: You may realize when information is missing from the sentence. Thus, your next step might be to include some of the missing information. On the other hand, you may decide to leave some of the nominalizations as is:

> **In this case, the Court recognized that police officers may coerce citizens during an arrest.**

Knowing how nominalizations can affect your writing can help you to make your points more explicitly when clarity is your goal and to blunt your message when it is appropriate to do so.

ii. Active and Passive Voice

Most writers know about "tense" as it relates to verbs; they consciously decide, for example, whether to write in present tense or past tense. Many, however, are unfamiliar with the concept of "voice." No matter what its tense, a verb can be cast in active or passive voice. Voice relates not to the tense of the verb, but to whether the verb's actor is in the subject position of the sentence or clause. If the verb's actor is in the subject position, the verb is said to be cast in "active voice"; if the verb's actor is not in the subject position, the verb is said to be cast in "passive voice." In almost every case in which the verb is cast in passive voice, the subject of the sentence is receiving the action of the verb rather than doing the action of the verb. Thus, in most cases, the subject of an active voice sentence or clause is "verbing"; the subject of a passive voice sentence or clause is "being verbed." Think of the subject passively receiving the action of the verb to help you remember the meaning of "passive voice":

> **The court decided the case. (Active voice; the subject [court] is verbing [deciding].)**

> **The case was decided by the court. (Passive voice; the subject [case] is being verbed [being decided].)**

Passive and active voice verbs, like nominalizations, are grammatically correct. Because active voice verbs can be understood more quickly, however, you should use active voice unless you have a specific reason to use passive voice. Passive voice is preferred on occasion:

1. if you don't know who the actor is or you want to hide or deemphasize the actor ("a decision was made to raise your tuition" hides the decision maker);
2. when you want to emphasize the object of the verb rather than the subject ("she was hit by a car" emphasizes the victim of the accident); or
3. when your sentence just works better with the object of the verb in the subject position (e.g., when the subject is unusually long or when the object is a more familiar person or concept than the subject).[18]

Look at these examples of similar information included in passive voice and active voice sentences. Try to decide which sentence might be better given various rhetorical situations:

> The statute was designed to limit the number of aliens who can bypass INS-mandated citizenship procedures.

> Congress designed the statute to limit the number of aliens who can bypass INS-mandated citizenship procedures.

> The evidence in question was obtained by observations made by a police officer looking into the window of an apartment.

> A police officer obtained the information for the warrant when he looked into the window of the apartment.

> A person's home, the place where he lives, has been recognized by this Court as the most important place in which to invoke Fourth Amendment protection.

> This Court has recognized that a person's home, the place where he lives, is the most important place in which to invoke Fourth Amendment protection.

As at least two of these illustrations show, using active voice results in shorter, more direct sentences. The point of this section, however, is not to say that you must eliminate all nominalizations and all uses of passive voice; rather, the point is that you should use nominalizations and passive voice only when you have a good reason to do so. When there is no reason to use them, use more direct, easier-to-understand subjects and verbs.

b.   Independent and Dependent Clauses

A second way that a writer can use sentence structure to persuade is by using dependent clauses to "hide" information that the writer wants

---

[18] *See* Mary Barnard Ray & Jill J. Ramsfield, *Legal Writing: Getting It Right and Getting It Written* 279-81 (4th ed., Thomson/West 2005).

to deemphasize. In grammatical terms, an independent clause is a clause that can stand on its own as a sentence, while a dependent clause cannot. Readers subconsciously put more emphasis on information in independent clauses and less emphasis on information in dependent clauses. It may help to think of information in a dependent clause as being in parentheses: The reader often sees it as a less important part of the sentence. Notice how switching information between the dependent and the independent clauses subtly changes the impression that the sentence gives the reader:

> First, although the area where the officer stood is close to Thompson's apartment, the communal nature of the grounds makes the claim of curtilage less valid.

> First, even though the officer stood in a communal area, the place where he stood was so close to Thompson's apartment that it increases the validity of the curtilage claim.

> Though the blinds were drawn at the time of the alleged search, there is no indication that Respondents drew them.

> Although there was no testimony at the trial about who closed the window blinds, the fact remains that at the time of the search the blinds were drawn.

> On the night in question, the blinds, though drawn, had a gap in them large enough for a citizen who passed by and an officer who stood a foot or more from the window to view easily the entire illuminated interior scene.

> On the night in question, the blinds had been drawn to cover the entire window, even though a small gap remained.

Again, all of these sentences are grammatically correct. The sentence you choose to write will depend on which information you want to emphasize and deemphasize.

c. Using Short Sentences for Emphasis

One guideline for sentence structure and length is the same for legal writing as for any kind of expository writing: Sentence variety is good. One short sentence can be effective. More than two short sentences are not. Compare the two examples below, and notice the impact of a short sentence and concrete language as compared to a long sentence and more abstract language:

> Thus, society will be prepared to recognize Respondents' expectation of privacy in Thompson's apartment as reasonable only if they were present on the premises for a purpose society deems permissible and valuable. Respondents, who introduced no evidence that they were anything other than temporary, transient visitors on the premises for

the sole purpose of conducting illegal business, simply do not belong to the class of individuals who have an expectation of privacy that society is prepared to recognize as reasonable.

Thus, society will be prepared to recognize Respondents' expectation of privacy in Thompson's apartment as reasonable only if they were present on the premises for a purpose society deems permissible and valuable. Respondents were there to bag cocaine. They simply do not belong to the class of individuals who have an expectation of privacy that society is prepared to recognize as reasonable.

To make the point even more emphatic, put the short sentence in a position of emphasis at the end of a paragraph:

Thus, society will be prepared to recognize Respondents' expectation of privacy in Thompson's apartment as reasonable only if they were present on the premises for a purpose society deems permissible and valuable. Respondents were there to bag cocaine.

Use this persuasive technique with care. If you use too many short sentences in your document, they will lose their dramatic effect.

11.4.5
EFFECTIVE WORD CHOICE

When it comes to word choice, the effective advocate must make decisions carefully. Certainly, it makes sense to choose words that have connotations that are more positive for your client's side. Think in terms of "claimed" instead of "stated," or "admitted" instead of "said." Once again, however, you must take care. It is easy to push this method into ridiculousness:

▽ BAD EXAMPLE

The officer was able to peer into the private window of the apartment because he abandoned the sidewalk, marched across the grass, and wedged himself behind bushes placed 24 to 48 inches away from the window. Record G-43.

△ GOOD EXAMPLE

The officer was able to approach a window belonging to the apartment by leaving the sidewalk leading up to the building, walking onto the grass and behind bushes located two to four feet away from the window. Record G-43.

Most writers know enough not to use exclamation points to emphasize points or to write in all capital letters to draw attention to a point. Yet many writers try to intensify their arguments with words that are just as ineffective as these techniques. *Clearly, obviously, of course,* and *it is evident that* have been so overused that they go beyond having no meaning to having a negative meaning. Many writers refer to them as "negative intensifiers."

Interestingly, scholars who studied briefs and court opinions observed that legal writers were more likely to use these intensifiers when they were on the losing side, or, for judges, when they were writing a dissent. They concluded that the writers felt "threatened" by being on the losing side, and subconsciously used more negative intensifiers in an "irrational attempt to 'attack' the winning side or to defend the losing argument."[19]

Instead of using a negative intensifier, identify and use "positive intensifiers." Positive intensifiers include *precisely, exactly, specifically, significantly*, and *explicitly*. These words are positive intensifiers because they signal that the writer will be giving the reader concrete information about what happened to parties before the court or in a case, about what a rule says, or about how a rule relates to the client's facts. Note the differences between the two examples below:

▽ BAD EXAMPLE

Second, the drawn blinds on the window of the apartment through which the police officer peered clearly indicated that the apartment was not open to public observation.

△ GOOD EXAMPLE

The blinds were drawn in the apartment precisely because the occupants did not want the apartment to be open to public observation. Whoever drew the blinds, that person was taking steps to prevent members of the public—and the police—from looking through the windows.

Of course, if you use a positive intensifier, you have to follow it up with the specifics that it promises, lest it become a negative intensifier:

△ GOOD EXAMPLE

The court specifically noted that its holding was not predicated on antiquated notions about the relative abilities of men and women; rather, the holding was predicated on the objectively verifiable fact that women could not serve in combat roles in the United States armed forces.

Whenever you use a positive intensifier, ask yourself how the law or the facts show that this information is *precisely, specifically,* or *significantly* true, and then include those details in your writing.

[19] Lance N. Long & William F. Christensen, *When Justices (Subconsciously) Attack: The Theory of Argumentative Threat and the Supreme Court*, 91 Or. L. Rev. 933, 958 (2013).

11.4.6
PERSUASIVE PUNCTUATION

Writers use punctuation marks to organize sentences and the words within sentences. They also use punctuation to show relationships between and among phrases and clauses within sentences. Legal writers can use punctuation marks to emphasize information and to imply relationships when argument is inappropriate. Three types of punctuation marks are particularly helpful: the semicolon, the dash, and the colon.

a.   The Semicolon

Semicolons are used in two circumstances. First, semicolons punctuate a list when items in the list contain internal commas. In legal writing, this situation occurs most frequently when writers cite multiple cases in support of a proposition. Second, semicolons separate two independent clauses. This technique is frequently used to highlight some sort of relationship between the two clauses, as in the following examples:

GOOD EXAMPLE

> Section 1409(a) does more than legislate on the basis of this stereotype beyond infancy; it applies this stereotype *forever.*

GOOD EXAMPLE

> The Supreme Court has allowed a warrantless search when a custodial arrest is performed largely because the suspect already will be subject to substantial interference with individual liberties; similar intrusions exist when a citation is issued in lieu of an arrest.

Semicolons can also be used to juxtapose information in a way that leads the reader to draw a conclusion. In *Minnesota v. Carter*, for example, the petitioner might want the reader to draw the conclusion that the respondents did not have a legitimate expectation of privacy in the apartment in which they were bagging cocaine. This conclusion could be supported by the lack of a connection between the respondents and Thompson, who lived in the apartment. In the statement of facts, it is inappropriate to argue, but the writer could use a semicolon to juxtapose two facts that might lead the reader to the desired conclusion:

GOOD EXAMPLE

> Nothing in the record indicates any personal or social relationship between Thompson and the Respondents; none of Respondents' personal effects were found in the apartment, and they did not present any evidence that they were overnight guests. See Record E-4, E-7, and G-2.

Because you can state conclusions rather than imply them within the argument, this method is used to greatest effect in the statement of the case. But you can always use semicolons to make clear a close relationship between two ideas. In any case, good writers are able to present information in a variety of ways. Proper use of semicolons separates sophisticated writers from unsophisticated ones; it's a good idea to learn to use them properly.

b.   The Dash

Mary Barnard Ray and Jill Ramsfield refer to the dash as "the gigolo of the punctuation world,"[20] and too many dashes may give your writing an inappropriately casual tone. The dash is used effectively, however, to highlight information in the middle of a sentence. Proper use of the dash consists of a space, two hyphens, and another space (at which point many word processing systems properly convert the two hyphens to a connected line called an *em dash*). When you use a dash on either side of an interrupting phrase, it creates white space on either side of the phrase and thus creates a position of emphasis within the sentence. Notice how the writer of a *Miller v. Albright* brief uses the dash to highlight a comparison between how the law treats the foreign-born children of United States citizens in different relationships:

GOOD EXAMPLE

> Children in the first two groups—those who are "legitimate" and those who have a United States citizen mother—are United States citizens by birthright. See 8 U.S.C. §1401(g) (1994). Children in the last group, however—those "illegitimate" children with United States citizen fathers—may receive their fathers' citizenship only after clearing several hurdles.

To avoid making your writing sound too casual, don't overuse the dash, and use it only to set off an interrupting phrase in the middle of a sentence rather than as a means to add an afterthought at the end of a sentence.

c.   The Colon

The colon is my favorite way to use punctuation for emphasis. Most writers use it only to introduce a long quotation or list, and it is properly used for that purpose. But it is very effectively used within sentences both to highlight information and to explain or elaborate on the information that came before the colon, as in these examples:

GOOD EXAMPLES:

> Through gaps in the drawn horizontal mini-blinds on the window, Officer Thielen observed the same scene the informant had described to him: two males and one female sitting at a kitchen table handling a white powdery substance. Record E-2.

---

[20] Ray & Ramsfield, *supra* note 18, at 109.

> In <u>Chimel</u>, this Court examined the search-incident-to-an-arrest exception to the warrant requirement and made note of the two major policy justifications for the search: preserving officer safety and preventing the destruction of evidence by the suspect. 395 U.S. at 763.

> The cases in which no substantial relation was found have one common element: They reject gender stereotypes that are little more than vestiges of past discrimination.

The information that comes after the colon elaborates on or explains the information that comes before the colon. In a sense, the colon prompts the reader to ask a "who, what, when, where, why, or how" question that the information after the colon answers. In the last example above, for example, the colon prompts the reader to ask "what is the common element?" The information after the colon answers this question.

The shorter the phrase or sentence after the colon, the more emphatic the use of the colon is. Note the differences among these examples: As the phrases get shorter, the sentences get more emphatic.

△ GOOD EXAMPLES

> As illustrated by the plight of Lorelyn and Charlie Miller, these burdens can become insurmountable: Section 1409(a) will prevent Mr. Miller and Ms. Miller from ever legally proving that they have a close family relationship unless this court refuses to accept the irrebuttable gender stereotype in Section 1409(a).

> The government argued that the observation was analogous to looking through a knothole or an opening in a fence: "If there is an opening, the police may look."

> The record indicates that Respondents engaged in only one activity while inside Thompson's apartment: bagging cocaine.

Grammatically, the information that precedes the colon should be a complete sentence. The information that comes after need not be. Do not capitalize the first word after a colon unless the information after the colon could be a separate sentence; even then, you may choose to leave it uncapitalized. If, like me, you fall in love with the colon, you should still avoid overusing it.

11.5
AVOIDING SPELLING, GRAMMATICAL, AND TYPOGRAPHICAL ERRORS

Avoiding mechanical errors does not really present an opportunity for persuasion. Your reader will not particularly notice or remark upon a brief that is free of these problems: Perfection in small things is a minimal expectation. Unfortunately, however, mechanical errors will have a negative effect. Many readers presume that someone who writes a document with mechanical errors cannot be trusted to conduct sound legal analysis. While the logic behind this attitude may be questionable, it's unmistakable that the attitude is there, and it provides one more reason why you should proofread diligently.

Chapter Twelve talks about effective proofreading methods, and Appendix A addresses common punctuation mistakes.

11.6
CREDIBILITY THROUGH DOCUMENT DESIGN

The way your document looks also creates an opportunity for persuasion. If it is neat, clean, visually easy to read, and complies with all local rules, you will impress the court with your competence, and your credibility will rise. Courts are beginning to recognize the benefits of effective document design, and to encourage—or require—that counsel keep readability in mind. The Seventh Circuit's Web site, for example, features a link called "Guidelines for Briefs and Other Papers" that links to a document explaining the importance of effective typography. The document notes the importance of effective document design:

> Choosing the best type[face] won't guarantee success, but it is worthwhile to invest some time in improving the quality of the brief's appearance and legibility.
>
> Judges of this court hear six cases on most argument days and nine cases on others. The briefs, opinions of the district courts, essential parts of the appendices, and other required reading add up to about 1,000 pages per argument session. Reading that much is a chore; remembering it is even harder. *You can improve your chances by making your briefs typographically superior. It won't make your arguments better, but it will ensure that judges grasp and maintain your points with less struggle.* That's a valuable advantage, which you should seize.[21]

Many small decisions can affect the ease with which the reader can read your brief. The reader's comfort level with the document itself can affect both your credibility and your chances for success as an advocate.

---

[21] United States Court of Appeals for the Seventh Circuit, *Requirements and Suggestions for Typography in Briefs and Other Papers* 4, http://www.ca7.uscourts.gov/Rules/type.pdf (last accessed Mar. 18, 2014) (emphasis added).

11.6.1
TYPEFACE

Even your choice of typeface can make a difference in the readability of your brief. Readers can more easily read typefaces that have "serif," that is, small lines as part of the beginning or ending strokes of each letter. The serifs (also known as "wings" or "feet") help the reader to connect the letters and thus move through the text more quickly and easily. Typefaces that do not have serif are called "sans serif" ("without serif") and are a little more difficult to read. Here are some serif and sans serif typefaces:

1. Times New Roman is a serif typeface.
2. Garamond is a serif typeface.
3. Bookman Old Style is a serif typeface.
4. Georgia is a serif typeface.
5. Courier New is a serif typeface.
6. Arial is a sans serif typeface.
7. **Raavi is a sans serif typeface.**

Although some people get emotionally attached to their favorite typefaces, you should base your decision on the reader's needs rather than your own preferences. Some courts mandate particular typefaces, while others mandate only categories of typeface. For example, a court might mandate a serif typeface or a proportionally spaced typeface. With proportionally spaced typefaces, the amount of space a letter takes up varies from letter to letter—an *i* takes less space than a *k*, for example. With monospaced fonts such as Courier, in contrast, each letter takes up the same amount of space.

Courier is monospaced: Bills make me ill.

Georgia is proportionally spaced: Bills make me ill.

Because proportionally spaced fonts are easier to read, you should use a proportionally spaced font unless court rules dictate otherwise.

11.6.2
CITATIONS AND EMPHATIC TEXT: <u>UNDERLINING</u>, *ITALICS*, **BOLDFACED TYPE**, AND CAPITALIZATION

Both the *ALWD Citation Manual* and the *Bluebook* allow the writer to choose between underlining and italics when citing cases and other titles. Although both underlining and italics have the same meaning vis-à-vis citation form, they are not equal. Both italics and underline distinguish text for a reader, but underlined text is more visible to the user: It can be seen with only a quick glance at the page, while italics usually take longer to notice. Try flipping through this textbook, which uses many examples with underlined citations, and note how the underlining jumps out at the eye. Even if you cannot read the words immediately, the underlining catches your eye and draws it to the underlined words. A busy judge or a clerk who is looking for your analysis of a particular case will have a much easier time finding that discussion if you use underlining instead of italics to designate case names and other titles.[22]

Whether you use underlining or italics for citation form, you should be consistent throughout all of your citations and all of the parts of your citations. For example, don't use italics for signal words but underlining for case names:

▽ BAD EXAMPLE

See, e.g., <u>Minnesota v. Carter</u>, 525 U.S. 83, 89 (1998).

△ GOOD EXAMPLES

<u>See, e.g.</u>, <u>Minnesota v. Carter</u>, 525 U.S. 83, 89 (1998).

See, e.g., Minnesota v. Carter, 525 U.S. 83, 89 (1998).

On the other hand, you may decide to use underlining for citations, but to use italics and boldfaced type as needed for emphasis (use bold for emphasis very rarely). This suggestion is somewhat radical; many readers expect a document to contain underlined words or italicized words, but not both. I believe, however, that this expectation is a mistaken carryover from the rule that underlining or italics should be used consistently in all *citations*. As a practical matter, you should use the graphic technique that will help the reader understand your point with minimal distraction. Boldfaced type and underlining provide the strongest emphasis; you will distract your reader if you use these methods to emphasize words that should receive only slight emphasis. Of course, as with many writing techniques, too little is better than too much. If you emphasize too many words, even with the subtle emphasis of italics, you will distract or annoy your reader and lose the benefit of the emphasis. Furthermore, studies show that underlining and italics each slow the reader's speed slightly.[23] If you emphasize only a few words or perhaps a line of text here and there, a minor slowdown will not be a problem. Too-frequent use of emphatic techniques, however, can slow the reader's progress too much.

---

[22] As noted in Chapters Nine and Ten, too much underlined text can interfere with reader comprehension; thus, underlining should not be used for headings, for example. However, I believe that it can be used effectively for citations because the underlined information in citations is rarely more than a few words.

[23] *E.g.*, Ruth Anne Robbins, *Painting with Print: Incorporating Concepts of Typographic and Layout Design into the Text of Legal Writing Documents*, 2 J. Assn. Legal Writing Dirs. 108, 118 (2004) (citations omitted).

Boldfaced type should almost always be reserved for headings alone. On extremely rare occasions, however, you may use boldfaced type for emphasis within your text. For example, if you have decided to include a long quotation of the text of a statute, you may be worried that your reader will skip the quotation. In that situation, italics would do little to show the reader the significant statutory language:

▽ BAD EXAMPLE

Section 1409(c) gives immediate citizenship to a foreign-born child of unmarried parents if the child's mother is a United States citizen at the time of birth:

> Notwithstanding the provision of subsection (a) of this provision [which requires fathers to meet certain requirements to establish the citizenship of their children], *a person* born, after December 23, 1952, outside the United States and out of wedlock *shall be held to have acquired at birth the nationality status of the mother, if the mother had the nationality of the United States at the time of such person's birth,* and if the mother had previously been physically present in the United States or one of its outlying possessions for a continuous period of one year.

8 U.S.C. §1409(c) (1994) (emphasis added).

If you use underlining or boldfaced type for the most crucial language in the statute, however, readers can glance at the quotation and easily read just the emphasized language as a coherent piece of text:

△ GOOD EXAMPLES

Section 1409(c) gives immediate citizenship to a foreign-born child of unmarried parents if the child's mother is a United States citizen at the time of birth:

> Notwithstanding the provision of subsection (a) of this provision [which requires fathers to meet certain requirements to establish the citizenship of their children], <u>a person</u> born, after December 23, 1952, outside the United States and out of wedlock <u>shall be held to have acquired at birth the nationality status of the mother, if the mother had the nationality of the United States at the time of such person's birth,</u> and if the mother had previously been physically present in the United States or one of its outlying possessions for a continuous period of one year.

8 U.S.C. §1409(c) (1994) (emphasis added).

Section 1409(c) gives immediate citizenship to a foreign-born child of unmarried parents if the child's mother is a United States citizen at the time of birth:

> Notwithstanding the provision of subsection (a) of this provision [which requires fathers to meet certain requirements to establish the citizenship of their children], **a person** born, after December 23, 1952, outside the United States and out of wedlock **shall be held to have acquired at birth the nationality status of the mother, if the mother had the nationality of the United States at the time of such person's birth,** and if the mother had previously been physically present in the United States or one of its outlying possessions for a continuous period of one year.

8 U.S.C. §1409(c) (1994) (emphasis added).

As these examples show, this technique can be used to allow the reader to read a complete phrase or clause without being distracted by language that is irrelevant to the issue under discussion.[24]

Finally, a word about using all capital letters for emphasis: Don't. In fact, unless court rules require it, you can write a very effective brief without ever using any words in all capital letters. Words written entirely in capital letters are more difficult to read; some studies indicate that we read lowercase text 5 to 10 percent faster than we do all-caps text.[25] Recent scholarship indicates that capital letters slow reading speed because of the typical reading style of sweeping over a few words at a time, and seeing only a few letters clearly with our direct vision. We see the rest of the letters with our peripheral vision, which is blurred, and which can distinguish small letters, with their varying shapes, much more easily than it can distinguish capital letters.[26] Of course, many writers use all capital letters to designate element headings such as "SUMMARY OF THE ARGUMENT" or "QUESTIONS PRESENTED." Most readers can tolerate this use reasonably well, but writing more than a few words in all capital letters will usually

---

[24] The Seventh Circuit discourages the use of underlining because it hides the descenders on certain lowercase letters, such as *y* and *g*. *Requirements and Suggestions, supra* note 21, at 5. Ruth Anne Robbins notes, however, that studies show that legibility depends mostly on the shape of the top half of the letter. Robbins, *supra* note 23, at 117 (citations omitted). This phenomenon would indicate that underlining should not interfere too much with legibility, particularly when only a few words are being underlined. Note that the degree to which underlining hides descenders varies with the font; a Times Roman underline hides more of the descender than a Georgia underline, for example. Of course, you should always obey a court's local rules and guidelines about typefaces.

[25] Ronnie Lipton, *The Practical Guide to Information Design* 113 (John Wiley & Sons, Inc. 2007).

[26] Ralf Herrmann, *How Do We Read Words and How Should We Set Them?* Wayfinding & Typography (June 14, 2011), available at http://opentype.info/blog/2011/06/14/how-do-we-read-words-and-how-should-we-set-them/ (last accessed Mar. 18, 2014) (illustrating blurred mixed-case type and all-caps type).

drive the reader to a new paragraph. Likewise, placing two- or three-line point headings in all caps almost guarantees that the reader will skip the headings.[27]

11.6.3
JUSTIFICATION

Justification refers to the alignment of the text. In most legal documents, text is aligned along the left side of the page, or "left justified." Some information, like page numbers in tables, is "right justified," or aligned along the right side of the page. Many word processing programs allow writers to use "full justification." Full-justified text is aligned evenly along the left and the right sides of the page. Sometimes, using full justification allows the writer to fit more words on the page because a program will compress some words to make them fit into a line. Unfortunately, the variable spaces in full-justified text interfere with readability. Although full-justified text may look more attractive from a distance, it is also more difficult to read.[28]

Most word processing programs have flush left, ragged right as their default justification. Do not be tempted to use full justification to save space or to "clean up" a ragged right edge. That ragged right edge helps your reader to read the document more efficiently.

11.6.4
EFFECTIVE TABLES

Because judges and clerks who read briefs often consult the tables of contents and authorities, it is important that these tables look good as well as contain accurate information. One of the four basic principles of design is alignment, and effective alignment is crucial in making tables look good. Page numbers and document elements should be aligned consistently, so that readers can easily find the information that they need.

In this excerpt from a table of contents, note how none of the elements are aligned; the table does not make obvious how the subparts relate to each other:

---

[27] See also Robbins, supra note 23, at 127 (noting that using all capital letters is "the worst thing you can do if you want your headings to be legible and easy to read").

[28] E.g., Securities and Exchange Commission, A Plain English Handbook: How to Create Clear SEC Disclosure Documents 44 (SEC 1998), available at http://www.sec.gov/news/extra/handbook.htm. See also Robbins, supra note 23, at 130-31.

▽ BAD EXAMPLE

In the next example, note how the writer uses alignment to make obvious the relationships between and among point headings. This method allows the user to find headings he or she cares about more easily or to choose which level of headings to review.

△ GOOD EXAMPLE

You may believe that you need not worry about design because in practice you will have an administrative assistant who will type and print the document. You should not presume, however, that your assistant will know or care about document design. You will have to face any consequences for the impression your document makes, so you must take responsibility not only for what your document says, but also for how it looks.

11.7
SUMMARY

Persuasive writing techniques cannot change bad law or weak facts to make a losing case a winner. They can, however, increase your chances of victory in a close case, and, when used properly, establish and maintain your credibility with the court.

POLISHING

12.1 Methods to Use on the Computer
12.2 Methods to Use on the Hard Copy
12.3 Proofreading Your Revisions
12.4 The Last Thing to Do with the Document
12.5 Summary

Unfortunately, many writers lose interest when they read advice about polishing the mechanics of a document because they think that people do not notice mechanics or that their administrative assistants will take care of mechanical problems. First of all, people do notice "the small stuff." Judge Wald, of the D.C. Circuit, has recommended that counsel "proofread with a passion":

> You cannot imagine how disquieting it is to find several spelling or grammatical errors in an otherwise competent brief. It makes the judge go back to square one in evaluating the counsel. It says—worst of all—the author never bothered to read the whole thing through, but she expects us to.[1]

Fairly or unfairly, many readers see mechanical mistakes as a sign of overall incompetence; too many typographical errors may lead the judge to mistrust the validity of the legal analysis. Justice Ginsburg has observed that if a brief is "sloppy" in regard to mechanics, "the judge may suspect its reliability in other respects as well."[2] In a 1994 case, a federal district judge dismissing a complaint ordered a sanctions hearing for the plaintiff's attorney, noting that the attorney's mechanical errors were evidence of a lack of due care:

> [Counsel] continues to submit documents to this Court with grammatical errors and misstatements. . . . Moreover, throughout the Amended Complaint [the attorney] repeatedly refers to his client as "he" instead of "she." These types of errors strongly suggest that Mr. Williams has not

---

[1] Patricia M. Wald, *19 Tips from 19 Years on the Appellate Bench,* 1 J. App. Prac. & Process 7, 22 (1999).

[2] Ruth Bader Ginsburg, *Remarks on Appellate Advocacy,* 50 S.C. L. Rev. 567, 568 (1999).

taken the appropriate care to avoid errors before submitting documents to this Court.[3]

To take a more practical view, failure to take care with polishing may cost you money. In a case that received wide publicity (including a story in the *New York Times*), an attorney whose courtroom work was praised had his fees for his written work cut in half—from $300 to $150 per hour—due in large part to sloppy proofreading.[4] When he was interviewed about the case, the federal judge who decided on the award of attorneys' fees commented that "no matter how good you are in front of the jury, most of your reputation's going to be built on what you write."[5]

The second reason you must learn polishing skills is that you probably cannot afford an assistant who can do this level of polishing. You must take responsibility for polishing the mechanics of your legal documents because your document reflects on your client and on your competence.

Polishing is hard for the same reason that revision is hard. Most people don't really see their writing when they review it. Instead, they see the document that they meant to write; their short-term memory interferes with their ability to see typographical errors or other problems. For that reason, this chapter identifies some objective methods for polishing that will help you to break up that relationship between your short-term memory and your document, and help you to catch mistakes in both your writing and your analysis.

The best way to proofread effectively is to put your writing away for a while. If you've ever gone back and read a document that you wrote last year, or even last month, you've probably noticed several mistakes or style problems that you missed when you wrote it. If you are trying to polish a document that you wrote this morning, your short-term memory makes it hard for you to see your mistakes. It knows what you wanted to say, and it tends to gloss over the mistakes.[6] Therefore, if you can get a draft done a week before your deadline, *don't* reread it and edit it every day. Instead, wait three days and do a thorough edit, and then wait three more days and

---

[3] *Styles v. Philadelphia Elec. Co.*, No. CIV.A.93-4593, 1994 WL 245469, at *3 (E.D. Pa. June 6, 1994) (cited in Judith D. Fischer, *Bareheaded and Barefaced Counsel: Courts React to Unprofessionalism in Lawyers' Papers*, 31 Suffolk U. L. Rev. 1, 27 (1997)).

[4] *DeVore v. City of Philadelphia*, 2004 U.S. Dist. Lexis 3635, at *6 (E.D. Pa. Feb. 20, 2004). The court noted that counsel's lack of care "caused the court, and I am sure, defense counsel, to expend an inordinate amount of time deciphering the arguments." *Id.* at *6-7.

[5] *All Things Considered, Magistrate Judge Jacob P. Hart Discusses His Fight to Get Lawyers to Clean Up Their Written Work* (Natl. Pub. Radio broadcast Mar. 4, 2004).

[6] Of course, getting a friend or colleague to review the document can also be helpful, since that person will not have the information in his or her short-term memory. In an academic setting, you should not use this method unless you have *specific* permission from your teacher. In a professional setting, asking a friend to review your work is fine; finding someone who has the time to help you is the hard part.

do a final edit.[7] Even a little time can make some difference. In a crunch, that might mean taking a 15-minute walk and then coming back to edit, but taking some time can make a difference.

A second effective polishing technique is to "start in the middle" when reviewing your work. Most writing teachers find that mechanical mistakes and other weaknesses show up more often in the second half of the document than in the first half. That's because many writers get bored with editing or polishing as they get closer to the end of the document; many give up before finishing the job. Even conscientious editors should give fresh eyes to different parts of the document at different times.

Generally, it is ineffective to proofread by reading the entire document very slowly once or twice, trying to catch every type of error. Instead, you should read the document through several times on the computer and several times in hard-copy form. Make surgical strikes, focusing on only one or two aspects of the document at a time. For example, you can review the document once just looking at citation form, another time just looking at topic sentences, and so on. This chapter discusses proofreading techniques for both the digital and hard-copy versions of the document.

12.1
METHODS TO USE ON THE COMPUTER

You can do some proofreading while your document is still in digital form. First, you may want to enlarge the font size while you proofread. Enlarging the font (say, to 20- or 22-point size) can have two benefits. First, you can focus more easily because you will have a smaller number of words on the screen at a time. Second, it will be easier to distance yourself from the text because the font change will significantly change the way the document looks. Proofreading on a screen also allows you to use your computer software's Find and Replace feature to your advantage. Although your eyes get tired, the computer never misses on a search, presuming you are searching precisely.

1. Pronoun search. Use the Find and Replace feature to search for *he, she, it, they,* and so on. Stop when you hit a pronoun and scrutinize it to make sure that the reader will have *no doubt* about the noun you are referring to (the antecedent). Also, make sure that you have not mistakenly used *they* in place of *it*. For example, a court or corporation should be referred to in the singular as *it*.

---

[7] *See also* Judge Stephen J. Dwyer, Leonard J. Feldman & Ryan P. McBride, *How to Write, Edit, and Review Persuasive Briefs: Seven Guidelines from One Judge and Two Lawyers*, 31 Seattle L. Rev. 417, 425 (2008).

2. Apostrophe search. If you tend to use too many apostrophes, use the Find feature to search for *s[apostrophe]* or *[apostrophe]s* so that you can scrutinize whether you've used each apostrophe correctly. If you use too few apostrophes, your task is a little harder. You could use the Find and Replace feature to find words that end in *s* by searching for *s[space]* or *s.[space]*. Once you are zeroed in on the potential problem words, consult grammar guidelines to see if you are using apostrophes correctly. Appendix A includes advice about some common apostrophe problems.

3. Quotation mark search. The rule in American English is that periods and commas *always* go inside quotation marks, even if you are quoting only one word or one letter:

⩔ BAD EXAMPLE

Judge Wald has noted that finding errors in a brief makes her "go back to square one in evaluating the counsel".

⩓ GOOD EXAMPLE

Judge Wald has noted that finding errors in a brief makes her "go back to square one in evaluating the counsel."

⩔ BAD EXAMPLE

The word "Aspen", which refers to both trees and a publisher, begins with the letter "A".

⩓ GOOD EXAMPLE

The word "Aspen," which refers to both trees and a publisher, begins with the letter "A."

To find errors of this type, use the Find feature to search for quotation marks, and check your punctuation. Also, check to make sure that all quotation marks come in pairs. Too often, when writers block and copy quotations, they place an opening quotation mark, then copy the language into the text, and neglect to insert the closing quotation mark. This is the punctuation equivalent of leaving the refrigerator door open, and it is very annoying to readers. Be sure to proofread specifically for this problem.

4. Citation search. To review your citations, search *[begin underline]* or *[begin italics]* or even *v.* to help you find citations and scrutinize them in isolation. Three types of errors are particularly common: (1) incorrect volume or page numbers, (2) misspelled party names, and (3) missing pinpoint page numbers. As noted earlier, presume that every citation should have a pinpoint. Even if you are just citing to a general principle from the case, find a page on which that general principle appears, and use it as the pinpoint.

While you are looking at your citations, take a look at your long-form citations and make sure that you have included the appropriate court abbreviation in the parenthetical. If you are not sure what court the case comes from, check the caption of the opinion. Note, for example, that F. Supp. 2d publishes only district court decisions, so any opinion printed in F. Supp. 2d (or in F. Supp.) cannot be a circuit court decision.

5. Spell-check. Run the spell-check early and often, but keep a few things in mind. First, keep your hand away from the mouse, or your finger off the button, so that you don't hit Replace or Skip by mistake. Second, don't hit Skip as soon as you see a party name or a case name; make sure that you've spelled each one properly and consistently.

Third, after completing spell-check, use the Find and Replace feature to search for typos that the spell-check function won't catch. In every document, look for *statue* for *statute, untied* for *united, form* for *from* (and vice versa), *reasonable* for *reasonably* (and vice versa), and *probable for probably* (and vice versa). You might consider setting your Quick Correct feature to change *pubic* to *public* to avoid that potentially embarrassing error. If your document is about *probable cause* or *reasonable doubt*, it is even more important to do this kind of search. I have read several briefs in which students claim that there was no "probably cause" for the defendant's arrest, or that the defense could not establish "reasonably doubt." Because both forms of certain problem words could appear in the text, search for each form separately and make sure each use is proper.

As you can see, the Find and Replace feature can help you to proofread on the computer in many different ways. You may be able to figure out other ways to make the computer's tireless brain work for you.

12.2
METHODS TO USE ON THE HARD COPY

Plan to print out a hard copy several times before you must file the document. Because your brain works differently when you are looking at a computer screen than when you are looking at a hard copy, you will undoubtedly find errors on the hard copy that you missed when reading the document on the computer.

1. Check paragraph length. You may have created some overlong paragraphs as you revised; they will be evident on the hard copy. Remember that there are two reasons to create a paragraph break: substance and graphics. Even if you have not moved on to a new subject, the reader may need the brief visual rest that a paragraph break provides. A good default is to look for at least two paragraph breaks per page (more is fine). If you have only one paragraph break, you must find a place to insert a hard return. Note that if you create an artificial paragraph break in this way, you may need to add a topic sentence to ensure that the reader can instantly understand how the paragraph is relevant to the point under discussion.

2. Check sentence length. If you have a problem with overlong sentences, edit for them by looking for periods. Take a pencil and make a slash mark at every period; you can do this without even reading the text. When you're done, review the slash marks. If you see several sentences in a row that are over four lines long, review them and try to shorten at least one. One good way to shorten long sentences is to look for verbs. If you have three verbs in one sentence, try giving each verb a subject and its own sentence. If you see several sentences that are only one line long—and you're not using short sentences for occasional, dramatic effect—try to combine a couple of the short sentences.[8]

3. Review the verbs. Readers subconsciously pay more attention to information in the verb position. Thus, go through your document and circle all of your verbs, trying not to read the sentences. You should scrutinize all vague verbs, including *is, are, was, were, made, involved, concerned, had*, and the like. Unless you are using them purposefully—e.g., in a persuasive document to deemphasize information, or because you are using passive voice to avoid an unusually long subject—you should look for the better verb hidden in the sentence and revise accordingly.

4. Review the signals to the reader. The best way to review signals to the reader is to review the "template items" identified in Chapter Ten. Look at the first paragraph (or two) of each heading section for needed legal backstory and roadmap. Look at the last paragraph of each heading section for a concluding statement connecting the analysis to the point being covered within that unit of discourse. Scan the first sentence of each paragraph to see how often your paragraphs begin with main points and include the phrase-that-pays. Scan through the document to make sure there are enough headings. If you go more than three or four pages without a new heading, scrutinize that section. Can you break that section down into two subsections? Have you gone onto a new point without labeling it with a heading? Similarly, review each roadmap and mini-roadmap, and then compare it to your headings. The roadmap should predict precisely the headings that follow.

5. Do a ruler-read. After you have taken these steps, read a hard copy aloud (as slowly as you can) backwards and forwards *with a ruler under each line as you read it*. Using the ruler helps to separate you from your text, breaking up that cozy relationship between your short-term memory and your document. When doing this ruler-read, include all extraneous materials like cover pages and tables; these sections often get short shrift when it comes to proofreading.

6. Repeat any or all of the above as needed. If you keep finding new mistakes when using these techniques, you need to keep proofreading. Do

---

[8] *See* Mary Barnard Ray & Jill J. Ramsfield, *Legal Writing: Getting It Right and Getting It Written* 371-72 (4th ed., Thomson/West 2005).

not print the final version of the document until you can read it through and find *no* mistakes.

12.3
PROOFREADING YOUR REVISIONS

Word processors have greatly improved the quality of written documents, but they are also responsible for a new type of editing error. In the past, when a writer revised a document, someone had to type the whole thing over again, and so it was fairly easy to substitute the new words and to leave the old words out. Now, with the constant editing that word processors allow, it is not uncommon to see both old and new versions of a phrase within a document: The writer typed the new phrase and forgot to delete the old one. Furthermore, writers who carelessly use the Find and Replace feature frequently find sentences like this in their writing:

▽ BAD EXAMPLE

On Saturday, the Mr. Johnson returned home.

The best way to avoid these types of errors is, once again, to focus your proofreading on different problems at different times. After each round of edits, print out the hard copy and highlight the words, lines, or paragraphs in which edits occurred. Read those sections in isolation, so that you don't get caught up in the meaning of the words. In addition, *never* use the Replace All feature; doing so causes mistakes like the one shown above because it's difficult to envision all of the contexts in which a word or phrase might appear. Instead, look at each use of the word you are replacing to avoid mistakes.

12.4
THE LAST THING TO DO WITH THE DOCUMENT

This section is really about the second-to-the-last thing to do with the document. The last thing you should do is file it with the court. But the last proofreading method you should use with your document is to read it aloud, out of order. Either start in the middle, start on the last page and then read the second-to-the-last page, and so on, or mix up the pages and read them in a random order. Whichever method you use, your goal is to pay attention to individual words and sentences rather than to get swept away by your no doubt fascinating discussion of the law.

12.5
SUMMARY

In practice, you will often need to write and file documents in a hurry, without time to polish and proofread in a leisurely way. Take the time now to develop an effective polishing process. When you submit documents that demonstrate professionalism in both content and presentation, you enhance your credibility and increase your opportunities for success in law practice.

ORAL ARGUMENT

Supreme Court Rule 28.1 provides that oral argument "should emphasize and clarify the written arguments in the briefs on the merits. Counsel should assume that all Justices have read the briefs before oral argument. Oral argument read from a prepared text is not favored."

Although most law students think of the oral argument first when they think of appellate advocacy and motions, most judges agree that the brief is more important than the oral argument. Justice Ginsburg has observed that "[a]s between briefing and argument, there is near-universal agreement among federal appellate judges that the brief is more important."[1] In many federal courts, most cases are decided without oral argument. Justice Ginsburg noted that the Fourth, Tenth, and Eleventh Circuits dispense with oral argument in about 70 percent of cases, and Judge Wiener pointed out that almost two-thirds of the appeals filed in the Fifth Circuit are decided without oral argument.[2] In many trial courts, oral argument is not presumed unless counsel requests it when a motion is filed; even then, the judge may not grant the request. Even in cases in which oral argument

---

[1] *See, e.g.,* Ruth Bader Ginsburg, *Remarks on Appellate Advocacy*, 50 S.C. L. Rev. 567, 567 (1999).
[2] *Id.* at 568. *See also* Jacques L. Wiener, Jr., *Ruminations from the Bench: Brief Writing and Oral Argument in the Fifth Circuit*, 70 Tul. L. Rev. 187, 189 (1995).

occurs, the brief usually has more to do with the outcome of the case. A 1986 article conducted a limited study of three appellate judges and noted that oral arguments changed the views they held before the oral argument in 31 percent, 17 percent, and 13 percent of the cases heard.[3]

This is not to say that oral argument is unimportant. After reading the briefs and relevant authorities, many judges form a sort of rebuttable presumption about how the case should be decided. The oral argument usually convinces them that their presumption was correct, but an ill-prepared attorney may convince them that they were wrong. As one judge observed, "if the court intends to rule in your favor, the easiest way to change the panel's mind is to be utterly unprepared or ineffective at oral argument."[4] The late Justice Brennan once observed, "I have had too many occasions when my judgment of a decision has turned on what happened in oral argument, not to be terribly concerned for myself were I to be denied oral argument."[5] Judge Bright, of the Eighth Circuit, has commented that "oral argument is an essential component of the decision-making process."[6] It is certainly responsible for generating more adrenalin.

13.1
PURPOSE OF ORAL ARGUMENT

The purpose of the oral argument is not to give an impressive speech. Rather, your goal as an oral advocate is simply to highlight your best arguments and to answer any questions that the judges have about the case. Judge Pierce has explained that oral arguments give judges "the opportunity to discuss . . . the issues they consider dispositive or particularly troublesome—issues that may not have been briefed or at least not briefed fully."[7] Justice Ginsburg has observed that questions during oral argument "give counsel a chance to satisfy the court on matters the judges think significant, issues the judges might puzzle over in chambers, and resolve less satisfactorily without counsel's aid."[8]

---

[3] *See* Myron H. Bright, *The Power of the Spoken Word: In Defense of Oral Argument*, 72 Iowa L. Rev. 35, 40 nn. 32-33 (1986).

[4] Judge Stephen J. Dwyer, Leonard J. Feldman & Robert G. Nylander, *Effective Oral Argument: Six Pitches, Five Do's, and Five Don'ts from One Judge and Two Lawyers*, 33 Seattle U. L. Rev. 347, 347 (2010).

[5] *Commission on Revision of the Fed. Court Appellate Sys., Structure and Internal Procedures: Recommendations for Change*, 67 F.R.D. 195, 254 (1975) (quoting Justice Brennan's comments at the 1972 Third Circuit Judicial Conference) (quoted in Lawrence W. Pierce, *Appellate Advocacy: Some Reflections from the Bench*, 61 Fordham L. Rev. 829, 833 (1993)).

[6] Bright, *supra* note 3, at 36.

[7] Pierce, *supra* note 5, at 833-34.

[8] Ginsburg, *supra* note 1, at 569. *See also* Wiener, *supra* note 2, at 199 (noting that oral argument "further crystallize[s] the issues [and enhances the court's] understanding of the factual and legal details, subtleties, and nuances of the case").

Judges use oral argument to test their presumptions about the case and to probe the case's limits, strengths, and weaknesses by asking counsel to clarify difficult issues or to speculate on the impact of a decision on future cases. Because of their intimate knowledge of the facts of the case and the relevant law, counsel for the parties are uniquely qualified to help the judges as they wrestle with the issues presented by the case.

13.2
FORMAT

In appellate arguments, the petitioner (or appellant) argues first, standing at a podium or lectern, and facing a panel of judges. Petitioner may reserve some of the allotted time for rebuttal. Counsel for respondent (or appellee) follows, after which counsel for petitioner may present a rebuttal. Time allotted to each side for argument varies from 10 to 30 minutes; in many courts, each side is allotted 15 minutes, and counsel for petitioner may reserve one, two, or three of those 15 minutes for rebuttal. Counsel for respondent does not have the opportunity for rebuttal.

In a motion argument, the party who has brought the motion argues first. Motions to dismiss are almost always brought by the defendant, but motions for summary judgment may be brought by either party. The formal requirements for motion oral arguments vary from court to court. Some courts have a "motion docket," where all motions are heard by the same judge, who may not be the judge that the case is assigned to for trial. Other courts may use a "motion day," once a week or on some other schedule. The typical method for oral argument is for a judge or judges to question an attorney standing at a podium, to use strict timekeeping methods, and to allow only the first speaker to present a rebuttal. Some trial judges, however, may dispense with some of these formalities. Because it is usually easier to move from more formal requirements to less formal requirements, this chapter presumes a more formal motion argument. In practice, of course, you should follow local rules and local customs.

13.3
INTELLECTUAL PREPARATION: WHAT DO YOU NEED TO KNOW?

You complete the most important preparation for the oral argument when you write the brief, for it is in writing the brief that you gain an understanding of the facts, issues, and authorities that control the case.

Nevertheless, there are two practical things that you must do in specific preparation for the oral argument. First, you must decide what points to argue and then prepare your argument. Second, you must gather the information that the court will expect you to know—to have at your mental fingertips—when you are at the podium.

13.3.1
DECIDING WHAT POINTS TO ARGUE

Your job on oral argument is not to present a summary of your brief.[9] Your short time at the podium will not be sufficient to discuss all of the issues and arguments that you raised in the brief. When planning your oral argument, identify the two or three points that are most necessary to convince the court of the justice of the result you seek. Frequently, these points will be those that could be resolved in favor of either party,[10] and thus, spending time on these points in oral argument will be particularly important. When deciding what points to argue, you may ignore points that you included for completeness but that are not crucial for your argument. For example, most statutory interpretation arguments include at least a short discussion of the statute's plain language, even if counsel believes that the plain language argument is a sure loser. In that situation, some unfortunate attorneys will begin an oral argument with what they plan to be a short discussion of plain language, thinking they will get past it and move to their more important arguments. Unfortunately, the court is not always in on the plan. As Florida Appeals Judge David Gersten warns, attorneys who try to address too many points may "get bogged down on questions on [their] weaker points and never get to the crux of [the] case."[11]

As you take notes on the points you will present to the court, write down citations to cases and statutes that support your assertions. Although you will not be reading from your notes, the act of writing down the points and their supporting authorities will help cement them in your mind.[12]

In your brief, you may have followed a CREXAC (Conclusion, Rule, Explanation, Application, Connection-Conclusion) model of analysis. When planning your oral argument, think in terms of a pared-down version of that model—more like "CRAC," if you will. That is, first, you should state the point, or the conclusion, that you want the court to agree with. Then support that conclusion by stating the rule that governs the

---

[9] *See, e.g.,* Karen J. Williams, *Help Us Help You: A Fourth Circuit Primer on Effective Appellate Oral Arguments,* 50 S.C. L. Rev. 591, 595 (1999).

[10] *Id.*

[11] Judge David M. Gersten, *Effective Brief Writing and Oral Argument: Gaining the Inside Track,* 81 Fla. B.J. 26, 29 (Apr. 2007).

[12] *See, e.g.,* Williams, *supra* note 9, at 594.

issue. If a case or statute is significant to your argument, you may mention it, but in oral argument, the rule is frequently more important than the citation to authority for that rule. On the other hand, you must be thoroughly familiar with all of the relevant authorities so that you may answer any questions about them. In addition, in some cases the relevant authorities become an important part of the argument.

Generally, the explanation part of the formula that was so important in the brief may be all but eliminated in the oral argument. The judges' eyes may glaze over during any lengthy recitation of authority case facts and holdings unless it is given in response to a specific question. How much support you should give for the rule varies from issue to issue. If the meaning of a rule, or which rule to apply, is at issue, you may need to spend more time talking about relevant authorities. In contrast, if you are arguing about how an established rule applies to the facts in your case, you should plan to go into more detail about your client's facts. Of course, you must still be prepared to discuss the relevant authorities if the court asks you questions about those authorities or about how they might apply to hypothetical situations.

After you have stated the rule and supported it (if needed), apply the rule to the facts by naming the particular facts that mandate the result that you seek. Remember that the meaning of the word *facts* in this context may vary from issue to issue. If the meaning of statutory language is at issue, for example, the facts may consist of the words from the statute. While the explanation section of the formula may be all but nonexistent in an oral argument, do not skimp on the application of law to facts. The judges will be particularly interested in why the facts of the case mandate the application of the rule in the manner that you suggest. Similarly, they will benefit from a detailed discussion of the result that occurs when the rule is applied to your facts.

Although planning your argument is useful, realize that you will rarely be permitted to proceed through the argument of an entire point without interruption.[13] Nonetheless, you should outline a full discussion of each of the points you plan to make during the argument. Doing so teaches you more about your case as you prepare to face the panel.

13.3.2
GATHERING INFORMATION

After you have planned your argument, make sure that you know the case, the issues, and the relevant authorities well enough to answer the court's questions. Although you should limit your prepared presentation to only two or three points, the court will probably ask you about other

---

[13] *See, e.g., id.* at 598.

issues. You must be prepared for all relevant—and some irrelevant—questions from the bench.

First, renew your acquaintance with the facts and procedure of the case. You should be able to answer the court's questions about the details of any relevant facts and be able to tell the court where in the complaint, the record, the decisions below, or the joint appendix certain facts have been recorded. Make sure that you understand all of the details surrounding the legally significant facts; very often, these factual details can make a legal difference. In *Bentsen v. Coors*, for example, counsel for the Coors Brewing Company spent a bit of time at oral argument discussing the difference between beer and ale.[14] Judge Wald has remarked that counsel's familiarity with the record can play a crucial role in the argument:

> The more arcane the subject matter . . . the more intimate with the record the advocate needs to be. All the questions of fact . . . that the brief may have raised in the judges' minds will surface at argument, and nothing frustrates a bench more than an advocate who does not know the answers. Your credibility as a legal maven spurts as soon as you show familiarity with the facts of the underlying dispute.[15]

Similarly, make sure you know the procedural details of the case. The judges may rely on you to clear up momentary confusion about what happened in the courts below.

Second, familiarize yourself with all filed briefs and the authorities cited in those briefs. You should be able to tell the court the facts, holding, or reasoning of any significant authority cases, and you should be able to explain how your case is similar to or distinguishable from those cases. Obviously, it is particularly important to be familiar with any mandatory authorities that are on point or that may be relevant. Furthermore, if you are asking the court to apply a multipart test, make sure that you understand all of the parts of the test, even those that are not controversial.[16]

Finally, and perhaps most importantly, figure out what you are asking for. What rule are you asking the court to create or apply? What will be the impact of that rule on future cases? Knowing the impact of a decision in your favor will enable you to respond effectively to hypotheticals posed by the court. On a related note, try to anticipate what concessions you may be asked to make. For example, you may be asked to concede that the rule in the case applies to a certain type of plaintiff or defendant, or that your client has or has not met all or part of the standard your opponent espouses. You should know which points you would (or should) concede

---

[14] *See* 1994 U.S. Tr. Lexis 163 at *45-46 (Nov. 30, 1994) (U.S. Sup. Ct. Oral Argument Tr.).

[15] Patricia M. Wald, *19 Tips from 19 Years on the Appellate Bench*, 1 J. App. Prac. & Process 7, 19-20 (1999).

[16] Williams, *supra* note 9, at 597.

immediately (those that have little or no effect on your argument), which points you can concede if pressed by the court (those that are important to your argument, but that do not determine victory), and which points you can never concede (any point that would cause you to lose the argument).

Not all judges try to force counsel to concede either minor or significant points, but it is wise to be prepared for the ones who do. Justice Ginsburg has pointed out that "questions are sometimes designed to nail down a concession that will show up in an opinion, perhaps in a footnote that reads: 'At argument, counsel conceded thus and so.' That doesn't mean lawyers should avoid concessions as inevitably damaging. As Judge Wald has observed, a concession once in a while can enhance a lawyer's credibility."[17]

Judge Karen Williams, of the Fourth Circuit, has also cautioned that judges may ask questions that try to get attorneys to "concede away [their] case[s]," stating that counsel should listen carefully to questions that seek concessions, to ensure that "the judge has accurately restated your argument. The judge may be leading you down the slippery slope to an absurd result. At the same time, nothing hurts an advocate's credibility with the court more than the failure to concede an obvious point."[18]

To sum up, at the end of your intellectual preparation for the argument, you should have a command of the issues you plan to discuss, the boundaries of the rule you are advocating, the concessions you are willing to make, the facts of your case, and knowledge of the cases and other authorities relevant to your argument and that of your opponent.

13.4
PREPARATION OF WRITTEN MATERIALS: WHAT SHOULD YOU BRING TO THE COURTROOM?

At a minimum, the well-prepared oral advocate should bring two things to the courtroom: the briefs that have been filed in the current hearing of the case, and the joint appendix or other record materials that are before the court. In the unusual (but not unheard of) event that the court should ask you to consider information on a particular page in the record or a brief, you want to have the materials there with you. If there is not enough room at the podium, you may leave them at counsel table so you can retrieve them if needed.

It is also appropriate to bring an outline or some form of notes up to the podium, but you should plan to make these materials succinct. Judge

---

[17] Ginsburg, *supra* note 1, at 569.
[18] Williams, *supra* note 9, at 599.

Wiener, of the Fifth Circuit, has advised that counsel should not "bring lots of documents to the lectern — shuffling books and papers and reading from them interrupts the flow of your presentation and paints a picture of an unprepared or bumbling advocate."[19]

It is the tradition at many law schools for students to use a manila folder for their notes; the students either write their notes on the four sides of the folder, or prepare them on a word processor and tape or staple them in place. The advantage of a manila folder is that it gives the advocate four pages that stay in order even if dropped. Also, four pages is about the maximum number that the oral advocate should try to look at. Many students use the interior of the folder for their main outline and store information about facts and cases, to be referred to if needed, on the outside.

If you want a more professional look, it is fine to use a *slim* three-ring binder instead of a manila folder. A binder will look better on the way to and from the podium, although the pages may be more difficult to turn. Furthermore, having a binder that allows multiple pages may tempt the advocate to write a more detailed outline, or even to write out the text of the argument. If you do use a binder, consider adding tabs to make turning the pages easier, and strive to include no more than four pages of notes.

Although the anxious advocate may believe that writing out a prepared speech will be a tonic to the nerves, reading from a prepared text is certain to antagonize the court. Supreme Court Rule 28.1 notes, delicately, that "[o]ral argument read from a prepared text is not favored." Judge Williams has made the point more directly, suggesting that reading the argument hurts both its style and its substance:

> The worst thing you can do is deliver a stiff presentation by attempting to read your argument verbatim. Such a presentation style is tedious and makes it difficult for you to answer questions from the bench. If you spend your time looking down at the podium reading your argument, you are likely to miss signals from the bench, and you cannot engage in a dialogue with the judges. Try to argue extemporaneously, or at least leave us with the impression that you are.[20]

Thus, when preparing materials to bring up to the podium, think in terms of words, phrases, and lists, rather than sentences, paragraphs, or pages. If you write full sentences, you will be tempted to read them because you will presume that a prefabricated sentence will sound better than an off-the-top-of-your-head remark. Remember, however, that the judges expect the oral argument to be, to some extent, a spontaneous dialogue. Most judges would rather hear an imperfect sentence from an advocate who is engaged in conversation with the court than perfect prose from a reader.

---

[19] Wiener, *supra* note 2, at 204.
[20] Williams, *supra* note 9, at 598.

Watch a few oral arguments on court Web sites, or read the transcripts, and you will see that many effective oral arguments are full of half-finished sentences and apparent lapses in grammar. This is because an oral argument is a conversation, not a speech.

Write your outline on full-sized paper rather than index cards, and use felt-tipped markers or large, boldfaced fonts to make your points easy to read. List your points in the order in which you plan to address them, and list supporting authorities under each point. You may want to write key words, or even the main phrases-that-pay, in boldfaced type across the top of the outline—or on every page of your materials—so that you have only to glance down at the podium to see words that will remind you of your main contentions.

Some advocates create both a case list and a fact list. On the case list, they list the name, citation, and relevant information (facts, reasoning, etc.) about each case. On the fact list, they list the legally significant facts and relevant background facts that either side might mention, noting where in the record each fact can be found. Creating these lists can be helpful, even if you never consult them during the argument. Both creating and studying them provides excellent opportunities to help you to commit important information to memory.

13.5
PRESENTING THE ARGUMENT

When planning your argument, think in terms of three parts: the Introduction, the Argument itself, and the Conclusion. You will spend most of your time at the podium on the Argument, but be sure to spend the needed time planning the Introduction and the Conclusion.

13.5.1
INTRODUCTION

Although your introductory material should be short (often less than a minute, and always less than two minutes), the introduction fulfills several important functions. A good introduction tells the court what is happening procedurally—who you are, who your client is, and what your client wants; it provides sufficient factual context, it outlines the argument and tells the court why you are asking for the result that you seek, and it grabs the court's attention by focusing the court on your theme.

As always, you must be aware of local rules and local practice. In some courts, you may be asked to "enter an appearance on the record" before either party begins the oral argument. If so, you will stand (as you should whenever you address the court), and state your name, your law firm, and the party you represent. The party speaking first may be asked if he or she is reserving rebuttal time. If you enter an appearance in this way, you may or may not be expected to take time in your formal presentation to restate your name and your client and to reserve rebuttal time.

Traditionally, advocates begin their arguments by saying, "May it please the court," although "Good afternoon, your honors" or any other respectful greeting will probably be acceptable to most judges.[21] Of course, you should review local rules to see if they require any particular opening, and, whenever possible, observe some arguments in that court before your debut so that you can learn the court's customs. In the United States Supreme Court, for example, advocates never introduce themselves, and they traditionally begin their arguments by addressing the Chief Justice directly, saying, "Mr. Chief Justice, and may it please the Court."[22]

However you begin your argument, you should never start without having the attention of the Judge, or, on a multi-judge panel, the Chief Judge or Justice. This requirement may mean that you have to wait a moment while the judge finishes with note-taking from a previous advocate, but the benefit it provides in professionalism is well worth any cost in time. Just stand at the podium and wait in silence for the judge to nod at you or to give you some other signal telling you to begin. Do not take notes or review your notes while waiting, because you want to be able to pick up on either verbal or nonverbal signals as soon as the judge is ready.

If you are the petitioner or the party supporting the motion, you may need to reserve rebuttal time at this point. The manner for reserving rebuttal varies from court to court. In the United States Supreme Court, for example, you do not set aside rebuttal time; you simply make your best effort to end your argument while you still have time remaining. In other courts, you may reserve time by speaking directly to the bailiff. In some courts, you may need to both request time from the bailiff and make the request orally from the podium. Section 13.7 provides more detail on preparing and making the rebuttal argument.

Your next task is to introduce yourself and your case. Judge Wiener has recommended opening with "a short, simple introduction: tell the panel your name, the name of your client, your client's role in the appeal . . . and in the trial . . . but refrain from blowing a lot of 'smoke' at the court

---

[21] Wiener, *supra* note 2, at 203.

[22] Because the United States Supreme Court has never had a Chief Justice who is a woman, the Court has no protocol for addressing a female Chief Justice. Some students who are faced with a female Chief Justice in a Moot Court setting address her as "Madame Chief Justice." While this may be acceptable, resorting to a foreign language strikes me as odd. Alternatives could include addressing the Chief by name, or by the title without the gender designator. Thus, either say, "Chief Justice (with a nod to the Chief), and may it please the Court," or "Chief Justice Sotomayor, and may it please the Court."

. . . . Begin your presentation with a short, attention-getting 'simple and direct' introduction of the points you plan to make."[23] Judge Williams has warned that the only uninterrupted time most oral advocates will have is at the beginning of the argument, and that they must use this time "to succinctly present the issue and explain to the court the most important reason why [they] should prevail. [They] may wish to use this time to give an outline of the points" to be covered during the argument.[24]

Many advocates spend too much time providing factual context. An oral argument does not have a formal statement of the case the way a brief does. You can presume that the court has read your brief and the relevant record materials. The Internal Operating Procedures of the United States Court of Appeals for the Third Circuit, for example, require that briefs and appendices be "distributed sufficiently in advance to afford at least four (4) full weeks' study in chambers prior to the panel sitting.[25] Rule 1.2 lays out the "Responsibility of Panel Prior to Scheduled Sitting," noting that "[t]his court has the tradition of carefully reading briefs and reviewing appendices prior to oral argument or conference."[26]

Most advocates can give enough factual context simply by articulating the issue. In the rare situation where more factual background is necessary, try to spend no more than one or two sentences on these facts. Ideally, the court should not even realize that you are laying out facts; if it does, it should do so only at the moment you move to your argument. Of course, later in the argument, you should discuss facts in detail as they relate to your points or in answering questions; in the introduction, however, you must be succinct.

Presenting a roadmap of the points you plan to cover has two advantages. First, it gives you at least one opportunity to make those points. With some "hot" courts, that opportunity may be the only one. Second, a roadmap provides the obvious benefit of telling the court the points you plan to address and the order in which you plan to address them. Some courts will let you proceed with your argument if you have named the points that the court is interested in; if you do not provide a roadmap, on the other hand, the judges may interrupt quickly to make sure that you discuss an issue that has provoked their interest. You should not state the points in your roadmap objectively (e.g., don't say, "First, I will address whether the statute passes the heightened scrutiny test"). Instead, state your points argumentatively, and use the roadmap to explain why you are asking for the result you seek.

---

[23] Wiener, *supra* note 2, at 201, 203.

[24] Williams, *supra* note 9, at 598.

[25] Internal Operating Procedures, U.S. Court of Appeals for the Third Circuit 1.1 (effective July 30, 2010), available at http://www2.ca3.uscourts.gov/legacyfiles/IOP_2010_final2.pdf (last accessed Mar. 21, 2014).

[26] *Id.* at 1.2.

If you are the first speaker, you may wish to grab the court's attention in the manner in which you describe the case or in your roadmap. Although you should not be overdramatic, you can be argumentative. If you are the respondent or the party opposing the motion, you may wish to grab the court's attention by referring specifically to a question that one of the judges asked of your opponent and explaining its significance to the case. There is no formula for what you should say to grab the court's attention. You must review your case and decide what aspect of the facts, the law, or your argument epitomizes the injustice you seek to have corrected. This is the time to exploit your argument's theme. Identify the common-sense reason why the court should decide the case in your favor.

If you must provide information about your name, your client, and a request for rebuttal, you may believe that the opportunity for an attention-getting opening is lost, but that is not necessarily true. Once you finish this logistical step, simply pause for a brief moment. Just as white space provides a position of emphasis in a written presentation, a pause provides one in an oral presentation. You should use the pause sparingly, but it can be an effective way to separate mundane identification information from the substance of your argument. If you believe that the issue is complex, and that the court needs some legal, factual, or procedural context before it can grasp the crucial point of your argument, move the dramatic statement of your thesis—and the pause—accordingly. That is, identify yourself (if needed), provide needed context, and then pause before stating your thesis in a dramatic way.

The sample introduction below is from a petitioner's argument in *Miller v. Albright*, 523 U.S. 420 (1998). Note that the advocate introduces herself, asks for rebuttal time, tells the court what she is asking it to do, pauses before describing the case in practical terms, and outlines the points that she will address in the argument:

> May it please the Court, I am Glenda de Guzman, and I represent the petitioner, Ms. Lorelyn Penero Miller. At this time I would like to reserve three minutes for rebuttal. Ms. Miller, who was the plaintiff below, is asking this Court to reverse the decision of the United States Court of Appeals for the District of Columbia Circuit. That court upheld the constitutionality of 8 U.S.C. Section 1409(a), which governs the citizenship of children born outside the United States to unmarried parents when only one of the parents has U.S. citizenship. Section 1409(a) distinguishes among these children based solely on the gender of the child's citizen parent. [Pause.]
>
> Section 1409(a) wrongly uses an irrebuttable gender stereotype to put a time limit on the relationship between a father and his children. This Court should find Section 1409(a) unconstitutional and reverse the decision below for two reasons. First, Section 1409's requirement that only fathers prove a close, personal relationship before their children can be declared citizens is

Using the Theme of Your Argument

Trial courts and intermediate appellate courts must follow the mandatory authorities of the Court(s) above them, if any on-point authority governs the case. Courts of last resort, however, and other courts deciding cases of first impression, are more likely to consider the impact that their decision will have on real-world situations.

Accordingly, you must know the commonsense reason behind what you are asking the court to do. Why would a decision in your favor be fair or just? In the case of *Miller v. Albright*, counsel for the young woman seeking citizenship could focus on the inherent unfairness of gender stereotypes or on the problems with imposing an arbitrary time limit on father-daughter relationships. Counsel for the government, on the other hand, might focus on Congress and the importance of respecting Congress's decisions in certain limited areas of law.

The theme is particularly important in oral argument. Having a theme in mind can help you keep the court focused on the reason for a decision in your favor. Frequently, when questions have led you away from the point of your argument, you can recover by returning to your theme. This does not mean that you can avoid answering a question. Instead, answer the question, and then remind the court of your theme. For example, if counsel for the government were asked about the irrebuttable gender stereotype in the statute, he or she could provide a substantive answer, but then say, e.g., "this Court has never examined this type of claim in an immigration statute, because the Court defers to Congress in this area."

In other words, a good theme is a statement that is true even in the face of your opponent's best point. A theme is not a statement of how a legal rule applies, because the court may accept or reject a statement of this type. Instead, it is based on *why* the court should apply the rule in a certain way. In the *Miller v. Albright* example, both themes are true: The Supreme Court has traditionally deferred to Congress in the area of immigration law, and gender stereotypes are inherently unfair.

Identifying and using a good theme gives you somewhere to "run" when you must concede the existence of a negative fact or legal precedent, and helps you to refocus the court's attention on the equities of your case.

premised on overbroad generalizations abut the relative capabilities of men and women, and thus violates the standard that this Court laid down in the VMI case just last year. Second, even if this Court should apply a less stringent test, Section 1409(a) is still unconstitutional because its concern with unreliable proof of paternity is neither facially legitimate nor rational in 1997.

In the second paragraph, the writer identified her broad themes: The statute should not use irrebuttable gender stereotypes, and it should not impose an arbitrary time limit. Before making this point, she identified the issue that the court is being asked to decide, and provided legal, procedural, and factual context. After stating her themes somewhat dramatically, she provided a roadmap that laid out the legal support behind these themes and told the Court the order in which she plans to proceed.

The respondent need not ask for rebuttal time and can spend much less time introducing the case. The Court should have any needed context thanks to the first speaker's argument.

The respondent should, however, strive to grab the court's attention by showing that he or she is "responsive" to the court's concerns. For example, a respondent representing the other side in the case of *Miller v. Albright* might begin the argument as follows:

> May it please the Court, I am Bradley Walent, and I am counsel for the Respondent, Secretary of State Madeline Albright. [Pause.] A moment ago, Justice Vargo asked counsel for Petitioner whether Section 1409(a) is or is not an immigration statute. Your honors, that question is at the very heart of this argument. This Court has consistently refused to interfere in Congress's decisions about immigration law, and this case is not the time to start. This Court should affirm the decision of the District of Columbia Court of Appeals precisely because Section 1409(a) is an immigration statute, and this Court has traditionally applied a deferential standard when reviewing federal immigration legislation. Furthermore, under that deferential standard, Section 1409(a) is facially legitimate, and it is rationally related to Congress's goal of promoting close, early family ties with U.S. relatives.

Although the respondent's attorney above did not use a traditional "first, second, third" roadmap, his introduction revealed his theme (deference to Congress), the two points that he planned to make, and the order in which he planned to make them: First, he planned to address the requirement that the Court use a deferential standard; second ("furthermore"), he planned to explain what happens when that deferential standard is applied.

The introduction will take up only a small percentage of your argument time, but you should plan it carefully so that you can obtain optimal benefits.

13.5.2
THE ARGUMENT ITSELF

We have already discussed substantive and organizational information regarding the argument itself; Section 13.6 below addresses how to handle questions during the argument. The transition point from the introduction to the argument is simple. After you have finished the introduction, simply move to your first point. Do not wait for the court to tell you to go on. Although many advocates provide a full sentence of transition between introductory material and the argument, rarely is such a formal shift necessary. Instead of saying, "Now that I have laid out the issues, I will address the first of the three points of my outline," it is usually more effective to be briefer, e.g., "turning to the first issue . . ." or even "First, . . ." A shorter transition saves both time and the court's patience. If you have prepared effectively, you can proceed to your first point, the rule governing it, the support for that rule (if needed), and the discussion of how that rule applies to the facts. Handling questions from the bench is discussed in Section 13.6.

13.5.3
THE CONCLUSION

Although the court will often control the amount of time you spend talking about particular points, the good advocate is aware of the passage of time and tries to provide an effective conclusion to his or her argument. In many courts, a podium light system is used: A green light is displayed throughout most of the argument; a yellow light signals that time is running short (how short varies from court to court—e.g., there may be two to five minutes remaining when the light turns on); and a red light signals that time is up. Counsel should never stop the court from asking questions in order to conclude. However, if the court is quiet, and the yellow light is on, counsel may decide to conclude rather than to launch into his or her final (and perhaps weakest) point. If you are arguing before the United States Supreme Court, or another court that requires you to preserve your time for rebuttal, you might look for a way to conclude early.

Like the conclusion to a brief, the conclusion to an oral argument should be short and sweet. At a minimum, it should tell the court what you want it to do. In an appellate argument, you will typically be asking the court to affirm, reverse, or reverse and remand a decision; in a motion argument, you will be asking the court to grant or deny the motion. If more time is available, counsel may want to recap the main reasons that support his or her conclusion, as in the following conclusion that might be appropriate for the petitioner in *Miller v. Albright*:

> Even in the area of immigration, Congress does not have the authority to pass a law that violates the Equal Protection Clause of the Constitution. Section 1409(a) denies equal protection to children of men who are U.S. citizens. Rather than promoting family ties between a father and a child, Section 1409(a) prevents those ties from developing further. For all of these reasons, this Court should reverse the decision of the District of Columbia Court of Appeals. Thank you.

If you are still in conversation with the court when your time elapses, you must acknowledge that time has run out and ask for permission to continue. If the court is asking you a question when your time elapses, pay careful attention to the question and plan your answer. Before answering, however, inform the court that time is up and ask if you may have time to answer the question. Most courts will give you permission. Unless you are asked still more questions, segue from your answer into your conclusion.

Even if you have a strong, dramatic conclusion planned, do not use it if time has already elapsed, even if the court has given you permission to continue. This is the time to move to a one-sentence conclusion, e.g., "Therefore, because Section 1409(a) makes unconstitutional distinctions based on gender stereotypes, this Court should affirm the decision below. Thank you."[27]

13.6
HANDLING QUESTIONS FROM THE BENCH

All of the hard work that you have completed to prepare you for the argument should have one purpose: enabling you to answer the court's questions.[28] Some questions may be answered by your argument itself—that is, you will have anticipated the court's concerns—but many others will come up the old-fashioned way: The court will interrupt your presentation and demand your attention. How you handle these interruptions says everything about your skill as an oral advocate and may even determine whether you win or lose your case.

The first thing you must do is let the court interrupt you. As Justice Ginsburg has noted, some attorneys—foolishly—try to squelch the court's questions by talking louder and more quickly when a judge tries to speak:

> A race the lawyer is bound to lose is the press-straight-on run when a judge attempts to interject a question. More than occasionally, I have repeated a lawyer's name three times before he gives way to my inquiry. Despite his strong desire to continue orating, the lawyer should stop talking when the judge starts.[29]

Remember that your job is not to "get through your stuff." Instead, you are there to find out what the judges are interested in, and so you should stop talking immediately when one of them tries to reveal an area of interest by asking a question. As one judge has noted, "questions are your friends."[30] Judge Williams has suggested that "[q]uestions are not interruptions, they are opportunities. The questions from the bench are the only indication of what issues are bothering the judges[,] and [the questions] may clue you in on what is preventing them from seeing the case your way."[31]

---

[27] For more information on making your conclusion effective, see Section 14.5.3.

[28] *See* Richard H. Seamon, *Preparing for Oral Argument in the United States Supreme Court*, 50 S.C. L. Rev. 603 (1999), for advice on preparing for oral argument primarily by anticipating and planning answers for the Court's questions.

[29] Ginsburg, *supra* note 1, at 569.

[30] Judge Bruce D. Willis, *Suggestions from the Bench: Things Judges Wish That Appellate Lawyers Would Do Differently*, 35 Wm. Mitchell L. Rev. 1281, 1285 (2009).

[31] Williams, *supra* note 9, at 599.

Thus, maintain eye contact so that you can see any nonverbal signals that one of the judges has a question. Speak slowly enough to allow the judges time to interject. If one of the judges makes the slightest noise or attempts to interrupt, you should stop speaking to give the judge a moment to ask a question. Use every technique possible to let the court know that you welcome its questions.

Do not presume that all questions will be hostile. On multi-judge panels, judges frequently use counsel to advance an argument that they already agree with, in hopes of gathering more votes. Justice Ginsburg has admitted that "[s]ometimes we ask questions with persuasion of our colleagues in mind, in an effort to assist counsel to strengthen a position."[32] Judge Williams has advised that "you may encounter a judge who is in favor of your position and spends time asking you easy questions that lead you to an even stronger version of your position."[33]

Second, you must listen to the question. Do not rush to give an answer. Oral argument is not a quiz show in which you must beat your opponent to the buzzer. Instead, listen carefully to make sure that you understand what the court is trying to do.[34] Some questions ask for a concession. At other times, as noted previously, a judge may try to advance your point of view by asking a question designed to reveal your best arguments. Some questions ask you to identify or explain a policy supporting your thesis or seek information about a case or other authority. Some questions focus on the point you are addressing, while others show that the court has moved on to a new issue. Listen to the question and assess what the court is asking before you try to answer.

If you do not understand the question, you may seek clarification. Ideally, you should try to articulate what you think the court has asked, e.g., "I'm not sure that I understand your question, Judge Lowe. I believe that you are asking whether this Court has ever invalidated an immigration statute." This statement does not demand an answer from a court, but it allows the court to correct you if you are mistaken. Tone is important here; do not emphasize the word "believe" in any way, lest you imply that you are struggling to understand a poorly worded question. Admittedly, the question may have been poorly worded (which is not surprising, since the judge may be figuring out the question while asking it), but you do not want to point this out to the court. After you signal that you may need clarification, pause very briefly to give the court an opportunity to correct you if needed. If no correction comes, simply answer the question as you

---

[32] Ginsburg, *supra* note 1, at 569.

[33] Williams, *supra* note 9, at 599.

[34] *See* Gersten, *supra* note 11, at 28 (noting that one of the two most common oral argument mistakes is "not listening to the judges' questions and the tenor of the discourse"); *see also* Dwyer, Feldman & Nylander, *supra* note 4, at 348-51 (identifying common categories of questions and describing how to deal with them effectively).

have stated it. Few judges will take offense at an attempt for clarification, as long as counsel does so in a respectful way.

Third, you should answer the question directly. Judge Williams has recommended that advocates "[r]espond immediately to a question with a 'yes,' 'no,' 'it depends,' or 'I don't know.'"[35] Some advocates, perhaps fearful that a direct answer will reveal a weakness in the case, try to launch into an explanation of the significance of the answer before they give the answer itself.[36] This tactic is a mistake because the court doesn't hear the explanation; it hears only that counsel has refused to answer a direct question with a direct answer.[37] Furthermore, you risk forgetting to answer the question directly or, more commonly, being interrupted before you can do so. The court will be much better able to listen to your explanation if you first satisfy the court's need for an answer to its question. Of course, it is very important that you *give* the explanation. Many attorneys refer to this kind of exchange as a "yes, but" answer. You must agree with the fact or legal rule that the court has laid before you, but you disagree as to its significance. It is perfectly appropriate to make a concession and then explain why that concession does not affect your argument.

Fourth, you should tie your answer to your argument. Judge Williams has advised, "Follow your short answer with a concise explanation and citation to the record or precedent as necessary."[38] This technique is just as important with friendly questions as it is with more challenging questions. If a judge asks you a question that advances your argument, you should use the opportunity to advance that point to its end. If you must answer a difficult question with a "yes, but" answer, you should answer a friendly question with a "yes, and" answer, as in "yes, and here's why." The judge who asks you a friendly question may well be disappointed if you do not do so. As one judge has noted, "a judge might ask you whether there is sufficient evidence in the record to support a jury's finding[.] [S]he is not asking because she thinks the evidence is insufficient, but because she wants you to describe that evidence in detail for the benefit of the other judges."[39]

After you have finished answering the question and explaining your answer, it is time to move back to your argument. Do not wait to be told to go on. If the court is not asking you a question, you have the floor, and you set the agenda. At this juncture, you must decide whether to return to the point you were making, or continue on to another point.

---

[35] Williams, *supra* note 9, at 599.

[36] *See also* Gersten, *supra* note 11, at 29 ("Answer the question honestly, even if you are afraid this might hurt your case. There is nothing worse than losing credibility with the court.").

[37] *See also id.* ("If you do not answer the question directly, or if you become evasive, the judge will find it difficult to listen to your argument because he or she will still be thinking about the unanswered question.").

[38] Williams, *supra* note 9, at 599.

[39] Dwyer, Feldman & Nylander, *supra* note 4, at 350.

If the court has asked a question that moves you to your second issue while you were still addressing your first, for example, you may be wise to continue with other support for that second point. The court may have been signaling you that it is not interested in the first issue, either because it already agrees with you or because there is no way that it will ever agree with you. In either circumstance, time is better spent on an issue in which the court has shown its interest.

If the court has asked you about an issue that you believe is irrelevant to the case, you must still answer the question, if you are able. You may let the court know that you think the question is irrelevant by respectfully pointing out the fact, legal rule, or other information that shows that the resolution of your case does not require resolution of the issue that it asked about, e.g., "Yes, your honor, that is true. However, in this case, Officer O'Donnell testified that he had no reason to believe that Ms. Restrepo was violating any laws when he conducted the search."

Similarly, do not dismiss hypothetical questions without an answer. Justice Ginsburg has expressed dismay over advocates' repeated dismissals of hypothetical questions with the pat answer, "That is not this case, your honor": "[The judge] knows, of course, that her hypothetical is not this case, but she also knows the opinion she writes generally will affect more than this case. The precedent set may reach her hypothetical."[40] When judges pose hypotheticals, they are testing the boundaries of the rule you suggest. The good advocate knows the boundaries of the rule he or she recommends, and so is able to explain how the proposed rule would govern the hypotheticals posed by the court.

13.7
REBUTTAL

Counsel for the petitioner or moving party should not reserve important *arguments* for rebuttal. Supreme Court Rule 28.5 provides that "counsel making the opening argument shall present the case fairly and completely and not reserve points of substance for rebuttal." In many courts, including the United States Supreme Court, counsel may not set aside time for rebuttal; counsel can preserve time for rebuttal only by stemming the tide of the justices' questions before his or her allotted time has elapsed. You may wish to reserve time strategically, depending on local custom. For example, some courts allow counsel to reserve time for rebuttal, and give counsel only the time reserved. Other courts, in contrast, give counsel the reserved time along with any argument time that was unused.

[40] Ginsburg, *supra* note 1, at 569-70.

If the court limits rebuttal to the time reserved, you should reserve a more generous amount of time; if the court adds unused argument time to the rebuttal, you can reserve less time. Be sure you understand your own local rules as to rebuttal before the day of your argument.

Although final decisions about what to say in rebuttal must be made on the spot, there are some guidelines you can follow to make your rebuttal more effective. First, remember that rebuttal is for rebuttal only.[41] Any point you make on rebuttal should be a response to a point made during your opponent's argument. Some courts will interrupt counsel who try to use rebuttal to "finish up" the main argument, saying, "Counselor, do you have any rebuttal to offer?"

Second, even though you must use rebuttal to respond to statements that opposing counsel has made during the argument, you should prepare for rebuttal while you prepare your argument. You can reasonably anticipate many of the points that your opponent will make. In a moot court argument, you might identify the points to which you have a "clean" response—that is, a response that will not draw painful questions from the bench. In real life, of course, you should identify the points that are most crucial to your argument, for you must address those points even if they result in painful questions.

Plan ahead, even make an outline, and then, during the argument, note which points your opponent actually makes. You might even jot down a word or phrase from your opponent's presentation to make your point more effective, e.g., "Your honors, counsel for Respondent stated that Ms. Miller's attempts to establish a relationship with her father were 'too little, too late.' This time limit on family relationships is precisely what is wrong with Section 1409(a)."

Third, don't sweat the small stuff. Unless an otherwise small error has legal significance in your case, rebuttal is not the time to point out that your opponent has given the wrong year in a case citation, confused the parties' names, or made some other picayune error. This kind of fussiness hurts you more than it helps you.

Finally, make your points and then sit down. Although this advice holds true at all stages in the argument, it is particularly important on rebuttal. When you stand up to give your rebuttal, address the court and then tell it how many points you plan to make, e.g., "Your honors, I have two points on rebuttal. First, counsel for Respondent stated . . . . This fact is irrelevant because . . . . Second, counsel cited . . . . That case does not apply here because . . . . Thank you."

Be aware that many courts do not listen passively to a rebuttal. Thus, you must be as prepared to answer questions during the rebuttal as you were during your main argument. It can be helpful, therefore, to let the

---

[41] *See, e.g.,* Wiener, *supra* note 2, at 199, 202.

court know how many points you intend to make; courts that have this knowledge may allow you to make all of your points, even if they have used up your time with questions.

13.8
WORD USE

Although the model for an oral argument is a conversation rather than a speech, in most cases it will be a more formal conversation than you are accustomed to. Because most law students have never seen an oral argument before law school, some may imitate lawyers' oral presentations that they have seen on television. Unfortunately, these presentations are almost always set during trials, such as opening and closing arguments, and the guidelines for an oral argument are different. For example, during an opening statement in a trial, counsel for each party may talk about what they will "show": "We will show you that the defendant was not anywhere near the scene of the crime . . . ." This statement refers to the testimony and exhibits that counsel plans to offer into evidence. It is inappropriate to imitate this language in an oral argument because, even in a motion argument, you will not be presenting evidence. Thus, you will not be "showing" the court anything.

Similarly, some students think they sound more lawyer-like if they speak in terms of "contentions," saying, e.g., "Petitioner contends that the First Amendment does not . . . ." Although this phrasing may have a lawyerly ring to it, most experienced attorneys do not use phrases like this. Announcing what you contend only reminds the court that your statements are merely contentions, rather than the truth. Instead of labeling all of your statements as contentions, just make the statement: "The First Amendment does not . . . ." If you need to, say silently to yourself before you begin to speak aloud, "The Petitioner contends that . . . ."

On a similar note, it is usually more appropriate to refer to the judges or justices by name rather than constantly saying "your honor." It is not so much that saying "your honor" is wrong; it is just as respectful and more natural, however, to use someone's name when you know it. Judge Willis notes that "many judges prefer to be addressed by name" and advises counsel to be certain of how to pronounce each name, and of whether the judges on a particular court are styled as "judges" or "justices."[42]

Of course, no one expects a flawless presentation. Just accept that you will probably use the wrong word from time to time. If you have actually misspoken, take the time to correct it: "The Fourth Amendment, excuse

---

[42] Willis, *supra* note 30, at 1284.

me, I mean to say the First Amendment . . . ." Do not bother to correct errors that are not misstatements. I have occasionally seen a nervous student begin a sentence by saying, "I contend that . . . ." I see in his face that he realizes he should avoid referring to himself, so he corrects himself: "I mean the Petitioner contends that . . . ." Suddenly, he remembers that I advised in class against using labels of any kind, and he freezes in dismay. No court will rule against you for a style error. This advice is meant to make your presentation as smooth as possible, but try not to become hypersensitive. Unless you say something offensive, if you make a style error, you should just keep going. To quote the old adage: "Least said, soonest mended."

13.9
PUBLIC SPEAKING TIPS

This point appears last because the most important public speaking tips—don't read to the court and maintain eye contact with the court—have been made previously in this chapter. The court is much more interested in the law and the facts of the case than it is in a professional oratorical style. That said, there are a few general pieces of advice that can help to make your presentation more effective.

First, speak loudly enough and slowly enough to be heard and understood. Visit the court before the day of your argument to find out what kind of amplification system, if any, is in use, and how effective it is. If you see several arguments in which the court is easily able to understand counsel who speak normally in front of a microphone that is six to eight inches from them, you can presume that you do not need to hold the microphone up to your lips in order to be understood. Make sure, however, to adjust the microphone so that it is pointing at your face, rather than your shirt front or the air above your head. If you realize you are speaking too quickly, try to slow down. If this is not possible, try to pause briefly between sentences to give the judges a chance to catch up, and for the court to ask you questions.

Second, avoid distracting gestures, mannerisms, and dress. Most courts appreciate normal hand gestures. They are distracted, however, by both arms waving at once or by hands that go beyond the boundaries of the podium (e.g., pointing at the judges). You should maintain a professional posture before, during, and after your time at the podium. While at the podium, stay *at the podium*. Most judges (and court recording systems) expect that the attorney will stand behind the podium for the entire argument. Generally, it is good advice not to touch your face or your clothes: don't adjust your collar or tie, run your fingers through your hair, scratch your ear, or jingle the coins in your pockets. If you are unsure whether you have any of these mannerisms, make a video of a practice argument, and then run through it at high speed. Any overused mannerisms will become obvious.

The standards for dress vary somewhat from court to court and are constantly evolving. When you are a student, choices like this affect only yourself and perhaps your grade; in practice, they may affect your client as well. Your goal should be to dress professionally, in a way that will not distract the court from your message. You must determine how to meet that standard in your particular courtroom. You might want to take a look at your outfit in the mirror to see how it looks not only when you are standing still, but also when you are sitting, bending, moving, and gesturing.

Third, just as you use sentence variety when writing, use vocal variety when speaking. Vary your speed and your tone of voice; don't speak, for instance, in the monotone that the actor Ben Stein has made famous. You can pause occasionally to let an important point sink in. Likewise, if a point is important, speaking slowly will draw the court's attention to it.

Finally, a word about your face. Realize that you are "on stage" from the moment you enter the courtroom until the moment you leave it. When you are at the podium, keep a poker face: Don't reveal your feelings, even if you are upset or confused by a question. In law school settings, you probably did not choose which side to argue, but you must still act as if you are confident in your argument. Too often, I have seen students react to a probing question with a look that says, "You are right; I'm sorry that I'm on this side of the case." Practice controlling your reactions now; the skill will come in handy in a variety of situations in which you have to project more confidence than you feel.

Remember also that the court can see you even while you are at counsel's table, and act professionally there as well. Judge Wiener has aptly illustrated the unprofessionalism of an attorney who overreacts to his or her opponent's argument:

> Don't "act out" while seated at the counsel table during your opponent's turn at the lectern. Most judges resent being distracted by seated counsel's body language and nonverbal comment—shaking or nodding your head, rolling your eyes, grimacing, squirming in your chair, and the like—in response to your opponent's remarks from the lectern or our questions from the bench. Just sit still and pay attention to opposing counsel and the court. Likewise, don't make a big production out of taking notes while your opponent is arguing. When you must look at your papers or take notes, do so unobtrusively and discreetly.[43]

---

[43] Wiener, *supra* note 2, at 205.

Because your goal on oral argument is to convince the court to adopt your point of view, you must take pains at every stage of the argument to impress the court with your credibility and your professionalism.

13.10
SUMMARY

All of this detailed advice may seem overwhelming to the new attorney, but it really boils down to a few points: Know what you're asking the court to do and what the impact of its holding will be. Know the facts and authorities behind your case so that you can answer questions about them. Treat the oral argument like a conversation, let the court interrupt you, and be willing to answer all of the court's questions. Dress and act professionally.

You should also know that the most common remarks I hear after a law student's first oral argument are: (1) "They didn't even ask me about everything I know!" and (2) "I want to do that again."

You'll do fine.

MOOT COURT COMPETITIONS

Each year, dozens of interscholastic moot court competitions take place around the country. There are two reasons to participate in a competition: to learn and to win. Everyone who participates in a moot court competition learns a great deal about the subject matter at issue and quite a bit about the practice of law. Nevertheless, despite the many tangible and intangible benefits of learning for the sake of learning, most teams still want to win. If you are a team member on an interscholastic moot court team, this chapter is meant to help you to enhance your learning experience in the hopes that it may help you to win.

Appellate advocacy is about mastery. You must master the facts in the case so that you can research and write effectively. You must master the law at issue so that you can explain why the law dictates the result that you seek. Moot court competitions are about demonstrating your mastery of the law and the facts through the vehicles of briefs and oral arguments.

Like the writing process generally, moot court competitions are also about making decisions. You and your teammates may be able to decide which competition to join or which side to argue. You will definitely have to decide how to divide your workload, how to assign the issues that the case presents, how to write the brief, and how to conduct the argument.

Like real practitioners, you will be able to seek advice, to greater or lesser degrees, from colleagues or mentors. Ultimately, however, you must decide which advice to take and which advice to leave alone.

Every year, when I meet for the first time with my team, and when I judge practice arguments for other teams, I tell them that they must decide whether they agree with my advice. I explain the reasons behind my suggestions, but they will be the ones at the podium during the competition. No matter whose advice they follow, they may well be victims of what I call "pet peeve-itis": Someone will deduct points from their score because they did or did not do something that happened to be a pet peeve of one of the judges. Therefore, they must sift through the often conflicting advice they will receive from the many people who judge their practice arguments and decide which advice best fits their theory of the case and their performance style.[1]

Because law practice is full of real-life decision making, one of the many benefits of moot court competitions is that they give students practice in making decisions in a context in which there will be real consequences: their victory or defeat in an argument round. The information in this book is meant to help you make those decisions, but it is *advice*. Only you and your teammates can decide how to use this advice.

14.1
TYPICAL COMPETITION REQUIREMENTS

The typical moot court competition requires a team of two or more students to complete an appellate brief and participate in a series of oral arguments. Competitors are usually provided a record of some kind, with varying amounts of factual and procedural information (e.g., depositions or affidavits, stipulations, complaints) and complete or excerpted "decisions below." They must then write a brief and file it with the competition by a certain date. Many competitions also require teams to file copies with the host of the competition and all of their potential opponents. Then, after some time to allow for practice arguments and for scoring of the briefs by the competition's representatives, the teams gather for oral argument rounds.

Unlike real-life attorneys, students in moot court competitions often argue both sides of the case, although they usually complete only one brief. The score in each round is typically based on a combination of the

---

[1] *See also* Sanford N. Greenberg, *Appellate Advocacy Competitions: Let's Loosen Some Restrictions on Faculty Assistance*, 49 J. Legal Educ. 545, 555 (1999).

team's brief score and oral argument score. In real life, the brief usually has much more impact than the oral argument, but in most moot court competitions, the oral argument is worth a higher percentage of the score. That said, however, the brief score is often dispositive: If the brief scores are spread over a broad range (as is common), the close oral argument scores that are awarded in many rounds can mean that the brief score will determine the winning team.

The requirements as to faculty participation vary; usually, the amount of outside help the students may receive during the briefing process is more limited than the help available after the brief is turned in. Sadly, some competitions even limit the amount of help students may receive during practice arguments. For many students, the learning that takes place during these practice arguments is invaluable. They learn not only about their own case, but also, by listening to the stories the practice argument judges tell about their real-life experience with cases of this type, they learn much about the practice of law. Thus, if you have a choice as to which competitions your school may enter or as to which team you wish to try out for, you may want to review the rules of the competitions you are interested in or talk to the coaches to see which competition's rules will give you the best possible experience.

Once you are on a team, your first task on receiving the materials for the competition should be to read the rules with a highlighter. Although you will need to be aware of formatting requirements (e.g., typeface and page limit specifications), your first focus should be on the requirements as to (1) the type of assistance that may be given, and (2) when that assistance may be given. A typical requirement is that no assistance may be given until after the brief has been submitted.

Do not rely on your coach to read the rules for you. You are the one who will be competing, and you must know the rules intimately. They are your "rules of civil procedure" for the competition, and you need to be aware of how they operate. Of course, you can consult your coach to answer questions or to decide if it is necessary to ask the competition administrator to interpret a rule. But you, as a team member, must take ultimate responsibility for your role in the competition.

14.2
DIFFERENCES BETWEEN MOOT COURT COMPETITIONS AND "REAL LIFE"

Although moot court competitions are meant to simulate real-life legal issues, no simulation experience can perfectly replicate real life. First, both your procedural facts and the client's case facts are limited to what you have been given. If your research reveals an issue that would be affected by a fact that has inadvertently been left out of the record, you cannot do more investigation to discover that fact, as you would in real life. It would be wise to read the record and do some basic research immediately after you receive the record materials; in this way, you may discover any legally significant gaps in the record while it is still early enough to consult competition administrators for guidance. This step would allow the competition to issue a clarifying memorandum to all of the competitors. If you find a gap too late, or if the gap is not significant, it might be appropriate to make a realistic assumption based on other facts in the record and include that assumption in your argument (e.g., "Assuming that Ms. Johnson had graduated from high school . . ."). Naturally, you should *not* make assumptions that are unrealistic or that will significantly affect the issues in the case, (e.g., "Assuming that the police did not provide Mr. Smith with valid *Miranda* warnings . . .").

Second, in a moot court competition, there are some expectations about what you will argue and what you will not argue. Many competitions provide the parties with the questions presented; others will include a grant of certiorari that allows the parties to argue "all issues fairly raised by the record," but will include a lower court opinion that clearly identifies two major issues.

Finally, style is often as important as substance in a moot court competition. It is not *more* important—most judges will notice significant misstatements of the law—but it has a much larger role in moot courts than it does in real life. In real life, the law and the facts will usually dictate the outcome, even though oratorical style may play a role in some extremely close cases. In moot court competitions, in contrast, the substantive points are earned not based on which side has the better substance, but on which side is best acquainted with the substantive arguments in the case, and which side can best express itself to the court when explaining that substance. Because most students become fairly well acquainted with the legal issues that the case presents, style differences may be the only significant distinctions between some competitors.

I should stress at this point that not all students need to aim for the *same* style. Over my many years of judging and coaching moot court competitions, I have seen several different effective styles. Students who speak softly (but loudly enough to be heard) can be as effective as students who speak loudly; students who gesture can be as effective as more sedate students. The main points of an effective style—maintaining eye contact, speaking loudly enough to be heard, listening when the court speaks, answering questions directly, supporting answers with reference to law and facts, and integrating answers into the argument—work with many different kinds of speaking styles.

14.3
CHOOSING WHICH SIDE TO BRIEF

If your school sends two teams to a particular competition, the rules usually dictate that one team must act as petitioner and one team must act as respondent. In that case, your choice of side will probably depend on a coin flip or some other arbitrary method. If your school sends only one team, however, you may be allowed to choose which side of the case to brief. Because you will be arguing both sides of the case at the competition, make this decision based mainly on how it relates to the brief. Presuming that there is no deadline for your decision (other than the brief deadline), you may want to begin researching and writing based on your gut instinct, but allow yourself to change sides if you later decide that the other side would be better.

Do not agonize too much over this decision; you cannot control how the judges will react to each side of the case. If the judges think that one side is much easier than the other, they may consciously or unconsciously award more points to what they perceive to be the more challenging side. On the other hand, if the judges are not overly perceptive of the relative difficulties of the two sides, they may award more points to the briefs that seemed to make the better arguments. Thus, you should choose the side that you think will allow you to write the better brief. If you think you are writing the easier side, be careful. Do not fall into the trap of failing to adequately brief issues because they seem easy or obvious to you.

14.4
WRITING THE BRIEF

The research, organization, and writing guidance throughout this book applies to any brief. In a moot court competition, however, you will be working collaboratively, and so other issues may arise. Most moot court competitions allow three students on a team. Some schools choose to have one person write the brief and the other two argue, but I do not recommend this structure. While it may make for an easier writing process (especially for the students who aren't writing), I believe that the final product is usually better if all three team members participate. More importantly, all three team members learn much more about their case, and about writing and oral argument, when all three participate in both writing the brief and arguing the case.

14.4.1
DIVIDING UP THE WORK

Because research and writing are parts of the analytical process necessary to fully understand the issues in a case, the people doing the arguing will be better prepared if they participate in the writing process. No less an authority than the late Chief Justice Rehnquist has noted the importance of the oral advocate's participation in the drafting of the brief:

> The questions you get in an oral argument are often ones that are not squarely covered in the brief—indeed that is probably the reason for the question from the bench. So an advocate who has not gone beneath the surface of the brief to understand how its parts fit together into a coherent argument will be at a considerable disadvantage. Even an advocate who has all but memorized the brief will be at this kind of disadvantage, if [he or she] has done no more than memorize it.[2]

Thus, if you are the one who conducted research, chose some cases to include in your argument and rejected others, and hammered out the analysis, you will be much better able to understand and respond to the questions from the bench. If you must argue an issue that you did not brief, try to read more than the cases that are cited in the brief. Get to know the area of the law thoroughly, so you can explain why certain authorities are relevant or irrelevant.

There is no one best way for two or three people to collaborate on writing a brief. Because revising and polishing should be team efforts, the first decision to be made is how to complete the first draft. Some teams divide up the two major issues—giving two of the team members one issue each, and then having the third member handle the "extras" such as the statement of the case, the summary of the argument, the table of contents, and other format requirements. If one of the two issues is much more challenging than the other, however, you may wish to divide that issue between two people, have the third person handle the second issue, and collaborate on the extras.

The most demanding method, and perhaps the most effective, would be to have all three team members conduct separate initial research on both issues with a short deadline. At that time, the team could meet and discuss the issues. Since three heads are better than one, this method would make best use of the intellectual strengths of all three team members. After the meeting, the team members could decide how best to divide up the continued research and the drafting of the arguments, and each writer would have the benefit of input from the other team member(s).

---

[2] William H. Rehnquist, *From Webster to Word-Processing: The Ascendance of the Appellate Brief*, 1 J. App. Prac. & Process 1, 5 (1999).

Even at this early stage of the writing process, it is important that you have a specific understanding of length and typeface requirements. For example, it wastes time to draft in Times Roman font if your final draft must be in Courier font. Similarly, if your competition requires that your citations follow a particular citation format, you should make sure that all of the citations are in that format from the very beginning. Find out the specific requirements of your competition, and write with those in mind from the start. Recording necessary citation information as you take your notes, and observing length limitations from early in your writing process, will help to prevent last-minute editing crises.

Completing multiple drafts guarantees a higher quality product. Whatever method is used to divide up the work, it is important to decide how many pre-final drafts you will complete and to set a date certain for each draft to be completed. Even if your faculty advisor cannot critique your brief before it is filed, he or she can require you to turn in drafts at certain times during the time allotted for writing. Decide how and when you are going to work together on critiquing the drafts.

14.4.2
CRITIQUING YOUR TEAMMATES' WORK

Often, teams that have begun the competition with much good will fall apart at the critiquing stage. Either their work doesn't progress because they don't meet regularly, or they are angered by the "stupidity" or the "rudeness" of their teammates. Do not let your desire to win the competition rob you of your basic good manners and civility. Remember that you will have to work with colleagues in this way when you practice law, and that you must treat them politely if you wish to keep your job. Treat your teammates with that same respect; meet the team's deadlines, and show up for meetings on time.

First, you must decide how to conduct your critiques. Some team members trade briefs and read each others' work separately, trading written comments with each other. Some teams find it more efficient to meet together and review each team member's contribution as a group. A combination of these two approaches may be best. If the team members exchange their work and review it separately, someone with questions about the law or the facts may review the record or research a narrow point in order to answer the question before the team meets. This is much more efficient than interrupting the discussion to hop on line or run to get a book (although you may end up doing this anyway, as the critique progresses).

Second, you must decide when to conduct your critiques. Plan ahead, and be aware of each team member's needs. While many teams are comfortable with the "all-nighter" method of collaboration, do not presume that this method will work for every member of the team. If one team member is on a law journal and has a deadline during the brief-writing time, plan around that date. If another team member has family responsibilities, plan to meet during the day if at all possible.

Finally, you must conduct the actual critiques with tact and respect. In practice, you will often be asked to critique the work of others (as well as deal with critiques of your own work). Start now to act like a professional. Some of the advice here is obvious. Avoid words with extreme negative connotations, such as *ridiculous* or *stupid*. If you believe that your teammate has made a mistake, use hedging language, such as "I believe" or "this may be," or the like. Your critiques will be easier to take—and will accomplish more—if they presume the writer is intelligent, but that you are having trouble understanding something.

In the alternative, critique by asking questions—questions that are as specific as possible about what is confusing you. Instead of saying, "This argument is wrong," ask, "How does this argument support a reversal?" Hearing your teammate's explanation may convince you of the validity of the argument and may inform all of you as to what further information needs to be included in the brief. On the other hand, if the argument is not valid, your teammate may recognize its weakness himself or herself when trying to explain it to you. By talking each argument out among the three of you, the team can get a good idea of the strengths and weaknesses of the various arguments, and then revise accordingly.

In addition, you may wish to hold a practice moot during the writing process. Although most rules prohibit, or at least limit, coaching during the brief-writing process, nothing prevents the three members of a team from conducting an "internal moot." Review the authorities relevant to your teammates' issues, and question each teammate in turn. Challenge the assumptions inherent in their arguments, and probe their knowledge of the relevant authorities. You could even spur their research by asking about the existence of other relevant cases, e.g., "Is there any case in which the court has held . . . ?" You can identify categories of questions before you begin and try to ask at least one question in every category. Some of the categories may be generic (e.g., standard of review, mandatory authorities vs. lower court authorities, etc.) while others may be specific to the substance of the problem. An internal moot can provide obvious substantive benefits, and it can also help the team rev up the sometimes dry process of churning out the brief.

Although you must be polite to each other as you work on the brief, you also have an obligation to raise issues that are bothering you. Effective collaboration is a balancing act. Each member of the team must feel comfortable raising questions about anything that is troubling. Once, after a competition, I was discussing an issue that I thought had not been briefed effectively with one of the team members. He told me that he, too, had seen the problem, but was self-conscious about raising it, since "the other two seemed to think everything was okay." Each team member has a responsibility to point out possible problems or mistakes. That is the best way to get the full benefit of three collaborators working on a brief.

On the other hand, you cannot beat an issue to death. After the team has fully considered a problem or concern and decided what action to take (or not to take), that should be the end of it. Even if you disagree with the outcome, don't sulk, and don't second-guess. Once the decision is made, it's over, unless new evidence appears.

14.4.3
POLISHING THE BRIEF

Particularly if you are not allowed to seek faculty assistance, you must work hard to see the brief through others' eyes as you edit and polish. Imagine that your most demanding professor is reading the brief. What would he or she say? Where would he or she find weaknesses, unsupported arguments, or inadequate analysis? When you are proofreading, imagine your most demanding editor—perhaps a parent, a professor, or a significant other.

The polishing advice given in Chapter Twelve applies here, but in some ways, perfection is even more important for a moot court brief than for any *one* professional brief. While your reputation will suffer over the long term if you consistently have small errors in your briefs, it would be extremely unusual for you to lose a case because of typographical errors, wrong font size, or some other minor error (of course, remember that cases can and have been dismissed because counsel missed deadlines or violated other more significant "format" rules of the court). In a close round in a moot court competition, in contrast, a few points off for citation form errors or for using the wrong font size can mean the difference between victory and defeat.

Thus, take care with your proofreading. Be sure to leave enough time to allow you to reprint the brief after correcting errors. Also, be sure to read the brief from beginning to end, from the docket number to the certificate of service.

14.5
PRACTICE ARGUMENTS

Hold as many practice arguments as you can. Practice arguments do two things: First, they teach you about your case by presenting new questions to you and giving you a chance to consider your answers.

Second, they give you needed practice to polish your performance for the competition.

You should recruit as many judges as you can beg, borrow, or steal. Ideally, you should begin to plan a schedule of practice arguments as early as possible. Rules often prohibit holding practice arguments until after the briefs are filed, but that doesn't mean you can't get them on your schedule. Take advantage of the time leading up to the brief due date to get as many practice arguments as possible on your post-due date schedule. The more different judges you have, the more different questions you will be exposed to, and the less frequently you will face an unexpected question at the competition. At each practice, one of the team members not at the podium should be assigned the task of recording all of the questions that are asked. The team can study them later to identify questions that require more research or thought. Furthermore, you will discover which questions you are most likely to hear at the competition, and you can take the time to develop strong answers to those questions.

The typical format for a practice argument is to treat it like a regular moot court: to time it in the way that it will be timed at the competition and to hold a critique after the argument. This format will be fine for most of your practices. For at least some practices, however—perhaps those with just your coach acting as judge—you may want to break the mold. If you get a question that stumps you, stop the clock and talk it out. Confer with your teammates or your coach as to the best way to handle the question. If you think you need to do more research, jot down ideas to help you get started.

This type of practice can help to improve the presentation of your most important points. Although in real life judges do not particularly care about diction, an advocate whose arguments are easier to understand will score more points than one who struggles to put his or her thoughts into words. If you have a good answer but cannot phrase it effectively, stop and take the time to figure out the best way to make your point. Strong subject-verb combinations and concrete language are even more important to easy comprehension in oral argument than they are in writing. Instead of saying, e.g., "The concerns over officer safety that justified the search incident to an arrest also justified the lesser intrusion presented by the issuance of a citation," say, "The search was justified because police officers are in as much danger when they give a driver a ticket as when they put a driver under arrest."

In addition to planning how you will answer questions, you should use your practice arguments to practice for "positions of emphasis" in the oral argument: the introduction and the conclusion. In addition, plan how to deal with predictable problems, like a cold court or your opponent's misstatements.

14.5.1

THE INTRODUCTION

Because virtually every moot court competition features two oralists on each team, the first speaker on each team faces another challenge. Instead of the usual introduction, he or she must introduce the case and explain which issues each team member will address. Doing so is courteous, for it helps the court to understand how things are organized. It is also smart because it reduces the chances that one team member will be asked about another's issues. After completing the introduction, pause before moving to your part of the argument; doing so will focus the court's attention.

There are two common ways to present your introduction. The first method is the objective method:

> **May it please the court. My name is Jennifer Manion, and along with my co-counsel, Susan Restrepo, I represent the Petitioners, Stitt & Gallagher, Inc. At this time I would like to reserve two minutes for rebuttal. Your honors, we are asking this Court to reverse the decision of the Eighteenth Circuit Court of Appeals, which held that Stitt & Gallagher violated Mr. Jasiunas's constitutional rights when it fired him. I will be addressing the privacy issue, and Ms. Restrepo will be addressing the issue of the applicability of the <u>McGuffin</u> test. [Pause.] Your honors, Stitt & Gallagher, Inc., did not violate Mr. Jasiunas's right to privacy when it dismissed him because of the contents of his e-mail messages. . . .**

On the other hand, you could deliver the same information in a more argumentative style:

> **May it please the court. My name is Jennifer Manion, and along with my co-counsel, Susan Restrepo, I represent the Petitioners, Stitt & Gallagher, Inc. At this time I would like to reserve two minutes for rebuttal. Your honors, this Court should reverse the decision of the Eighteenth Circuit Court of Appeals for two reasons. The first reason, which I will explain, is that Stitt & Gallagher, Inc., did not violate Mr. Jasiunas's right to privacy when it dismissed him because of the contents of his e-mail messages. The second reason, which Ms. Restrepo will explain, is that plaintiffs such as the Respondent are not entitled to recover under the <u>McGuffin</u> test. [Pause.] Your honors, the Respondent has no privacy right in e-mails that he sends on company time.**

Although both introductions do the job and get the message across, the second example is more argumentative and may be seen as more persuasive. You must identify the introduction that works best for you.

14.5.2
PLANNING FOR AWKWARD MOMENTS

a. The Cold Court

Most practice arguments are before "hot" courts that are well prepared and pepper the team with questions. You should also practice, however, for a "cold" court. In real life, a cold court is not a problem. You can make the points you think are most important and sit down, even if only a few minutes of your time have elapsed. In a competition setting, however, a quiet court is a problem; you will have less of a chance to demonstrate your vast knowledge of the case and its governing authorities. Furthermore, some competitions require that you spend at least ten minutes of your time at the podium, and deduct points if you fail to do so. Thus, during your practice arguments, figure out what to do if you have a panel that has nothing to say to you.

Essentially, you must impress every panel with your skill as an orator and your knowledge of the law. If you have a quiet panel, the first thing to do is to slow the pace of your speech. Although many advocates could benefit by speaking more slowly, talking too fast is even more of a problem with a quiet court. If you are talking quickly, you are going through your material quickly, and you may not have enough to say to use up the minimum time required. If you talk more slowly, you take up more time; furthermore, you provide more opportunities for the judges to interrupt you. On a silent panel, the judges may be too intimidated by their own silence to break into your rat-a-tat delivery. If you pause fairly often—but not so often as to be noticeable—a judge may venture into the breach with a question.

Second, you must develop a strategy for impressing the quiet court. You impress a hot court when the judges ask you tough questions and you answer them. But how do you impress a court that won't ask you any tough questions? One method is to go out of your way to refer to authority for the legal propositions you state. Give details from the cases that show why they support your assertions. Cite to the record whenever you mention a particularly significant fact.

Another way to impress a quiet court is to "ask yourself" the tough questions. In your practice rounds, identify any apparently tough questions for which you have a strong answer. Keep those questions in mind for when you have a quiet court. For example, let's say that one of your practice judges asked, "Won't allowing foreign-born children to establish parentage at any time discourage early bonds between fathers and children?" You could "ask yourself" that question by stating, "Allowing foreign-born children to establish parentage at any time will not discourage early bonds between fathers and children. First, as this Court noted in McGuffin . . . ."

Some advocates try to wake up a quiet court by making bombastic statements in the hope that someone on the court will rise to the bait and challenge the assertion. While this technique may loosen the logjam if it succeeds, it is a risky proposition. If no one challenges your assertion, you may end up sounding foolish or ignorant.

b.   Dealing with Opponents' Misstatements of Law or Facts

Oral arguments serve a different purpose in moot courts than in real life. In real life, as noted above, judges often read the briefs before the argument and form a rebuttable presumption as to how the case will turn out. They will often question the attorneys about specific points made in the briefs, and attorneys may challenge specific points that the other party has made in a brief.

Furthermore, in real life the oral argument is only a small part of the decision-making process. After the oral argument, the judges may cast an initial vote on the outcome of the case and justify that decision with a written opinion. Claims made in the oral argument or the brief will be tested by the research and analysis of the judges and their clerks. Finally, a majority opinion and, perhaps, concurring or dissenting opinions, will convey the court's decision on the issue.

In a moot court argument, on the other hand, the judges have often not seen any briefs in the case; they are relying only on the record and on bench materials. They may question counsel on very narrow points of law, but they cannot challenge specific statements that appeared in the briefs. Furthermore, the oral argument ends the decision-making process. The brief will have received a score earlier, and that score will be combined with a score that the judges give on the spot, right after the argument. If either side makes claims about the law or the facts, those claims will be evaluated immediately, without reference to cases cited, or, most likely, the record (even though judges will usually have the record with them).

This difference between moot courts and real arguments makes detailed mastery of the law and the facts even more important for moot courts than for real-life arguments. In real life, if your opponent innocently misstates a fact or misinterprets the meaning of a case, there is a good chance that the error will be discovered during the decision-making process, and that your opponent's misstatement will have no impact on the decision. In a moot court, however, if the two sides contradict each other as to the facts or the law, the judges must decide immediately which advocate to believe. Some students try to prevail in this battle merely by contradicting their opponents, sometimes forcefully. I believe that the best signals of credibility are citations to the record or the opinions at issue.

Thus, if your opponent mistakenly mischaracterizes a fact that is crucial to the argument, you can best correct it—professionally and politely—with a citation to the record:

> Counsel for Respondent stated that the arrest occurred at 6:45 P.M. While that is true, that is not the crux of Petitioner's argument. If I may direct the Court's attention to page 3 of the record; on that page, in the second paragraph, Officer Perek explicitly stated that Defendant was "taken into custody" after church "that morning." This is the time when <u>Miranda</u> warnings should have been given.

If your opponent mischaracterizes an authority case, your best bet is to counter that characterization with language from the opinion that shows that your interpretation is the correct one:

> Counsel for Petitioner has said that the <u>McGuffin</u> Court limited the impact of <u>Miranda</u> to the time after "arrest." This is inaccurate. On page 372 of the decision, the <u>McGuffin</u> Court specifically noted that <u>Miranda</u> warnings must be given not only upon arrest, but before any custodial interrogation.

At first glance, memorizing specific page numbers may seem to be a daunting task. However, you will discover that throughout your practices, you are memorizing many "sound bites" about the facts and authorities relevant to your case. Get in the habit of including the page number when you talk about these elements. After all, the page number is just one more word to remember, and the benefits in credibility are worth the slight cost of brainpower. Of course, you must decide whether your performance arguments should include page numbers every time you mention a crucial fact, or a crucial point from an authority case. While the specific page numbers can be effectively used to contradict an opponent's misstatement of the law or the facts, using them throughout the argument can look like showboating. On the other hand, some judges are duly impressed by counsel's ability to provide such specific support for statements about the law and the facts.

Keep in mind that although citations to cases are unusual in real life, citations to the record are not. If you have had the opportunity to observe more than a couple of oral arguments, you have probably seen a judge ask counsel where a particular fact can be found in the record. Upon receiving the answer, most judges turn to the page to start reviewing the facts immediately. Thus, memorizing certain page numbers can be a skill worth developing.

Perhaps the best way to prepare for this situation is to make a "cheat sheet" for both the law and the facts. Make a chart of the most significant facts, and note their location in the record. Similarly, identify the two or three cases that are most significant to each argument, and identify a statement from the case that crystallizes the point that each side might use the case to make. Not every case will yield effective arguments for each side; when they don't, search for something you can use to argue the case on one side and to distinguish it on the other. Preparing a cheat sheet will help you to learn the law and the facts, provide you with a study guide, and give you a ready reference to take to the podium if needed.

14.5.3
THE CONCLUSION

Although the argument's conclusion may take less than a minute of your time, it is important to do it right because it represents the last impression that the court will have of you. To make life more interesting, your conclusion should be structured differently depending on what is happening when your time runs out or is about to run out. Your first job is to be aware of your time. At the competition, talk to the bailiff before the round, and make sure that he or she is sitting where you can see the time cards. If the bailiff is planning to sit in an inconvenient place, don't be shy about asking for a change in seating arrangements. The whole purpose of keeping time is for the participants and the judges to know how much time has elapsed.

Second, during the argument, pay attention to the time cards. In real life, many courts give extra time at the podium only grudgingly; in some courts, your microphone will be turned off when time elapses. At a competition, presume that time limits are strictly observed. If you are still at the podium when your time elapses, you must *acknowledge* the end of your time and ask the court's permission if you wish to continue speaking. You should plan ahead and have a few different exit strategies planned for the various possible scenarios.

First, you may have a quiet panel. In this case, after you see the two-minute card (or a while after you have seen the five-minute card), transition into a rather lengthy conclusion. State your two or three best points affirmatively, and then say, "for these reasons, this Court should affirm [or reverse] the decision below. Thank you."

Second, you may have a panel that keeps you frantically answering questions every minute of your time. If you have lost track of your time and see the "stop" card as you pause after answering a question, *don't* go into a lengthy formal conclusion. I have seen too many oralists stop a stirring colloquy to turn to a wooden, obviously prefabricated conclusion. If you are surprised by the "stop" card, you may simply say, "I see that my time is up. Thank you." If you are a little braver, most courts will let you get away with a little more: "I see that my time is up. We ask that the Court affirm [or reverse] the decision below. Thank you." Do not presume that you must end by asking for relief. As long as you have asked for it at some point in your argument, it is perfectly appropriate—and often effective—to end with a simple "thank you."

A sidebar on handling an active court: saying the words "in conclusion" will cause many courts to stop paying attention and look to their score sheets. While this technique is generally not advised even in competition (and is almost never appropriate in real life), it may be helpful if you have a relentless court. Saying "in conclusion" (when you see that you have only a minute or so left) may quiet the court enough to allow you to end on a strong point. In the alternative, one of my moot court team members would sometimes use the two-minute sign as an opportunity to say, "I see that my time grows short." This statement always made the judges sit up and take notice of the time, and often, they relaxed and let him finish the argument in peace.

Third, you may be in the middle of answering a question, or the court may be in the middle of asking a question, when the time elapses. If the court is talking, wait until the question is asked before noting the end of your time. If you are speaking, stop immediately. In each case, begin your next statement by saying, "I see that my time is up. May I answer [or finish answering] your question?" Almost every court will allow you to answer. I do not recommend asking for time to conclude in this situation. Instead, finish your answer with a few words that encompass one of your assertions, and then segue to a brief "and therefore, this Court should reverse the decision below."

14.6
PROFESSIONALISM

Naturally, you will treat the court and your opponents with respect at all times. You may certainly address a judge as "your honor," but it is more realistic, and more effective, to use names. Ask the bailiff if there will be name plates, or if he or she can tell you who will be sitting where. Of course, it is much better to call a judge "your honor" than to use the wrong name; one of the counsel for the Florida secretary of state provided an unintended moment of levity during the 2000 election oral arguments by addressing Justice Stevens—twice—as "Justice Brennan." Justice Brennan had retired from the bench in 1990 and died in 1997.

You should dress professionally, as well. My general guideline is to dress as if you are interviewing for an important job. Unfortunately, your choices are rather limited; you are expected to wear conservative colors, with no distracting accessories. You may decide that personal choices of this kind are important to you, and so you may wish to push the envelope a bit. As long as you look professional, most reasonable judges will not change your score for this type of choice. Some judges may, however, want to discuss your appearance during the critique. If this happens, listen respectfully, thank the judge for his or her opinion, and then continue to make your own decisions. This advice holds true for the entire critique. As long as you are polite, you may certainly ask a question to clarify advice that a judge gives you, but it is both unprofessional and fruitless to argue with the court on a point of law or a method of presentation.

Finally, you must deal with your opponents professionally. Before the argument, it is courteous to introduce yourself, shake hands, and wish them luck. After the round, you should shake hands again and congratulate your opponents before conducting any private postmortems with your coach or teammates.

Whatever the result of the round, accept the news with dignity. If you win, don't high-five your teammates or shoot your fist into the air. If you lose, don't lay your head on the table (as I have seen people do!). Again, shake hands with your opponents, congratulate them on a job well done, and wish them luck or accept their good wishes, as appropriate.

Through my many years of coaching I, alone, have gained this unique insight: *People do not like to lose.* In every competition, every team but one has to lose at some point. It is all right to feel bad when you lose a round or are eliminated from a competition. But don't get carried away. Don't berate yourself, your teammates, or your coach. Some postmortem analysis is to be expected, and may be helpful, but postmortems are best in moderation. Especially if you lose in a preliminary round, don't let it knock you for a loop, for you may still advance in the tournament. If you get too upset over an early loss, however, you may hurt your performance in a later round, ensuring that you are eliminated from the competition.

14.7
SUMMARY

Even though moot court competitions do not replicate the practice of law, participating gives you practice in collaboration and decision making as well as in legal writing and oral argument. Take full advantage of the learning opportunities that the competition presents, and remember that you need three things to win: a good brief, good oral arguments, and good luck. I hope this chapter helps you with the good briefs and oral arguments; the good luck is up to you.

Appendix A

FOR REFERENCE: CITATION FORM AND PUNCTUATION INFORMATION

Because even lawyers still make grammatical and citation form mistakes, this appendix provides basic information about these pesky problems. Review it now, and keep it handy when you are polishing your final draft.

A.1
PUTTING CITATIONS IN THEIR PLACE

Sections A.1 to A.4 address four basic concerns about citations: (1) when to cite and not to cite, (2) requirements for and common mistakes in long-form and short-form citations, (3) how to adjust sentence structure to accommodate citation form, and (4) statutory citations.

A.1.1
WHEN TO CITE

There are four common occasions that call for a citation:

(1) When you are either **quoting or paraphrasing** language from another source, you must cite the source of the language.

(2) When you state a legal proposition, you must cite to authority for that proposition. This rule applies even when the legal proposition could be part of a lawyer's general knowledge. In a formal document, all legal propositions must be supported by a citation to authority, preferably authority from the controlling jurisdiction.

(3) The first time you tell the reader about an authority—whether by quoting language from it, by paraphrasing a summary of it, or by referring to it generally—you must cite to that authority in full.

(4) *Each time* you tell the reader—through a quote or a paraphrase— what a court held, found, reasoned, decided, or stated, you must cite to the page to which you refer.

A.1.2
WHEN NOT TO CITE

Naturally, there are many times when you need not cite to an authority. There are two occasions, however, that present dilemmas to many legal writers.

(1) It is appropriate to omit some or all citations to authority within the summary of the argument, within point headings, and within a question presented, even though these items might include legal propositions. Consult Chapter Nine (and local practice) for more guidance on these matters.

(2) When you are comparing the facts of your case to the facts of an authority case that you have already introduced and explained within the same general discussion, you usually don't need to cite to the authority again. Citations are also omitted when you refer to a common law rule that you've already cited, e.g., "Thus, the rule in McGuffin should apply in this case."

A.2
COMMON CASE CITATION FORMATS

A.2.1
LONG FORM

The guidelines below are based on both ALWD and Bluebook citation rules, although they do not cite to particular rules.[1] They explain common

---

[1] For complete ALWD guidelines, consult Association of Legal Writing Directors & Coleen M. Barger, *ALWD Guide to Legal Citation* (5th ed., Aspen 2014). For complete Bluebook guidelines, consult *The Bluebook: A Uniform System of Citation* (19th ed., Harv. L. Rev. Assn. 2010). You should be aware that more states are now requiring public domain citations in certain documents.

mistakes and discuss which elements are most significant to readers and users of legal documents.

The typical long-form case citation includes five elements:

(1) **The case name.** For most cases, the name of the case consists of one name on each side of the "v." Do not use a party's first name (unless it is part of a corporate party name, e.g., "Larry King, Inc.") and do not use more than one name, even if there are multiple plaintiffs and defendants. To use abbreviations precisely, consult the appropriate rules; in general, never abbreviate the first word in a party name, and never use *et al.* in a citation. Case names should be underlined or italicized. Some writers mistakenly underline or italicize an entire citation, whether to a case or a statute, because they have seen entire citations underlined in hypertext on a Web site or another online resource. Statutory citations are *never* italicized or underlined; in cases, *only* the case name (e.g., *"Smith v. Jones"*) should be italicized or underlined. Because the eye is drawn to underlined words more than to italicized words, I recommend underlining unless local rules or practice dictate otherwise.

(2) **Where the case and the information cited to can be found**. This element is the most important part of the citation for a reader who is actually looking up a case that you've cited. Provide the volume of the reporter, the designated reporter abbreviation, and the page on which the case begins.

(3) **The pinpoint citation.** With every cite, you should include the specific page to which you are citing ("pinpoint cite"). Although it is tempting not to bother with the pinpoint cite, you may be frustrating or angering a busy clerk if you leave it out. Some writers tell themselves that pinpoints are unnecessary because they are just citing to the case "generally." This excuse is usually a cop out. In almost every situation, you are at least citing to the case's holding. Make the clerk's life easier—and increase the chance that the judge will understand that the case stands for the point you say it does—by providing pinpoints that take the clerk to the parts of the case that prove your argument.

Some local rules will will require you to provide "parallel cites," that is, citations to two different reporters that contain the same case. Although providing parallel citations is not fun for the writer, take it seriously if it is required.

(4) **The year of decision**. This element is the simplest: put the year of the decision into parentheses. Even readers who aren't fussy about minor citation form errors care deeply when you leave the date of decision out of a long-form citation. Because the date of a decision affects its current validity, readers always want to know the year in which authority cases were decided. Note that for some non-standard citations (e.g., to slip opinions), you may need to include not just the year, but the month and day of the decision as well.

(5) **Which court decided the case**. It is even more important for the reader to know the deciding court than to know the year of decision. If the

reporter title conveys this information "unambiguously," you don't need to include this information elsewhere within the citation. For example, the "U.S. Reports" (abbreviated as "U.S.") publish only decisions of the United States Supreme Court, so no further information is needed. On the other hand, "F.3d," for example, publishes decisions of all of the federal courts of appeal, so when citing to decisions in that reporter, you need to put the correct circuit into the parentheses with the date.

Knowing which court decided the case is vital for a reader who wants to determine whether a case is controlling. Therefore, even readers who are not fussy about citation form want to know which court decided the case. Make sure to include this important element in your citation

GOOD EXAMPLES

Donchatz v. Corn, 101 U.S. 101, 105 (2010).
Ohio v. Burpee, 101 N.E.2d 122, 128 (Ohio 2010).
Maloon v. Hagen, 101 F. Supp. 2d 122, 128 (N.D. Ohio 2010).

A.2.2
SHORT FORM

The most basic guideline is that you should omit the date and court information. Otherwise, use of short form depends on context.

If you are citing again to the *last-cited and last-mentioned* authority, you may use the id. form. "Id." replaces the name of the case, the volume of the reporter, and the abbreviation of the reporter. Thus, if you cited again to the case of Donchatz v. Corn, you could use the following short form if you were citing to a different page in the opinion:

Id. at 107.

If you were citing to the same page, you would use "Id." alone. If you are citing to an already-cited opinion, but (a) you have cited to or *mentioned* another authority in the meantime, *or* (b) there is any doubt that the reader will know to which authority you are referring, use a short form that identifies the name of the case. Make sure to use an identifiable case name; if one of the parties is a governmental entity, for example, use the name of the other party in the short-form cite. If you were citing again to Ohio v. Burpee, but there had been an intervening cite, use either of the following formats:

Burpee, 101 N.E.2d at 125.
Ohio v. Burpee, 101 N.E.2d at 125.

Note that it is *never* appropriate to use supra when citing cases in a brief, nor is it appropriate to use a case name cite without including reporter information. Thus, the two examples below are both wrong:

▽ BAD EXAMPLES

> Maloon, supra, at 126.
> Sanders at 135.

A.2.3
CITING TO LANGUAGE FROM CONCURRING, DISSENTING, OR PLURALITY OPINIONS

Unless your citation indicates otherwise, the reader will presume that you are citing to language from a majority opinion. Thus, when you cite to language from a plurality opinion, a concurrence, a dissent, etc., you must indicate as much in a parenthetical after the citation. Use this parenthetical even if you have mentioned the type of opinion cited in your text; it's also true for both long-form and short-form citations. Thus, the following citations are all correct:

> Donchatz v. Corn, 101 U.S. 101, 125 (2006) (plurality opinion).
> Id. at 155 (Williams, J., dissenting).
> Sanders, 101 N.E.2d at 135 (Moyer, C.J., concurring in part and dissenting in part).

A.3
CHANGING SENTENCE STRUCTURE TO ACCOMMODATE CITATION FORM

Many writers instinctively begin sentences with a citation:

> In McGuffin v. Consolidated Ice Cream Board, 44 N.E.2d 33, 39 (Ind. 1981), the court found that ice cream is a "traditional dessert" within the meaning of the Mousse Statute.

This sentence is hard to read because the citation takes up a lot of space within the sentence. In addition, this structure puts too much emphasis on the citation and not enough emphasis on the substance of the sentence. To solve this problem, some writers would separate the case name from the rest of the citation:

▽ BAD EXAMPLE

> In McGuffin v. Consolidated Ice Cream Board, the court found that ice cream is a "traditional dessert" within the meaning of the Mousse Statute. 44 N.E.2d 33, 39 (Ind. 1981).

This technique creates another problem because separating the case name from the rest of a long-form citation can confuse the reader. If a reader sees the name alone, the reader may presume that the writer is using a short form and wonder why he or she does not recognize the case name; the reader may even take a moment and try to recall the case. Upon reaching the end of the sentence, the reader would see "full citation" information and then realize that this was the first citation. Because suspense is the enemy of good legal writing, I recommend against this structure. There is a way to write a readable sentence and still use correct citation form:

⚠ GOOD EXAMPLE

Ice cream is a traditional "dessert" within the meaning of the Mousse Statute. <u>McGuffin v. Consolidated Ice Cream Bd.</u>, 44 N.E.2d 33, 39 (Ind. 1981).

This sentence emphasizes the rule itself. If you wanted to emphasize the court that decided the case, you could write the sentence this way:

⚠ GOOD EXAMPLE

The Indiana Supreme Court has held that ice cream is a "traditional dessert" within the meaning of the Mousse Statute. <u>McGuffin v. Consolidated Ice Cream Bd.</u>, 44 N.E.2d 33, 39 (Ind. 1981).

Thus, write the sentence in a way that lets you put the citation in a separate sentence at the end. Ideally, you should look at all of your citations to make sure that as few as possible are within textual sentences. Of course, if the material in the first half of a sentence comes from a source, and the second half comes from a different source (or no source), you might mislead your reader if you put a citation at the end of the sentence. In that situation, you might choose to revise so that each sentence contains information from only one source.

Your sentence structure will change depending on what you want to emphasize, but you rarely want to emphasize the citation itself. At least three of the four previous sample sentences are technically correct, but they each emphasize something different. Notice also that in two of the examples above, the word *Board* is spelled out, while in the other two examples, the word is abbreviated. Citation rules usually instruct legal writers to spell out case names that appear in textual sentences (with a few exceptions), but allow them to abbreviate case names that appear in citation sentences (also with a few exceptions).

Of course, if you have already cited to a case and wish to refer to it again, it is appropriate to use the case name only, as in the following example:

⚠ GOOD EXAMPLE

Ice cream is a "traditional dessert" within the meaning of the Mousse Statute. <u>McGuffin v. Consolidated Ice Cream Bd.</u>, 44 N.E.2d 33, 39 (Ind. 1981). In <u>McGuffin</u>, the court examined the ingredient lists for

the plaintiff's product before finding that it was a traditional dessert. 44 N.E.2d at 39.

Opening the second sentence with "In <u>McGuffin</u>" provides an effective transition. Because the case name is in the sentence, a "just the numbers" short form is permissible.

A.4
STATUTORY CITATIONS

The first thing to remember when citing statutory citations is to consult the appropriate charts in ALWD or another citation guide. Look up the jurisdiction that you are citing to and check the recommended method. Note that some citation guides illustrate statutory citations using large and small capitals, they generally advise writers to use this convention mostly in law review articles, not in briefs. Thus, presume that you should use ordinary roman type, without underlining or italics, for statutory citations.

The second thing to remember about statutory citations is that you must include a date for the statute, and that the date required is the date on the book and/or pocket part (supplement) that the language appears in. (Neither citation guide contemplates citing statutory material to a computer database.) ALWD Rule 14 and Bluebook Rule 12 address statutory citations.

Thus, a correct citation to a statute that appears partially in a bound volume dated 2011 and partially in a pocket part dated 2014 would be as follows:

Okla. Stat. tit. 19, § 222.22 (2011 & Supp. 2014).[2]

If the entire statute appeared in the pocket part (or at least the entirety of what the writer referenced), the citation would be as follows:

Okla. Stat. tit. 29, § 122.22(h) (Supp. 2014).

If the language cited appeared entirely in the bound volume, the citation would be as follows:

Okla. Stat. tit. 15, § 111.22(a) (2011).

Note that although your instincts may be to provide the date of enactment or amendment, that information is not required. You may decide to add this information, however, if you think it is relevant to your analysis:

---

[2]Note that the supplements to the United States Code are numbered; thus, you might have a cite like this: 29 U.S.C. § 122 (2009 & Supp. II 2013).

> Okla. Stat. tit. 19, § 222.22 (2011 & Supp. 2014) (effective May 27, 1987).

Finally, the third thing to remember about citing statutes is that you can use a short form to refer to statutes. The statute cited in the first example above could be cited later in the discussion by title and section number, as in "tit. 19, § 222.22," or simply by section number, as in "§ 222.22." Note that you should never start a sentence with an abbreviation or a symbol. If you wish to open the sentence with a short-form reference to a statute, spell out the first word, e.g., "Title 19, § 222.22, provides . . ." or "Section 222.22 provides. . . ."

One more note: If your citation guide allows citation to a database (e.g., ALWD rule 14.2(f)(2)), look to the website's currency information to provide the needed date information for the parenthetical. On LexisAdvance, the "current through" information is printed at the top of the page, underneath the statutory citation. On WestlawNext, look for a hotlink that says "currentness."

EXAMPLES

> Ohio Rev. Code § 4506.19 (West, WestlawNext through Files 1 to 94 of the 130th GA (2013-2014)).

> 42 U.S.C. § 2000c (LexisNexis, Lexis Advance through PL 113-96, with gaps of 113-79 and 113-93, approved 4/3/14).

Note that not every statutory compilation online contains a "current through" date. Some note only a reference to the last legislative enactment. In that situation, you might consult a resource of the legislature to determine the date of that enactment, or consult an alternative resource (that has a date) for the statutory enactment.

A.5
COMMON PUNCTUATION PROBLEMS

Unfortunately, many legal writers still have problems with basic punctuation; perhaps even more unfortunately, others will judge the competence of these writers based on punctuation mistakes. This section addresses some of the most common punctuation problems and gives commonsense advice on how to avoid them.

A.5.1
APOSTROPHE PROBLEMS

Many apostrophe problems are caused by mixing homonyms (words with different meanings that sound alike), while others are caused by a misunderstanding of the rules of possessives. This section addresses each in turn.

a. Common Homonym Problems

Many writers confuse *their*, *theirs*, and *they're*, while others confuse *its* and *it's* or *your*, *yours*, and *you're*. Making one of these errors is a sure way to irritate your reader and give an impression of carelessness. It's worth the time to study these explanations and make sure you understand the differences.

Their, Theirs, *and* They're

Use *their* to modify a noun that belongs to more than one person or entity.

⚠ GOOD EXAMPLE

This animal is their dog.

Use *theirs* to stand alone as a possessive pronoun when the noun possessed is in another part of the sentence or is in a previous sentence.

⚠ GOOD EXAMPLE

This animal is theirs.

Theirs never takes an apostrophe.

They're is a contraction meaning "they are."

⚠ GOOD EXAMPLE

They're happy to admit that this animal is their dog. The fleas are also theirs.

It's *and* Its

It's is a contraction of "it is" and, less often, of "it has."

⚠ GOOD EXAMPLES

It's time to go.
It's been a long day.

Its is the possessive form of the pronoun *it*.

⚠ GOOD EXAMPLE

The company formed its board of directors within one week of incorporation.

Note: The *it's/its* rule may be easier to remember if you don't apply logic. Just remember that someone made the arbitrary rule that the possessive of *it* does not take an apostrophe. Perhaps an easier rule to remember is that the only time *it* does take an apostrophe is when the word is used as a contraction. Because contractions are rare in formal legal writing, you should avoid using *it's*.

To find and correct *it's/its* problems, use your Search feature to search the word *it's* and then *its* and check them both against this handy reference (or any grammar reference).

Your, Yours, *and* You're

A *your/yours* mistake is particularly grating to fussy readers. Use *your* to modify a noun belonging to you.

⚠ GOOD EXAMPLE

This animal is your dog.

Use *yours* to stand alone as a possessive pronoun when the noun possessed is in another part of the sentence or is in a previous sentence.

⚠ GOOD EXAMPLE

This animal is yours.

Yours never takes an apostrophe.

You're is a contraction meaning "you are."

⚠ GOOD EXAMPLE

You're sure that this animal is your dog? Well, then, the fleas are also yours.

b. Rules of Possessives

Making a Singular Noun Possessive

If you wish to make a singular noun possessive, add an apostrophe and then an *s*. Typically, the word following the possessive noun will be the thing that belongs to the noun; on rare occasions, the thing belonging to the noun will be implied.

⚠ GOOD EXAMPLES

This house belongs to Bill (no possessive noun, so apostrophe not needed).
This is Bill's house (possessive form needed; "owned" noun in sentence).
This house is Bill's (possessive needed; "owned" noun implied).

Although there is some controversy on this point, most formal writers (including the *New York Times*) add an *[apostrophe] s* to make a singular noun possessive, even when the singular noun already ends in *s*.

⚠ GOOD EXAMPLES

This house belongs to Mr. Burns.
This is Mr. Burns's house.
This house is Mr. Burns's.
The delay in the vote was Congress's fault.
The delay in the vote can be blamed on Congress.
The fault was Congress's.

Adding *[apostrophe]* *s* when making any singular noun possessive is preferable because most people pronounce the added *s* without any problem. Furthermore, as a practical matter, one rule is easier to remember than two.

Making a Plural Noun Possessive

About this point there is no controversy. When you are making a plural noun possessive, and that plural noun already ends in *s*, add an apostrophe without an *s*.

⚠ GOOD EXAMPLES

This house belongs to the Dukes.
This is the Dukes' house.
This house is the Dukes'.

If the plural noun does not end in *s* (e.g., *children*), add *[apostrophe]* *s*.

⚠ GOOD EXAMPLES

These toys belong to the children.
These are the children's toys.
These toys are the children's.

A.5.2
SEMICOLON USE

Effective use of semicolons separates sophisticated writers from unsophisticated ones; it's worth taking a little time to learn to use them properly. Here are a few basic semicolon rules:

1. Use a semicolon to separate independent clauses[3] *not* joined by a coordinating conjunction.[4] For example:

⚠ GOOD EXAMPLE

Mr. Sanders refused to transfer to the production room; the salary of production room workers is $5,000 per year less than Mr. Sanders's current salary.

Writers often use semicolons to imply a relationship between the points made in each of the two independent clauses. In the previous example, the writer is implying a cause and effect relationship between the salary of production room workers and the reason that Mr. Sanders refused the transfer to the production room.

---

[3] An independent clause is a clause that can stand on its own as a sentence.
[4] The seven coordinating conjunctions are *and, but, or, for, nor, yet,* and *so.*

2. Use a semicolon when two independent clauses are joined with a conjunctive adverb.[5]

⚠ GOOD EXAMPLE

The salary of production room workers is $5,000 less per year than that of copy editors; therefore, Mr. Sanders refused an opportunity to transfer to the production room.

Note: Do not assume that every conjunctive adverb separates two independent clauses and therefore needs a semicolon; instead, realize that conjunctive adverbs can also appear in many other sentence structures.

3. Always use semicolons to separate items in a series if one or more of the items has internal commas. For example:

⚠ GOOD EXAMPLE

The plaintiff has owned residences at 5 Main Street, Quechee, Vermont; 4560 Hickory Street, Mishawaka, Indiana; and 303 Jackson Street, Columbus, Ohio.

You may use a couple of different techniques to search for semicolon problems. If you use too *many* semicolons, use the Find feature on your computer to search for and scrutinize your semicolons. If you use commas where semicolons belong, first, train your reader's "ear" by reading about and doing exercises on semicolon use. Second, scrutinize your longer sentences and/or your lists.

A.5.3
COMMON COMMA PROBLEMS

Although the simple little comma arrives on the punctuation scene with the baggage of many rules, only three of the most common problems are addressed here. Two rules concern when you should have a comma, and the other rule concerns where you should not have a comma.

1. Use commas between items in a series of more than two items. Make sure to put a comma before the conjunction, as in "tall, dark, and handsome."

Some informal writers swear that you should eliminate the comma after the second-to-the-last item in a series (in our example, after *dark*), but this advice is bad for legal writing. There have been law cases in which a will, a contract, or a statute had to be litigated because of a missing

---

[5]The most common conjunctive adverbs are *accordingly, also, besides, consequently, furthermore, hence, however, indeed, instead, likewise, meanwhile, moreover, nevertheless, still, then, therefore,* and *thus*. For more information, *see* Anne Enquist & Laurel Currie Oates, *Just Writing* § 8.1.6(c) (4th ed., Aspen 2013).

comma. Thus, in legal writing, make sure to include the comma before the conjunction.

▽ BAD EXAMPLE

Mr. Johnson is tall, dark and handsome.

△ GOOD EXAMPLE

Mr. Johnson is tall, dark, and handsome.

▽ BAD EXAMPLE

Ms. Gomez researched the law, wrote the motion and filed the motion.

△ GOOD EXAMPLE

Ms. Gomez researched the law, wrote the motion, and filed the motion.

2. Place a comma before a coordinating conjunction separating two independent clauses.

The most common coordinating conjunctions are *and* and *or*. When a coordinating conjunction creates a compound noun or verb, there is only one independent clause, and no comma is necessary.

△ GOOD EXAMPLES

Mr. Johnson is tall and handsome.
John laughed all the way to the bank and then made a large deposit.

However, if the two parts of the sentence are independent clauses, they should be separated with a comma.

△ GOOD EXAMPLES

Mr. Johnson is tall, and he is handsome, too.
John laughed all the way to the bank, and then he made a deposit.

For most people, the hard part about using this comma properly is correctly identifying an independent clause. Usually, you can identify an independent clause by looking for an independent subject and a verb, as long as the clause is not introduced by a subordinating conjunction. In the sentence "John laughed all the way to the bank and then made a deposit," there is a verb (*made*) after the *and*, but there is no separate subject—the subject from the first, independent, clause carries over into the second, dependent, clause. However, in the sentence "John laughed all the way to the bank, and then he made a deposit," you find a separate subject (*he*) for the verb (*made*) in the second clause, which means that it is an independent clause. Although this rule is not foolproof, it can help you separate the dependent clauses from the independent clauses.

3. Unless a clause intervenes, do *not* put a comma between a subject and a verb.

▼ BAD EXAMPLE

The infamous rule against perpetuities, is hard to understand.

▲ GOOD EXAMPLES

The infamous rule against perpetuities is hard to understand.
The infamous rule against perpetuities, which is the bane of many lawyers, is hard to understand.

This appendix is by no means comprehensive. If you have problems that are not covered here, you may wish to consult Anne Enquist & Laurel Currie Oates, *Just Writing* (4th ed., Aspen 2013), or Mary Barnard Ray & Jill J. Ramsfield, *Legal Writing: Getting It Right and Getting It Written* (5th ed., West 2010).

FOR REFERENCE: COURT WEBSITE INFORMATION

Almost every court posts relevant rules on its website. These rules may include the applicable state or federal rules of civil procedure as well as local rules and standing orders.

The rules of the United States Supreme Court, which have been referenced throughout the text, can currently be found at this website: http://www.supremecourt.gov/ctrules/2013RulesoftheCourt.pdf

Some federal courts combine the generally applicable rules with their own local rules. At the following link, for example, the tenth circuit's local rules are interspersed with the relevant Federal Rules of Appellate Procedure: http://www.ca10.uscourts.gov/sites/default/files/clerk/FRAP%20RULES%20FINAL%202014-11-15-2013.pdf

Other courts may post their local rules as a separate document, as this link shows: http://www.state.il.us/court/AppellateCourt/LocalRules/3rd.pdf

If you are writing a motion brief, remember that many trial courts do not use rules to articulate formal requirements for these briefs. Nevertheless, consult the appropriate civil or criminal rules, the local rules, or the court's standing orders for any existing requirements for motion briefs or oral arguments. This link shows a standing order regarding civil motions for summary judgment: http://www.ohsd.uscourts.gov/judges/dlott/standing%20order%20civil%20may%202014.pdf

Instead of a formal "standing order," some judges may post tips or guidelines for practitioners: http://www.ohsd.uscourts.gov/judges/frost/Practice%20Pointers%20revised%201-2013.pdf

If you are looking for the rules of a particular court, search for the court by its full name, and then look on the main page for a link to the court's rules. Be careful when searching. Sites other than the court's official website may give you inaccurate information or no information due to "link rot" or other problems. Be sure to link to the court's official website (perhaps designated with a "dot-gov" url) so that you can be certain to have the most up-to-date rules. Useful search terms include phrases like "standing orders," "standard orders," "general orders," "forms and procedures," and, of course, "local rules."

SAMPLE BRIEFS

Many writing professors worry about providing samples because some students follow them too closely, imitating structure, arguments, or style that may have been appropriate for the issues in the sample but may not be appropriate for the issues in the student's brief. Furthermore, no sample is perfect. In the following sample student briefs, I have included annotations that identify strengths, explain possible problems, or point out unusual structures that may not be appropriate in different cases. By design, not all possible problems are identified. You should not, of course, rely on the law in these samples. Your professor may have you critique the sample briefs as part of your course work, or may identify other issues that you should consider when deciding whether certain samples are effective models for certain types of briefs.

The sample appellate briefs in this appendix follow Supreme Court rules as to format, and the sample motion brief follows a commonly acceptable motion format. All of the sample briefs follow publishing conventions rather than word processing conventions. Thus, for example, briefs that you prepare for a law school course may need to be double-spaced (other than headings and double-indented quotations), may require different margins, and may require other different spacing conventions. Of course, you should always consult local rules, whether those rules are rules of a court or rules of a classroom.

No. 97-1147

IN THE SUPREME COURT OF THE UNITED STATES
FALL TERM, 1998

————————————————

STATE OF MINNESOTA,

Petitioner,

v.

WAYNE THOMAS CARTER and MELVIN JOHNS,

Respondents.

————————————————

ON WRIT OF CERTIORARI TO THE SUPREME COURT OF MINNESOTA

————————————————

BRIEF FOR THE PETITIONER

Sarah Student
55 West 12th Avenue
Columbus, Ohio 43210
Counsel for the Petitioner

QUESTIONS PRESENTED ❶

1. Should the Court expand the class of individuals who can claim a legitimate expectation of privacy under the Fourth Amendment to include a temporary invitee who is present on the premises only to conduct an illegal business activity? ❷

2. Should a police officer standing in a publicly used apartment common area, who is able to plainly see an apartment interior, be required to shield his eyes because the observation would constitute a Fourth Amendment ''search''?

❶ You are not *required* to have more than one question presented, but you may if your case presents more than one dispositive issue. See §9.1 for more information on drafting questions presented.

❷ The writer uses "expand" early in the question and "illegal business activity" at the end of the question to make the opponent's premise seem ridiculous and to encourage the reader to answer "of course not."

i

TABLE OF CONTENTS

3 The brief has no "parties to the proceedings" page because all parties are listed on the cover page.

4 These two subheads do not contain the word *because*—they are the "becauses" for point heading B: They show why society is not prepared to recognize the Respondents' expectation of privacy as reasonable.

5 Heading 2 presents an alternative, in case the court disagrees with heading 1. These two subheads are the "becauses" for point heading 2: They show why the Respondents' activity was not valuable to society under the standard.

6 This heading is a policy argument, noting that it's just a bad idea generally to have too many people claiming a legitimate expectation of privacy. *Note that it does not label itself as a policy argument.*

7 These two subheads are the "becauses" for point heading A: They show how the place that Officer Thielen stood proves that no Fourth Amendment search occurred.

8 These two subheads are the "becauses" for point heading B: They show how Officer Thielen's actions prove that no Fourth Amendment search occurred.

9 This brief has an unusually high number of headings and subheadings. For information about deciding how to break your argument into parts and subparts, see §9.4.3.

TABLE OF AUTHORITIES

United States Supreme Court Cases:

10 If a case name or other authority name is particularly long, use a "hanging indent" like this so that only case names appear at the left margin.

11 Notice that the writer does not use *passim* with these frequently cited cases. *Passim* should be used *only* when citation is so frequent that listing the pages would not help the reader to find the pages on which the authority is cited. The reader can use the table of authorities to note the most significant authorities at a glance and then to find the places in the brief in which those authorities are used as support.

STATE COURT CASES

12 Separating all of the state court opinions into separate categories may provide more categorization than is necessary. When deciding whether to create categories, ask (1) whether court rules or orders require or prefer the extra categories, or (2) whether the extra categories would help the reader, the user, or both.

IN THE SUPREME COURT OF THE UNITED STATES 🔴13

No. 97-1147

STATE OF MINNESOTA,

Petitioner,

v.

WAYNE THOMAS CARTER and MELVIN JOHNS,

Respondents.

ON WRIT OF CERTIORARI TO THE SUPREME COURT OF MINNESOTA

BRIEF FOR THE PETITIONER

OPINIONS BELOW

The decision of the Supreme Court of Minnesota reversing the trial court's decision in State v. Carter is reported at State v. Carter, 569 N.W.2d 169 (Minn. 1997). The decision of the Supreme Court of Minnesota reversing the trial court's decision in State v. Johns is reported at State v. Johns, 569 N.W.2d 180 (Minn. 1997). The decision of the Minnesota Court of Appeals affirming the trial court's decision in State v. Carter is reported at State v. Carter, 545 N.W.2d 695 (Minn. Ct. App. 1996). The decision of the Minnesota Court of Appeals affirming the trial court's decision in State v. Johns is unreported and can be found at Record D-1. The trial court's decisions in State v. Carter and in State v. Johns, denying the motion to suppress, are unreported and can be found at Record E-1.

JURISDICTION

The judgment of the Supreme Court of Minnesota was entered on September 11, 1997. Petitioners filed the Petition for Writ of Certiorari on December 29, 1997. On March 9, 1998, this Court granted the Petition. The jurisdiction of this Court rests on 28 U.S.C. §1257 🔴14 (1997).

CONSTITUTIONAL PROVISION INVOLVED

The pertinent part of the Fourth Amendment to the United States Constitution provides: "The right of the people to be secure in their persons, houses, papers and effects, against unreasonable searches and seizures, shall not be violated." U.S. Const. amend. IV.

1

13 Note that the use of "internal captions" is not required. If you do not include a complete internal caption of this type, it is helpful to at least include a one-line heading indicating the type of document, e.g., "Brief for the Petitioner."

14 This statute is one of the two statutes that are most frequently the basis of jurisdiction in the United States Supreme Court. Be sure to cite the statute that is appropriate for your case.

STANDARD OF REVIEW

The Minnesota Supreme Court erred as a matter of law when it reversed the trial court's decision. This Court accepts the trial court's findings of fact unless clearly erroneous, but decides questions of law de novo. See United States v. U.S. Gypsum Co., 333 U.S. 364, 395 (1948). A finding is clearly erroneous when, although there is evidence to support it, the reviewing court on the entire evidence is left with the definite and firm conviction that a mistake has been committed. Id. at 395. When the Court reviews conclusions of law de novo, it makes an independent review, and is free to arrive at its own holding. See First Options of Chicago v. Kaplan, 514 U.S. 938, 947 (1995). **15**

STATEMENT OF THE CASE

This Court is being asked to reverse a Minnesota Supreme Court judgment that Respondents were entitled to suppress evidence on Fourth Amendment grounds. The issue at hand is the constitutionality of an officer's naked-eye observation of Respondents as they bagged cocaine in an apartment in which they were neither residents nor overnight guests. **16**

On May 15, 1994, a confidential informant reported to Officer Jim Thielen that drug activity was occurring in a nearby apartment. Record E-l. The informant specified that he or she had viewed the occupants of 3943 South Valley View, Apartment 103, sitting at a table placing a white powdery substance into plastic bags. Record E-2. The informant, who also gave the officer details about a car the informant believed the apartment occupants were using, said that he or she had seen the drug activity from outside the apartment's ground-level window when the informant had walked past the window. Record G-9, G-39. **17**

At approximately 8:00 P.M., in response to the informant's report, the officer drove to the apartment complex and then walked on a grassy common area to a spot one to one-and-a-half feet from the window of Apartment 103. Record G-45, G-13. From his location in the apartment complex yard, Officer Thielen could see into the interior of Apartment 103. Record E-2. At no time during his observation did Officer Thielen place his hands along the window. Record G-13. He used no flashlight or other device to supplement his natural senses. **18**

Though the grassy area on which Officer Thielen stood featured some shrubs and trees, the shrubs were not planted immediately in front of the apartment window to create an enclosure that prevented the public from gaining entrance to the area. See Record E-10. The area outside the window was one on which residents and nonresidents regularly walked and interacted with others. Record G-44, G-32, G-68. Children commonly played there, and on at least one occasion a bicycle was left directly outside Thompson's window. Record G-71. **19**

Through gaps in the drawn horizontal mini-blinds on the window, Officer Thielen observed the same scene the informant had described to him: two males and one female sitting at a kitchen table handling a white powdery substance. Record E-2. One male placed the powder onto the table, then passed the substance to the second male, who placed the powder into plastic bags. Id. The second male gave the plastic bag to the female, who cut off the ends of the bag for sealing. Id. The officer observed the activity for 15 minutes, during which time the three individuals filled five or six bags. Record G-13, G-14.

Officer Thielen then contacted South Metro Drug Task Force Officer Kevin Kallestad, who applied for warrants to search the apartment and the car that the informant

15 Because the writer never discusses the significance of findings of facts in her argument, she need not draw the Court's attention to the standard of review for such findings.

16 Note that the writer provides context by telling the Court what it is being asked to decide. While the facts included are certainly more sympathetic to the petitioner's argument, they are facts and not legal conclusions, and thus are appropriately used here.

17 Note the use of the words "specified" and "details" to heighten the credibility of the informant's information.

18 Here, the writer creates a position of emphasis with a paragraph break, to emphasize the things that the officer did not do and that are crucial to her argument.

19 This record was a complex one; notice how the writer assembled facts from various places in the record ("E-10," "G-44, G-32, G-68"). The citations increase the reliability of the fact statement and make it easy for the Court to check the validity of the facts.

indicated may have belonged to the apartment occupants. Record F-7. At approximately 10:30 P.M., police stopped the car as it left the premises. Record E-3. Officer Thielen recognized the driver, Respondent Wayne Thomas Carter, and the passenger, Respondent Melvin Johns, as the males he had observed in the apartment. Record G-21, G-22. Officer Thielen identified Carter as the individual he had seen putting the white substance onto the table and dividing it into piles and Johns as the man who placed the piles into the bags. Id.

Respondents were arrested, and when police executed a search warrant on the vehicle, they discovered pagers, a scale, and more than 40 grams of a white mixture that later tested positive for cocaine. Record E-3. After Respondents' arrests, police returned to the apartment and arrested its occupant, Kimberly Thompson. When police executed a search warrant on the apartment, they found plastic bags and cocaine residue on the kitchen table. State v. Carter, 569 N.W.2d 169, 172 (Minn. 1997).

Both Petitioner and Respondents stipulated that the sole lessee of Apartment 103 was Kimberly Thompson. **20** Officer Thielen identified Thompson as the woman he had viewed cutting off the ends of the baggies and placing the baggies in piles. Record E-3. Nothing in the record indicates any personal or social relationship between Thompson and the Respondents. See Record E-4. No evidence was presented that Respondents lived at Apartment 103 long term, were overnight guests, or were related to the leaseholder. See Record E-7. Both Respondents are residents of Chicago, Illinois, and no evidence was presented as to their status in the apartment except that the officer viewed them from outside the window for a short period of time on May 15, 1994. See Record E-3, E-4. None of Respondents' personal effects or clothing were found on the premises. See Record G-2.

At trial, Respondents moved to suppress all evidence obtained as a result of Officer Thielen's initial observation of the apartment, on the grounds that his observation constituted a warrantless search. Record E-7. On December 16, 1994, the District Court for the First Judicial District in the County of Dakota denied Respondents' motion to suppress. Record E-5. The court held that Respondents had no standing to challenge the officer's observations through Thompson's window, because Respondents failed to present any evidence that their expectations of privacy were expectations that society is prepared to recognize as reasonable. Record E-7. The district court further held that the officer's observation was not a Fourth Amendment search. The court found that Officer Thielen's observation was made from a grassy common area outside the curtilage of the apartment and that the observation was limited to scenes in plain view, and therefore, the observation did not violate any reasonable expectation of privacy. Record E-9. **21**

After Respondents were found guilty, they appealed to the Minnesota Court of Appeals. The Minnesota Court of Appeals affirmed in State v. Carter, concluding that Carter did not have standing to bring a motion to suppress the evidence. State v. Carter, 545 N.W.2d 695, 697 (Minn. Ct. App. 1996). The Minnesota Court of Appeals also affirmed in State v. Johns, concluding that the officer acted reasonably in walking to the window and in continuing to observe. State v. Johns, No. C9-95-1765, 1996 WL 310305, at *2 (Minn. Ct. App. June 11, 1996). Respondents appealed to the Supreme Court of Minnesota, which reversed the trial court's judgment. State v. Carter, 569 N.W.2d 169 (Minn. 1997); State v. Johns, 569 N.W.2d 180 (Minn. 1997). The State filed a Writ of Certiorari, arguing that Carter and Johns lacked a legitimate expectation of privacy in Thompson's apartment and that Officer Thielen's observation was not a search. The Supreme Court granted certiorari to review the decision of the Minnesota Supreme Court. **22**

20 This paragraph gives details to support the assertion that Respondents had no expectation of privacy in the apartment. The paragraph starts with a topic sentence, focusing on the "sole lessee," and backs it up with details that will lead the reader to conclude that respondents' sole connection with the apartment was to use it to bag cocaine.

21 Notice how the writer goes into more detail on the holdings at the trial court level, which were in the petitioner's favor. Take care not to go into *exhaustive* detail; that will usually backfire.

22 The petitioner ends on a positive note, observing that the Court has granted certiorari to her client.

23 Notice the difference between the objective opening of a fact statement and the argumentative opening of the summary of the argument. Ideally, the opening sentence or sentences of the summary of the argument should crystallize your main point or points in a dramatic and easily understandable way. Because this case has two distinct issues (and two distinct questions presented), this writer uses two sentences to state the issues.

24 This paragraph gives an overview of the two main points of the argument; the rest fleshes out the more specific arguments.

25 Although the writer uses many legal assertions that would usually require citations, the writer follows summary of the argument conventions by not citing to them, focusing on the arguments rather than authority at this stage. For this summary, it may well have been appropriate for the writer to cite <u>Minnesota v. Olson</u>, <u>Katz v. United States</u>, and <u>California v. Ciraolo</u> because those cases are particularly crucial to the argument. For a discussion of when citations are appropriate in the summary, see §9.3.

SUMMARY OF THE ARGUMENT

People who bag cocaine near a window in another's basement apartment do not have a reasonable expectation of privacy. Further, an officer does not conduct a search when he observes this activity simply by looking through a gap in the blinds while standing in a common area outside the apartment. **23** Accordingly, this Court should reverse the Minnesota Supreme Court's judgment.

The Minnesota Supreme Court incorrectly reversed the trial court's denial of Respondents' motion to suppress. First, it erroneously ruled that Respondents had a legitimate expectation of privacy while in another's apartment for the sole purpose of illegally bagging cocaine. Second, it wrongly held that an officer conducted a search when he merely observed criminal activity in plain view from an area outside the apartment's curtilage. **24**

This Court's Fourth Amendment jurisprudence demonstrates that the Minnesota Supreme Court's ruling was erroneous. In order to invoke the Fourth Amendment's protections, an individual must prove that he had a legitimate expectation of privacy. An individual possesses a legitimate expectation of privacy when he demonstrates that he has both a subjective expectation of privacy and an expectation of privacy that society is prepared to view as reasonable.

Respondents were sitting at an illuminated kitchen table facing a window of a basement apartment and packaging cocaine. Respondents should have realized that a passerby could have looked into the apartment and noticed the illegal activity occurring within the apartment. Thus, Respondents can claim no subjective expectation of privacy.

Additionally, any subjective expectation of privacy Respondents possessed is not one that society is prepared to recognize as reasonable in light of longstanding social customs that serve functions recognized as valuable by society. As non-overnight guests, they lacked the connection with the premises that legitimizes an expectation of privacy. Even if shorter-term guests can claim the protection of the Fourth Amendment, only those short-term guests who are present for socially permissible and valuable reasons qualify for Fourth Amendment protection. Respondents were present only to conduct criminal business activities, and therefore did not have an expectation of privacy that was reasonable in light of longstanding social customs that serve functions recognized as valuable by society.

Furthermore, even assuming that Respondents are entitled to invoke the Fourth Amendment's protections, no Fourth Amendment search occurred. A search occurs only when governmental agents intrude upon an area in which an individual has a reasonable expectation of privacy. **25** A reasonable expectation of privacy is violated when an officer intrudes upon the home or its curtilage, the area immediately surrounding the home that shares the same private characteristics as the home. Conversely, there is no violation of a reasonable expectation of privacy, and therefore no search, when an officer merely stands outside the curtilage of a residence and observes what is in plain view.

In the case at bar, the officer stood in a publicly accessible common area outside the apartment's curtilage. The officer used only his natural senses to observe what was in plain view. He conducted his observation without physical intrusion, without the use of any device, and in a manner that any member of the public could have employed. The officer's conduct violated no reasonable expectation of privacy and therefore was not a Fourth Amendment search.

For the above reasons, this Court should hold that Respondents had no legitimate expectation of privacy in the apartment and that the observations of the officer did not constitute a search. This Court should reverse the Minnesota Supreme Court's judgment.

ARGUMENT

I. **As temporary business invitees present in another's residence for the sole purpose of packaging drugs, Respondents had no legitimate expectation of privacy and, thus, may not invoke the Fourth Amendment's protections.**

Individuals invited to another's residence temporarily and for the sole purpose of conducting illegal business do not possess a legitimate expectation of privacy. Respondents, who were present in Thompson's apartment for a very short period of time and for the sole purpose of packaging drugs, have no legitimate expectation of privacy and thus, may not invoke the Fourth Amendment's protections. Therefore, this Court must reverse. [26]

[27] The Fourth Amendment to the United States Constitution guarantees "[t]he right of the people to be secure in their persons, houses, papers, and effects, against unreasonable searches and seizures." U.S. Const. amend. IV. Only individuals who demonstrate a legitimate expectation of privacy can claim the protection of the Fourth Amendment. Minnesota v. Olson, 495 U.S. 91, 95 (1990); Smith v. Maryland, 442 U.S. 735, 740 (1979).

In order to demonstrate a legitimate expectation of privacy, an individual must satisfy a two-pronged test set forth in Katz v. United States, 389 U.S. 347 (1967). First, an individual must exhibit an actual, subjective expectation of privacy in the searched premises at the time of the alleged search. Id. at 361 (Harlan, J., concurring). Second, the individual's expectation must be one that society is prepared to recognize as "reasonable." Id. The expectation must be reasonable in light of "longstanding social customs that serve functions recognized as valuable by society." Olson, 495 U.S. at 98. The proponent of a motion to suppress bears the burden of proving that he or she had a legitimate expectation of privacy. See Rakas v. Illinois, 439 U.S. 128, 130-31 n.1 (1978).

[28] In the case at bar, Respondents failed to demonstrate a subjective expectation of privacy. Respondents engaged in illegal acts in a well-lit room directly in front of a window that faced a public area. Even assuming Respondents did possess a subjective expectation of privacy, Respondents failed to show that their subjective expectation of privacy was one that was reasonable in light of longstanding social customs that serve functions recognized as valuable by society. Respondents were temporary invitees whose activities within the apartment were both criminal and commercial. Bagging cocaine is not a social custom that serves functions recognized as valuable by society.

[29] Respondents had neither a subjective expectation of privacy nor an expectation of privacy that society is prepared to recognize as reasonable, so they cannot claim a legitimate expectation of privacy. Having demonstrated no legitimate expectation of privacy, they may not assert a Fourth Amendment challenge. Because this Court should be extremely reluctant to expand the class of persons who can claim legitimate expectations of privacy, and because Respondents have not demonstrated that they fit within any group that has such a claim, this Court should reverse.

[26] This paragraph gives a quick summary of the writer's whole argument for this section. Because this argument alone is dispositive, it's appropriate to state that the Court must reverse if it accepts the argument.

[27] In these two paragraphs, the writer continues to provide legal backstory for her roman I argument. Note how she starts with the Fourth Amendment—the central rule at issue—and then moves to the cases that lay out the rules about "expectation of privacy," which is the rule at issue in this section (roman I) of the argument.

[28] In this paragraph, the writer applies the rule to the facts in a conclusory way to support her assertion that the respondents have no legitimate expectation of privacy. It would be appropriate to do this even more succinctly.

[29] In this paragraph, the writer provides a roadmap to the specific arguments that will be addressed as subpoints within the roman I heading. Note that not all roadmaps must contain enumerated points.

A. Respondents failed to meet their burden of proving that they had a legitimate expectation of privacy because they introduced absolutely no evidence regarding their status in Thompson's apartment.

Respondents bore the burden of proving that they had a legitimate expectation of privacy that entitled them to invoke the Fourth Amendment's protection. Respondents failed to introduce any evidence whatsoever regarding their status in Thompson's apartment and, therefore, failed to meet their burden of proof. Because Respondents have proved no legitimate expectation of privacy, this Court must reverse.

The proponent of a motion to suppress bears the burden of establishing that his or her own rights were violated by the challenged search. **30** Before a criminal defendant can bring a motion to suppress evidence on the basis that it was obtained in violation of the Fourth Amendment, the defendant must show that he or she is a proper party to assert the claim of illegality and to seek the remedy of exclusion. See Rakas v. Illinois, 439 U.S. 128, 130-31 n.1 (1978); Simmons v. United States, 390 U.S. 377, 389-90 (1968); Jones v. United States, 362 U.S. 257, 261 (1960) (indicating that "it is entirely proper to require of one who seeks to challenge the legality of a search as the basis for suppressing relevant evidence that he allege, and if the allegation be disputed, that he establish, that he himself was a victim of an invasion of privacy"). The defendant in a criminal trial bears the burden of proving that his or her expectation of privacy was a reasonable one. Florida v. Riley, 488 U.S. 445, 455 (1989) (O'Connor, J., concurring).

31 In the present case, Respondents made a motion to suppress on Fourth Amendment grounds, Record E-7, and therefore bore the burden of proving they had a legitimate expectation of privacy. Yet the record is entirely devoid of evidence of any connection between Respondents and the apartment that would give rise to a legitimate expectation of privacy. The trial court explicitly found that "[n]o evidence was presented as to [Respondents'] status in the apartment" other than that Officer Thielen viewed Respondents packaging cocaine inside the apartment for a very short time on May 15, 1994. Record at E-4. The record's sparseness is attributable only to Respondents' failure to introduce evidence regarding their status.

Having failed to meet their burden of proving a legitimate expectation of privacy, Respondents cannot attempt to assert a Fourth Amendment claim. This Court must reverse.

B. Respondents had no legitimate expectation of privacy because any subjective expectation they might have had while temporarily in another's home for the sole purpose of conducting illegal business was not one society recognizes as reasonable.

Even assuming that Respondents possessed a subjective expectation of privacy, Respondents failed to establish that their subjective expectation of privacy was one that society views as reasonable as required by the second prong of the Katz test. Katz v. United States, 389 U.S. at 361 (Harlan, J., concurring). **32** Respondents' expectation was not one society is prepared to recognize as reasonable because (1) society is prepared to recognize as reasonable only the privacy expectations of overnight guests, and (2) even if society is prepared to recognize as reasonable the privacy expectations of non-overnight guests, society is not prepared to recognize as reasonable the privacy expectations of business invitees present only to commit the crime of packaging drugs.

30 Although a writer may sometimes violate convention by failing to cite to authority for legal assertions (more typically, as in a summary of the argument; less typically, in a roadmap, as in the previous paragraph), the writer *should* have a citation to legal authority here. For guidance on when readers expect citations to authority, see §6.5.1.

31 This argument is placed first because it must come first logically. However, because the writer has other arguments that she believes will carry more weight, she does not complete a thorough analysis of her point.

32 The backstory here is appropriately quite minimal, but it provides context for the argument and follows up with a roadmap to the subpoints.

6

1. The Olson rule dictates that only overnight guests have a connection to a premises that gives rise to a legitimate expectation of privacy.

Respondents, who introduced no evidence that they were anything other than temporary, transient visitors on the premises for the sole purpose of conducting illegal business, simply do not belong to the class of individuals who have an expectation of privacy that society is prepared to recognize as reasonable. Therefore, they do not have a legitimate expectation of privacy in Thompson's apartment and cannot assert a Fourth Amendment challenge to any alleged search of the premises.

33 In 1990, this Court established the rule that "status as an overnight quest is alone enough to show that [a defendant had] an expectation of privacy in the home that society is prepared to recognize as reasonable." Minnesota v. Olson, 495 U.S. 91, 96-97 (1990). **34** In Olson the Court found that a defendant suspected of driving the getaway car used in a robbery-murder had a legitimate expectation of privacy in his girlfriend's duplex sufficient to challenge a warrantless entry into the duplex. **35** Id. at 100. Olson, who had been at the duplex for several days, had a change of clothes at the duplex and had spent the previous night there. Id. at 97 n.6. **36** This Court reasoned that because staying overnight with a host is a socially necessary practice, and because all citizens share the expectation that an overnight guest's host will respect the guest's privacy, Olson had a sufficient interest in his girlfriend's home to assert a Fourth Amendment challenge. Id. at 98-99. His expectation of privacy was one that society recognizes as reasonable. Id. **37**

In establishing the rule that overnight guests have a legitimate expectation of privacy sufficient to challenge a Fourth Amendment search, the Olson Court repeatedly emphasized the overnight nature of the defendant's stay, thus illustrating that the holding does not cover a shorter-term guest. Id. at 97-100. No language in the opinion expressly states that the holding extends beyond overnight guests. The Court's reasoning and examples indicate that the Fourth Amendment protects only those who permanently reside on the premises and those who expect the same protection because they reside on the premises overnight.

The Olson Court discussed at length the social custom of staying overnight with friends or family when traveling to a strange city and the concomitant expectation of privacy that comes with seeking overnight shelter in another's home. The Court reasoned that an expectation of privacy arises because "[we] are at our most vulnerable when we are asleep because we cannot monitor our own safety or the security of our belongings." Id. at 99. While the police found Olson in his host's closet at 3 P.M., the Court's analysis indicated that he had earned the right to assert Fourth Amendment rights in the home because he was an overnight guest in the home the night before. Id. **38**

The factors that gave Olson the right to challenge a search of the residence all hinged on his overnight status. The overnight guest, not the shorter-term invitee, will have a "measure of control over the premises" when "the host is away or asleep." Id. at 99. The overnight guest, not the shorter-term invitee, is most likely not to "be confined to a restricted area of the house." Id. The overnight guest, not the shorter-term invitee, has a host who is "willing to share his house and his privacy with his guest." Id.

7

33 Here, the writer provides the rule in the topic sentence, but, appropriately saves the citation for the end of the sentence.

34 The writer explicitly states the rule here and uses the explanation section of the formula to (1) demonstrate how the rule was applied in Olson, and (2) demonstrate that the Olson Court did not intend the rule to be expanded to guests other than "overnight" guests. In the application section, she will show that the respondents cannot be characterized as overnight guests and thus cannot benefit from this rule.

35 This sentence provides readers with many of the elements necessary for a complete case description: the issue ("standing" to challenge a warrantless entry into the duplex), the disposition of that issue (his status was sufficient to allow him to challenge the entry), and some of the facts (he was in his girlfriend's duplex).

36 Here are more details on the facts, provided because the issue of whether someone is an overnight guest is a fact-intensive inquiry.

37 These last two sentences provide the Court's reasoning. Though some lower courts have been confused as to the scope of the Olson rule, the reasoning in Olson and this Court's emphasis on Olson's overnight status indicate that the holding does not extend to invitees who are not overnight guests.

38 The analysis of Olson is lengthy only because it is the source of the rule and illustrates one of the most controversial issues in the case.

39 The writer should
identify how many circuits
have decided this issue,
and cite at least one that
has gone the other way,
so that the Court does
not leave the brief to go
looking for the answer.

40 Note that strong
parentheticals will have
three or four of the needed
case description elements
of issue, facts, disposition,
and reasoning.

41 Disposition is indicated
here.

42 Issue is indicated here.

43 Reasoning is implied
here.

44 Facts are indicated
here.

45 Facts are indicated
here.

46 Disposition is indicated
here.

47 Issue is indicated here.

48 These analyses are
good, but in order to
provide a complete
picture, the writer should
identify how many
courts have decided
this issue the other way.
Otherwise, she is seen to
be hiding the ball, and
the Court may doubt
the significance of these
cases.

49 Facts are indicated
here.

50 Disposition is indicated
here.

51 Issue is indicated here.

Furthermore, a significant number of courts that have examined <u>Olson</u> have applied the <u>Olson</u> rule narrowly. **39** Several courts have held that temporary, non-overnight presence for the purpose of illegal drug activity clearly falls outside of the <u>Olson</u> rule. <u>See, e.g.,Terry v. Martin</u>, 120 F.3d 661, 664 (7th Cir. 1997) (**40** holding that the legitimate expectation of privacy realized by overnight guests did not extend **41** to confer Fourth Amendment standing **42** on temporary visitors **43** present in an apartment for the purpose of buying heroin **44**); <u>United States v. Hicks</u>, 978 F.2d 722, 724 (D.C. Cir. 1992) (holding that a guest who used an apartment to distribute cocaine **45** had no **46** legitimate expectation of privacy **47**).

Additionally, a number of lower courts have flatly declined to extend <u>Olson</u> to casual or temporary visitors. **48** <u>See State v. Wise</u>, 879 S.W.2d 494, 505 (Mo. 1994) (holding that a defendant who was in an apartment to use the telephone **49** had no **50** legitimate expectation of privacy **51**); <u>Villarreal v. State</u>, 893 S.W.2d 559, 561 (Tex. Ct. App. 1994) (declining to extend the <u>Olson</u> expectation to an invited guest who had not stayed overnight but "was welcome to stay if he wanted to"). Some courts have even declined to extend <u>Olson</u> to cover party guests. <u>See, e.g.</u>, <u>Fisher v. State</u>, 665 So. 2d 1014 (Ala. Crim. App. 1995); <u>Lewis v. United States</u>, 594 A.2d 542, 546 (D.C. 1991). For example, in <u>Lewis,</u> the court held that a party guest who happened to fall asleep for several hours in a bedroom could not assert a Fourth Amendment challenge to a search of the apartment. <u>Id.</u> at 545. The court ruled that because Lewis offered no evidence that he had been invited to spend the night or intended to do so, he had not shown a legitimate expectation of privacy. <u>Id.</u> The court reasoned that a mere guest who is not spending the night is substantially different from the overnight guest who receives standing under <u>Olson</u>. <u>Id.</u>

In the present case, the record bears no evidence that Respondents were invited overnight guests. <u>See</u> Record E-4. Respondents were not lessees of the apartment. Record G-5. While Respondents were residents of another state, the record provides no evidence as to Respondents' status in the apartment or any link they may have had with it or with the lessee. <u>See</u> Record E-3. Indeed, the only evidence of Respondents' connection to the apartment is the police officer's testimony that he saw Respondents bagging cocaine inside the apartment for a period of 15 minutes. Record E-3. The sparseness of the record and the complete absence of evidence that Respondents intended to spend the night lead only to the conclusion that Respondents were temporary visitors who could not claim any parallel characteristics to the overnight guest in <u>Olson</u>. Record E-8.

The Minnesota Supreme Court conceded that "it is undisputed that Carter failed to produce any evidence that he was a 'guest' of Thompson's, let alone an 'overnight guest.'" <u>State v. Carter</u>, 569 N.W.2d 169, 175 (Minn. 1997). Given this Court's emphasis on the special privacy concerns of sleeping guests and the social custom of staying overnight, Respondents do not fall within the <u>Olson</u> rule and cannot claim an expectation of privacy that society is prepared to recognize as reasonable. Thus, they have no legitimate expectation of privacy and are not entitled to claim the protection of an Amendment that was not designed for their use.

> **2. Even if the Olson rule extends to non-overnight guests, Respondents' expectation of privacy is unreasonable because they were present only to conduct illegal business that is not valuable to society.**

If <u>Olson</u> does not stand for the proposition that only overnight guests may assert a Fourth Amendment challenge, it at least stands for the proposition that only a very limited category of guests may do so. The limited category includes only those guests whose connections to the home give rise to an expectation of privacy that society is prepared to recognize as reasonable. See Olson, 495 U.S. at 98-99. Respondents failed to demonstrate that their expectation of privacy was one society is prepared to recognize as reasonable. The Minnesota Supreme Court found that Respondents demonstrated an expectation of privacy that society is prepared to recognize as reasonable because they were present in the apartment "to conduct a common task." State v. Carter, 569 N.W.2d 169, 176 (Minn. 1997). This Court should reverse the decision of the Minnesota Supreme Court because (1) the distribution of drugs is not a longstanding social custom that serves functions recognized as valuable by society, and (2) Respondents were not "guests" in a home but rather were business invitees on the property for a purely commercial purpose, and therefore lost the Fourth Amendment protection normally associated with the home.

a. Illegal drug distribution is not a longstanding social custom that serves functions recognized as valuable by society.

Respondents, whose purpose for being on the premises was purely criminal, cannot claim that their expectation of privacy was reasonable in light of longstanding social customs that serve functions recognized as valuable by society. Therefore, they do not have a legitimate expectation of privacy in Thompson's apartment and cannot assert a Fourth Amendment challenge to any alleged search of the premises.

Society is prepared to recognize an individual's expectation of privacy as reasonable only when the individual was present on the premises for a purpose society deems permissible and valuable. Rakas, 439 U.S. at 144 n.12 (indicating that a legitimate expectation is one that is rooted in "understandings that are recognized and permitted by society"). In Olson, this Court held that an overnight guest's expectation of privacy was legitimate because the act of staying overnight is a "longstanding social custom that serves functions recognized as valuable by society." Olson, 439 U.S. at 98.

Generally, lower courts applying the Olson test have looked to the social utility of the defendants' activities when determining whether finding a legitimate expectation of privacy will promote a "longstanding social custom that serves functions recognized as valuable by society." First, in 1992, a California court found that a defendant who moved to suppress items seized at his brother's apartment while the defendant was babysitting there had a legitimate expectation of privacy. People v. Moreno, 3 Cal. Rptr. 2d 66, 70 (Cal. Ct. App. 1992). The court cited Olson and indicated that, "[l]ike 'staying overnight in another's home,' babysitting 'is a longstanding social custom that serves functions recognized as valuable by society.'" Id. at 70. **52** Because the babysitter's activity was permissible and valuable to society, society was prepared to recognize his expectation of privacy as reasonable. He therefore had a legitimate expectation of privacy and could challenge a Fourth Amendment search. Id.

52 The writer should include the Olson cite parenthetically here.

Second, in 1993, a court in the District of Columbia found that a defendant who regularly visited a home to feed and care for the homeowner's mentally disabled adult son had a legitimate expectation of privacy "rooted in understandings that are recognized and permitted by society." Junior v. United States, 634 A.2d 411, 419 (D.C. 1993). Society benefits when a caretaker executes his responsibilities within a home. Because the activity in Junior served functions recognized as valuable by society, society was prepared to recognize the caretaker's expectation as reasonable. Thus, he had a legitimate expectation of privacy and could challenge a Fourth Amendment search. Id.

9

In contrast, this Court has repeatedly recognized that the possession, use, and distribution of illegal drugs represent "one of the greatest problems affecting the health and welfare of our population" and thus "one of the most serious problems confronting our society today." Treasury Employees v. Von Raab, 489 U.S. 656, 668, 674 (1989). The Court has expressed concern about the grave threat that illegal drugs, particularly cocaine, pose to society in terms of violence, crime, and social displacement. Harmelin v. Michigan, 501 U.S. 957, 1002 (1991). Certainly, this Court does not view illegal drug possession as a longstanding social custom that serves a function recognized as valuable by society. Rather, this Court has insisted that illegal drug activity is socially unacceptable and has held that the states have a great interest in prohibiting it. See, e.g., Employment Div., Dept. of Hum. Res. of Or. v. Smith, 494 U.S. 872 (1990) (holding that the Free Exercise Clause of the First Amendment does not prohibit application of Oregon drug laws to the ceremonial ingestion of peyote).

In the case at bar, Respondents cannot claim that their expectation of privacy was one that society is prepared to recognize as reasonable. The record indicates that Respondents engaged in only one activity while inside Thompson's apartment: bagging cocaine. Record at E-2. Respondents failed to introduce any evidence of any other purpose for their presence. See Record at E-4. Unlike the defendant in Olson, Respondents were not engaged in any longstanding social custom that serves functions recognized as valuable by society. Instead, Respondents were present at another's home for the sole purpose of committing a crime.

Because Respondents' criminal activity was not a longstanding social custom that serves functions recognized as valuable by society, Respondents' expectation of privacy was not one that society recognizes as reasonable. Therefore, Respondents had no legitimate expectation of privacy and cannot assert a Fourth Amendment challenge.

b. Respondents were present for a purely commercial purpose and were not entitled to the Fourth Amendment protection associated with the home.

Respondents were not present in a "home," but were on property for a purely commercial purpose. Respondents therefore are not entitled to the Fourth Amendment protection normally associated with the home and cannot claim that their expectation of privacy was one society is prepared to recognize as reasonable.

This Court has recognized that business premises invite lesser privacy expectations than do residences. See G.M. Leasing Corp. v. United States, 429 U.S. 338, 353 (1977); see also 1 Wayne R. LaFave, Search and Seizure § 2.4(b), at 429 (2d ed. 1987). Similarly, while the home is afforded the full range of Fourth Amendment protections, see Silverman v. United States, 365 U.S. 505, 511 (1961), when the home is converted into a commercial center to which outsiders are invited to transact unlawful business, that business is not entitled to the great measure of sanctity afforded to homes. See Lewis v. United States, 385 U.S. 206, 211 (1966).

In Lewis, this Court held that a defendant who used his home for the felonious sale of narcotics could not claim a violation of any reasonable expectation of privacy when an undercover officer entered the home to purchase marijuana. Id. The Court emphasized that the officer never saw, heard, or took anything that was not contemplated and intended by the defendant as a necessary part of his illegal business. Id. at 210. Because the property was properly characterized as a place of business, the defendant could not contend that the officer had violated any expectation of privacy that society is prepared to recognize as reasonable. Id. at 211.

Utilizing the same reasoning, the D.C. Circuit held that a visitor who used another's apartment solely to conduct drug transactions could not claim Fourth Amendment protection. United States v. Hicks, 978 F.2d 722, 723-24 (D.C. Cir. 1992). The court reasoned that the defendant "treated the apartment as a base for his business operation, not as a sanctuary from outsiders." Id. at 724. "Hicks was not engaging in any longstanding social custom that serves functions recognized as valuable by society. Quite the opposite." Id. The court held that while the defendant may have been legitimately in the apartment, in the sense that the apartment tenant permitted his presence, the defendant did not have any legitimate expectation of privacy in the apartment because he was present only to engage in illegal business. Id.

In the present case, Respondents, like the defendants in Lewis and Hicks, were present on property for the sole purpose of conducting criminal business. Record at E-4. As the Minnesota Court of Appeals noted, Respondents' claims that they were predominantly social guests in the apartment are "inconsistent with the only evidence concerning [their] stay in the apartment, which indicates that [they] used it for a business purpose—to package drugs." State v. Carter, 545 N.W.2d 695, 698 (Minn. Ct. App. 1996). Officers found Respondents in possession of 40 grams of cocaine, pagers, and a scale, Record E-3, illustrating that Respondents treated the apartment as a base for a business operation, not as a sanctuary from outsiders.

Like the apartments in Lewis and Hicks, the property in the present case had been converted into a commercial center to which outsiders were invited for purposes of transacting unlawful business. The business therefore was not entitled to the great measure of sanctity afforded to homes. Like the officer in Lewis, Officer Thielen observed only activities that were a necessary part of Respondents' illegal business. During the entire time Officer Thielen watched the apartment occupants, the occupants did nothing but divide and package cocaine. See Record at E-2, G-14.

Thus, Respondents, who were conducting a purely commercial activity, were not visitors to a "home" and were not engaging in longstanding social customs that serve functions recognized as valuable by society. While Respondents may have been legitimately in the apartment, in the sense that Thompson permitted their presence, Respondents did not have any legitimate expectation of privacy in the apartment because they were present only to conduct illegal business. Because Respondents' expectation of privacy was not one that society recognizes as reasonable, this Court must reverse.

C. Respondents may not claim a legitimate expectation of privacy because by engaging in criminal acts in a well-lit room, directly in front of a window facing a widely used common area, they exhibited no subjective expectation of privacy.

Respondents, who engaged in criminal activity in an illuminated room directly in front of a window that faced a widely used common area, manifested at most a hope that no one would view their unlawful acts. Respondents exhibited no actual, subjective expectation of privacy. Therefore, they cannot claim a legitimate expectation of privacy in Thompson's apartment and may not assert a Fourth Amendment challenge to any alleged search of the premises. **53**

An individual seeking to establish possession of a legitimate expectation of privacy must first demonstrate an "actual (subjective) expectation of privacy." Katz v. United States, 389 U.S. 347, 361 (Harlan, J., concurring). "What a person knowingly exposes to the public, even in his own home or office, is not the subject of Fourth Amendment protections." Id. at 351.

53 The writer articulates her conclusion in the first paragraph; in the second paragraph, the writer articulates the rule.

11

54 The writer then explains the rule, first by talking about a case in which the phrase-that-pays was met, and then by discussing a case in which the phrase-that-pays was not met.

55 Notice how the writer applies the rule to the facts. First, she states explicitly that the phrase-that-pays does not equal her client's facts. She follows that statement with necessary details and by distinguishing her client's case from one of the authority cases cited in the explanation section.

A person exhibits a subjective expectation of privacy when his or her conduct demonstrates his intent to keep activity private. See id. at 352. In Katz, the defendant exhibited a subjective expectation of privacy when he closed the door to a telephone booth to prevent being overheard. Id. Katz did not knowingly expose his activity to the public; rather, his conduct demonstrated his intent to keep the activity private. Id. Therefore, the government "[v]iolated the privacy upon which he justifiably relied" when it attached an electronic surveillance device to the telephone booth. Id. Because Katz had a subjective expectation of privacy, and that expectation was one society is prepared to recognize as reasonable, he had a legitimate expectation of privacy and was entitled to assert a Fourth Amendment challenge. Id. **54**

In contrast, when individuals in all probability know that information or activities will be revealed to others, the individuals demonstrate no actual, subjective expectation of privacy. For example, a defendant challenged the government's installation of a pen register to record his telephone calls in Smith v. Maryland, 442 U.S. 735, 736 (1979). This Court held that the defendant likely entertained no actual, subjective expectation of privacy in phone numbers he dialed, as all telephone users realize that they must convey phone numbers to the telephone company and that the telephone company records the information. Id. at 742.

Smith illustrates that even an individual who has taken cautionary measures to protect his or her activity from public exposure may fail to exhibit a subjective expectation of privacy if those cautionary measures are in fact inadequate to safeguard the activity from public inspection. See id. at 743. The Smith Court held that the defendant did not demonstrate an actual, subjective expectation of privacy merely by using his home phone rather than some other phone. The Court reasoned that the defendant's conduct, although perhaps "calculated to keep the contents of his conversation private," could not have preserved the privacy of the number he dialed. Id. Thus, despite what may have been some effort to maintain secrecy, the defendant exhibited no actual, subjective expectation of privacy as to the exposed information. Id. Similarly, in a 1984 decision, this Court suggested that a defendant who hid his marijuana crop from the public view with two fences may have "manifested merely a hope that no one would observe his unlawful gardening pursuits" and not an actual, subjective expectation of privacy. California v. Ciraolo, 476 U.S. 207, 211-12 (1985).

In the case at bar, Respondents' behavior and location within the apartment indicate that they had no actual, subjective expectation of privacy. **55** Respondents manifested at most a hope that no one would observe their unlawful pursuits inside Thompson's apartment. Nothing in the record indicates Respondents took any action to preserve their privacy. Unlike the defendant in Katz, Respondents introduced no evidence of conduct that demonstrated an intent to keep their activity private. Though the blinds were drawn, there is no indication that Respondents drew them. See Record at E-2, E-10. On the night in question, Respondents were present in a first-floor apartment that had several windows at ground level. Record G-26. The windows faced a public area that apartment residents and nonresidents frequented. Record G-69, G-70. As darkness fell in early evening, Respondents sat illuminated under a chandelier light at a table directly in front of one of these windows. Record G-13. Only a pane of glass and a set of blinds that featured a series of laths, Record G-50, separated Respondents from the adjacent common area. On the night in question, the blinds, though drawn, had a gap in them large enough for a citizen who passed by and an officer who stood a foot or more from the window to view easily the entire illuminated ulterior scene. Record G-13.

An individual in Respondents' position would have known and expected that a passerby could look through the gaps in the blinds and see into the illuminated kitchen.

Thus, Respondents could not have actually expected that their illegal activities would go unnoticed. **56** Absent a subjective expectation, Respondents do not have a legitimate expectation of privacy and cannot assert a Fourth Amendment challenge to an alleged search of the premises. Therefore, this Court must reverse.

D. This Court should maintain its reluctance to expand the class of individuals who may claim a legitimate expectation of privacy and invoke the exclusionary rule.

Because the arguments for limiting the use of the exclusionary rule are compelling, this Court should continue its reluctance to expand the class of persons that may invoke the rule. The Court should reverse the case at bar because doing so recognizes (1) the significant counter interests in public safety and the proper functioning of the justice system and (2) the fundamental constitutional doctrine that an individual may not assert the rights of a third party.

Each application of the exclusionary rule "exacts a substantial social cost," as "[r]elevant and reliable evidence is kept from the trier of fact and the search for truth at trial is deflected." Rakas, 439 U.S. at 138. While recognizing the deterrent aim of the exclusionary rule, the Rakas Court emphasized that "misgivings as to the benefit of enlarging the class of persons who may invoke that rule are properly considered when deciding whether to expand standing to assert Fourth Amendment violations." Id. Expanding the class of individuals who may invoke the exclusionary rule to include persons whose own rights were not violated would be harmful to our system of justice and detrimental to effective police work.

Because of the potential harm, this Court has expressly ruled that only individuals whose rights were infringed by the search itself may urge suppression of the fruits of a Fourth Amendment violation. Alderman v. United States, 394 U.S. 165, 175 (1969). The additional benefits of extending the exclusionary rule to other defendants would not "justify further encroachment upon the public interest in prosecuting those accused of crime and having them acquitted or convicted on the basis of all the evidence which exposes the truth." Id.

Under core principles of constitutional law, a person may seek a remedy for a constitutional violation only if he or she belongs "to the class for whose sake the constitutional protection is given." Hatch v. Reardon, 204 U.S. 152, 160 (1907). A person asserting a constitutional claim must show an adverse interest based upon an alleged violation of his or her own rights, rather than the violation of the rights of some third party. See, e.g., Tileston v. Ullman, 318 U.S. 44, 46 (1943). This Court has repeatedly rejected attempts to vicariously assert violations of Fourth Amendment rights. See, e.g., Rakas, 439 U.S. at 150; Brown v. United States, 411 U.S. 223, 230 (1973). In 1980, this Court held that defendants charged with crimes of possession may claim the benefits of the exclusionary rule only if their own Fourth Amendment rights have in fact been violated. United States v. Salvucci, 448 U.S. 83, 85 (1980). To allow otherwise, the Court said, "serves only to afford a windfall to defendants whose Fourth Amendment rights have not been violated," id. at 95, an outcome that cannot be tolerated in light of the significant public interests in curbing crime and in fairly and accurately determining defendants' guilt or innocence at trial.

Extending the Olson holding to protect Respondents in the present case would afford Respondents a windfall. The apartment where Respondents were observed was not their home, see Record G-5, and, as discussed above, they had no legitimate expectation of privacy there. They simply do not belong to the class for whose sake the

56 In this paragraph, the writer rearticulates her conclusion, and provides "Bacon links" to other relevant parts of her argument.

13

constitutional protection is given. Extending the right to invoke the exclusionary rule to individuals in Respondents' situation would hamper effective police work and unacceptably thwart the truth-finding functions of judge and jury. Allowing Respondents to assert third-party rights before this Court would be contrary to decades of established case law and contrary to good public policy. Therefore, this Court must reverse.

II. Officer Thielen's conduct was not a Fourth Amendment search because he stood in a location where any member of the public might have stood and observed the criminal activity in a manner any member of the public might have employed.

57 This umbrella section includes legal backstory and roadmap.

57 Even if Respondents may invoke the Fourth Amendment's protections to challenge a search of Thompson's residence, no Fourth Amendment search occurred in the case at bar. Because the officer's naked-eye observation from the apartment common area was not a Fourth Amendment search, this Court must reverse.

A search occurs only when governmental agents intrude upon an area in which a person has a "reasonable" expectation of privacy. See California v. Ciraolo, 476 U.S. 207, 212 (1986). A reasonable expectation of privacy exists when an individual manifests a subjective expectation of privacy in the place from which the observation occurred and demonstrates that his or her subjective expectation is one that society recognizes as reasonable. See Katz v. United States, 389 U.S. 347, 361 (1967) (Harlan, J., concurring). A "search" suggests "some exploratory investigation, or an invasion and quest, a looking for or seeking out." 1 Wayne R. La Fave, Search and Seizure § 2.1(a), at 301 (2d ed. 1987) (quoting C.J.S. Searches and Seizures § 1 (1952)).

[I]t has been held that a search implies some sort of force, either actual or constructive, much or little. A search implies a prying into hidden places for that which is concealed and that the object searched for has been hidden or intentionally put out of the way. While it has been said that ordinarily searching is a function of sight, it is generally held that the mere looking at that which is open to view is not a "search."
Id.

This Court examines two factors in determining whether a Fourth Amendment search occurred: (1) the location from which the observation occurred and (2) the manner in which the observation occurred. See Ciraolo, 476 U.S. at 213; 1 Wayne R. LaFave, Search and Seizure § 2.3(f), at 497 (2d ed. 1987). An examination of these two factors in the present case indicates that no Fourth Amendment search occurred. The observation in the present case took place from a publicly accessible location outside the apartment's curtilage, where the officer had a right to be. The officer observed in a manner that could have been carried out by any private passerby, without physical intrusion or the use of any device, and with only the aid of his natural senses to detect what was in plain view. Under these circumstances, the officer violated no reasonable expectation of privacy. Thus, Officer Thielen's observations were not a Fourth Amendment search.

A. No Fourth Amendment search occurred because the officer merely viewed what was in plain view from a publicly accessible common area outside the apartment's curtilage, where Respondents had no reasonable expectation of privacy.

In the case at bar, no Fourth Amendment search occurred because Respondents had no reasonable expectation of privacy in the location where the officer stood when he observed the criminal activity occurring within the apartment. **58** The officer (1) was standing on a public area, outside the apartment's curtilage; and (2) viewed only what was in plain view from this lawful vantage point. Because Officer Thielen merely stood where any other member of the public might have stood and viewed what any other member of the public might have viewed, the officer's behavior was not a search.

1. The unenclosed, publicly used common area where Officer Thielen stood was not within the curtilage of the apartment.

Officer Thielen made his observation of the apartment from an unenclosed, publicly accessible location that was regularly used by tenants of a multi-unit apartment complex. Because the observation was made from an area outside the curtilage of the apartment where Respondents were located, the observation violated no reasonable expectation of privacy. Therefore, the observation was not a search.

A person possesses a reasonable expectation of privacy, and thus, a search occurs, when an officer makes an observation from a location within the curtilage of a private home. See Oliver v. United States, 466 U.S. 170, 180 (1984). Curtilage, "the land immediately surrounding and associated with the home," is "the area to which extends the intimate activity associated with the 'sanctity of a man's home and the privacies of life.'" Id. (quoting Boyd v. United States, 116 U.S. 616, 630 (1886)). Whether an area is curtilage depends upon four factors: (1) the proximity of the area to the home, (2) whether the area is included within an enclosure surrounding the home, (3) the nature of the uses to which the area is put, and (4) steps taken by the resident to protect the area from observation. See United States v. Dunn, 480 U.S. 295, 301 (1987). The primary focus of the curtilage test is whether the area "harbors those intimate activities associated with domestic life and the privacies of home." Id. at 304.

This Court uses the curtilage concept to recognize that certain areas are so intimately linked with the home, both physically and psychologically, that privacy expectations are as heightened in those areas as they would be within the home itself. 4 William Blackstone, Commentaries 225 (1902). Courts have ruled that curtilage can include garages, Martin v. United States, 183 F.2d 436, 439 (4th Cir. 1950); barns, Rozencranz v. United States, 356 F.2d 310, 313 (1st Cir. 1966); smokehouses, Roberson v. United States, 165 F.2d 752, 754 (6th Cir. 1948); greenhouses, Florida v. Riley, 488 U.S. 445, 452 (1989) (plurality opinion); and backyards, California v. Ciraolo, 476 U.S. 207, 213 (1986). Because curtilage is afforded the same protection as the private residence, an invasion of the curtilage violates a reasonable expectation of privacy. Oliver, 466 U.S. at 180.

On the other hand, an officer violates no reasonable expectation of privacy when he or she merely observes a scene in plain view from outside the curtilage. Dunn, 480 U.S. at 304. In Dunn, officers observed a drug laboratory inside the defendant's barn while standing outside the curtilage. Id. at 304. This Court held that even if the barn itself had been within the curtilage, the defendant could claim no reasonable expectation of privacy because the scene was plainly visible from outside the curtilage. The police officers could look into the barn without violating the Fourth Amendment. Id.

Applying the four-factor curtilage test to the location where Officer Thielen stood reveals that the location is not within the curtilage of Thompson's apartment. First, as the trial court correctly noted, although the area where the officer stood is close to Thompson's apartment, the communal nature of the grounds "detracts from the closeness of the claimed curtilage area" to Thompson's apartment. Record E-10. The trial court in the case at bar characterized the place where the officer walked as a "grassy

58 This umbrella material would be even better with just one "see" citation to provide needed legal context.

15

common area." Record at E-2. Apartment complex common areas are by nature in close proximity to many apartments, and no single apartment lessee can make a special claim to them. Cases in lower courts have recognized that it is "well-settled that observations made by law enforcement officials from the common areas of multi-unit dwellings ordinarily do not violate a resident's reasonable expectation of privacy." United States v. Acevedo, 627 F.2d 68, 69 n.1 (7th Cir. 1980). **59**

The privacy expectation in apartment common areas "is often diminished because it is not subject to the exclusive control of one tenant and is utilized by tenants generally and numerous visitors attracted to a multiple occupancy building." 1 Wayne R. LaFave, Search and Seizure § 2.3(f), at 414 (2d ed. 1987). See, e.g., United States v. Holland, 755 F.2d 253, 255 (2d Cir. 1985) (holding that individual tenants in multi-tenant buildings have no legitimate expectation of privacy in common hallway areas, even when guarded by locked doors); Acevedo, 627 F.2d at 69 n.1 (holding that a surveillance officer's observation of an undercover heroin purchase while standing in a gangway to the side of an apartment complex did not violate expectation of privacy); State v. Hines, 323 So. 2d 449, 450 (La. 1975) (holding that apartment tenants have no reasonable expectation of privacy as to the "common yard open to the public").

Second, the location where Officer Thielen stood was not within any enclosed area attached to Thompson's apartment. No fence surrounded the area. Record E-10. Shrubs and bushes were planted near where Officer Thielen stood, Record G-43, but the trial court found that none were planted "immediately in front of the window to create an enclosure-type space that prevents the public from gaining entrance to the area." Record E-10. The trial court found no evidence that the shrubs were planted for privacy reasons rather than for aesthetic reasons. Record E-11.

Third, the record unquestionably indicates that the area in the case at bar was publicly used. Officer Thielen stood in a common area open to all residents and utilized by nonresidents as well. Record E-10, G-69. Children regularly played on the lawn. Record E-11. Passersby often left the sidewalk to walk freely across the area. Id. The trial court found that a bicycle parked next to Thompson's window illustrated that the public had access to the area directly in front of Thompson's apartment. Record E-10, G-71. Indeed, the informant who reported the illegal activity to Officer Thielen said that he had noticed Respondents when he himself was walking past the window. Record G-39.

Finally, the record contains no evidence whatsoever that Thompson took personal measures to protect the area outside her window as if it were her own curtilage. See Record E-11. Indeed, as a tenant in a multi-unit complex, she could not protect the area outside her window as her own. In this regard, the present case is distinguishable from cases involving single-family homes. Unlike the owner of a single-family home, Thompson was only one of many individuals who could access and use the common area outside her window. Individuals who share a building with other tenants who are entitled to use the area without giving notice or seeking permission cannot reasonably expect privacy from uninvited individuals. See, e.g., United States v. Fields, 113 F.3d 313 (2d Cir. 1997) (holding that a police officer's observation of defendants cooking and bagging crack cocaine through a partially covered first-floor apartment window was not a Fourth Amendment search, and distinguishing the case from cases involving single-family dwellings).

Thompson and her guests did not put the area outside her apartment window to private use. The area did not "harbor those intimate activities associated with domestic life." Oliver, 466 U.S. at 180. Under the Dunn test, the area where Officer Thielen stood does not fall within the curtilage of the apartment. An observation of a scene in plain view from the location where Thielen stood is not a Fourth Amendment search.

2. The apartment interior was in plain view from Officer Thielen's lawful vantage point.

Because Thielen was located outside the curtilage of the apartment, he was free to observe any scene in plain view. Respondents' activities within the apartment were in plain view from Thielen's lawful vantage point. Thus, Thielen's observation violated no reasonable expectation of privacy and did not constitute a Fourth Amendment search.

The Fourth Amendment protection of the home "has never been extended to require law enforcement officers to shield their eyes when passing by a home on public thoroughfares." California v. Ciraolo, 476 U.S. 207, 213 (1985). While a person's home is, for most purposes, a place where he or she expects privacy, activities that the homeowner "exposes to the 'plain view' of outsiders are not protected." Katz v. United States, 389 U.S. 347, 361 (1967) (Harlan, J., concurring).

Illegal activities in plain view from outside the curtilage are not protected even if the police observation is specifically directed at identifying illegal activity. United States v. Puna, 480 U.S. 294 (1987) (holding that an officer's observation into a barn was not a Fourth Amendment search and stressing it was irrelevant that the observation was motivated by a law enforcement purpose); Ciraolo, 476 U.S. at 212, 213. In Ciraolo, the defendant was growing marijuana in a 15-by-25 foot plot in his backyard. He surrounded the yard with a 6-foot outer fence and a 10-foot inner fence. Id. at 209. Officers flew over the defendant's house in a private airplane and readily identified the illegal plants using only the naked eye. Id. The government argued that the observation was analogous to looking through a knothole or an opening in a fence: "If there is an opening, the police may look." Id. at 220. This Court agreed with the government, holding that the observation was not a Fourth Amendment search. The airspace was outside the curtilage of the apartment, and the Court reasoned that the scene would have been in plain view to any member of the public flying in the same airspace. Thus, the officers violated no reasonable expectation of privacy. Id. at 213-14.

In the case at bar, the officer merely observed a scene that was in plain view from his lawful vantage point. As was discussed above, the area in which Officer Thielen stood was outside the curtilage of the apartment. While standing outside the curtilage, the officer plainly viewed Respondents' unlawful activities. Record E-2. While Officer Thielen did go to the common area outside the apartment window in response to the report from the informant, Record G-11, his motivation is irrelevant. The illegal activity was in plain view regardless of Officer Thielen's motivation. Just as the Fourth Amendment does not require police traveling in public airways to refrain from observing what is visible to the naked eye, the Fourth Amendment did not require Officer Thielen to refrain from viewing what could be seen from the public area outside Thompson's window.

Activities that Respondents exposed to the plain view of outsiders were not protected by the Fourth Amendment. Because Respondents' activities within the apartment were in plain view from Thielen's lawful vantage point, Thielen's observation violated no reasonable expectation of privacy. Therefore, the officer's observation was not a Fourth Amendment search. This Court must reverse.

17

B. No Fourth Amendment search occurred because Officer Thielen, who used only his natural senses to observe the apartment without physical intrusion, took no extraordinary measures.

60 Again, note the succinct legal backstory and roadmap.

60 Officer Thielen's manner of observation violated no reasonable expectation of privacy. No reasonable expectation of privacy exists when an officer takes only ordinary measures, using only his or her natural senses, to view what any private passerby could have viewed with no physical intrusion. See California v. Ciraolo, 476 U.S. 207, 213-14 (1985). Because Officer Thielen took no extraordinary measures to view the inside of the apartment, his observation violated no reasonable expectation of privacy. Therefore, the observation was not a Fourth Amendment search.

As Professor LaFave has noted, when the police "resort to the extraordinary step of positioning themselves where neither neighbors nor the general public would be expected to be, the observation or overhearing of what is occurring within a dwelling constitutes a Fourth Amendment search." 1 Wayne R. LaFave, Search and Seizure § 2.3(f), at 414 (2d ed. 1987). Conversely, if police merely observe a scene in the same manner as any member of the public might have viewed it, they have taken no extraordinary measure and have violated no reasonable expectation of privacy. Texas v. Brown, 460 U.S. 730, 749 (1983). The measures taken by Officer Thielen were not extraordinary because (1) any member of the public might have achieved the same view, and (2) Officer Thielen neither used an electronic device nor physically invaded the apartment. Because the officer took no extraordinary measure, he violated no reasonable expectations of privacy and did not conduct a search. Therefore, this Court must reverse.

1. Officer Thielen did no more than any other member of the public might have done to achieve a view of the apartment interior.

Officer Thielen, who merely positioned himself to achieve a view that any other member of the public might have achieved, violated no reasonable expectation of privacy. Because the general public could have taken the same measures Officer Thielen took, the fact that the officer changed position to achieve the view is irrelevant. The officer's measures were not extraordinary. Therefore, the officer's conduct did not constitute a search.

Officers do not take extraordinary measures when they merely position themselves to achieve a particular view from a public place. Texas v. Brown, 460 U.S. 730, 749 (1983). A measure that could have been taken by a member of the public is an ordinary measure, not an extraordinary measure. So long as a member of the public might achieve the same plain view, the officer violates no reasonable expectation of privacy. Id.

In Brown, an officer on a traffic stop bent down at an angle so that he could see the inside of the defendant's car. Id. at 734. The officer changed his position to better view the interior of the defendant's glove compartment. Id. This Court held that the fact that the officer changed his position to peer into the vehicle was "irrelevant to Fourth Amendment analysis." Id. at 740. The officer did not take any extraordinary measure and did not conduct a Fourth Amendment search. Id. The Brown Court noted that "[t]he general public could peer into the interior of [the car] from any number of angles" and that there is no reason an officer "should be precluded from observing as an officer what would be entirely visible to him as a private citizen." Id. The Court held that there is no reasonable expectation of privacy shielding scenes that may be viewed "by either inquisitive passersby or diligent police officers." Id. What mattered to the

18

Court was not whether the officer remained in one position or whether he casually or accidentally obtained the view, but rather whether it would have been <u>possible</u> for a member of the general public to obtain the same view. <u>Id.</u>

It is significant to note that some ordinary measures that might be taken by members of the public are less than polite. This Court's reasoning in <u>Brown</u> indicates that impolite measures are not necessarily extraordinary measures. <u>Id.</u> "Peering through a window or a crack in a door or a keyhole is not, in the abstract, genteel behavior, but the Fourth Amendment does not protect against all conduct unworthy of a good neighbor." <u>State v. Smith</u>, 181 A.2d 761 (N.J. 1962). **61** Police have a duty to investigate, and "in striking a balance between the rights of the individual and the needs of law enforcement," the Fourth Amendment does not protect individuals from observations that impolite neighbors might have made. <u>Id.</u>

Applying the law to the case at bar, Officer Thielen's affirmative steps to obtain the best view of the interior of the apartment simply cannot be classified as extraordinary measures. <u>See</u> Record G-29. Looking through a gap in the blinds may not be polite behavior, but it is something a neighbor or passerby <u>could</u> do, which is sufficient under <u>Brown</u> to place the conduct outside the Fourth Amendment.

Like the officer in <u>Brown</u>, Officer Thielen observed a scene that could have been viewed by either inquisitive passersby or diligent police officers. The Fourth Amendment simply did not preclude Officer Thielen from observing as an officer what he could have viewed as a private citizen. Officer Thielen's movement to secure a better view, <u>see</u> Record G-30, is irrelevant to the Fourth Amendment analysis.

The officer's movement was not an extraordinary measure. His manner of observation did not violate any reasonable expectation of privacy and therefore did not constitute a search. Thus, this Court must reverse.

61 What issue was the New Jersey court looking at when it made this pronouncement? The reader should be able to relate the quotation to the relevant issue and the disposition of that issue, at the very least.

2. Officer Thielen made no physical intrusion and used no device to enhance his natural senses.

Officer Thielen's observation, which was conducted without the aid of any device and without any physical intrusion of the premises, involved no extraordinary measures. Therefore, the observation violated no reasonable expectation of privacy and did not constitute a search.

This Court has repeatedly suggested that an officer does not take extraordinary measures when he simply observes an area without physically invading it. <u>See Florida v. Riley</u>, 488 U.S. 445, 449 (1989) (plurality opinion); <u>California v. Ciraolo</u>, 476 U.S. 207, 213 (1986). Although the <u>Katz</u> Court indicated that the reach of the Fourth Amendment cannot turn on the presence or absence of a physical intrusion into an enclosure, 389 U.S. at 353, <u>Katz</u> dealt with government officers supplementing their natural senses with electronic listening devices. In subsequent cases involving officers using only their natural senses, this Court has repeatedly indicated that the home is "not necessarily protected from inspection that involves no physical invasion." <u>Riley</u>, 488 U.S. at 449.

In <u>Riley</u>, the Court held that there was no search when police observed marijuana in a defendant's greenhouse from a helicopter circling above the greenhouse. The Court emphasized that there was no evidence that the helicopter interfered with the normal use of the greenhouse, that intimate details connected with the use of the home were observed, or that there was undue noise or threat of injury. <u>Id.</u> at 452. Because there was no physical invasion, the Court reasoned, the officers violated no reasonable expectation of privacy. <u>Id.</u>

19

In the case at bar, the record indicates absolutely no physical intrusion into Thompson's dwelling. The observation was completely visual, never disturbing the people inside the apartment. See Record D-3. Officer Thielen used no electronic device. He did not even utilize a flashlight. Record G-13. Nothing in the record suggests that the officer removed any obstacles or disturbed any portion of Thompson's dwelling. See Record G-46. The officer stood a foot or more from the apartment window. See Record E-2. Never did he even place his hands along the window. See Record G-13. Officer Thielen could not hear the occupants' conversation. See Record G-14. No evidence suggests that the officer's presence in any way interfered with the use of the home. Indeed, during the entire time Officer Thielen observed, the occupants did nothing but illegally package cocaine. See Record G-14.

Thus, like the defendant in Riley, Respondents were completely undisturbed by the officer's observations. Like the defendant in Riley, Respondents cannot claim the officer took extraordinary measures. Officer Thielen did not violate any reasonable expectation of privacy. Because the officer's observation was not a Fourth Amendment search, this Court must reverse.

CONCLUSION

Respondents had no legitimate expectation of privacy in Thompson's apartment and therefore cannot assert a Fourth Amendment challenge. Even if Respondents were entitled to assert a Fourth Amendment challenge, Officer Thielen's nonenhanced use of his natural senses to observe criminal activity inside the residence from a public area outside the curtilage of the residence was not a search. This Court should reverse the decision of the Minnesota Supreme Court.

Respectfully submitted,

Sarah Student

Sarah Student
55 West 12th Avenue
Columbus, Ohio 43210-1391
Counsel for the Respondents

November 2, 1998

CERTIFICATE OF SERVICE

This document certifies hand delivery of one copy of the foregoing brief to my opponent's mailbox on this second day of November, 1998.

Sarah Student

Sarah Student

20

CERTIFICATE OF COMPLIANCE ⓺

This document certifies that this brief was completed using WordPerfect software, Times New Roman font, in 12-point type. It contains 12,876 words. The brief complies with the length requirements of this Court.

This document further certifies that the author of this brief has complied with all applicable honor code requirements, including the requirement that the author may not consult briefs or memoranda prepared on behalf of parties or amici to this case.

Sarah Student
_____

Sarah Student

⓺ Rule 33.1(h) of the United States Supreme Court Rules now requires a Certificate of Compliance in some circumstances, so this sample includes an example of a Certificate of Compliance. This Certificate is geared toward the requirements of an appellate advocacy course. If you are asked to include a Certificate of Compliance, in school or in practice, be sure to identify and follow the requirements of the relevant local rules.

No. 97-1147

IN THE SUPREME COURT OF THE UNITED STATES

FALL TERM, 1998

————————————

STATE OF MINNESOTA,

Petitioner,

v.

WAYNE THOMAS CARTER and MELVIN JOHNS,

Respondents.

————————————

ON WRIT OF CERTIORARI TO THE SUPREME COURT OF MINNESOTA

————————————

BRIEF FOR THE RESPONDENTS

————————————

Susan Scholar
55 West 12th Avenue
Columbus, Ohio 43210
Counsel for the Respondents

QUESTIONS PRESENTED

I. Under the Fourth Amendment, does an invited guest in a private residence **1** have a legitimate expectation of privacy from government or police observation of activity occurring wholly within that private residence, where lowered Venetian blinds almost completely cover the only windows to the residence?

1 The words "invited guest" and "private residence" create an image that supports the respondents' argument that they had a legitimate expectation of privacy.

II. Under the Fourth Amendment, does an officer's unwarranted and purposeful sight observation **2** into a clearly private residence, made while standing within inches of the apartment and peering through gaps in the covered window of the apartment, constitute an unlawful invasion of curtilage?

2 Notice how the writer uses the nominalized "sight observation" instead of "look" to make the police action seem more complex.

TABLE OF CONTENTS

3 This argument is not dispositive, even though it is designated by a roman numeral. The Respondents must prove both that they have standing to raise a Fourth Amendment challenge and that Officer Thielen's behavior constituted a search. Many legal writers think that only dispositive points may be the basis for roman numeral headings, but some good writers break that rule where, as here, each of the points is dispositive for the writer's opponent. When deciding whether to create a roman numeral heading for a nondispositive point, you might consider (a) the significance of the point to your argument, (b) whether the point is dispositive of your opponent's argument, and (c) whether the enumeration will still reveal the logical relationships between and among your points.

TABLE OF AUTHORITIES

IN THE SUPREME COURT OF THE UNITED STATES

———

No. 97-1147

STATE OF MINNESOTA,

Petitioner,

v.

WAYNE THOMAS CARTER and MELVIN JOHNS,

Respondents.

———

ON WRIT OF CERTIORARI TO THE SUPREME COURT OF MINNESOTA

———

BRIEF FOR THE RESPONDENT

———

OPINIONS BELOW

The order of the Minnesota District Court, County of Dakota, denying the motion to suppress evidence against Respondents Carter and Johns is reprinted in the record at E-l. The opinions of the Court of Appeals of Minnesota affirming denial of motion to suppress evidence are reported at State v. Carter, 545 N.W.2d 695 (Minn. Ct. App. 1996), and State v. Johns, No. C9-95-1765, 1996 WL 310305 (Minn. Ct. App. June 11, 1996). The opinions of the Supreme Court of Minnesota reversing denial of the motion to suppress evidence are reported at State v. Carter, 569 N.W.2d 169 (Minn. 1997), and State v. Johns, 569 N.W.2d 180 (Minn. 1997).

JURISDICTION

The judgment of the Supreme Court of Minnesota was entered on September 11, 1997. The petition for the writ of certiorari was filed on December 29, 1997, and this Court granted the petition on March 3, 1998. The jurisdiction of this Court rests on 28 U.S.C. §1257 (1995).

CONSTITUTIONAL PROVISION INVOLVED

The Fourth Amendment to the United States Constitution provides:

The right of the people to be secure in their persons, houses, papers, and effects, against unreasonable searches and seizures, shall not be violated, and no Warrants shall issue, but upon probable cause, supported by Oath or affirmation, and particularly describing the place to be searched, and the persons or things to be seized.

1

STANDARD OF REVIEW

This is an appeal from the Supreme Court of Minnesota's reversal of the trial court, which decided that evidence in this case is admissible under the Fourth Amendment to the United States Constitution. Interpretation of the United States Constitution is subject to de novo review. Ornelas v. United States, 517 U.S. 690 (1996); United States v. United States Gypsum Co., 333 U.S. 364 (1948).

STATEMENT OF THE CASE

This case involves a claim by Defendants-Respondents Wayne Thomas Carter and Melvin Johns, challenging, under the Fourth Amendment, the constitutionality of evidence used in their conviction. The evidence in question was obtained by observations made by a police officer looking into the window of an apartment where the Respondents were guests of the apartment's leaseholder. Record E-3. **4**

On May 15, 1994, Officer Jim Thielen of the Eagan, Minnesota, Police Department received information from an unidentified source that the source had observed people inside a nearby apartment "bagging" a white powdery substance. Record E-2. The source also stated that a blue Cadillac parked at the apartment building belonged to the individuals inside the apartment. Record E-2. After collecting additional information from the source, Officer Thielen proceeded to the apartment in question. The officer was able to approach a window belonging to the apartment by leaving the sidewalk leading up to the building, walking onto the grass and behind bushes located two to four feet away from the window. Record G-43.

By standing approximately twelve to eighteen inches from the window, Officer Thielen was able to observe the occupants' activities inside the apartment for approximately fifteen minutes. Record E-2, G-53. Because the blinds were closed, the officer could observe the activities only by looking through a gap in the blinds. Record G-49. He then returned to his original location at a nearby fire station parking lot, where he contacted a superior officer to inform him of his findings and to request instructions. Record G-53, G-54. Officer Thielen reported that he observed two individuals bagging a powdery substance on the kitchen table of the apartment. Record E-2.

Based on Officer Thielen's observations, Officer Kallastad proceeded to obtain search warrants for the apartment and the vehicle that the informant had identified. Record E-3. Investigation of the Respondents revealed that they were guests in the apartment in question, which was leased by a Kimberly Thompson. Record E-3. Based on findings (of a substance later determined to be cocaine) from the vehicle and apartment searches, Respondents were arrested on two counts of controlled substance crime in the first degree. Record E-4. **5**

At trial, the Respondents pleaded not guilty and challenged Officer Thielen's surveillance through the window of the apartment as an unwarranted search within the meaning of the Fourth Amendment, moving to suppress all evidence obtained as a result of that surveillance. Record E-5. The District Court ruled that Respondents did not have standing to challenge Officer Thielen's observations of Thompson's apartment and denied the motion. Record E-4. On September 21, 1994, Respondents were convicted in the Minnesota District Court for the County of Dakota based on evidence obtained by officers the night of May 15. Record E-3.

On appeal to the Court of Appeals of Minnesota, Respondents argued that they had proper standing to challenge the evidence under the Fourth Amendment because their status as invited house guests is a status that society is willing to recognize as legitimate

4 Contrast this opening with the petitioner's opening. Both are accurate, yet each highlights different information.

5 This information is accurate, but it purposely does not go into as much detail about the alleged crime.

for purposes of expectations of privacy. State v. Carter, 545 N.W.2d 695, 697 (Minn. Ct. App. 1996). The Court of Appeals again rejected the motion to suppress, holding that case precedent required a guest to stay overnight in order to have standing under the Fourth Amendment. Having rejected Respondents' claim of standing, the court affirmed the lower court without discussing the merits of Officer Thielen's search. Id. at 698.

The Supreme Court of Minnesota reversed the Court of Appeals, and held that the Respondents had standing to assert a Fourth Amendment challenge to the search in question because they had demonstrated an adversary interest in the outcome of the case and because Respondents had a legitimate expectation of privacy in the observed apartment. State v. Carter, 569 N.W.2d 169, 174 (Minn. 1997). The court also held that the officer's observations into the apartment did constitute a search within the meaning of the Fourth Amendment and that the search was not reasonable. Id. at 169. **6**

6 Respondents give more details about the holdings in their favor — but not exhaustive detail.

SUMMARY OF ARGUMENT

Invited guests in another's home have a legitimate expectation of privacy that protects them from unreasonable searches and seizures under the Fourth Amendment. Furthermore, observations made from directly outside an apartment into the window of the apartment constitute a search within the meaning of the Fourth Amendment because of an intrusion into curtilage. The Supreme Court of Minnesota correctly found that any time a person has demonstrated an expectation of privacy that society is prepared to recognize as reasonable, he will enjoy a constitutionally guaranteed protection from unwarranted search and seizure. Carter, 569 N.W.2d at 176. Furthermore, the court also held that any time government observations invade the curtilage of a place where there is a legitimate expectation of privacy, a search has taken place. Id. at 178.

This Court has gone to great lengths to refine its application of the Fourth Amendment. Conclusively, cases have held that government agents do not have free reign to intrude into and tamper with the private lives of citizens without probable cause or warrant. The key to this case, and others before it, is that if (1) a person has demonstrated a subjective expectation of privacy in the particular circumstances and (2) all evidence suggests that society recognizes that expectation of privacy to be reasonable, then the police cannot invade that privacy without a warrant. This Court's analysis has shown that the Fourth Amendment, perhaps once thought to primarily protect a "man in his own castle," actually extends protection to people as guests in others' homes, in their own offices and workplaces, in telephone booths, and in automobiles, from unreasonable searches of their private activities and personal effects.

The Supreme Court of Minnesota also properly labeled Officer Thielen's surveillance as an illegal search. When Officer Thielen stood within inches of a window and looked into a private residence where the victims of the search were going about their private affairs, he was conducting a search. Whether a search has taken place within the meaning of the Fourth Amendment depends on whether the officers intruded into a privately protected area, or an area so intimately connected or tied to a private place that it constitutes curtilage. If the area intruded into is curtilage, where a person has a reasonable expectation of privacy, agents may not search that area without warrant and may not enter the area of curtilage.

In this case, Respondents have demonstrated a legitimate expectation of privacy as guests in a host's home. Their host's home is a private residence and therefore enjoys protection from unwarranted physical intrusion. As a place where Respondents had a legitimate expectation of privacy, the apartment is also given protection from unwarranted observations that are conducted from immediately outside the apartment. The Respondents therefore respectfully request that this Court affirm the judgment of the Supreme Court of Minnesota.

ARGUMENT

I. An invitee in a residence has a legitimate and reasonable expectation of privacy under the Fourth Amendment and has protection from all unwarranted searches and seizures while demonstrating an expectation of privacy from public intrusion.

In this case, two people who had the right to be protected from unwarranted search and seizure were denied that right. Respondents' legitimate expectation of privacy was invaded when a Minnesota police officer peeked through a small opening in the window blinds of a private residence where the Respondents were guests; thus, the officer conducted a search of the activities within, without warrant. See Carter, 569 N.W.2d at 173. This Court has consistently construed the Fourth Amendment as protecting all citizens from intrusions of unreasonable searches and seizures that invade wholly private actions conducted within the sanctity of a recognizable private home. See, e.g., Minnesota v. Olson, 495 U.S. 91, 98 (1990).

Invocation of the Fourth Amendment against evidence obtained in this case is appropriate because (1) the Respondents had a reasonable expectation of privacy from unwarranted searches while invitees in an acquaintance's residence; (2) the nature of the Respondents' presence on the searched premises was such that society recognizes them as possessing a legitimate expectation of privacy; and (3) Respondents' legitimate expectation of privacy gives them proper standing to challenge evidence under the Fourth Amendment.

A. A person has a legitimate and reasonable expectation of privacy that society is prepared to acknowledge while he is an invited guest in another person's private residence.

When the Respondents left the public streets and entered the private home of their host, they had a legitimate expectation of privacy: They believed they were protected against unwarranted government observation. This Court has said that people will be recognized as having a legitimate expectation of privacy if they demonstrate an expectation that their activities are treated as private, and if it can be shown that their expectation of privacy is reasonable in the given situation. Katz v. United States, 389 U.S. 347, 361 (1967) (Harlan, J., concurring). In Katz, conversations obtained by FBI wiretapping efforts could not be used as evidence to convict a man for transmitting wagering information by public telephone because the defendant clearly demonstrated a legitimate expectation of privacy while using the public telephone. Id. at 348.

This Court reasoned in Katz that a person using a public telephone is the type of person who has a legitimate expectation of privacy because most people who enter a phone booth and shut the door assume no one else is listening to the conversation. Id. at 361. Thus, even though a phone booth is accessible to the public, it can also be a temporary private place where the occupant legitimately expects privacy.

Legitimate expectations of privacy and society's acceptance of those expectations are used by this Court to determine when the protection of the Fourth Amendment goes beyond one's own home, and in which places a person is rightfully protected from unwarranted intrusions by the government. For example, in 1990, this Court held that an overnight guest has a legitimate expectation of privacy in his host's home. <u>Minnesota v. Olson</u>, 495 U.S. 91, 98 (1990). The <u>Olson</u> Court held that Olson's unwarranted arrest was an illegal seizure because Olson, as an invited overnight guest in the apartment, had a sufficient interest in the privacy of his host's home to be free from unwarranted search and seizure. <u>Id.</u> at 96-97. Furthermore, that subjective expectation of privacy was found to be reasonable because staying overnight in another's home is a socially recognized custom: "We will all be hosts and we will all be guests many times in our lives. From either perspective, we think that society recognizes that a houseguest has a legitimate expectation of privacy in his host's home." <u>Id.</u> at 98.

<u>Olson</u> did not specifically require a person to be an overnight guest or even a guest in order to have a legitimate expectation of privacy.[1] The legitimacy of Olson's expectation was upheld, not specifically because he was a guest, but because the circumstances in which the police intruded upon him were the type in which most people would normally expect to enjoy a right to privacy. <u>Id.</u> at 96-97. This was also true in <u>Katz</u>, where a privacy interest was found in a person using a public phone booth, who was neither a guest nor located in a residence. 389 U.S. at 352. Thus, the facts of the particular circumstances, coupled with the overriding values and expectations of society, will determine whether the victim of a search and seizure had a legitimate expectation of privacy and, thus, should not have been searched.

This Court has also rejected the argument that a person must have a legal property interest in the premises to challenge a search. <u>Olson</u>, 495 U.S. at 97. <u>Olson</u> drew its conclusions from a similar case in which the defendant challenged a search warrant used for his arrest while a guest in a friend's apartment. <u>Jones v. United States</u>, 362 U.S. 257, 265 (1960) (overruled on other grounds). The government claimed Jones could not challenge the search warrant because he had no legal property interest in the premises where he was located. This Court held that Jones could challenge the search because he was "legitimately on the premises." <u>Id.</u> at 265. This Court later refined the <u>Jones</u> "legitimately on the premises" test to mean that "a person can have a legally sufficient interest in a place other than his own home," and the "Fourth Amendment protects him from unreasonable government intrusion into that place." <u>Rakas v. Illinois</u>, 439 U.S. 128, 141-42 (1978).

The Fourth Amendment similarly extends to the Respondents in this case. Respondents were legitimately on the premises of their host's home because they were invited guests. The Respondents, having shown a legitimate expectation of privacy while there, had a legally sufficient interest in being safe from unreasonable government intrusion.

B. A person has demonstrated his expectation of privacy when he takes action to protect himself from public observation.

As guests in another's home, Respondents had a legitimate expectation of privacy because people expect certain protections in the home as they conduct themselves either

---

[1] This Court recognized that the status of overnight guest in <u>Olson</u> was enough to show he had a legitimate expectation of privacy. However, the analysis did not rest wholly on whether he was an overnight guest, but said an unlawfully searched overnight guest was one example of "a mistaken premise that a place must be one's 'home' in order for one to have a legitimate expectation of privacy there." <u>Id.</u> at 96. Thus, a person can have a legitimate expectation of privacy in places other than his own home, and <u>Olson</u> was one example where the defendant demonstrated such a legitimate expectation. <u>Olson</u> left open the interpretation of what other situations will demonstrate a legitimate expectation of privacy.

5

as guests or hosts. This Court has used several factors to determine whether a socially acknowledged, legitimate expectation of privacy exists. E.g., Jones, 362 U.S. at 265 (examining how the individual used the location where the search occurred); United States v. Chadwick, 433 U.S. 1, 7-8 (1977) (looking at intention of the framers of the Constitution and Fourth Amendment and how they might react to a particular situation); Payton v. New York, 445 U.S. 573, 589 (1979) (considering common understandings among people of which areas deserve protection from government intrusion); see also Rakas, 439 U.S. at 139 (finding that no single factor can determine the legitimacy of a Fourth Amendment claim). **7**

7 Note that these parentheticals are less effective because they tell what the court *considered*, but not what the court did. Note also that they make the writer's roadmap harder to perceive.

These cases suggest that courts should, in each case, examine the conduct of the parties involved and think about the expectations and actions of ordinary people if put in similar circumstances. This Court has found that there are many situations in which Fourth Amendment protection extends beyond the scope of one's own home and even beyond private residences. For example, this Court held that a search warrant was required to search the personal belongings inside a footlocker because, by placing their personal belongings inside the double-locked footlocker, respondents manifested an expectation that the contents would be free from public intrusion. Chadwick, 433 U.S. at 9-10. This expectation was no different from that of a person who locks the doors of his home against intrusion. Id. Also, Katz extended Fourth Amendment protection to evidence obtained by eavesdropping on a conversation held in a public telephone booth. 389 U.S. at 359. Both Chadwick and Katz demonstrate that the legitimacy of a privacy interest within the meaning of the Fourth Amendment depends not solely on the location of activities or belongings, but also on whether a privacy interest will be recognized by society in the given situation. See also United States v. Jeffers, 342 U.S. 48, 52 (1951) **8** (finding that **9** since the Fourth Amendment prohibits unreasonable searches and seizures to both house and effects, **10** a judicial warrant was required **11** to search a hotel room where the defendant was staying); Mancusi v. Deforte, 392 U.S. 364, 369 (1968) (requiring a search warrant to search a business office where a legitimate expectation of privacy was demonstrated).

8 This parenthetical is more effective because it includes the four elements that promote effective case descriptions.
9 This phrase indicates the court's reasoning.
10 This phrase indicates the issue and the disposition of that issue.
11 This phrase indicates the significant facts.

In the present case, the nature of the Respondents' time as guests in the searched premises establishes that they possessed a legitimate expectation of privacy. First, Respondents had the leaseholder's permission to be in the apartment, Record G-4, G-5, as did the victims of the searches in Olson and Jones. Olson, 495 U.S. at 97 n.6; Jones, 362 U.S. at 265.

Second, Respondents were inside the apartment for a minimum of two and one-half hours. Record E-2, E-3. The issue of how much time must be spent in a location before a privacy right exists has been an area of some confusion. **12** Other courts have not found a legitimate privacy expectation when the defendants were only briefly present on the premises. See generally United States v. Maddox, 944 F.2d 1223, 1234 (6th Cir. 1991) (finding the defendant could not have a reasonable expectation of privacy when it was shown he was nothing more than a short-term party guest); Prophet v. United States, 602 A.2d 1087, 1091 (D.C. 1992) (holding that a defendant who arrived minutes before police at his friend's house could not challenge entry). These cases are distinguishable from the present case because in those cases the defendants were not personally authorized or acknowledged as private guests in the home, were only present at the residence for a matter of minutes, or were unable to establish any personal connection to the people or objects within the apartment. In this case, Respondents were two of only three persons present, and their presence had the personal acknowledgment of the leaseholder. Record G-5.

12 If this is a significant issue, perhaps it should be treated separately, with a separate heading. Generally, it burdens the reader when the writer returns to rule explanation after beginning rule application.

Finally, for the two-and-one-half-hour period of time Respondents remained in the apartment, they engaged in activity with the leaseholder and each other. Record

E-3, E-4. The type of activity engaged in by the victims of a search is wholly irrelevant to the Fourth Amendment analysis. For example, in Katz, even though agents had hard-core evidence of the defendant's criminal activity, this Court would not allow it as evidence because the evidence was, itself, obtained illegally. 389 U.S. at 355. Similarly, in this case Respondents should not be denied their constitutionally protected right under the Fourth Amendment because evidence obtained by disobeying the order of the Fourth Amendment might prove criminal conduct. **13**

> **13** Note that these parentheticals are less effective because they tell what the court *considered*, but not what the court *did*. Note also that they make the writer's roadmap harder to perceive.

C. A person properly asserts Fourth Amendment protection when he has an adverse interest in the outcome of the case and when there has been a violation of some protected individual right, namely privacy.

Since the Respondents have demonstrated that they had a reasonable expectation of privacy as invited guests in another's home, they have proper standing to assert their Fourth Amendment claims. Standing for a Fourth Amendment claim requires a party to establish an adversary interest or personal stake in the outcome of the case. Baker v. Carr, 369 U.S. 186, 204 (1962). A party also must show that the adversary interest is based upon the violation of some individual right, rather than the rights of some other party. Jones, 362 U.S. at 261. The adversary interest requirement is easy to meet in this case. Any criminal defendant who faces jail time because of evidence offered against him surely has an adversary interest in the outcome. For the second part, this Court has held that determination of whether a search infringed a Fourth Amendment right depends on the person claiming such a right having a legitimate expectation of privacy in the invaded place. Rakas, 439 U.S. at 143.

Furthermore, as a general policy consideration, the Fourth Amendment must equally protect all citizens, regardless of whether or not the searched activities are tainted with criminal conduct. The Fourth Amendment was not framed to extend protection only to those citizens who can prove their activities are lawful. Rather, the protection from search and seizure extends as a right to "the people," and all citizens have always enjoyed the protections of the Constitution, without distinction between the alleged criminality or noncriminality of their actions. U.S. Const. amend. IV. This Court pointed out that the Fourth Amendment's protection of a person's security and personal liberty "has never been forfeited by his conviction of some public offense." Weeks v. United States, 232 U.S. 383, 391 (1914) (disallowing evidence of an illegal lottery enterprise that police officers obtained by searching the previously arrested defendant's home without warrant).

The policy of the Fourth Amendment is simple: Illegal and unwarranted searches are not justified just because they uncover illegal activities. If the government does not conduct its affairs legally, it cannot possibly expect to demand the same of its citizens. The Fourth Amendment, therefore, unreservedly protects Respondents' right to enter their host's home and be safe from unwarranted observation and intrusion by police officers. **14**

> **14** Because the reader will be moving on to heading II, it would be more effective if this heading provided a more thorough conclusion as to the writer's point about the respondents' legitimate expectation of privacy.

II. A police officer conducts a search within the meaning of the Fourth Amendment when he observes actions taking place inside a private residence from within inches of the residence's window, because the area is so close to the home that it qualifies as part of the residence's curtilage.

The central value of the Fourth Amendment is its protection of the sanctity of a person's home from unlawful intrusion. Silverman v. United States, 365 U.S. 505, 511 (1961) (stating that the very core of the Fourth Amendment is "the right of a man to retreat into his own home and there be free from unreasonable government intrusion"). Alongside protection of the home comes protection of the area immediately surrounding the home, known as curtilage— "the area to which extends the intimate activity associated with the 'sanctity of a man's home and the privacies of life.'" Oliver v. United States, 466 U.S. 170, 180 (1983) (quoting Boyd v. United States, 116 U.S. 616, 630 (1886)).

Curtilage is a unique concept and is not always defined strictly in terms of proximity to a home. In Katz, this Court said the Fourth Amendment protects those areas where an individual has a legitimate expectation of privacy. 389 U.S. at 360 (Harlan, J., concurring). There can be no claim of a legitimate expectation of privacy in areas surrounding the home that are open fields. California v. Ciraolo, 476 U.S. 207, 213 (1986) (holding that those areas that are knowingly and clearly exposed to a public vantage point are open fields and have no protection under the Fourth Amendment). However, other areas are so intimately tied to the home that they require protection under the Fourth Amendment because people legitimately expect privacy while in those areas. See Oliver, 466 U.S. at 178 (saying that an individual may demand privacy for activities in the area immediately surrounding the home).

In the present case, Officer Thielen's behavior constituted a search for three reasons. First, the area intruded upon was so intimately tied to the apartment itself that Respondents had a legitimate expectation that the government would not intrude upon the area, and thus intrude upon their privacy. Second, the area in question is curtilage even though the apartment lessee did not have property rights in the yard. This is so because curtilage is based on whether an individual has a legitimate expectation of privacy, not on whether the individual has a legal property interest. See, e.g., Jones, 362 U.S. at 266 (rejecting lower courts' attempts to deny Fourth Amendment standing based on lack of property rights). Third, even if Officer Thielen did not intrude into the apartment's curtilage to make the observations, he conducted an unlawful search because he demonstrated awareness that the Respondents' activities were taking place inside a privately protected area.

> **A. The area immediately outside of the apartment where the Respondents were guests qualifies as curtilage because there can be a reasonable expectation of privacy despite lack of property rights in the building or land in question.**

Protection of curtilage does not depend on the person claiming a legitimate expectation of privacy having a property interest in the intruded-upon area. This Court has specifically rejected attempts by lower courts to deny Fourth Amendment standing based on a defendant's status as a guest or invitee. Jones, 362 U.S. at 266 (holding that a defendant properly had standing to challenge probable cause of a search warrant used to seize narcotics, despite being a guest and not the owner of the searched premises). In the present case, Respondents should be afforded the same curtilage protection as a homeowner, whose home sits on private property, because a guest in a private residence has the same legitimate expectation of privacy in an apartment as a homeowner has in his home.

This Court pointed out in Katz that the belief "that property interests control the right of the Government to search and seize has been discredited." 389 U.S. at 353 (citing Warden, Md. Penitentiary v. Hayden, 387 U.S. 294, 304 (1967)). Katz set down the principle that the Fourth Amendment was designed to "protect people, not places," and that courts need to examine whether there is a legitimate expectation of privacy, not whether officers committed a technical trespass. Id. at 351. This was shown in Silverman when police officers, without warrant, stationed themselves in a neighboring home and inserted listening devices into the ground near a heating duct, allowing them to overhear incriminating gambling conversations inside the defendant's home. <u>Silverman</u>, 365 U.S. at 506. The officers never entered the home in question, but simply invaded the area immediately surrounding it and listened to the conversations within. <u>Id.</u> at 506. This Court found the officers' efforts to be an unlawful search of the defendant's home because, even though there was no actual trespass, there was still an intrusion into a "constitutionally protected area." <u>Id.</u> at 512.

Because protection from search and seizure does not depend on ownership or trespass of the invaded building or land, protection of curtilage likewise should not depend on ownership of an area that is normally considered curtilage. <u>Silverman</u> shows that a search can occur even when agents do not intrude upon private property. This Court has also said that an actual trespass is "neither necessary nor sufficient to establish a constitutional violation." <u>United States v. Karo</u>, 468 U.S. 705, 713 (1984). In <u>Karo</u>, although it was held that Karo's Fourth Amendment rights were not violated by the public installation of a monitoring beeper that Karo later carried into his house, the Court pointed out that privacy interests would be impaired by the monitoring of a beeper in a private residence without a warrant, even when agents did not physically enter private property. <u>Id.</u> at 713.

Additionally, <u>Katz</u> showed the irrelevance of property rights under the Fourth Amendment in holding that a public phone booth is protected from intrusions because the phone user has a legitimate expectation that he or she will be free from government eavesdropping. 389 U.S. at 361 (Harlan, J., concurring). This Court has also suggested that Fourth Amendment protection may extend to individuals within commercial buildings if a person has taken reasonable steps to exclude the public. <u>E.g.</u>, <u>See v. City of Seattle</u>, 387 U.S. 541, 543 (1967) (holding that a businessman has a constitutional right to conduct his business and be free from unreasonable intrusion); <u>Camara v. Municipal Court of San Francisco</u>, 387 U.S. 523, 528 (1967) (stating that the basic purpose of the Fourth Amendment is to "safeguard the privacy and security of individuals against arbitrary invasions by government officials," regardless of location).

The extension of Fourth Amendment protection to curtilage allows the privacy and security of a privately protected place to be more fully safeguarded. In the present case, the Respondents did not have any property rights in the apartment or the property on which the apartment building was situated. Record E-7. However, as guests in a private residence, Respondents had the same legitimate expectation of privacy as a homeowner on private property. It would be inconsistent to apply the safeguard of curtilage to some places that enjoy Fourth Amendment protection and not to others. Because guests inside a rented apartment enjoy the same Fourth Amendment protection as a homeowner in a privately owned home, both deserve equal protection against unwarranted invasion into the exterior area that is closely tied to the intimacies of the home or apartment. Therefore, observations made from the immediate exterior of the private residence where Respondents were guests should be inadmissible as evidence because the observations constitute an illegal search from within the apartment's curtilage.

B. The observations of Respondents' activities constitute an unwarranted search because the police officer invaded the curtilage of the apartment by being physically within inches of the apartment's window and walls, having left the normal walkway area to do so.

The government may only make unwarranted observations of activities that are conducted in the open and can be seen naturally by the public at large. <u>Ciraolo</u>, 476 U.S.

at 211 (noting that officers' observations from public areas failed to constitute a search only because the defendant's activities were open for all the public to see); United States v. Dunn, 480 U.S. 294, 303 (1987) (finding that curtilage protects the activities and privacies of the home from unwarranted observation, as compared to a nearby barn where police could freely see activities within); Katz, 389 U.S. at 352 (pointing out that physical penetration of the area where privacy is claimed is no longer a requirement of the Fourth Amendment inquiry). However, in this case, the police officer's observations were made from within inches of the apartment walls. Record G-13. This constitutes an intrusion into curtilage because the officer intruded into an area where Respondents legitimately did not expect people to intrude. The officer approached so closely to the apartment that he was able to observe the activities within, even with the window blinds shut.

The Respondents' activities took place in an enclosed, shielded area and are fundamentally different from activities conducted in openly visible areas. In Ciraolo, officers' observations from an airplane of marijuana growing in the defendant's yard were held not to be an unwarranted search within the meaning of the Fourth Amendment. 476 U.S. at 214. Similarly, in Dunn, observations of drug activity inside an open barn by officers located outside of the defendant's gate did not qualify as a search because defendants did little to shield activities from public observation. 480 U.S. at 303. This Court pointed out that the barn in Dunn, even though located on private property next to the defendant's home, was not so intimately associated with the home to qualify as curtilage, and observation of such an open place from a public vantage point was not a search. Id. at 304.

The steps that Officer Thielen took to reach his vantage point show that he invaded the apartment's curtilage. The facts in these "open fields" cases are distinguishable from the present case. In Dunn and Ciraolo, the observed activities were conducted so as to be easily and readily available to observation by the public at large. This Court said that the defendants in those cases could not possibly be recognized to have any legitimate expectation of privacy when the activities were so readily accessible to the public view. Dunn, 480 U.S. at 303; Ciraolo, 476 U.S. at 213. There was, however, no public view of the activities in this case. Respondents' activities occurred only within a private residence. Record E-3. Those activities could not be observed unless a person took the extreme action of locating himself within inches of the residence's windows. It was necessary to approach the residence very closely because the window blinds were closed, and activities could only be observed by peeking through a small gap in the blinds. Record G-49.

A reasonable person should still expect a right to privacy, even though others may be able to enter onto his or her land, or even peer into his or her windows, without committing a trespass. E.g., Katz, 389 U.S. at 351 (holding that "even an area accessible to the public [sic], may be constitutionally protected"). This is the reality of any person who lives in or is a guest in an apartment. Apartment lessees depend on socially accepted concepts of privacy to be protected from invasions into those areas that are intimately connected to the shelter of the apartment, since ownership and control over such areas are, in most cases, impossible. It is also reasonable that apartment lessees would have the same expectation of privacy from government invasion on the immediate exterior of the apartment, as a person who actually owns the land and walls invaded upon. A person's home, the place where he lives, has been recognized by this Court as the most important place protected by the Fourth Amendment. Payton, 445 U.S. at 589 (pointing out that the Fourth Amendment protects an individual's privacy in a variety of settings, but none is more clearly defined than the protection of a person's home). If not for the police officer's entrance into the curtilage of their host's apartment, Respondents' activities could not have been observed. **15**

15 Be careful not to end a heading section with a statement that leaves a question. Instead, explain the legal significance of your assertions as they relate to the ultimate assertion in your document, or at the minimum, in that heading section.

C. It should have been evident to the police officer making the observations that he was intruding into the privacy of the home because of the circumstances under which he made the observations.

The police officer observing Respondents was on notice that his actions were an invasion of privacy for three reasons. First, the apartment was a private residence, and the officer knew it. Record G-68, G-69. Respondents' host lived there, slept there, and conducted the other daily activities of life there. Record E-7. Second, the window of the apartment through which the police officer peered clearly indicated the apartment was not open to public observation. The blinds on the window had been drawn, with the exception of one small, defective gap. Record G-49. Finally, the officer could see the activities inside only by purposefully walking onto the grass, behind a bushy area, and within mere inches of the window to look inside. Record G-13. Simply because the yard area of an apartment is open to public traffic does not mean the public is free to peer inside, nor that a leaseholder and her guests are unreasonable to expect to be free from such eavesdropping. This Court has been reluctant to accept that police officers may freely observe in any manner from areas simply because they have a legal right to be there. Florida v. Riley, 488 U.S. 445, 454, 457 (1989) (4-1-4 decision) (O'Connor, J., concurring) (Brennan, J., dissenting) (disagreeing with the Justices in the plurality, saying that the true test of legality of observation should be measured by the regularity and frequency of public intrusion into such an area).

It is socially recognized that the windows of a home are not portals through which one may observe the intimacies of life occurring within. This concept is not novel. People go into their homes, shut the doors, and close the blinds precisely because home is the place where a person may find respite from the scrutiny of the outside world. Similarly, when someone is invited, as a guest, to join in such a respite, that guest rightfully expects to enjoy the same type of escape and privacy from the outside. The case law presented supports Respondents' right to be free from the unwarranted intrusion that police conducted while they were in the sanctity of their host's home, the intrusion of which eventually led to their arrest and conviction.

CONCLUSION

Because the Fourth Amendment protects all people who, like Respondents, demonstrate a legitimate expectation of privacy to be free from unwarranted search and seizure while invited guests in a host's home, and because officers, as in this case, may not intrude into the curtilage of a privately protected area without a warrant, this Court should affirm the decision of the Supreme Court of Minnesota granting Respondents' motion to suppress evidence collected against them in an unwarranted search.

Respectfully submitted,

Susan Scholar

Susan Scholar
55 West 12th Avenue
Columbus, Ohio 43210-1391
Counsel for the Petitioner

November 2, 1998

CERTIFICATE OF SERVICE

This document certifies hand delivery of one copy of the foregoing brief to my opponent's mailbox on this second day of November, 1998.

Susan Scholar

Susan Scholar
55 West 12th Avenue
Columbus, Ohio 43210-1391
Counsel for the Petitioner

12

No. 96-1060

IN THE SUPREME COURT OF THE UNITED STATES

October Term, 1996

Lorelyn Penero Miller,

Petitioner,

v.

Madeleine K. Albright,
Secretary of State of the United States,

Respondent.

ON WRIT OF CERTIORARI TO THE
UNITED STATES COURT OF APPEALS
FOR THE DISTRICT OF COLUMBIA CIRCUIT

BRIEF FOR THE PETITIONER

Simon J. Scholar
1356 School Street
Metropolis, Ohio
555-555-5555

Counsel for the Petitioner

QUESTION PRESENTED

Does the irrebuttable presumption ❶ that all men are different from all women with respect to their relationships with their "illegitimate" ❷ children, codified in 8 U.S.C. § 1409(a) (1994), violate the Fifth Amendment to the United States Constitution?

❶ The writer varies the common question-presented structure to emphasize the negative concept of "irrebuttable presumptions," which are generally frowned upon.

❷ Word in quotation marks to show that author does not agree that children born out of wedlock should be characterized as "illegitimate."

i

PARTIES TO THE PROCEEDING

Petitioner Lorelyn Penero Miller and Secretary of State Warren Christopher were plaintiff-appellant and defendant-appellee, respectively, below. Respondent Secretary of State Madeleine K. Albright was substituted for Mr. Christopher when Ms. Albright succeeded Mr. Christopher as Secretary of State of the United States. Secretary Albright is responsible under 22 U.S.C. § 211(a) (1994) for granting and issuing United States passports. Charlie R. Miller, Ms. Miller's father, was added as a co-plaintiff below by Ms. Miller; the United States District Court for the Eastern District of Texas dismissed his claims for lack of standing, and Mr. Miller is not a party to the appeal before this Court.

TABLE OF CONTENTS

3 This writer, appropriately, begins with an argument about which test to apply because the appropriate test is in controversy. If the *test* is not in controversy, but how to *apply* the test *is* in controversy, a section like this is unnecessary.

TABLE OF AUTHORITIES

No. 96-1060

IN THE SUPREME COURT OF THE UNITED STATES

October Term, 1996

Lorelyn Penero Miller,

Petitioner,

v.

Madeleine K. Albright,
Secretary of State of the United States,

Respondent.

ON WRIT OF CERTIORARI TO THE
UNITED STATES COURT OF APPEALS
FOR THE DISTRICT OF COLUMBIA CIRCUIT

BRIEF FOR THE PETITIONER

OPINIONS BELOW

The opinion of the United States Court of Appeals for the District of Columbia Circuit is reported as <u>Miller v. Christopher</u> **4** at 96 F.3d 1467 (D.C. Cir. 1996). The opinion of the United States District Court for the District of Columbia is reported as <u>Miller v. Christopher</u> at 870 F. Supp. 1 (D.D.C. 1994).

4 Although providing case names is usually not necessary in this section, it is helpful where, as here, the case name was different below.

JURISDICTION

The judgment of the United States Court of Appeals for the District of Columbia Circuit was entered on October 8, 1996. The petition for the writ of certiorari was filed on January 6, 1997, and this Court granted the petition on April 28, 1997. This Court has jurisdiction pursuant to 28 U.S.C. § 1254 **5** (1994).

5 This statute is one of the two statutes that are the most common sources of jurisdiction for cases before the United States Supreme Court.

STATUTORY AND CONSTITUTIONAL PROVISIONS INVOLVED

The pertinent part of the Fifth Amendment to the United States Constitution provides that "[n]o person shall be . . . deprived of life, liberty, or property, without due process of law."

1

The pertinent part of the Fourteenth Amendment to the United States Constitution provides that "[n]o State shall . . . deny to any person within its jurisdiction the equal protection of the laws."

Title 8 of the United States Code provides in pertinent part as follows:

The following shall be nationals and citizens of the United States <u>at birth</u>:
(g) <u>a person born outside the geographical limits of the United States and its outlying possessions of parents one of whom is an alien, and the other a citizen of the United States</u> who, prior to the birth of such person, was physically present in the United States or its outlying possessions for a period or periods totaling not less than five years, at least two of which were after attaining the age of fourteen. . . .

8 U.S.C. § 1401(g) (1994) (emphasis added).

Title 8 of the United States Code then modifies 8 U.S.C. § 1401 (g) by providing that, in the case of a person born outside of marriage and outside of the United States to an American father and an alien mother, that person will be a United States citizen as of the date of birth <u>only</u> if the following four conditions are met:

(1) a blood relationship between the person and the father is established by clear and convincing evidence,

(2) the father had the nationality of the United States at the time of the person's birth,

(3) the father (unless deceased) has agreed in writing to provide financial support for the person until the person reaches the age of 18 years, and

(4) while the person is under the age of 18 years —

(A) the person is legitimated under the law of the person's residence or domicile,

(B) the father acknowledges paternity of the person in writing under oath, or

(C) the paternity of the person is established by adjudication of a competent court.

8 U.S.C. § 1409(a) (1994). The different treatment given to "illegitimate" children based on the gender of their United States citizen parents is further emphasized by 8 U.S.C. § 1409(c), which provides in pertinent part:

Notwithstanding the provision of subsection (a) of this provision [which requires fathers to meet certain requirements to establish the citizenship of their children], a person born, after December 23, 1952, outside the United States and out of wedlock <u>shall be held to have acquired at birth the nationality status of the mother, if the mother had the nationality of the United States at the time of such person's birth</u>, and if the mother had previously been physically present in the United States or one of its outlying possessions for a continuous period of one year.

8 U.S.C. § 1409(c) (1994) (emphasis added). **6**

5 The writer uses this unusual method of introducing and juxtaposing statutes to emphasize the unreasonableness of the statutes governing U.S. citizen fathers as compared to those governing U.S. citizen mothers.

STATEMENT OF THE CASE

This is an action for declaratory judgment pursuant to 28 U.S.C. § 2201 (1994). Petitioner Lorelyn Penero Miller seeks a declaration that 8 U.S.C. § 1409(a) (1994) violates the Equal Protection Clause of the Fourteenth Amendment to the United States

Constitution, as applied to the federal government by the Fifth Amendment to the United States Constitution.

Petitioner Lorelyn Penero Miller was born on June 20, 1970, in the Republic of the Philippines. App. 15. Her mother, Luz Penero, was a citizen of the Republic of the Philippines. Id. Her father, Charlie R. Miller, is a citizen of the United States and was so at the time of Ms. Miller's birth. Mr. Miller and Ms. Miller's mother were never married; Ms. Miller's birth certificate does not list the name or nationality of her father as a result. App. 15. On July 27, 1992, Mr. Miller obtained a voluntary paternity decree from a court in his home state of Texas establishing that Ms. Miller is his daughter.

In 1986, 8 U.S.C. § 1409(a)(4) was amended to lower from twenty-one to eighteen the age limit that restricted a father's ability to pass his citizenship to a foreign-born child. Because of the effective date of that amendment, Ms. Miller would be able to satisfy 8 U.S.C. § 1409(a)(4) if she met its requirements before she turned twenty-one.

On February 11, 1992, Ms. Miller applied to the United States Department of State for registration as a United States citizen and for the issuance of a passport. App. 16. The State Department ultimately denied her application on November 5, 1992, because (1) Ms. Miller had failed to obtain the paternity decree before Ms. Miller's twenty-first birthday as required by 8 U.S.C. § 1409(a)(4), and (2) Mr. Miller had failed to agree in writing (while Ms. Miller was still under twenty-one) that he would financially support her until she turned twenty-one. App. 8. Mr. Miller was denied the opportunity to pass his United States citizenship to his daughter simply because he was late completing some paperwork and because he is a man. The paperwork obstacles that Mr. Miller failed to negotiate apply only to fathers; if Mr. Miller were a mother, Ms. Miller would have been a citizen from birth. **7**

Ms. Miller sought relief from the United States District Court for the Eastern District of Texas on March 31, 1993, alleging that the gender and "illegitimacy" distinctions contained in 8 U.S.C. § 1409(a) violated the Fifth Amendment to the United States Constitution. App. 6, 9. Ms. Miller subsequently added Mr. Miller as a co-plaintiff, but the district court dismissed his claims for lack of standing. Miller v. Christopher, 870 F. Supp. 1, 3 (D.D.C. 1994). Based upon Secretary Christopher's residence in Washington, the district court granted the Secretary's motion to transfer venue to the United States District Court for the District of Columbia. Miller v. Christopher, 96 F.3d 1467, 1468 (D.C. Cir. 1996). On April 29, 1994, the district court found that Ms. Miller lacked standing and granted the Secretary's motion to dismiss. Id.

Ms. Miller appealed that decision to the United States Court of Appeals for the District of Columbia Circuit on June 29, 1994. App. 1. Her appeal presented three separate claims. First, she argued that the district court erred in finding that she lacked standing; second, she argued that 8 U.S.C. § 1409(a)(4) violates the Fifth Amendment's equal protection guarantees; and third, she argued that she meets the requirements of 8 U.S.C. § 1409(a)(4) because the voluntary paternity decree "legitimated" her as of her date of birth. Miller v. Christopher, 96 F.3d at 1469-70.

The Court of Appeals found that Ms. Miller did have standing to invoke federal jurisdiction, but that Mr. Miller's voluntary paternity decree did not "legitimate" Ms. Miller as of her date of birth. Id. at 1469, 1472-73. Neither of those findings is under review in this Court.

The Court of Appeals also found that the gender and "illegitimacy" distinctions contained in 8 U.S.C. § 1409(a)(4) did not violate the equal protection principles of the Fifth Amendment to the United States Constitution. Id. at 1470-73. The Court of Appeals found that the case was controlled by this Court's decision in Fiallo v. Bell, 430 U.S. 787 (1977).

7 This borders on argument, but it states only facts: It is true that these obstacles are placed only in front of fathers. Be careful not to use language that characterizes facts in a way that affects the legal issues before the court.

In her opinion concurring in the judgment, Judge Wald took the unusual step of noting the inconsistency between <u>Fiallo</u> and this court's recent equal protection jurisprudence:

> <u>Fiallo</u> is a Supreme Court decision directly on point and, as a result, we have no choice but to hold section 1409(a) constitutional. Yet I think it is important to underscore the extent to which <u>Fiallo</u> is out of step with Court's current refusal to sanction "official action that closes a door or denies opportunity to women (or to men)" based on stereotypes or "overbroad generalizations" about men and women. <u>Virginia</u>,—U.S.—, 116 S. Ct. at 2275. <u>Fiallo</u> is a precedent whose time has come and gone; it should be changed by Congress or by the Supreme Court.

<u>Miller v. Christopher</u>, 96 F.3d at 1477 (Wald, J., concurring in the judgment). **8**
This Court granted Ms. Miller's petition for a writ of certiorari on April 28, 1997.

SUMMARY OF THE ARGUMENT

Congress may not use an irrebuttable gender stereotype to implement its policy decisions, even if those policy decisions concern immigration law. Accordingly, this Court should reverse the decision below. This Court faces two **9** tasks when deciding this case. First, the court must select the appropriate level of scrutiny to apply to the statute codifying the irrebuttable gender stereotype; second, the Court must apply that level of scrutiny to the statute. Both tasks are made easier by this court's repeated insistence that antiquated, sexist notions about the relative roles of men and women in our society have no place in our law.

The Court's first task — the selection of the appropriate level of scrutiny — is complicated by the fact that the irrebuttable gender stereotype is embedded in a naturalization statute, and the Court has traditionally given extreme deference to Acts of Congress in the naturalization arena. This complication is readily overcome.

This Court should give heightened scrutiny, not extreme deference, to the irrebuttable gender stereotypes embedded in naturalization legislation. First, this Court has refused to defer to Congress in the past when Congress has infringed on constitutional rights via immigration and naturalization legislation, and the Court has likewise refused to defer to Congress in the past when gender stereotypes have infected legislation in areas traditionally under almost complete congressional control. Second, there is a significant distinction between congressional power to set policy and congressional power to enforce that policy: The Constitution regulates implementation more closely than it regulates the formation of policy itself. Third, and finally, this Court should apply heightened scrutiny to this statute because the questionable practices of the past should not be permitted to taint today's decisions. **10**

The Court's second task — the application of the appropriate level of scrutiny to the statute — is straightforward. At the heart of the statute is a distinction between mothers and fathers that is the result of the archaic, sexist, stereotypical thinking that continues to plague our society. Section 1409(a) embodies the antiquated view of a family in which the woman's role is to nurture children and the man's role is to pay the bills. Section 1409(a) does not merely suggest that this is the case; section 1409(a) declares that this gender stereotype is true in all cases.

The plight of Lorelyn Miller and her father illustrates this problem with section 1409(a) especially well. Ms. Miller and Mr. Miller are a family and wish to live like one in the United States; section 1409(a) denies them that opportunity because they did

8 Giving this much information from the opinions below is usually not necessary or appropriate; it is appropriate here because a respected judge recommended overruling the main on-point decision.

9 The writer takes an unusual step by seeming to lay out two "objective" tasks for the court to follow. However, he is setting up his argument that the court's existing decisions mandate the result he seeks.

10 This sentence is almost identical to a point heading; generally, your summary should reflect the phrases-that-pay and *themes* of the point headings, but should not be identical to the headings.

not jump through the bureaucratic hoops quickly enough. There is absolutely nothing that they can now do to defeat the operation of the gender stereotype codified in section 1409(a). Now that Ms. Miller is over twenty-one, section 1409(a) operates as a conclusion that she and her father <u>cannot</u> have the close family relationship that allows a parent to transmit citizenship to a child.

In short, section 1409(a) declares that all women will automatically have a close family relationship with their children, and that all men will not have such a relationship unless it is established in connection with the financial support of those children before they reach the age of majority. There is no justification for the presence of this irrebuttable gender stereotype in our law. The application of heightened scrutiny is not necessary in order to rid the law of this anachronism; the choice of how closely to examine the statute will determine nothing more in this case than the degree of mismatch between the irrebuttable gender stereotype in question and the reality of the modern world. **11**

11 It is also appropriate to end the summary by reminding the court of what it is asked to do (affirm or reverse). This writer has chosen to end on a dramatic note instead.

12 An "introduction" labeled as such is unusual in effective appellate briefs. A more argumentative heading might be better here.

ARGUMENT

I. Introduction. **12**

The statute in question in this case, 8 U.S.C. § 1409(a) (1994), classifies children born of a United States citizen and a noncitizen into three groups: those who are "legitimate"(i.e., those whose parents are married), those who are "illegitimate" and have a United States citizen for a mother, and those who are "illegitimate" and have a United States citizen for a father. Children in the first two groups — those who are "legitimate" and those who have a United States citizen mother — are United States citizens by birthright. <u>See</u> 8 U.S.C. § 1401(g) (1994).

Children in the last group, however — those "illegitimate" children with United States citizen fathers — may receive their fathers' citizenship only after clearing several hurdles. Even if paternity is established by "clear and convincing evidence," as required by section 1409(a)(1), and even if the father was a United States citizen at the time of the child's birth, as required by section 1409(a)(2), section 1409(a)(3) and (a)(4) deny citizenship to an "illegitimate" child of a United States citizen father and a noncitizen mother <u>unless</u> the father agrees in writing to support that child until age eighteen <u>and</u> the child is either "legitimated," the father acknowledges paternity, or paternity is established by adjudication, <u>before</u> the child reaches the age of eighteen.

This Court has previously noted that Congress made these classifications and enacted these statutory hurdles out of a concern for "a perceived absence in most cases of close family ties, as well as a concern with the serious problems of proof that usually lurk in paternity determinations." <u>Fiallo v. Bell</u>, 430 U.S. 787, 799 (1977).

Those "problems of proof" do not lurk in 1998 the way they did in 1977. Furthermore, this Court soundly rejected decision making based on "perceived" notions of how men and women act in <u>United States v. Virginia</u>, 116 S. Ct. 2264 (1996). This Court should reverse the decision of the Court below and allow Ms. Miller to receive her birthright of United States citizenship.

II. This Court should require an "exceedingly persuasive justification" for the irrebuttable gender stereotype codified in 8 U.S.C. § 1409(a) because extreme deference to congressional use of such gender stereotypes is unwarranted.

This Court has recently reaffirmed its unwillingness to countenance the use of gender stereotypes as proxies for more rational decision making. <u>United States v. Virginia</u>,

116 S. Ct. 2264, 2274 (1996) (requiring "[p]arties who seek to defend gender-based government action [to] demonstrate an 'exceedingly persuasive justification' for that action" and characterizing this approach as "skeptical scrutiny of official action denying rights or opportunities based on sex"). Although naturalization legislation has traditionally been given extremely deferential review by this Court, Fiallo, 430 U.S. at 792, the time has come for this Court to enforce the Equal Protection Clause in all contexts and strike down irrebuttable gender stereotypes wherever they are found.

Respect for a coordinate branch of government does not require this Court to turn its back on the Constitution's demand for equal protection of the laws. The extreme deference that has historically characterized this Court's review of naturalization legislation is more the result of momentum than logic. The approach taken in Fiallo typifies this extreme deference. The Fiallo Court held that naturalization legislation is constitutional if Congress had merely a "facially legitimate and bona fide reason" for enacting it, and basing its decision on a 1972 immigration case. Fiallo, 430 U.S. at 792 n.4 (citing Kleindienst v. Mandel, 408 U.S. 753, 770 (1972)) (articulating a standard of review for First Amendment challenges to immigration legislation).

As the Fiallo Court admitted, quoting Justice Frankfurter, "much could be said for the view" that Congress does not have unchecked power over immigration "were we writing on a clean slate." Id. (quoting Galvan v. Press, 347 U.S. 522, 530-32 (1954)). The Fiallo Court then refused to examine the issue anew, however, finding itself "not prepared to deem ourselves wiser or more sensitive to human rights than our predecessors, especially those who have been most zealous in protecting civil liberties under the Constitution." Id.

Petitioners respectfully contend that this Court is, indeed, more sensitive to human rights than its predecessors. This Court's unflinching application of the Equal Protection Clause in Virginia makes that clear. Furthermore, as will be discussed in detail below, the Fiallo Court's alleged impediments to a more exacting review of naturalization legislation are illusory.

No legal standard prevents this Court from reviewing the appropriateness of the Fiallo standard because the choice of standard is a decision of law, and this Court reviews decisions of law de novo. United States v. Singer Mfg. Co., 374 U.S. 174, 177 (1963). The time has come for this Court to give the irrebuttable gender stereotypes found in naturalization legislation the same scrutiny given to irrebuttable gender stereotypes found in other areas of the law. **13**

A. 8 U.S.C. § 1409(a) should not escape meaningful judicial review merely because Congress acted at the height of its powers.

The Equal Protection Clause of the Fourteenth Amendment is applicable to Congress via the Fifth Amendment. See, e.g., Bolling v. Sharpe, 347 U.S. 497, 505 (1954). In United States v. Virginia, this Court held that legislation based on gender stereotypes should receive "skeptical scrutiny" upon review. 116 S. Ct. at 2275. There is no reason to use a different standard when reviewing section 1409(a) simply because it is immigration legislation.

The first reason offered by the Fiallo Court for its extremely deferential standard is that "'over no conceivable subject is the legislative power of Congress more complete than it is over' the admissions of aliens." Fiallo, 430 U.S. at 791 (quoting Oceanic Navigation Co. v. Stranahan, 214 U.S. 320, 339 (1909)). **14** The quoted statement does not address the question whether congressional power over naturalization is free from any meaningful judicial review; it merely points out that this power is more

13 This paragraph illustrates a method for including standard of review information when the court rules do not ask for a separate section. The writer inserts the information into introductory material. This introductory material also serves as a roadmap in the sense that it identifies the *themes* that this section of the document will be exploring, and thus prepares the reader for what will follow. Although it is effective, a more traditional roadmap is usually more helpful to a busy reader.

14 Because knowing the origin of the quotation does not help the reader to understand its significance, this citation might best be replaced with the notation "(citation omitted)." If the writer wants to discount the *Fiallo* Court's reasoning by showing that it is relying on ancient authority, he should do so more directly.

complete than congressional power over other areas of the law. It is a relative statement that addresses the power of Congress over naturalization by comparing that power
to other powers. It wisely does not attempt to place any power of Congress above the
Constitution, because even when congressional power is at its apex, it may not violate
the Constitution. Marbury v. Madison, 5 U.S. (1 Cranch) 137, 180 (1803) (holding that
the Constitution is the "supreme law of the land" and that only those laws made pursuant to the Constitution are to be recognized).

This Court has previously recognized that specific, constitutional grants of authority to Congress do not allow Congress to ignore the rest of the Constitution. Almeida-
Sanchez v. United States, 413 U.S. 266, 272-75 (1973). The Almeida-Sanchez Court
struck down a statute that authorized searches and seizures without probable cause
within "reasonable distances" from any external boundary of the United States. Id. at
275. The Court reasoned that the Naturalization Clause of the Constitution — Article
I, section eight, clause four, which empowers Congress to "establish a uniform Rule of
Naturalization"— did not permit Congress to enact a statute that violated the Fourth
Amendment's guarantee against unreasonable searches and seizures. Id. at 272-75.
Similarly, the Court refused to apply the highly deferential "rational basis" standard to
a draft registration statute that exempted women, even though "judicial deference to
such congressional exercise of authority is at its apogee when legislative action under
the congressional authority to raise and support armies and make rules and regulations
for their governance is challenged."Rostker v. Goldberg, 453 U.S. 57, 70 (1981).

This Court's holdings in Almeida-Sanchez and Rostker show that Congress is
never free from meaningful judicial review. The draft registration statute that received
heightened scrutiny in Rostker did not violate the Constitution because men and women
were undeniably dissimilarly situated by operation of the ban on women in combat
roles. 453 U.S. at 79. **15** A skeptical scrutiny of the gender distinction in section
1409(a) will not reveal any such statutory distinction between mothers and fathers;
the distinction is based on nothing more than a gender stereotype. Congress should
not be permitted to dodge this scrutiny merely because it is legislating in the area of
immigration.

15 This analysis goes
beyond the focus of section
II, which is merely to
establish which test should
be applied, rather than to
apply the test.

B. Even unreviewable naturalization policy choices may not be imple-
mented by patently unconstitutional methods.

The power over naturalization is a fundamental sovereign attribute involving some
purely political decisions. It does not necessarily follow, however, that the enforcement
of those decisions must be free from judicial review as a consequence. The Fiallo Court
based its deferential review on its claim that the "power to expel or exclude aliens is a
fundamental sovereign attribute exercised by the Government's political departments
largely immune from judicial control." 430 U.S. at 792 (citing Shaughnessy v. Mezei,
345 U.S. 206, 210 (1953)). It also noted that "the power over aliens is of a political
character and therefore subject to only narrow judicial review."Fiallo, 430 U.S. at 792
(citing Hampton v. Mow Sun Wong, 426 U.S. 88, 101 n.21 (1976)). The Fiallo Court's
reluctance to apply less deferential review is not supported by this Court's decisions.
This Court has not hesitated to apply meaningful review to the implementation of
political decisions. For example, the power over domestic law enforcement is also
a fundamental sovereign attribute, but "[w]here rights secured by the Constitution
are involved, there can be no rulemaking or legislation which would abrogate
them."Miranda v. Arizona, 384 U.S. 436, 490 (1966). The result reached in Miranda

recognized that the government has wide latitude in choosing which activities to criminalize, but that it may not enforce those policy choices in an unconstitutional manner.

As far back as 1896, this Court held that Congress cannot criminally penalize aliens without due process. See Wong Wing v. United States, 163 U.S. 228, 240 (1896) (distinguishing Congress's authority to control borders from constitutional limits on criminal penalties). As recently as 1954 this Court admitted that "[p]olicies pertaining to the entry of aliens . . . are peculiarly concerned with the political conduct of government," but noted that "in the enforcement of these policies, the Executive Branch of the Government must respect the procedural safeguards of due process." Galvan v. Press, 347 U.S. 522, 531 (1954) (holding that aliens must receive due process when the executive branch seeks to enforce the law against them). These cases addressed due process concerns in the implementation of policy. This Court should address equal protection concerns in the implementation of policy, as well. To hold otherwise would bifurcate the Constitution into one part that must be obeyed and another part that may be ignored with impunity.

Furthermore, this Court has the authority to review acts of the other branches of the federal government to ensure that they comply with the Constitution. See Marbury v. Madison, 5 U.S. (1 Cranch) 137, 150 (1803). This authority springs from the fact that the people of the United States — not the federal government — are sovereign. McCulloch v. Maryland, 17 U.S. (4 Wheat.) 316, 403-05 (1819) ("The government proceeds directly from the people. . . . In form, and in substance, it emanates from them."). The people are the collective holders of the power over naturalization. They have created a federal government to exercise that power, but they have done so through a Constitution that requires the government to adhere to specified norms. One function of this Court is to watch over the other branches of government and to ensure, on behalf of the people, that the Constitution is obeyed. To conclude that legislation can escape meaningful review in this Court when Congress acts in politically sensitive areas is to conclude that Congress itself is sovereign, and that this Court has no power to review its actions on behalf of the people.

Such a conclusion must be rejected because it would artificially place Congress above the Constitution. The Constitution gives Congress the power to set naturalization policy; but, as Marbury v. Madison made clear, Congress may never act in violation of the Constitution. In this case, this Court must use a heightened standard when reviewing Congress's decision to require close family ties before allowing some United States citizens — but not others — to pass on their citizenship to their foreign-born children.

C. Past practices in violation of the Constitution should not be permitted to corrupt today's decisions.

As Judge Wald noted in her concurring decision below, "Fiallo is out of step with [the] Court's current refusal to sanction 'official action that closes a door or denies opportunity to women (or to men)' based on stereotypes or 'overbroad generalizations' about men and women." Miller v. Christopher, 96 F.3d 1467, 1477 (1996) (Wald, J., concurring) (citing United States v. Virginia, 116 S. Ct. at 2275). Judge Wald went on to state explicitly that "Fiallo is a precedent whose time has come and gone; it should be changed by Congress or the Supreme Court." Miller, 96 F.3d at 1477 (Wald, J., concurring).

The Fiallo Court tried to justify its holding by noting that "in the exercise of its broad power over immigration and naturalization, 'Congress regularly makes rules that would be unacceptable if applied to citizens.'" 430 U.S. at 792 (quoting Mathews v. Diaz, 426 U.S. 67, 80 (1976)). To the extent that this reasoning indicates that the Fiallo

Court deferred to the weight of past practice when enforcing the Constitution, the Fiallo Court erred, and Petitioner respectfully contends that this Court would err if it continued to follow the Fiallo line of cases.

This Court did not hesitate to end a long history of constitutional abuse when it enforced the Equal Protection Clause and first struck down a statute based upon an antiquated gender stereotype. Reed v. Reed, 404 U.S. 71 (1971) (unanimously striking down state law requiring that men be chosen over similarly situated women when selecting estate administrators). Likewise, this Court should not hesitate to end another long history of constitutional abuse by striking down the use of irrebuttable gender stereotypes in naturalization legislation.

Even the extremely deferential Fiallo Court noted that this Court's cases "reflect acceptance of a limited judicial responsibility under the Constitution even with respect to the power of Congress to regulate the admission and exclusion of aliens."Fiallo, 430 U.S. at 794 n.5. This Court's responsibility to enforce the Constitution goes beyond merely checking to see if Congress had a "facially legitimate and bona fide reason" for legislating on the basis of an irrebuttable gender stereotype.

In the twenty years since Fiallo was decided, our society has grown to more fully appreciate the fundamental flaw inherent in creating legislative distinctions based on gender. It is time to enforce the Equal Protection Clause across the board and apply "skeptical scrutiny" to any use of irrebuttable gender stereotypes. Without an "exceedingly persuasive justification," the use of these stereotypes in any context undermines this Court's pronouncement in Virginia that gender-based classifications "must not rely on overbroad generalizations about the different talents, capacities, or preferences of males and females."Virginia, 116 S. Ct. at 2275.

Because section 1409(a) is a federal law that makes a distinction based on gender, it should be reviewed using the "skeptical scrutiny" standard that this Court set forth in United States v. Virginia.

>   **III.The use of an irrebuttable gender stereotype in 8 U.S.C. §1409(a) is not "substantially related" to the achievement of the government's objective, and there is no "exceedingly persuasive justification" for the stereotype's use.**

This Court recently clarified the level of scrutiny applicable to gender-based classifications. See United States v. Virginia, 116 S. Ct. 2264 (1996). **16** The government must now show "at least that the challenged classification serves important governmental objectives and that the discriminatory means employed are substantially related to the achievement of those objectives." Virginia, 116 S. Ct. at 2275 (internal punctuation and citations omitted). Furthermore, the Court will apply "skeptical scrutiny," and "parties who seek to defend gender-based government action must demonstrate an exceedingly persuasive justification for that action." Id. at 2274 (internal punctuation omitted).

16 Generally, it is more effective to begin point heading sections with a more argumentative statement of an assertion you want the court to agree with.

Petitioner Lorelyn Miller does not challenge the government's important objective of allowing United States citizenship to flow only through close family relationships. Petitioner does challenge, however, the government's assertion that there is an exceedingly persuasive justification for the use of an irrebuttable gender stereotype in the statutory scheme devised to achieve that objective.

The government's use of an irrebuttable gender stereotype in section 1409(a), as explained by the Fiallo Court and the court below, is predicated on two erroneous assumptions: (1) that all men, without exception, will not form close family ties with their "illegitimate" children unless that relationship is formed as a by-product of the financial support of those children, and (2) that proof of the paternity of an "illegitimate" child is much less reliable than proof of maternity of that child. See Miller v. Christopher, 96 F.3d 1467, 1472 (D.C. Cir. 1996); United States v. Fiallo, 430 U.S. 787, 797-800 (1977).

Congress concluded from these assumptions that the United States should make it more difficult for American fathers to pass their citizenship on to their "illegitimate" children by establishing procedural hurdles (in section 1409(a)) that (1) burden all of these fathers and their children regardless of whether they have close family ties, and (2) burden all of these fathers and children regardless of how accurately paternity can be proven. As illustrated by the plight of Lorelyn and Charlie Miller, these burdens can become insurmountable: Section 1409(a) will prevent Mr. Miller and Ms. Miller from ever legally proving that they have a close family relationship unless this Court refuses to accept the irrebuttable gender stereotype in section 1409(a).

A. 8 U.S.C. § 1409(a) is unconstitutionally overinclusive and, therefore, is not "substantially related" to the achievement of the government's objective.

The first inquiry under the Virginia test is whether congressional use of the irrebuttable gender stereotype found in section 1409(a) is "substantially related" to the government's concededly legitimate objective of conditioning citizenship on close family ties. This Court's equal protection jurisprudence makes it clear that very few gender-based distinctions are "substantially related" to the governmental objectives they purport to advance.

The cases in which no substantial relation was found have one common element: They reject gender stereotypes that are little more than vestiges of past discrimination. For example, in 1971, this Court unanimously found no substantial relationship between a state law that favored men over women as executors, and the state's objective of reducing intrafamily controversy. Reed v. Reed, 404 U.S. 71, 77 (1971). In language particularly relevant to the case before this court, the Reed Court expressed its unwillingness to countenance the use of an irrebuttable gender stereotype in lieu of a simple hearing on the merits: **17**

To give a mandatory preference to members of either sex over members of the other, merely to accomplish the elimination of hearings on the merits, is to make the very kind of arbitrary legislative choice forbidden by the Equal Protection Clause of the Fourteenth Amendment; and whatever may be said as to the positive values of avoiding intrafamily controversy, the choice in this context may not lawfully be mandated solely on the basis of sex.

Id. at 76-77 (emphasis added).

This Court has also struck down a gender-based distinction in a statute that allocated government benefits to families with dependent children based on the sex of the parent who had lost his or her employment. Califano v. Westcott, 443 U.S. 76, 96 (1979). The statute was struck down because it did not substantially relate to the achievement of the government's objective, which was to allocate resources only to those families truly in need. Id. at 88. In striking down the statute, the Westcott Court apparently recognized — as this Court should, as well — that not every family consists of a wage-earning father and a child-rearing mother.

Congress may make gender-based distinctions if the reason for the distinction is based in fact and not stereotypes. Rostker v. Goldberg, 453 U.S. 57, 67 (1981). In Rostker, the Court held constitutional a statute that exempted women from registering

17 Notice how the writer uses long quotes sparingly, and introduces them effectively with a focusing, or NPR introduction.

for the military draft, noting that, with respect to military service, men and women were not similarly situated due to another statute: Men could serve in combat positions, but women could not. Id. Thus, a statute that exempted women from registering for the draft was substantially related to the government's legitimate goal of providing for an induction system that would produce combat soldiers. Id. The Court specifically noted that its holding was not predicated on antiquated notions about the relative abilities of men and women; rather, the holding was predicated on the objectively verifiable fact that women could not serve in combat roles in the United States armed forces. Id.

The application of the "substantial relationship" test to section 1409(a) is straight-forward. **18** In a limited sense, section 1409(a) is related to the government's objective of conditioning citizenship on close family ties: Section 1409(a) will certainly prevent citizenship from flowing to some children who do not deserve it. The fatal flaw in section 1409(a), though, is that it is overinclusive. Section 1409(a)'s various hurdles exclude from citizenship those children — like Ms. Miller — who are deserving of citizenship under the standards of the statute due to their close family ties with their United States citizen parents.

> **18** This topic sentence is too subtle for a brief. The sentence should signal more strongly what the result will be when the test is applied to the client's case.

The degree to which section 1409(a) is overinclusive is a function of the degree to which the assumptions underlying section 1409(a) are invalid. Thus, because the assumptions underlying section 1409(a) — that paternity is hard to establish reliably and that women and men are destined to occupy different roles — are substantially incorrect, the use of these irrebuttable stereotypes is not substantially related to the government's objective.

The gender stereotypes underlying section 1409(a) are the very sort of archaic generalizations that modern equal protection jurisprudence seeks to eradicate. This Court has repeatedly recognized that the government "must not rely on overbroad generalizations about the different talents, capacities, or preferences of males and females." Virginia, 116 S. Ct. at 2276 (citing Weinberger v. Wiesenfeld, 420 U.S. 646, 643, 648 (1975); Califano v. Goldfarb, 430 U.S. 188, 223-24 (1977)). If we as a society have learned anything about gender in the twenty years since Fiallo was decided, it is that women and men may not be conclusively pigeon-holed solely on the basis of their gender.

The facts of this case support this rather obvious conclusion. Ms. Miller is twenty-seven years old. Although she is not a minor, and although she neither needs nor receives the financial support of her father, she and Mr. Miller have a close family relationship. By the terms of the stereotype underlying section 1409(a), all men — including Mr. Miller — irrebuttably do not form close family relationships with their adult "illegitimate" children. To uphold the rationality of this irrebuttable stereotype is to deny the existence of Mr. Miller and those other men who, for whatever reason, form relationships with their "illegitimate" children later in life. To uphold the validity of this irrebuttable stereotype is to deny reality. This Court should reject the validity of this irrebuttable stereotype and acknowledge that there is no substantial relationship between the use of the stereotype and the government's goal of fostering close family relationships.

B. There is no "exceedingly persuasive justification" for the use of an irrebuttable gender stereotype in 8 U.S.C. §1409(a) because less discriminatory methods would achieve the government's objective.

Even if the irrebuttable gender stereotype codified in section 1409(a) could somehow be found to be substantially related to the government's objective, the statute must still be found unconstitutional because there is no "exceedingly persuasive justification" for the use of that irrebuttable gender stereotype. See Virginia, 116 S. Ct. at 2276. Even if this Court finds that the stereotype is generally valid, Congress need not have made it operate conclusively and irrebuttably, with no safety-valve provision for fathers like Mr. Miller. A rebuttable presumption might be justifiable if individuals are given the opportunity to show that they do not fit the mold, but any stereotype that mechanically and permanently penalizes people because of their gender offends the very core of the Constitution's equal protection guarantees. This Court recognized as much in Reed, 404 U.S. at 76-77, and Westcott, 443 U.S. at 90. The Court should recognize that basic truth again today. **19**

19 This subsection would be more effective if the writer provided support for his assertions and analysis of how the "exceedingly persuasive justification" language has been analyzed in the past.

IV. 8 U.S.C. § 1409(a) violates the Equal Protection Clause even under an extremely deferential level of scrutiny because Congress had no "facially legitimate and bona fide" reason for using an irrebuttable gender stereotype.

The irrebuttable gender stereotype codified in section 1409(a) is so irrational that it fails even the Fiallo Court's extremely deferential level of scrutiny. As the Fiallo Court itself recognized, this Court's cases "reflect acceptance of a limited judicial responsibility under the Constitution even with respect to the power of Congress to regulate the admission and exclusion of aliens." 430 U.S. at 794 n.5. Even if this Court does not use the Virginia "skeptical scrutiny" standard, there is still ample reason to conclude that section 1409(a) violates the Constitution's equal protection guarantees.

The Fiallo Court held that naturalization legislation is constitutional if Congress had merely a "facially legitimate and bona fide reason" for enacting it. 430 U.S. 792 n.4 (citing Kleindienst v. Mandel, 408 U.S. 753, 770 (1972)). In this test, all that is necessary is that the use of the irrebuttable gender stereotype be legitimate and reasonable. Section 1409(a) fails even this easy examination.

The Fiallo Court assumed that all men are different from all women with respect to their relationships with their "illegitimate" children, referring any concerns about this gender stereotype to Congress. 430 U.S. at 799 n.9. Congress's failure to abandon this gender stereotype in the twenty years since Fiallo was decided has left this Court no choice but to reject it today. This Court has repeatedly held that it is unconstitutional to legislatively assume that one's gender conclusively determines one's personality, noting in 1994 that "[t]oday we reaffirm what, by now, should be axiomatic: Intentional discrimination on the basis of gender by state actors violates the Equal Protection Clause." J.E.B. v. Alabama, 511 U.S. 127, 136-37 (1994); see also United States v. Virginia, 116 S. Ct. 2264 (1996); Mississippi Univ. for Women v. Hogan, 458 U.S. 718, 725 (1982) ("Care must be taken in ascertaining whether the statutory objective itself reflects archaic and stereotypic notions"); Duren v. Missouri, 439 U.S. 357, 370 (1979) (striking down a state's practice of excluding women from jury service on equal protection grounds where the only rationalization for the practice was based on a stereotype).

Furthermore, this Court has previously struck down the perpetual, irrebuttable application of this very stereotype regarding relationships between fathers and their "illegitimate" children. Caban v. Mohammed, 441 U.S. 380, 389 (1979). The Caban Court used equal protection grounds to strike down a statute that distinguished between mothers and fathers of "illegitimate" children based on their presumed relationships with those children after infancy. The Court noted that "[e]ven if unwed mothers as a class were closer to their newborn infants, this generalization concerning parent-child relations would become less acceptable as a basis for legislative distinctions as the age of the child increased." Id. Section 1409(a) does more than legislate on the basis of this stereotype beyond infancy; it applies this stereotype <u>forever</u>. Ms. Miller is long past infancy, but the stereotypical assumptions about her relationship with her father govern her to this day. The irrebuttable gender stereotype that distinguishes between the relative proclivities of men and women towards their offspring is not a "facially legitimate and bona fide reason" for the gender-based distinctions codified in section 1409. As Justice Marshall pointed out in his dissent to <u>Fiallo</u>, "[t]he majority does not even engage in the modest degree of scrutiny required by [Kleindienst]. . . . That failure, I submit, is due to the fact that the statute could not even pass that standard of review." <u>Fiallo</u>, 430 U.S. at 806 n.6 (Marshall, J., dissenting). Justice Marshall was right. Given all that we know about the dangers of irrebuttable gender stereotypes, the stereotype embedded in section 1409(a) is neither facially legitimate nor bona fide.

CONCLUSION

Because the irrebuttable gender stereotype codified in 8 U.S.C. § 1409(a) (1994) violates the equal protection guarantees of the Fifth Amendment to the United States Constitution, this Court should declare section 1409(a) unconstitutional and remove one more vestige of gender discrimination from our laws. The decision of the United States Court of Appeals for the District of Columbia Circuit should be reversed.

Respectfully submitted,

_____

Simon J. Scholar
1356 School Street
Metropolis, Ohio
555-555-5555

November 3, 1997

CERTIFICATE OF SERVICE

This document certifies hand delivery of one copy of this brief to Edward Enemy, 456325 Student Mailboxes, Metropolis, Ohio, on November 3, 1997.

_____

Simon Scholar

IN THE
UNITED STATES DISTRICT COURT
FOR THE SOUTHERN DISTRICT OF OHIO EASTERN DIVISION

Nathan Herman, Plaintiff,	))))	
v.	)))	Case No. C72-09-275 **6** Memorandum in Support of
Sports-R-Us Publications, Inc.,	)))	Defendant's Motion to Dismiss
Defendant.	)))	

6 Consult court documents and local custom to determine how to format the caption.

INTRODUCTION

This Motion responds to Plaintiff's wrongful discharge Complaint. After **7** Sports-R-Us terminated Plaintiff, who was an at-will employee, he filed suit and alleged (1) that his smoking-related complaints at work were made in support of an Ohio public policy, (2) that his termination was somehow related to those complaints, and (3) that his termination therefore constituted the tort of wrongful discharge in violation of public policy. Defendant Sports-R-Us files this Motion to Dismiss under Fed. R. Civ. P. 12(b)(6). Plaintiff's Complaint fails to state a plausible claim upon which relief can be granted because it does not contain sufficient facts that would allow the plaintiff to demonstrate any causal connection between his termination and his alleged complaints about smoking. Even if he were able to demonstrate that connection, his complaint does not state a claim upon which relief can be granted because adequate statutory remedies protect society's interests in the public policy. Defendant files this Memorandum to support its Motion.

7 The theme for Counsel for Defendant is that Plaintiff looked for a reason to sue after he got fired, and that he is trying to make a "federal case" out of a small workplace complaint. Instead of addressing facts chronologically, she starts by talking about the termination, and implies that he came up with the idea about his complaints after he was terminated.

STATUTES INVOLVED **8**

Ohio Rev. Code Ann. § 3794.02 (C) (Westlaw, current through Files 1 to 94 of the 130th GA (2013-2014)) provides in pertinent part:

> (C) No person or employer shall discharge . . . or in any manner retaliate against an individual for exercising any right, including reporting a violation, or performing any obligation under this chapter.

Ohio Rev. Code Ann. § 3794.09 (Westlaw, current through Files 1 to 94 of the 130th GA (2013-2014)) provides in pertinent part:

> (A) Upon the receipt of a first report that a proprietor of a . . . place of employment or an individual has violated any provision of this chapter, the department of health or its designee shall investigate the report and, if it

8 Generally, if your statutes involved are this lengthy, you should include them in an appendix rather than in this introductory material. Counsel for Defendant includes them here because they advance one of defendant's arguments: that the relevant statutes provide adequate protection for the public policy. Simply seeing the volume of statutory language may send a signal to the court that the statutory protection is adequate.

concludes that there was a violation, issue a warning letter to the proprietor or individual.

(B) Upon a report of a second or subsequent violation of any provision of this chapter by a proprietor of a . . . place of employment or an individual, the department of health or its designee shall investigate the report. If the director of health or director's designee concludes, based on all of the information before him or her, that there was a violation, he or she shall impose a civil fine upon the proprietor or individual in accordance with the schedule of fines required to be promulgated under section 3794.07 of this chapter.

. . . .

(D) The director of health may institute an action in the court of common pleas seeking an order in equity against a proprietor or individual that has repeatedly violated the provisions of this chapter or fails to comply with its provisions.

Ohio Rev. Code Ann. § 3794.07 (B) (Westlaw, current through Files 1 to 94 of the 130th GA (2013-2014)) provides in pertinent part:

The amount of a fine for a violation of 3794.02 (A) and (B) shall not be less than one hundred dollars and the maximum for a violation shall be twenty five hundred dollars. The amount of a fine for a violation of 3794.02 (D) shall be up to a maximum of one hundred dollars per violation. Each day of a violation shall constitute a separate violation. The schedule of fines that apply to a proprietor shall be progressive based on the number of prior violations by the proprietor. . . .

The fine schedule shall set forth specific factors that may be considered to decrease or waive the amount of a fine that otherwise would apply. Fines shall be doubled for intentional violations.

Ohio Rev. Code Ann. § 4101.15 (Westlaw, current through Files 1 to 94 of the 130th GA (2013-2014)) provides in pertinent part that "[n]o employer . . . shall violate this chapter or Chapter 4121. [sic] of the Revised Code . . . ."

Ohio Rev. Code Ann. § 4101.99 (Westlaw, current through Files 1 to 94 of the 130th GA (2013-2014)) provides in pertinent part:

(A) Whoever violates section 4101.15 of the Revised Code shall be fined not less than fifty nor more than one thousand dollars for a first offense; for each subsequent offense such person shall be fined not less than one hundred nor more than five thousand dollars.

Ohio Rev. Code Ann. § 4101.16 (Westlaw, current through Files 1 to 94 of the 130th GA (2013-2014)) provides in pertinent part:

Every day during which any person, or corporation, ... or employee thereof fails to observe and comply with any order of the bureau of workers' compensation, or to perform any duty enjoined by this chapter and Chapter 4121. [sic] of the Revised Code, constitutes a separate violation of the order or chapters.

Ohio Rev. Code Ann. § 4121.17 (Westlaw, current through Files 1 to 94 of the 130th GA (2013-2014)) provides in pertinent part:

(A) Upon petition by any person that any employment or place of employment is not safe or is injurious to the welfare of any employee or frequenter, the bureau of workers' compensation shall proceed with or without notice to make an investigation as is necessary to determine the matter complained of.

(B) After such hearing as is necessary, the bureau may enter any necessary order relative thereto to render the employment or place of employment safe and not injurious to the welfare of the employees therein or frequenters thereof.

(C) Whenever the bureau learns that any employment or place of employment is not safe or is injurious to the welfare of any employee or frequenter, it may of its own motion summarily investigate the same, with or without notice, and issue such order as is necessary thereto.

STATEMENT OF THE CASE

Sports-R-Us Publications, Inc. files this Memorandum to support its Motion to Dismiss Nathan Herman's Complaint. Herman's Complaint alleges that he was wrongfully discharged in violation of the public policy of the State of Ohio. Compl. ¶ 1. Herman claims that his discharge was in violation of public policy as found in various Ohio Statutes. Compl. ¶ 20.

Herman began his at-will employment with Sports-R-Us in its Columbus office on May 23, 2002, and his complaint states that at the time he began his employment, he signed an agreement acknowledging that he was an "employee at-will." Compl. ¶¶ 8, 9. Herman worked at Sports-R-Us for 11 years, receiving average and occasionally above-average evaluations during that time. Compl. ¶ 10. Sports-R-Us terminated Herman's at-will employment on August 30, 2013. Compl. ¶ 16. Columbus Manager Kenneth Wagner informed Herman of his termination and did not provide a reason. Compl. ¶¶ 16, 17.

Six **9** months after he was terminated, Plaintiff filed a lawsuit in federal court against his former employer. In his complaint, Plaintiff alleged that he had been fired because of occasional complaints he had made about the smoking that occurred outside of the entrance to Defendant's offices. Compl. ¶ 12. Plaintiff alleges that beginning in early 2013, three of Defendant's employees routinely smoked cigarettes in the area immediately adjacent to Defendant's main entrance. Compl. ¶ 12. Plaintiff claims that he complained about the smoking to Susan Restrepo, his supervisor, at least five times between February 15, 2013, and August 25, 2013. Compl. ¶ 14. Herman alleges that each time he complained, he informed Restrepo that smoking in that location "violated Ohio law." Id. Herman does not allege that he specified any particular law that was being violated by the employees who were smoking outside the building. See id. **10**

Plaintiff now claims that he was wrongfully discharged in violation of the public policy of the State of Ohio. Compl. ¶ 24. Plaintiff alleges that "Mr. Wagner terminated [him] . . . unlawfully and without a sound business reason, because of Nathan Herman's complaints about violations of the law in the Defendant's workplace." Compl. ¶ 18.

Notably, although Plaintiff alleges that Wagner terminated his employment, Compl. **11** ¶¶ 16, 18, he does not allege that he had made any complaints to Wagner, nor **12** does he allege that Susan Restrepo ever informed Wagner about Plaintiff's complaints about the outdoor smoking.

9 Again, the writer's theme is that plaintiff is grasping at straws to find an illegal reason for his termination. Thus, she first provides the fact that he was terminated; only then does she go back and give details about the events that allegedly led to the termination. This organization violates a traditional chronological organization, but it advances the writer's strategic goals.

10 It is appropriate to identify significant facts that were not alleged. Usually, a citation is not appropriate, because you can't cite to something that was not alleged. Here, the writer uses a "see" cite to signal the paragraph in which the information should have appeared.

11 This citation is appropriate in the middle of a sentence because only the first half of the sentence refers to allegations from these paragraphs.

12 Again, the writer is specifying what was not alleged to emphasize what she will characterize as a significant gap in the complaint.

Herman filed his Complaint on February 3, 2014. Sports-R-Us timely files this Motion **13** to Dismiss.

ARGUMENT

This Court should grant the motion to dismiss of Defendant Sports-R-Us. Plaintiff's complaint does not state a claim upon which relief can be granted. The United States Supreme Court has ruled that to survive a motion to dismiss, a complaint must "state a claim to relief that is plausible on its face." <u>Bell Atlantic Corp. v. Twombly</u>, 550 U.S. 544, 570 (2007) (affirming the grant of a defendant's motion to dismiss because the complaint did not state a "plausible" claim for relief). The Supreme Court has explained that a claim has "facial plausibility" when the complaint includes "factual content that allows the court to draw the reasonable inference that the defendant is liable for the misconduct alleged." <u>Ashcroft v. Iqbal</u>, 556 U.S. 662, 678 (2009) (holding that the complaint did not plead sufficient facts). Further, the facts alleged must be sufficient to "raise a right to relief above the speculative level." <u>Bell Atlantic Corp.</u>, 550 U.S. at 555. These facts must be more than a "formulaic recitation of the elements of a cause of action." <u>Twombly</u>, 550 U.S. at 555. Likewise, **14** "[t]hreadbare recitals of the elements of a cause of action, supported by mere conclusory statements, do not suffice." <u>Iqbal</u>, 556 U.S. at 678.

Plaintiff Nathan Herman's Complaint, alleging **15** wrongful discharge in violation of public policy, does not meet this standard. Under Ohio law, an employer can generally **16** discharge an at-will employee for any reason or for no reason. <u>Painter v. Graley</u>, 639 N.E.2d 51, 55 (Ohio 1994) (holding in summary judgment that employee did not meet the requirements of a claim for wrongful discharge in violation of public policy). One of the rare exceptions to this general rule is when the discharge violates public policy. <u>Id.</u> at 55-56. To prevail upon a public policy claim, Plaintiff must establish each of the following four elements:

1. That clear public policy existed and was manifested in a state or federal constitution, statute, or administrative regulation, or in the common law (the *clarity* element).
2. That dismissing employees under circumstances like those involved in the plaintiff's dismissal would jeopardize the public policy *(the jeopardy* element).
3. **17** [That] [t]he plaintiff's dismissal was motivated by conduct related to the public policy (the *causation* element).
4. [That] [t]he employer lacked overriding legitimate business justification for the dismissal (the *overriding justification* element).

<u>Id.</u> at 57 n.8 (citation and internal punctuation omitted). The first two elements are questions of law, whereas the last two elements are questions of fact. <u>Collins v. Rizkana</u>, 652 N.E.2d 653, 658 (Ohio 1995).

This Court should grant Defendant's Motion to Dismiss. Even **18** if Plaintiff has adequately pled the first and fourth elements, Plaintiff's complaint does not include facts regarding the third **19** element, causation, that are sufficient to raise his right to relief above the speculative level. The complaint includes only a "formulaic recitation" of the causation claim, and does not even include an allegation that the manager who fired him was aware of his alleged complaints about smoking.

4

Further, **20** even if this Court finds that Plaintiff has alleged facts that could allow him to establish causation, it is not plausible that the Plaintiff will be able to establish jeopardy, the second element: Plaintiffs cannot establish the jeopardy element if there are adequate remedies in the statutes that underlie the public policy claim. <u>Leininger v. Pioneer Nat'l Latex,</u> 875 N.E.2d 36, 42-43 (Ohio 2007). The statutes that the Plaintiff cites allow the imposition of both fines and administrative oversight to ensure that the public policy goals in the statutes are realized.

Accordingly, because the Plaintiff's complaint will not allow him to establish at least two of the four required elements, this Court should grant Defendant's Motion to Dismiss. **21**

A. Plaintiff's Complaint does not plead sufficient facts regarding causation to raise his right to relief above the speculative level.

This Court should find that Plaintiff's Complaint does not plead sufficient facts regarding causation "to raise [his] right to relief above the speculative level." <u>Bell Atlantic Corp. v. Twombly</u>, 550 U.S. 544, 555 (2007). The facts alleged in the complaint must be more than a "formulaic recitation of the elements of a cause of action." <u>Twombly</u>, 550 U.S. at 555. Further, "[t]hreadbare recitals of the elements of a cause of action, supported by mere conclusory statements, do not suffice." <u>Iqbal</u>, 556 U.S. at 678. **22** Plaintiff has alleged only that Wagner terminated him "because of [his] complaints about violations of the law in the Defendant's workplace." Compl. ¶¶ 18, 24. This conclusory allegation does not satisfy the requirements for establishing causation or for surviving a motion to dismiss.

To satisfy the causation element, the Plaintiff must establish that his dismissal "was motivated by conduct related to the public policy." <u>Painter v. Graley</u>, 639 N.E.2d at 57 n. 8. Case law discussing the causation element of wrongful discharge claims is sparse, but the United States Court of Appeals for the Sixth Circuit has applied the causation analysis that courts use when they decide Title **23** VII retaliation claims. See <u>Herlik v. Cont'l Airlines, Inc.</u>, No. 04-3790, 2005 WL 2445947, at *4 (6th Cir. Oct. 4, 2005) (citing to a Title VII retaliation case as authority for its causation analysis when reviewing summary judgment decision).

Courts deciding retaliation cases have held that a plaintiff can establish causation by either direct evidence or indirect evidence. See <u>DiPietro v. Morgan Stanley DW Inc.</u>, 517 F. Supp. 2d 1016, 1022 (S.D. Ohio 2007). Plaintiff's complaint states that Wagner did not give a reason for firing him, Compl. ¶ 17, so Plaintiff must establish causation by indirect evidence.

This Court should find that Plaintiff's Complaint does not raise his right to relief above the speculative level for two reasons. First, **24** Plaintiff does not identify any other indicia beyond a temporal connection that might support causation. See **25** <u>Miller v. TMT Logistics, Inc.</u>, 3:07CV3180, 2009 WL 1850313, at *3 (N.D. Ohio June 25, 2009). Second, Plaintiff never alleges that the firing supervisor knew about his complaints. See <u>Herlik v. Cont'l Airlines, Inc.</u>, No. 04-3790, 2005 WL 2445947, at *4 (6th Cir. Oct. 4, 2005).

Plaintiff has not pleaded sufficient facts regarding causation. Plaintiff is not permitted to force this Court to speculate as to his ability to establish causation. Therefore, this Court should grant Defendant's Motion to Dismiss. **26**

20 This brief addresses only two elements. Instead of giving an enumerated roadmap, it articulates and briefly supports its two major contentions.

21 The writer appropriately ends the umbrella by stating the brief's ultimate conclusion.

22 This umbrella focuses first on the pleading standard because the language re: factual pleading is crucial to the Defendant's argument.

23 The Defendant plans to use analysis that courts have used when analyzing analogous Title VII issue; here, she justifies the use of these cases by noting courts that have applied this standard to public policy exception cases. You can apply rules from analogous cases even if no court has ever done so, but doing so is obviously more persuasive with a court's "blessing."

24 This paragraph articulates a more traditional roadmap.

25 The writer uses "see" for both citations because neither court talked about her client's case; she is drawing the inference that they support her argument.

26 The four-part test is a disjunctive test for the defendant: he needs victory on only one element to convince the court to grant the motion. Accordingly, it is appropriate to end this roadmap by referencing the ultimate goal of the brief.

1. Plaintiff does not identify any other indicia beyond a temporal connection that might establish an inference of causation.

This Court should grant Defendant's motion to dismiss because Plaintiff does not identify any other indicia beyond a temporal connection that might establish an inference of causation. Courts have sometimes found that a "very close" temporal connection can establish causation in retaliatory discharge claims, but something more than temporal proximity between the termination and the public policy-related action is usually required. See Nguyen v. City of Cleveland, 229 F.3d 559, 565 (6th Cir. 2000) (in Title VII case, refusing to agree with the plaintiff's argument that the sixth circuit "follows a rule that temporal proximity . . . is alone sufficient to establish causation"). Courts applying this test have indicated that "a temporal connection coupled with other indicia of retaliatory conduct may be sufficient to support a finding of a causal connection." Randolph v. Ohio Dep't of Youth Servs., 453 F.3d 724, 737 (6th Cir. 2006).

27 The writer cites two cases in which courts found other indicia, so that she can contrast the facts of her case with those of the authority cases.

Even mildly retaliatory actions by the employer can provide the other **27** indicia. Id. In Randolph, the employee plaintiff claimed she had been discharged in retaliation for reporting sexual harassment and assaults. Id. at 736. She had reported the assaults, was placed on administrative leave soon after, and was discharged about seven months later. Id. at 737. The court found that investigations during the intervening period into the employee's conduct provided the other indicia necessary to survive summary judgment on the causation element. Id.

28 The court did not explicitly make this statement about its belief; the writer uses the word "apparently" to signal that she has drawn a conclusion.

Threatening statements by the employer can also provide the other indicia. See Abbott v. Crown Motor Co., 348 F.3d 537, 543-44 (6th Cir. 2003). In Abbott, the employee was terminated eleven months after volunteering to testify against his employer. Id. The employee's supervisor twice threatened the employee during the intervening period. Id. The court apparently **28** believed that the two intervening threats constituted other indicia which produced enough evidence of causation to survive summary judgment. See id.

But when an employee can point to nothing more than a tenuous temporal connection, Ohio courts usually will not infer causation. When interpreting Ohio's retaliatory discharge law, courts have "consistently held that temporal proximity, without more, cannot establish causation." Miller v. TMT Logistics, Inc., 3:07CV3180, 2009 WL 1850313, at *3 (N.D. Ohio June 25, 2009) (holding that the employee could not survive summary judgment on his retaliatory discharge claim when the only evidence of causation was a temporal connection of three months).

Plaintiff does not identify any indicia besides a temporal connection that might produce an inference of causation. He does not state that his supervisor ever threatened him or retaliated against him in response to his complaints. Plaintiff merely states that he complained three times to Restrepo and that Wagner discharged him about five days after his last complaint. Compl. ¶¶ 14, 16. Plaintiff's complaint refers to no other facts that might indicate a causal connection between the two events. Therefore, this Court should find that Plaintiff has not pleaded sufficient facts to raise his right to relief above the speculative level, and it should grant the motion to dismiss.

2. Plaintiff's Complaint does not allege that his firing supervisor knew of his complaints.

This court should find that Plaintiff has not pleaded facts that are sufficient to raise his right to relief above the speculative level because his Complaint does not allege that his firing supervisor knew of his complaints regarding smoking. To establish causation in wrongful discharge claims, the employee must show that the firing supervisor knew of the employee's complaints regarding the public policy. E.g., Herlik v. Cont'l Airlines, Inc., No. 04-3790, 2005 WL 2445947, at *4 (6th Cir. Oct. 4, 2005) (plaintiff could not survive summary judgment because he could not show that the firing supervisor knew of the Plaintiff's safety complaints); Sollitt v. KeyCorp, 1:09-CV-43, 2009 WL 2588329, at *7 (N.D. Ohio Aug. 21, 2009) vacated and remanded to state court on other grounds, 463 F. App'x 471 (6th Cir. 2012) (plaintiff could not survive summary judgment because he could not show that the firing supervisor knew of the Plaintiff's complaints regarding fraud).

A failure to plead **29** specific, supporting facts is fatal to a complaint in the motion to dismiss context. See Bargo v. Goodwill Indus. of Kentucky, Inc., 969 F. Supp. 2d 819, 823 (E.D. Ky. 2013). In Bargo, the court granted a motion to dismiss an age discrimination claim because the plaintiff had offered "no factual allegations to show that she was terminated based on age." Id. The court refused to accept as true the "legal conclusions" that the reason given for her termination was "pre-textual and merely a mask to cover-up the pattern of age discrimination." Id. Similarly, in a 2010 case, the Eastern District of Tennessee refused to infer that a plaintiff met age standards for an ADEA claim when the plaintiff had merely alleged that she was part of the "protected class" but had not specifically pled her age. Hughes v. Am.'s Collectibles Network, Inc., 3:09-CV-176, 2010 WL 890982 at *4 (E.D. Tenn. Mar. 8, 2010).

Plaintiff Nathan Herman's complaint contains insufficient allegations relevant to the causation element. Plaintiff claims that he complained to his supervisor, Susan Restrepo. Compl. ¶ 14. Plaintiff then alleges, however, that he was fired by a different supervisor, Kenneth Wagner. Compl. ¶¶ 16-18. What Plaintiff does not allege is that Wagner knew of his complaints to Restrepo. Because Plaintiff does not state that Wagner knew of his complaints, Plaintiff has neglected to plead a fact that is a crucial part of the causation element. This Court must accept all facts "*in* the complaint" as true. Ashcroft v. Iqbal, 556 U.S. at 678 (emphasis added). However, Plaintiff may not force this Court to add necessary factual allegations to his Complaint. Plaintiff has omitted a fact crucial to establishing the required element of causation. Therefore, this Court should grant the motion to dismiss because Plaintiff has not pleaded facts sufficient to raise his right to relief above the speculative level.

B. It is not plausible that Plaintiff will be able to establish the jeopardy element.

Even if this court finds that plaintiff has adequately pled causation, it should grant Defendant's Motion to Dismiss because Plaintiff will not be able to establish the jeopardy element of his wrongful discharge claim.

To establish the jeopardy element at trial, Plaintiff must establish that "dismissing employees under circumstances like those involved in the plaintiff's dismissal would jeopardize the public policy." Painter v. Graley, 639 N.E.2d at 57 n. 8. This issue presents a question of law to the court. Collins v. Rizkana, 652 N.E.2d at 658. This court must grant Defendant's motion to dismiss because Plaintiff's complaint will not allow him to establish that his discharge jeopardizes public policy, and his complaint therefore does not plausibly **30** entitle him to relief.

The Ohio Supreme Court has held that a claim cannot meet the jeopardy test if the statutes that manifest the public policy provide remedies that render a tort claim unnecessary for the protection of that public policy. Leininger v. Pioneer Nat'l Latex, 875

29 The previous paragraphs in the explanation section addressed how the legal standard operates and why "knowledge" is crucial to causation. This paragraph focuses on how courts have used the pleading standard. Neither of the cases cited is a public policy case, so the writer specifies the cause of action. They are similar to this case in that the plaintiff in each case did not include enough specific facts in the complaint.

30 Unlike the causation element, the jeopardy element is a question of law. For this issue, the problem is not that the plaintiff did not plead sufficient facts. Rather, the problem is that the law does not apply to the facts in a way that will entitle him to relief.

N.E.2d 36, **31** 42-43 (Ohio 2007).[1] In <u>Leininger</u>, the court granted summary judgment in favor of an employer who had allegedly violated a public policy against age discrimination. <u>Id.</u> at 38. The court noted that state statutes provide remedies for age discrimination and held that it is "unnecessary to recognize a common-law claim [for wrongful discharge] when remedy provisions are an essential part of the statutes upon which the plaintiff depends for the public policy claim and when those remedies adequately protect society's interest by discouraging the wrongful conduct." <u>Id.</u> at 42-43.

The jeopardy rule focuses upon society's interests and not upon the plaintiff's interests, so it is irrelevant whether the "remedies" provided inure to the benefit of the plaintiff. See <u>Leininger</u>, 875 N.E.2d at 43-44. The core issue is whether, absent a wrongful discharge claim, society's interests in the public policy will be jeopardized. See <u>id.</u> at 42-43. In <u>Leininger</u>, the Supreme Court of Ohio found the remedies adequate, concluding that the statutory remedies granted to the plaintiff would protect society's interests by dissuading the employer's wrongful conduct. <u>Id.</u> at 44.

But statutory remedies not granted to the plaintiff can also adequately protect society's interests. See <u>Tracy</u>, 2009 WL 690255, at *5. In <u>Tracy</u>, the United States District Court for the Southern District of Ohio stated that "the jeopardy element is to protect society's interests, not necessarily a specific plaintiff." <u>Id.</u> at *5 n. 2. The statute at issue in <u>Tracy</u> did not provide the plaintiff with any compensatory or equitable relief. <u>Id.</u> at *5. Nonetheless, the court found that the statute allowed individuals to bring suit on behalf of the government and protected them from retaliation by the employer. <u>Id.</u> The court held that the plaintiff could not meet the jeopardy element because "there [was] an adequate remedy available to satisfy the public policy concerns." <u>Id.</u> The court's focus was upon society's interests, not the plaintiff's individual interests. See <u>id.</u>

Statutory remedies designed to punish the employer have also been found adequate to protect society's interests. <u>DeMell v. Cleveland Clinic Found.</u>, No. 88505, 2007 WL 1705094, at *4 (Ohio Ct. App. June 24, 2007). In <u>DeMell</u>, an Ohio Court of Appeals held that statutory remedies consisting of regulatory agency inspection with civil and criminal liability for violations were adequate to protect society's interests. <u>Id.</u> The plaintiff had argued that the statutory remedies were inadequate "because the statute impose[d] only a criminal penalty rather than a civil remedy." <u>Id.</u> at *3. The court disagreed, ruling that "'[g]iven the regulatory oversight and the civil and criminal penalties, the public policy . . . is adequately protected.'" <u>Id.</u> at *4 (quoting <u>White v. Sears. Roebuck & Co.</u>, 837 N.E.2d 1275, 1282 (Ohio Ct. App. 2005)).

Admittedly, a remedy may be inadequate to protect society's interests if it is merely **32** discretionary. <u>Greeley v. Miami Valley Maint. Contractors, Inc.</u>, 551 N.E.2d 981,984 (Ohio 1990). In <u>Greeley</u>, the Supreme Court of Ohio concluded that a discretionary fine was inadequate to protect society's interests in the absence of a wrongful discharge claim. <u>Id.</u> The court held that "[t]o permit an employer to discharge an

31 This writer could have created a separate section that applied the Himmel test and argued that it was an alternative way to succeed on the jeopardy element. Instead, she chose to dismiss the Himmel test, justifying her decision by noting that both state and federal courts have applied the Leininger test, and that the Leininger test was approved by the Ohio Supreme Court three years after the Sixth Circuit used the Himmel test. This argument has merit, of course, because federal courts are obliged to use Ohio rules when analyzing Ohio law.

32 Here, the writer identifies a case in which a court has found that the remedy is inadequate. By her use of the word merely, she tries to signal that a remedy must be *very* minimal in order to be found to be inadequate.

[1] In <u>Leininger</u>, decided in 2007, the Supreme Court of Ohio articulated Ohio's test for the jeopardy element. <u>Leininger,</u> 875 N.E.2d at 41-44 (setting forth the jeopardy test). Admittedly, three years earlier, the United States Court of Appeals for the Sixth Circuit used a different test. See <u>Himmel v. Ford Motor Co.</u>, 342 F.3d 593, 599 (6th Cir. 2004) (applying a three-pronged approach to jeopardy). However, Ohio federal courts currently use the <u>Leininger</u> test. See, e.g., <u>Tracy v. Northrop Grumman Sys. Corp.</u>, No. 1:08cv126, 2009 WL 690255, at *5 (S.D. Ohio March 12, 2009) (applying the <u>Leininger</u> jeopardy test). Ohio state courts also use the <u>Leininger</u> test. See, e.g., <u>Ripley v. Montgomery</u>, No. 07AP-6, 2007 WL 4564572, at *7 (Ohio Ct. App. Dec. 31, 2007) (applying the <u>Leininger</u> jeopardy test).

employee who is subject to wage withholding would be condoning the violation of a statute and the frustrating of a court order—all by simply paying a small fine which may (or may not) be imposed by the court." Id.

Accordingly, **33** a plaintiff cannot meet the jeopardy element if the relevant statutes contain remedies that are mandatory and that would protect or advance the public policy by dissuading the defendant from committing the wrongful conduct. Statutes that do not compensate a discharged employee can meet these requirements as long as they include sufficient administrative or criminal consequences.

> **33** In this paragraph, the writer articulates a rule summary.

The statutes Plaintiff cites as the public policy basis of his claim all contain **34** non-discretionary remedies that are adequate to protect society's interests. See Compl. ¶ 20; Ohio Rev. Code Ann. §§ 3794.02, 4101.99, 4121.17. The Smoke Free Workplace Act contains three enforcement mechanisms. First, the department of health can issue a warning letter. § 3794.09(A). Second, upon a subsequent reported violation the department "shall impose a civil fine." § 3794.09(B). The minimum fine the department can impose is $100, and the maximum is $2,500. Id. Every day that the employer contravenes the statute counts as a separate violation. Id. Third, "[t]he director of health may institute an action in the court of common pleas seeking an order in equity against a proprietor or individual that has repeatedly violated the provisions of this chapter or fails to comply with its provisions." § 3794.09(D). If an employer discharged an employee for reporting a violation, the department of health could, therefore, seek an injunction requiring the employer to reinstate the employee. See §§ 3794.02(C), 3794.09(D).

> **34** Here the writer begins her rule application.

Likewise, the safe workplace act that Plaintiff relies on imposes significant fines upon employers who violate provisions. It mandates a fine of $50 - $1,000 for the first offense and $100 - $5,000 for subsequent offenses. § 4101.99(A). Every day that the employer contravenes the statute counts as a separate violation. § 4101.16. It is true that the United States District Court for the Northern District of Ohio indicated that the safe workplace act did not provide remedies. Jenkins v. Cent. Transp., Inc., 09CV525, 2010 WL 420027, at *6 (N.D. Ohio Jan. 29, 2010) (finding no remedies under the safe workplace act and granting the plaintiff's motion to remand). That statement, however, was not accurate because the safe workplace act does provide significant remedies. See § 4101.99(A). In Jenkins, the court was ruling on a motion to remand, and apparently neither party disputed whether the statute contained any remedies. See id at 1, 6.

Finally, § 4121.17 is enforced through agency action and fines. §§ 4101.15, 4121.17. Section 4121.17(A) orders the bureau of workers' compensation to investigate reported violations. Then, "[after] such hearing as is necessary, the bureau may enter any necessary order relative thereto to render the employment or place of employment safe." § 4121.17(B). The fines imposed for a violation of § 4121.17 are identical to those imposed for a violation of the safe workplace act. §§ 4101.15, 4101.99.

Thus, all three statutes cited by Plaintiff provide significant remedies. These remedies, like those available under the statutes cited in Leininger, Tracy, and DeMell, are all adequate to protect society's interests. The legislature designed the hefty fines to enforce the statutes. Added to these fines are pressure from the specified agencies and the very real possibility of a judicial injunction. If the Plaintiff had *reported* the alleged violations to the relevant authorities instead of merely complaining, the statutory remedies available would likely have ended the alleged misconduct. The remedies these statutes provide are completely adequate to protect society's interests.

Unlike the statute providing for a merely discretionary fine in Greeley, each of these statutes *mandates* that the state take significant action against the employer.

35 Here, the writer connects the legal standard—regarding the adequacy of the statutory remedies—to the motion standard—regarding the plausibility of the claim.

Therefore, **35** this Court should find that the statutory remedies adequately protect society's interests and thus conclude that it is not plausible that Plaintiff can meet the jeopardy element. Since Plaintiff has failed to state a plausible claim upon which relief can be granted, this Court should grant Defendant's Motion to Dismiss

CONCLUSION

Plaintiff Nathan Herman's complaint does not satisfy the minimum pleading requirements as articulated by the Supreme Court of the United States. Plaintiff's complaint does not plead sufficient facts regarding causation that would raise his right to relief above the speculative level. Further, it is not plausible that Plaintiff will be able to establish the jeopardy element because there are available, adequate statutory remedies that already protect society's interests. In short, Plaintiff has failed to adequately plead a claim for relief that is plausible on its face. Therefore, this Court should grant Defendant's Motion to Dismiss.

Penelope Pupil

Respectfully submitted,
Penelope Pupil
Counsel for the Defendant
1223 Schoolhouse Street
Columbus, OH 43215
Attorney No. 12-34567

CERTIFICATE OF SERVICE

I certify that I have delivered a copy of this document to Rebecca H. Vargo, Counsel for the Plaintiff, Nathan Herman. The copy was delivered in person April 23, 2014, to her offices at 345 Court Street, Columbus, Ohio.

Penelope Pupil

Respectfully submitted,
Penelope Pupil
Counsel for the Defendant
1223 Schoolhouse Street
Columbus, OH 43215
Attorney No. 12-34567

Index